Confronting the Shadow State

OXFORD MONOGRAPHS IN INTERNATIONAL LAW

The aim of this series is to publish important and original pieces of research on all aspects of international law. Topics that are given particular prominence are those which, while of interest to the academic lawyer, also have important bearing on issues which touch the actual conduct of international relations. Nonetheless the series is wide in scope and includes monographs on the history and philosophical foundations of international law.

RECENT TITLES IN THE SERIES

Irresolvable Norm Conflicts in International Law
The Concept of a Legal Dilemma
Valentin Jeutner

Institutionalizing State Responsibility
Global Security and UN Organs
Vincent-Joël Proulx

The Power of Process
The Value of Due Process in Security Council Sanctions Decision-Making
Devika Hovell

Jurisdiction in International Law
Second edition
Cedric Ryngaert

Confronting the Shadow State

An International Law Perspective on State Organized Crime

HENRI DECŒUR

OXFORD
UNIVERSITY PRESS

OXFORD
UNIVERSITY PRESS

Great Clarendon Street, Oxford, OX2 6DP,
United Kingdom

Oxford University Press is a department of the University of Oxford.
It furthers the University's objective of excellence in research, scholarship,
and education by publishing worldwide. Oxford is a registered trade mark of
Oxford University Press in the UK and in certain other countries

First Edition published in 2018

Impression: 1

Published in the United States of America by Oxford University Press
198 Madison Avenue, New York, NY 10016, United States of America

British Library Cataloguing in Publication Data
Data available

Library of Congress Control Number: 2018930539

ISBN 978–0–19–882393–3

Printed and bound by
CPI Group (UK) Ltd, Croydon, CR0 4YY

‘La conscience règne et ne gouverne pas.’

Paul Valéry, *Mauvaises pensées et autres*

General Editor's Preface

Relatively little attention has been paid to the insidious phenomenon of 'state capture', the effective appropriation and systematic exploitation for mostly private gain of the institutions of government and public assets of a state by holders of high office. 'Kleptocracy', as the phenomenon is also known, makes a mockery of a people's permanent sovereignty over its natural resources and its right to development, beggaring countless millions worldwide. More disheartening still, perhaps, is the reticence surrounding the diversion of the institutional and material resources of a state by its high officials for organized criminal activities, such as trafficking in drugs, arms, clandestine nuclear material, and human beings, with a view to profit.

This is not to say that nothing has been done, including by means of international law, about the global scandals of public-sector corruption and organized crime. An alloy of self-interest and cosmopolitan civic virtue on the part of certain states and the dogged labours of intergovernmental and non-governmental organizations have given rise to a raft of sectoral, regional, and universal conventions and specific conventional provisions aimed at preventing, putting a stop to, and punishing corrupt practices on the part of rent-seeking state officials and the private-sector actors who pander to them. For its part, transnational organized crime is the subject not only of a universal convention to which 189 states are presently parties but also of three additional protocols to it.

It is Henri Decœur's thesis, however, that, aside from their practical limitations, these current international legal efforts adequately capture neither the moral essence nor material harm caused by what he terms 'state organized crime'. In *Confronting the Shadow State: An International Law Perspective on State Organized Crime*, Dr Decœur proposes establishing state organized crime as a specific international crime, to be suppressed by combined means of a purpose-dedicated universal convention, action by the United Nations Security Council under Chapter VII of the Charter of the United Nations, and prosecution by an international criminal court or tribunal. His principled and pragmatic arguments are thoughtful and imaginative and his background account at times arresting. Many are likely to consider his programme utopian, but the same was routinely said of the abolition of slavery, the outlawry of aggressive war, and the establishment of a permanent international criminal court, all of them eventually achieved, if in practice manifestly imperfectly, via international law. *Confronting the Shadow State* merits and rewards an open mind.

CR, RO'K

Oxford and London
March 2018

Table of Contents

III. INTERNATIONAL LEGAL MECHANISMS FOR THE SUPPRESSION OF STATE ORGANIZED CRIME

Table of Cases

INTERNATIONAL TRIBUNALS AND TREATY BODIES

International Criminal Court

International Criminal Tribunal for Rwanda

International Criminal Tribunal for the former Yugoslavia

DOMESTIC COURTS

United States of America

Table of Treaties

Abbreviations

ACJHR	African Court of Justice and Human Rights
ACJHR Statute	Protocol on the Statute of the African Court of Justice and Human Rights
ARSIWA	Articles on Responsibility of States for Internationally Wrongful Acts
AU	African Union
AU Convention on Corruption	African Union Convention on Preventing and Combating Corruption
CIA	Central Intelligence Agency (United States)
Convention against Torture	Convention against Torture and Other Cruel, Inhuman or Degrading Treatment or Punishment
ECCC	Extraordinary Chambers in the Courts of Cambodia
FATF	Financial Action Task Force
Framework Decision on the European arrest warrant	Council Framework Decision on the European arrest warrant and the surrender procedures between Member States
Genocide Convention	Convention on the Prevention and Punishment of the Crime of Genocide
ICC	International Criminal Court
ICC Statute	Rome Statute of the International Criminal Court
ICCPR	International Covenant on Civil and Political Rights
ICJ	International Court of Justice
ICTR	International Criminal Tribunal for Rwanda
ICTY	International Criminal Tribunal for the former Yugoslavia
ILC	International Law Commission
Inter-American Convention against Arms Trafficking	Inter-American Convention against the Illicit Manufacturing of and Trafficking in Firearms, Ammunition, Explosives, and Other Related Materials
ISIL	Islamic State in Iraq and the Levant
MİT	National Intelligence Organization (Turkey)
OECD Convention on Bribery	Convention on Combating Bribery of Foreign Public Officials in International Business Transactions
SCSL	Special Court for Sierra Leone
STL	Special Tribunal for Lebanon

UN Charter	Charter of the United Nations
UN Drug Convention	United Nations Convention against Illicit Trafficking in Narcotic Drugs and Psychotropic Substances
UNCAC	United Nations Convention against Corruption
UNCTOC	United Nations Convention against Transnational Organized Crime
UNCTOC Firearms Protocol	Protocol against the Illicit Manufacturing of and Trafficking in Firearms, Their Parts and Components and Ammunition
UNCTOC Human Trafficking Protocol	Protocol to Prevent, Suppress and Punish Trafficking in Persons, Especially Women and Children
UNCTOC Migrants Smuggling Protocol	Protocol against the Smuggling of Migrants by Land, Sea and Air
UNODC	United Nations Office on Drugs and Crime
VCLT	Vienna Convention on the Law of Treaties

Introduction

A few weeks after the coup that deposed former Guinean President Lansana Conté in December 2008, the state television broadcast the confession of his son and of other senior government officials telling the story of the former regime's involvement in the drug trade. Cocaine shipments from Latin America, loaded on board airplanes carrying the insignia of the Red Cross, were received at Conakry international airport by the presidential guard, transported in truck convoys under the supervision of the head of the intelligence services, and smuggled to Europe in diplomatic pouches. The drug deals were negotiated in the president's VIP salon at the airport and in the first lady's villa.[1]

This short description of the inner workings of a 'narco-state'[2] sheds light on the extent of the involvement of senior state officials in organized criminal activities in certain countries. It reinforces the view that organized crime exercises a 'destabilizing and corrupting influence on fundamental social, economic and political institutions',[3] but challenges the underlying assumption commonly found in the literature that organized criminal groups are autonomous agents competing with, and weakening, the authority of the state.[4] Where state organs themselves directly participate in organized criminal activities, organized crime may become for the state a tool of political, economic, and social control.

It is, then, not exaggerated to speak of 'state organized crime'.[5] State organized crime constitutes an advanced form of system criminality where the perpetrators,

[1] 'Guinea narcostate revealed in TV confessions', *The Washington Times* (15 March 2009). See also US diplomatic cable, Embassy Conakry, 'Guinea – Narco-trafficking Crackdown Bonanza' (27 February 2009) 09CONAKRY131.

[2] The concept of 'narco-state' has gained currency to refer to a number of states alleged to be involved in drug trafficking. See e.g. Alain Labrousse and Michel Koutouzis, *Géopolitique et géostratégies des drogues* (Economica, 1996), at 32–35, 41–46, 90–96.

[3] UN General Assembly, Resolution 49/159, 23 December 1994, UN Doc A/RES/49/159.

[4] See e.g. Thomas Feltes and Robin Hofmann, 'Transnational Organized Crime and Its Impact on States and Societies' in Pierre Hauck and Sven Peterke (eds), *International Law and Transnational Organized Crime* (Oxford University Press, 2016) 42, in particular at 57–62; Susan Strange, *The Retreat of the State: The Diffusion of Power in the World Economy* (Cambridge University Press, 1996), at 118–21.

[5] The term 'state-organized crime' was originally coined by Chambliss to describe covert operations carried out by the state for policy purposes, involving criminal activities such as piracy, assassinations, enforced disappearances, or the smuggling of drugs or arms. According to Chambliss, state-organized crime 'consists of acts defined by law as criminal and committed by state officials in the pursuit of their job as representatives of the state' and in furtherance of official state policy. See William J Chambliss, 'State-Organized Crime – The American Society of Criminology, 1988 Presidential Address' (1989) 27 *Criminology* 183.

abusing their authority as officials of the state, use the state's material and human resources to commit or facilitate the commission of crimes for the purpose of profit.[6]

This phenomenon is not a new one. History has shown that sovereigns are sometimes keen to turn to criminal means to generate the revenue needed to pursue their agenda. States facilitated or directly engaged in criminal activities where significant economic interests were at stake. Privateering, for example, generated substantial revenue in addition to weakening the enemy's economy. In some instances, it was hardly distinguishable from unlawful state-sponsored piracy.[7] The correlation between the exercise of sovereign power and organized crime is most tellingly illustrated by the modern history of opium, starting with the trade in opium by the great colonial empires in the late eighteenth and nineteenth centuries. Despite a ban on opium in China, opium produced in regions under the rule of the British East India Company was smuggled into China by British companies while the United Kingdom government collected tax revenues from the production and sale of opium.[8] When China seized and destroyed illicit opium shipments, the United Kingdom responded with military force, triggering the first Opium War.[9] A hundred years later, Japan funded its war effort in East Asia by taking over and developing the manufacturing of opium, heroin, and cocaine in Manchukuo and Formosa, and facilitating the smuggling of drugs into China, in spite of Japan's ratification of the International Opium Conventions. Narcotics factories were supervised by the Japanese Finance Ministry, while a special branch of the Japanese army was in charge of regulating the drug trade in occupied territories.[10]

[6] Note that as a matter of international law, even *ultra vires* acts and acts committed for private ends may be characterized as acts of the state: see Chapter 2, Section B.1. This is recognized by criminologists: see Dawn L Rothe, *State Criminality: The Crime of All Crimes* (Lexington Books, 2009), at 6 (defining state criminality as '[a]ny action that violates international public law, and/or a state's own domestic law when these actions are committed by individual actors acting on behalf of, or in the name of the state, even when such acts are motivated by their personal economical, political, and ideological interests').

[7] Although privateering was an established practice of naval warfare governed by precise customary rules, in practice abuses were frequent and many states commonly treated foreign privateers as pirates: see Patrick Villiers, *Les corsaires : des origines au traité de Paris du 16 avril 1856* (Jean-Paul Gisserot, 2007), at 4–6, 10; Jean Merrien, *Histoire des corsaires* (L'Ancre de Marine, 1992), at 140; Virginia West Lunsford, *Piracy and Privateering in the Golden Age Netherlands* (Palgrave MacMillan, 2005), at 2–3. The states of the Barbary Coast, placed under the rule of the Ottoman Empire, directly engaged in piracy: see Vespasien V Pella, 'La répression de la piraterie' (1926) 15 *Recueil des cours de l'Académie de droit international* 145, at 161–62, 176. On the evolution of international law regarding privateering, see Roberto Sandiford, 'Évolution du droit de la guerre maritime et aérienne' (1939) 68 *Recueil des cours de l'Académie de droit international* 555, at 571–73. Privateering was formally banned under international law in 1856 by the Declaration Respecting Maritime Law, Paris, 16 April 1856, entered into force on 16 April 1856, reproduced in Natalino Ronzitti (ed), *The Law of Naval Warfare: A Collection of Agreements and Documents with Commentaries* (Martinus Nijhoff, 1988), at 61 ff.

[8] See generally David Edward Owen, *British Opium Policy in China and India* (Yale University Press, 1934); Michael Greenberg, *British Trade and the Opening of China 1800–42* (reprinted edn, Cambridge University Press, 1969).

[9] The Opium Wars were respectively settled in 1842 by the Nanjing treaty (Treaty between China and Great Britain, 29 August 1842, 93 CTS 465) and in 1858 by the Tianjin treaty (Treaty of Peace, Friendship and Commerce, between Great Britain and China, 26 June 1858, 119 CTS 163).

[10] See generally John M Jennings, *The Opium Empire: Japanese Imperialism and Drug Trafficking in Asia, 1895–1945* (Praeger, 1997). Japan's involvement in drug trafficking was documented by the International Military Tribunal for the Far East in its judgment: see 'Majority Judgment' in Neil Boister

It can be seen from these examples that state organized crime has a far-reaching impact on the international plane. As this book will show, state organized crime poses a concrete threat to international peace and security. In addition to fuelling armed conflicts and funding terrorism, it violates human rights, undermines the rule of law, and adversely affects the economy of developing countries. It is a phenomenon that challenges traditional representations of the mechanics of domestic governance and international relations. Untangling 'the complex and murky relations between criminals and political elites in many parts of the world [can help] explain much not only about local politics, but regional and global trends in world politics as well'.[11] State organized crime is the expression of complex political and economic forces which govern informal structures of power entrenched within the state. Such structures, commonly referred to as a 'shadow state',[12] 'rhizome state' (*État rhizome*),[13] or 'deep state',[14] can be observed in different forms in many states in all regions of the world and from across the spectrums of economic development and systems of government. As proceeds of organized crime reach unprecedented levels,[15] illicit capital accumulation and diversion by state officials occur in massive proportions. If not properly addressed, state organized crime will continue to undermine the foundations of the international legal order as well as the potential of many countries to experience a peaceful and sustainable development.

Yet the magnitude of the harm caused internationally by state organized crime is not always manifest, as the involvement of governments in organized criminal activities is often cloaked in secrecy. State organized crime remains a marginal object of interest, in particular for international legal studies. This book proposes to contribute to an enhanced understanding of the implications of this phenomenon on the international plane, by examining state organized crime from the perspective of public international law. An enquiry into international law's potential for addressing state organized crime is indeed both relevant and necessary. State organized crime involves the primary subject of international law—the state—and impacts other subjects of international law, be it states, corporations, or individuals. State organized crime raises a number of questions from the perspective of different branches

and Robert Cryer (eds), *Documents on the Tokyo International Military Tribunal: Charter, Indictment, and Judgments* (Oxford University Press, 2008) 71, at 364–65, 430.

[11] Roy Godson, 'The Political-Criminal Nexus and Global Security' in Roy Godson (ed), *Menace to Society: Political-Criminal Collaboration around the World* (Transaction Publishers, 2003) 1, at 1.

[12] See generally William Reno, *Corruption and State Politics in Sierra Leone* (Cambridge University Press, 1995).

[13] Jean-François Bayart, *L'État en Afrique : La politique du ventre* (rev edn, Fayard, 2006), at 270 ff.

[14] Penny Green and Tony Ward, *State Crime: Governments, Violence and Corruption* (Pluto Press, 2004), at 86–104.

[15] Estimates published in 2011 by the United Nations Office on Drugs and Crime (UNODC) suggest that flows related to drug trafficking and other transnational organized crime activities amounted to approximately US$ 650 billion per year in 2000–2009, which was equivalent to 1.5% of global GDP. In 2009, the totality of criminal proceeds worldwide amounted to about US$ 2.1 trillion (3.6% of global GDP). As much as US$ 1.6 trillion (2.7% of global GDP) of illicit money is estimated to have been successfully laundered through the financial system in 2009. See UNODC, *Estimating Financial Flows Resulting from Drug Trafficking and Other Transnational Organized Crimes* (United Nations, 2011), at 36, 38, 42.

of international law, such as the law of state responsibility, the law of treaties, international criminal law, and international security law. On an ethical-normative plane, state organized crime stands at odds with core principles of the international legal order. In an attempt to address these important issues, this book provides an analysis of the rules and mechanisms of international law relevant to the suppression of state organized crime, as well as a normative argument for developing international legal mechanisms specifically designed to address this phenomenon.

As Chambliss pointed out, '[t]he fact that some of the most serious social harms [...] are not defined as crime makes the study of state crime in the global age even more urgent'.[16] The analysis performed in this volume shows that state organized crime remains largely unaddressed and unchecked by international law. Existing international law rules and mechanisms, such as the law of state responsibility or crime-suppression conventions designed to ensure individual criminal responsibility under domestic law for organized crime and corruption, are inadequate for the task of combating state organized crime. With the aim of prompting reflection on the implications of the participation of state organs in organized crime and on international law's potential for addressing this phenomenon, the book intends to provide a normative justification for addressing state organized crime at the international level and for establishing it as an international crime.[17] It also puts forward proposals to develop an international legal framework for the suppression of state organized crime, sketching draft provisions for an international convention for the suppression of state organized crime, and considering the potential role of the UN Security Council and of international criminal courts and tribunals, respectively, in holding perpetrators accountable.

Before proceeding with the argument, the concept of state organized crime should be clearly delineated. Because 'the conceptual, definitional, and methodological issues in the realm of state crime are especially daunting',[18] some terminological clarifications are in order.

Terminology

Using the concept of state organized crime in a piece of legal scholarship comes with challenges. First, it must succeed in convincing international lawyers that a term borrowed from criminology, with conceptual underpinnings specific to that discipline, can be useful for the purposes of legal analysis. Secondly, it must convince criminologists that the concept of 'state-organized crime' commonly known in their field may be altered to reflect particular ontological assumptions about profit-driven state criminality and to fit applicable legal concepts. As will be explained shortly, for

[16] William J Chambliss, 'Foreword' in Dawn L Rothe and Christopher W Mullins (eds), *State Crime: Current Perspectives* (Rutgers University Press, 2011) vii, at viii.

[17] A definition of the concept of 'international crime' is provided in Chapter 5, Section B.1.

[18] David O Friedrichs (ed), *State Crime*, vol I: *Defining, Delineating and Explaining State Crime* (Ashgate, 1998), at xvi.

the purposes of this book the concept of state organized crime should be read more narrowly than the concept of 'state-organized crime' used in criminology. Attentive readers will have noticed that liberty was taken to remove the hyphen, in order to reflect this distinction.

To begin with, in the term 'state organized crime' the word 'state' is understood as an organized political structure equipped to carry out governmental and administrative functions and possessing the monopoly over the use of coercive power within a given territory. In that sense, it does not refer to the state as a formal legal entity, as it is understood in public international law, but to the government of the state and more generally to the individuals acting as organs or agents of the state. This choice of terminology is intended to reflect the limits, from the perspective of political sciences, of the legal-formal distinction between 'the state' and the individuals acting on its behalf in circumstances where crimes are committed by state officials in their official capacity. It is not intended, however, to call into question the validity or pertinence of such distinction in public international law. As a result, the use of the term 'state organized crime' does not imply in any way that a state, as an abstract entity and vehicle for identity and responsibility under international law, can commit a crime in the legal-technical sense and face criminal responsibility. The *dictum* of the Nuremberg International Military Tribunal holds true: 'Crimes against international law are committed by men, not by abstract entities'.[19] That is not to say, however, that the criminal conduct of individuals acting as organs or agents of the state may not constitute an internationally wrongful act of the state giving rise to state responsibility under international law.[20]

Secondly, contrary to the term known to criminologists, state organized crime as understood in this volume does not encompass every type of criminal activity involving a state. Rather, state organized crime is a particular form of 'organized crime'. While attempts to define the concept of 'organized crime' for academic or crime-suppression purposes have given birth to widely disparate definitions, most have in common two key elements: a certain degree of organization of the perpetrators, and the existence of a specific financial or economic motive for engaging in criminal conduct.[21] Under international law, the commonly accepted definition of organized crime is to be found in the United Nations Convention against Transnational Organized Crime[22] (UNCTOC, or Palermo Convention). UNCTOC defines an 'organized criminal group' as 'a structured group of three or more persons, existing

[19] *Trial of the Major War Criminals before the International Military Tribunal, Nuremberg*, vol XXII: *Proceedings, 27 August – 1 October 1946* (Nuremberg, 1948), at 466. See also *United States v Wilhelm von Leeb and others* (*High Command* case) in *Trials of War Criminals before the Nuremberg Military Tribunals under Control Council Law No 10* (US Government Printing Office, 1949–1953), vol XI, at 508 ('The State being but an inanimate corporate entity or concept, it cannot as such make plans, determine policies, exercise judgment, experience fear or be restrained or deterred from action except through its animate agents and representatives').

[20] See Chapter 2.

[21] See generally Letizia Paoli and Tom vander Beken, 'Organized Crime: A Contested Concept' in Letizia Paoli (ed), *The Oxford Handbook of Organized Crime* (Oxford University Press, 2014) 13.

[22] United Nations Convention against Transnational Organized Crime, 15 November 2000, entered into force on 29 September 2003, 2225 UNTS 209.

for a period of time and acting in concert with the aim of committing one or more serious crimes or offences [...] in order to obtain, directly or indirectly, a financial or other material benefit'.[23] Simply put, as a matter of international law the lure of profit is an essential feature of organized crime. Organized criminal groups tend to deploy their efforts in lucrative activities, typically activities of an economic nature (such as illicit trade in prohibited goods, or the providing of illicit services) or related to some form of extortion (such as protection rackets, or corruption). In keeping with this premise, this book is concerned solely and exclusively with crimes committed or facilitated by state officials for the purpose of profit, such as drug trafficking, illicit exploitation of natural resources, currency counterfeiting, corruption, embezzlement of public funds, and money laundering.

That is not to say that state organized crime may not pursue an agenda that goes beyond the satisfaction of plain material interests. As a matter of law, it is accepted that proceeds of organized crime may be used, for example, to further political objectives.[24] This has two important consequences for the purposes of our analysis. First, all criminal activities involving a financial or other material benefit will fall under the definition of state organized crime, irrespective of whether the final purpose for the perpetrator is to obtain personal profit or to further a political agenda. Secondly and correlatively, this definition excludes conduct that is not at least partly motivated by the perspective of a financial or other material benefit. As a result and as a general rule, crimes that do not entail any form of profit as a constitutive element, including crimes committed purely for political or ideological motives, such as terrorism, and other crimes involving the use of armed violence traditionally considered to be 'state crimes' *par excellence* such as aggression, genocide, crimes against humanity, and war crimes remain beyond the scope of this study. Exceptionally, however, where it can be established that such crimes were committed for the purpose of obtaining a financial or other material benefit, the latter may fall within the scope of the definition of state organized crime. This caveat is important, as crimes known as 'core' international crimes may in some instances be driven by material considerations.[25]

The question of which specific offences may be committed in the form of 'organized crime' and, by extension, of which crimes fall within the definition of state organized crime does not need to receive a definite answer. For the sake of consensus, this volume refers to conduct considered a criminal offence in the eyes of international law,[26] in particular conduct that states parties to international crime-suppression conventions are required to criminalize in their domestic law.

Lastly, it is necessary to delineate the circle of perpetrators. State organized crime is different from petty corruption involving low-level civil servants. It commonly involves the highest authorities of the state—individuals entrusted with prominent

[23] Ibid, Art 2(a). [24] See Chapter 3, Section A.7. [25] See Chapter 1, Section B.3.

[26] This approach is in line with the dominant view in the literature: see Dawn L Rothe and David O Friedrichs, 'The State of the Criminology of Crimes of the State' (2006) 33 *Social Justice* 147, at 151; William J Chambliss, 'Commentary by William J. Chambliss' (1995) 26 *Society for the Study of Social Problems Newsletter* 9; Ronald C Kramer, 'State-Organized Crime, International Law and Structural Contradictions' (2016) 24 *Critical Criminology* 231, at 235–36; Jean-François Bayart, Stephen Ellis, and Béatrice Hibou, *The Criminalization of the State in Africa* (Indiana University Press, 1999), at 15–16.

public functions who have the power to devise and control the implementation of state policies, and who have the authority to harness the resources of the state to further their agenda. This element is what makes state organized crime distinctly 'wrong' when compared to regular forms of organized crime and corruption.[27] The definition of state organized crime should accordingly reflect the specific harm and wrongfulness inherent in the involvement of the most powerful officials of the state in organized crime. For the purposes of this study, state organized crime is therefore defined as being committed by 'a public official in a position to shape or influence the actions of a state'. This functional definition is similar to that used to define the perpetrators of the crime of aggression.[28] As a result, not any case of organized crime or corruption involving public officials may fall within the definition of state organized crime.

To sum up, for the present purposes state organized crime can be defined as the use, by a public official in a position to shape or influence the actions of a state and acting in concert with a structured group, of the resources of the state to commit or facilitate the commission of acts criminalized in international law, in order to obtain a financial or other material benefit.

Methodology

A few words should be said about the methodology followed in this volume to establish the factual basis necessary to postulate the existence, and analyse the mechanics, of state organized crime. Information related to the criminal conduct of senior state officials is, by nature, sensitive, and therefore not easily accessible and often to be taken with a grain of salt. The criminological analysis of the phenomenon of state organized crime, conducted in Chapter 1, relies on prima facie reliable secondary sources, such as published research in criminology and political sociology; publications of international organizations, non-governmental organizations, independent think-tanks, or domestic commissions of inquiry; judicial decisions and official records of judicial proceedings; press articles and reports from established newspapers and press agencies; and government documents such as US diplomatic cables released by WikiLeaks.[29]

[27] A normative argument regarding the wrongfulness of state organized crime is expounded in Chapter 5, Section C.

[28] For a more detailed explanation, see Chapter 6, Section A.1(a).

[29] Available and searchable online at https://wikileaks.org/plusd/. US diplomatic cables released by WikiLeaks were considered prima facie reliable and admitted into evidence by the Special Court for Sierra Leone. See *Prosecutor v Charles Ghankay Taylor*, Case no SCSL-03-01, Decision on the Urgent and Public with Annexes A-C Defence Motion to Re-Open Its Case in Order to Seek Admission of Documents Relating to the Relationship between the United States Government and the Prosecution of Charles Taylor, 27 January 2011.

Outline of the Argument

The argument of the book is advanced in three steps. First, as a preliminary matter, a criminological analysis identifies the distinctive characteristics of state organized crime. Secondly, the book analyses the applicability, potential, and limits of the norms and mechanisms of international law relevant to the suppression of state organized crime. It discusses whether and under which conditions the involvement of state organs or agents in organized crime may amount to an internationally wrongful act giving rise to the international responsibility of the state. Turning to an analysis of mechanisms of individual criminal responsibility, the book also highlights a number of practical and normative shortcomings of the legal framework established by relevant crime-suppression conventions requiring states parties to take action to punish individuals involved in organized crime and corruption. Thirdly, the book sketches proposals to develop an international legal framework designed to hold perpetrators of state organized crime accountable. It presents a normative justification for criminalizing and suppressing state organized crime at the international level, proposes draft provisions for an international convention for the suppression of state organized crime, and discusses the potential role of the UN Security Council and of international criminal courts and tribunals, respectively, in holding perpetrators accountable.

Chapter 1 (Part I) describes the phenomenon of state organized crime. It analyses the context in which state organized crime occurs, highlighting the criminogenic mechanisms at play in 'shadow states' and kleptocratic regimes. It discusses the motives underlying the involvement of state officials in organized crime, showing that state organized crime may be committed not only for the perpetrators' personal profit, but also in pursuit of state policy or broader ideological objectives such as international terrorism. It further identifies the actors involved in state organized crime and the means through which it is perpetrated, stressing that state organized crime is committed by senior state officials abusing their authority and using the material and human resources of the state for criminal purposes. State organized crime is posited as a criminological concept to comprehend diverse forms of government misconduct driven by profit, including partnerships with organized criminal groups, the plundering of a country's resources by kleptocratic rulers, and high-level corruption schemes.

Our enquiry into international law's capacity to address state organized crime (Part II) begins in Chapter 2 with an analysis of issues of state responsibility. This chapter discusses whether and under which conditions the involvement of senior public officials in organized crime may amount to an internationally wrongful act of the state. As a preliminary matter, the chapter opens with general considerations concerning the nature of state responsibility for criminal acts committed by individuals acting as organs or agents of the state. The chapter then analyses the issue of attribution of conduct to a state, showing that the conduct of state officials using the resources of the state to commit or facilitate the commission of organized criminal activities may in many cases be considered attributable to the state. This chapter then discusses whether the participation of the organs or agents of a state in organized crime may constitute a breach of an international obligation of the state. It seeks to determine whether state participation in organized crime is prohibited as such under international law, whether pursuant to the provisions of crime-suppression conventions pertaining to organized crime and corruption, or pursuant to customary international law. To that end, it examines the potential legal implications of state organized crime under general principles of international law and under different branches of international law, examining in turn the obligation to perform treaty obligations in good faith, the obligation of states to prevent acts contrary to the rights of other states within their territory, the obligation not to intervene in the internal affairs of another state, the obligation not to infringe another state's sovereignty over its natural resources, the obligation not to engage in pillaging in the context of an armed conflict, and the obligation under international human rights law to uphold the protection from slavery, servitude, and forced labour. Finally, this chapter discusses the conditions under which other states may be entitled to invoke the responsibility of a state involved in state organized crime where that state may be considered to have committed an internationally wrongful act. The conclusion reached is that, while state participation in organized crime may in certain cases give rise to the international responsibility of the state, overall primary and secondary rules of international law fail to regulate and attach legal consequences to the involvement of states in organized crime.

In Chapters 3 and 4, the book turns to an analysis of the rules and mechanisms of international criminal law relevant to the criminal responsibility of individuals involved in organized crime and corruption. These chapters identify the practical and normative shortcomings, for the specific purpose of combating state organized crime, of the substantive and procedural law laid out in relevant crime-suppression conventions. This part of the book lays the foundation of the argument for establishing state organized crime as an international crime, expounded in Chapter 5, and for the proposals put forward in subsequent chapters.

Chapter 3 begins by outlining the obligations of states parties to the various international instruments on organized crime and corruption, examining provisions on the criminalization of conduct under domestic law, the establishment of jurisdiction, the obligation to extradite or prosecute suspected offenders, international cooperation in criminal matters, and the confiscation and seizure of proceeds of crime.

Chapter 4 then highlights the limits of applicable crime-suppression conventions in cases of state organized crime, analysing the practical and normative shortcomings of relevant treaty provisions as well as external procedural bars such as the international law of immunities. A number of issues are identified in this chapter. First, the applicable law is fragmented into different legal regimes implemented unevenly across national jurisdictions. Secondly, the current international crime-suppression model is likely to be ineffective in politically sensitive cases because of its reliance on a territorial approach to jurisdiction. Thirdly, certain principles governing extradition proceedings and mutual legal assistance in criminal matters, such as the political offence exception, the discrimination clause, and the 'essential interests' clause, can be relied on by suspected offenders or requested states parties to undermine international cooperation and law enforcement. Fourthly, the narrow formulation of the obligation *aut dedere aut judicare* in the relevant conventions can in certain circumstances allow offenders to escape responsibility. Fifthly, the legal regime established by the relevant instruments remains subject to the international law of jurisdictional immunities, which in certain cases shields state officials from foreign criminal proceedings as well as state property from measures of foreign judicial constraint in confiscation proceedings. Finally, and most importantly, this chapter argues that the existing law does not take into consideration the involvement of state organs and resources in organized crime, and therefore fails to fulfil a crucial expressive function.

In view of the limits of the existing law, Part III of the book sketches the contours of an international legal framework dedicated specifically to the suppression of state organized crime, focusing on mechanisms designed to hold perpetrators responsible.

Chapter 5 makes a theoretical argument for establishing state organized crime as an international crime, whether by means of a treaty or through a decision of the UN Security Council. It opens with general reflections on the function of criminalization to identify guiding principles and to establish a theoretical framework within which to make the argument, discussing the dynamics of international criminalization and identifying grounds underlying the genesis of existing international crimes. It shows that conduct considered by states to be eligible for criminalization as a matter of international law tends to present certain features, suggesting that international criminalization serves the purpose of protecting specific interests. In light of this theoretical framework, this chapter argues that state organized crime ought to be criminalized because it threatens interests that states deem worthy of protection by way of international criminalization, constituting as it does an abuse of state authority, a threat to international peace and security, a violation of internationally guaranteed human rights, and a subversion of the rule of law and of the proper functioning of interstate cooperation. This chapter also suggests that the positing of state organized crime as an international crime would fulfil an important expressive function.

Chapter 6 then proposes the adoption and discusses the contents of a multilateral treaty by which states parties would undertake to criminalize state organized crime specifically, to adopt provisions in their domestic law to allow for more effective law enforcement, and to refrain from participating in or supporting organized criminal activities. The proposed treaty is designed to remedy certain of the limits of the existing law. First, it would provide an appropriate legal basis for prosecuting and punishing individuals involved in state organized crime. Secondly, it would enhance domestic criminal law enforcement by creating a broad obligation for states parties to establish both territorial and extraterritorial jurisdiction over the proposed crime, and by widening the scope of the obligation *aut dedere aut judicare*, with a view to pressuring states parties genuinely to initiate proceedings against suspected offenders present in their territory. Thirdly, it would open the door for the international responsibility of a state involved in organized crime. Last but not least, it would fulfil a necessary expressive function.

This volume also explores other means to suppress state organized crime at the international level, as an alternative or a complement to the proposed treaty. Chapter 7 discusses the potential role of the UN Security Council in the suppression of state organized crime. It suggests that in situations involving armed violence or a terrorist threat, state organized crime can be characterized as a threat to the peace, which opens the door for the adoption by the Security Council of binding measures under Chapter VII of the UN Charter. This chapter proposes that the Security Council require UN member states to establish state organized crime as a criminal offence in their domestic law and to cooperate to bring offenders to justice. It is suggested that a Security Council decision could usefully complement or provide a substitute for a multilateral treaty for the purpose of establishing state organized crime as an international crime. In addition, this chapter proposes that the Security Council require member states to freeze the assets of state officials and entities suspected of being involved in state organized crime. Such sanctions would fulfil prescriptive, expressive, and preventive functions. This chapter argues that the proposed measures can be taken in conformity with the UN Charter and that they would be in line with the contemporary practice of the Security Council.

Lastly, Chapter 8 discusses the potential role of international criminal courts and tribunals in prosecuting individuals suspected of being involved in state organized crime. Operating on the premise that a number of obstacles undermining law enforcement at the domestic level could be overcome by an international criminal court or tribunal, it outlines the potential merits and challenges of prosecuting offenders before such courts or tribunals. It identifies potential advantages common to international criminal courts and tribunals, namely the unavailability of jurisdictional immunities as a procedural bar, the greater likelihood of a genuine investigation, the existence of formal rules to deal with concurrent claims of jurisdiction, the capacity to address complex cases of system criminality, and the expressive potential of international criminal courts and tribunals. It then considers the respective advantages and disadvantages of different institutional mechanisms that could be used or adapted for the prosecution of state organized crime, examining in turn the International Criminal Court (ICC), international ad hoc tribunals, and the future criminal chamber of the African Court of Justice and Human Rights (ACJHR). It reaches the conclusion that, while international criminal courts and tribunals may in some circumstances appear better equipped to deal with cases of state organized crime than their domestic counterparts, recourse to an international criminal court or tribunal would come with difficulties perhaps even greater than those associated with prosecuting offenders domestically.

PART I

STATE ORGANIZED CRIME

1

The Phenomenon of State Organized Crime

This chapter describes the phenomenon of state organized crime, defined as the use, by a public official in a position to shape or influence the actions of a state and acting in concert with a structured group, of the resources of the state to commit or facilitate the commission of acts criminalized in international law, in order to obtain a financial or other material benefit. The chapter begins with a succinct introduction to state organized crime as a criminological concept, before discussing in turn the context, the motives, the actors, and the means of state organized crime. The concern of this chapter is purely descriptive and analytical, with a view to setting the stage for the discussion of legal considerations in subsequent chapters.[1]

A. Conceptualizing State Organized Crime

To understand what state organized crime is, a good starting point is to note that states and organized criminal groups share common features. Both exercise authority through a power structure and the use of coercive force. Both operate economic enterprises.[2] Tilly has shown that there is conceptually little difference between a state in the making, collecting taxes to fund a war against political enemies, and a protection racket, extorting money in an effort to overcome competitors and extend its territorial influence.[3] The resemblance is evident in the case of the Islamic State in Iraq and the Levant (ISIL), which used coercion to levy taxes in occupied cities to fund its war in Syria and Iraq.[4] Whether ISIL is a criminal organization using violence for

[1] Note that the cases discussed in this chapter are cited to illustrate specific aspects or mechanisms of state organized crime. It is not claimed that the facts of each particular case, when considered as a whole, are necessarily constitutive of state organized crime as I have chosen to define it. A legal definition of the constitutive elements of state organized crime as a criminal offence is proposed in Chapter 6, Section A.

[2] Susan Strange, *The Retreat of the State: The Diffusion of Power in the World Economy* (Cambridge University Press, 1996), at 110–11.

[3] See Charles Tilly, 'War Making and State Making as Organized Crime' in Peter B. Evans, Dietrich Rueschemeyer, and Theda Skocpol (eds), *Bringing the State Back In* (Cambridge University Press, 1985) 169, at 171. As early as the fifth century, Saint Augustine noted: 'Justice being taken away, then, what are kingdoms but great robberies? For what are robberies themselves, but little kingdoms? The band itself is made up of men; it is ruled by the authority of a prince, it is knit together by the pact of the confederacy; the booty is divided by the law agreed on' (Aurelius Augustine, *The City of God*, first published 426, trans Marcus Dods, vol 1 (T & T Clark, 1913), at 139).

[4] See Madjid Zerrouky, 'Mossoul, une machine à cash pour l'EI', *Le Monde* (3 April 2017).

Confronting the Shadow State: An International Law Perspective on State Organized Crime. Henri Decœur. Published 2018 by Oxford University Press.

the purpose of extortion, or whether it used legitimate state-like authority to collect taxes within its jurisdiction, is a matter of perspective.

Such structural and functional similarities, however, do not necessarily lead to competition and confrontation between a state and organized criminal groups operating within its territory or its sphere of influence. The nature and degree of interplay between the state and organized criminal groups are contingent on the interests of each party in a given political, economic, and cultural context.[5] When agendas coincide, this relationship may range from occasional collaboration to full-blown symbiosis,[6] a situation in which state organized crime is likely to occur.

Traditional criminological concepts can help conceptualize the 'what', the 'how', and the 'why' of state organized crime. To begin with, state organized crime involves different types of profit-driven crimes, principally 'market-based crimes' such as drug trafficking, but also 'predatory crimes' involving the use of violence, such as pillaging in the context of an armed conflict.[7] State organized crime is also a form of 'state-initiated crime', which 'occurs when [the perpetrators], employed by the government, engage in organizational deviance at the direction of, or with the tacit approval of, the government'.[8] The kind of criminal involvement on the part of public officials that amounts to state organized crime therefore requires more than a merely passive facilitation of criminal activities committed by private entities through a policy of *laissez-faire*. State organized crime requires an active contribution from senior public officials acting in their official capacity and using the resources of the state for criminal purposes. Finally, not unlike 'white-collar crime', state organized crime can be conceptualized in turn as 'occupational crime' (that is, crime committed in the course of activity within an organization but for personal ends), and as 'organizational crime' (that is, crime committed in furtherance of an organization's goals).[9] State officials may engage in organized criminal activities to

[5] For an analysis of the motivational and structural factors shaping the relationship between the state and organized crime, see generally Roy Godson, 'The Political-Criminal Nexus and Global Security' in Roy Godson (ed), *Menace to Society: Political-Criminal Collaboration around the World* (Transaction Publishers, 2003), at 8–17.

[6] See Peter A Lupsha, 'Transnational Organized Crime versus the Nation-State' (1996) 2 *Transnational Organized Crime* 21, at 30–32 (distinguishing between a 'parasitical' stage and a 'symbiotic' stage). For a concrete illustration of this evolution in Kyrgyzstan, see Erica Marat, 'The State-Crime Nexus in Central Asia: State Weakness, Organized Crime, and Corruption in Kyrgyzstan and Tajikistan', Silk Road Paper (Central Asia-Caucasus Institute and Silk Road Studies Program, 2006), at 93 (noting: 'If earlier political actors had been connected with criminal elements illegally and in a subversive way, following the controversial parliamentary elections in February–March 2005, the relations between criminals and politicians took on a new form. New hybrids of power relations developed within the state between criminals and politicians. Common economic interests between criminal and political actors merged within the state apparatus. Both groups could operate in sync in maintaining licit and illicit businesses while simultaneously representing the state and enjoying legal status').

[7] For an attempt to conceptualize and provide a typology of profit-driven crimes, see Robin T Naylor, 'Towards a General Theory of Profit-Driven Crimes' (2003) 43 *British Journal of Criminology* 81.

[8] On the difference between 'state-facilitated' and 'state-initiated crime', see Ronald C Kramer, Raymond J Michalowski, and David Kauzlarich, 'The Origins and Development of the Concept and Theory of State-Corporate Crime' (2002) 48 *Crime & Delinquency* 263, at 271–72.

[9] The distinction between occupational and organizational crime was coined in Marshall B Clinard and Richard Quinney, *Criminal Behavior Systems: A Typology* (Holt, Rinehart and Winston, 1967). On the latter, see Laura Shill Schrager and James F Short, 'Toward a Sociology of Organizational Crime' (1977) 25 *Social Problems* 407, at 411–12 (defining organizational crime as 'illegal acts of omission or

generate personal profit, or to further the state's objectives. In some cases where the line separating private and public interests is tenuous, the pursuit of personal profit by rulers may be institutionalized and become part of an organizational policy of the state. State organized crime is a cross-over phenomenon which blurs the boundaries between traditional criminological concepts, as the following analysis will evidence.

B. The Context of State Organized Crime

State organized crime usually, although not exclusively, arises in situations involving a relationship of symbiosis between state organs and organized criminal groups. In kleptocratic regimes, where this relationship reaches a particular degree of sophistication, state organized crime may even operate as a mode of governance. In the worst cases, state organized crime may also harness armed violence to generate revenue, triggering and fuelling armed conflicts.

1. Symbiosis between state organs and organized crime

Symbiosis is defined as the 'interaction between two different organisms living in close physical association, typically to the advantage of both'.[10] For two entities to cohabit in a state of symbiosis, each must provide something needed by the other. This is what happens when the interests of the state and those of organized criminal groups converge to give rise to a mutually beneficial *quid pro quo*. State officials may turn to organized criminal networks for financial or political support, or to attain strategic policy objectives. In return, privileged connections with policy-makers allow criminals to prosper.[11] Corrupt officials can notably be requested to use their authority to protect individuals connected to organized crime, for instance by forwarding them classified information or by tampering with evidence to hinder law enforcement.[12]

While cases of outright collusion between the state and organized criminal groups remain relatively exceptional, it is important to keep in mind that such symbiosis

commission of an individual or a group of individuals in a legitimate formal organization in accordance with the operative goals of the organization, which have a serious physical or economic impact on employees, consumers or the general public').

[10] Oxford English Dictionary, online version.

[11] See Phil Williams, 'Transnational Organized Crime and the State' in Rodney Bruce Hall and Thomas J Biersteker (eds), *The Emergence of Private Authority in Global Governance* (Cambridge University Press, 2002) 161, at 176–77; Godson (n 5), at 8–9 (interestingly emphasizing the criminals' need for social recognition and mobility).

[12] This is what happened in Bulgaria, leading to the resignation of Interior Minister Rumen Petkov in April 2008. According to a leaked intelligence report, Interior Ministry officials forwarded classified internal documents to a criminal group trading in synthetic drugs, and received money from illegal alcohol producers in return for information and the destruction of incriminating evidence. See 'Dirty Politics: One Resignation is not Enough to Clean up Bulgaria', *The Economist* (17 April 2008); US diplomatic cable, Embassy Sofia, 'Interior Minister Resigns under Mounting Pressure' (15 April 2008) 08SOFIA229.

does not occur in a vacuum. Rather, it is often rooted in established informal practices of the high-level sphere of international business and politics that remain mostly unknown to the general public until they hit the headlines of the press. In this peculiar context, the border between licit and illicit activities may be as difficult to delineate as it is easy to overstep. This 'grey zone' provides a fertile environment for collusion between senior government officials and individuals connected to or involved in organized crime. For instance, government officials may seek the support of key individuals belonging to the well-connected business elite of a foreign kleptocratic state to provide the input needed to secure a strategic transaction. In France, a former Interior minister is currently under investigation for his alleged role in facilitating the passing by the Belgian parliament of a bill allowing a prominent businessman and close associate of Kazakh President Nursultan Nazarbayev, facing corruption charges in Belgium, to strike a deal with the prosecution to avoid trial and conviction. It is reported that Nazarbayev demanded that France use its influence in Belgium to get his friend out of trouble as a precondition to the purchase by Kazakhstan of French-made military helicopters.[13] This example provides an informative glance into the inner workings of the so-called 'shadow state', and highlights the prevalence of corruption in the symbiosis between the business elite and senior state officials in both kleptocratic and democratic states.

The same processes are at play in alliances between the state and organized criminal groups. Organized criminal groups may act as power brokers for services needed by the state. The influence of organized crime can be particularly determinant in regions where the state has little authority or legitimacy: in Sicily, where the mafia traditionally fulfilled an important social role by maintaining law and order, figures of local organized crime acted as facilitators to secure political arrangements and votes in local communities.[14] Influential organized crime figures may also prove useful as peace brokers. In Myanmar, the good offices of drug lord Lo Hsing Han were employed by former Burmese Prime Minister Khin Nyunt to negotiate a ceasefire agreement with local rebel groups. In exchange, Lo Hsing Han was granted leeway to traffic heroin in Myanmar and to launder his proceeds in Singapore.[15]

A situation of symbiosis may also arise where organized criminal groups control strategic territory. For example, in the 1960s and 1970s successive military governments in Thailand forged an unofficial alliance with rebel groups involved in opium trafficking in Burma to keep the northern borderlands under control, at the same time allowing the Thai army and police to collect an informal tax on opium caravans entering Thai territory. In exchange, opium warlords were guaranteed a safe haven in Thailand to conduct their trade and operate heroin laboratories.[16] Furthermore,

[13] Fabrice Lhomme and Gérard Davet, 'Le Kazakhgate : une affaire d'Etat', *Le Monde* (9 July 2015).

[14] Diego Gambetta, *The Sicilian Mafia: The Business of Private Protection* (Harvard University Press, 1996), at 182–87.

[15] US diplomatic cable, Embassy Rangoon, 'Dropping the Hammer on Crony Steven Law' (28 December 2007) 07RANGOON1211; US diplomatic cable, Embassy Rangoon, 'Burmese Businessman on GOB-U.S. Relations, Ethnic Conflict, and 2010 Elections' (23 September 2009) 09RANGOON644; John Sweeney, 'How Junta protects Mr Heroin', *The Guardian* (8 April 2001).

[16] Alfred W McCoy, *The Politics of Heroin: CIA Complicity in the Global Drug Trade* (rev edn, Lawrence Hill Books, 2003), at 414–15.

smuggling networks may be used by the state as sources of intelligence and instruments of subversion in neighbouring states, a tactic used by South African security forces to root out foreign bases of the African National Congress.[17] Last but not least, politicians may also have recourse to organized criminal groups to intimidate rivals.[18]

Symbiosis between organized criminal groups and the state is the dominant paradigm for conceptualizing the involvement of public officials in organized crime. For instance, in its 2013 resolution on organized crime and corruption, the European Parliament declared that:

> criminal organizations can take advantage of a grey area of collusion with other parties, merging for the purpose of carrying out certain activities with white-collar perpetrators [including] public officials at all levels of decision-making, politicians [...], who, while not actually belonging to criminal organizations, have mutually lucrative business relations with them.[19]

The predominance of such paradigms, not only in criminology and political sciences, but also in crime-suppression strategies, is symptomatic of a fundamental epistemological problem. The interplay between organized crime and the state cannot be properly understood by maintaining a hermetic separation between these two concepts, as if 'organized crime' were an autonomous entity pursuing its own purposes within its own 'underworld', and as if it were inconceivable that state officials acting in their official capacity could be members of an organized criminal group or constitute one in their own right. As pointed out above, there are structural and functional similarities between states and organized criminal groups.[20] It is crucial to recognize that organized criminal groups are generally not fixed and permanent entities,[21] and

[17] See e.g. Stephen Ellis, 'The New Frontiers of Crime in South Africa' in Jean-François Bayart, Stephen Ellis, and Béatrice Hibou, *The Criminalization of the State in Africa* (Indiana University Press, 1999), at 62.

[18] For instance, in the late 1980s prominent Japanese politician Kanemaru Shin, who had received illegal campaign contributions from the organized crime *milieu*, helped former Prime Minister Noboru Takeshita hire criminals to silence right-wing opponents: see Eiko Maruko, 'Mediated Democracy: *Yakuza* and Japanese Political Leadership' in Felia Allum and Renate Siebert (eds), *Organized Crime and the Challenge to Democracy* (Routledge, 2003) 202, at 202, 214. See also the case of Kyrgyzstan, discussed in Marat (n 6), at 66 (adding: 'In this manner, the criminalization of the state takes place at the initiative of state officials and not the non-state criminal figures').

[19] European Parliament, 'Resolution on Organized Crime, Corruption and Money Laundering', 23 October 2013, Doc no P7_TA(2013)0444, para I.

[20] Recall Section A of this chapter.

[21] Joseph Albini observes that '[r]ather than being a criminal secret society, a criminal syndicate consists of loosely structured relationships functioning primarily because each participant is interested in furthering his own welfare' (Joseph L Albini, *The American Mafia: Genesis of a Legend* (Appleton-Century-Crofts, 1971), at 288). For example, in West Africa 'it is particularly misleading to think of organized crime groups as being solid structures resembling major corporations of crime' with a rigid hierarchy. West African criminal networks 'are generally characterized by their great fluidity and flexibility'. See UNODC, *Transnational Organized Crime in the West African Region* (United Nations, 2005), at 2, 15–18.

that the boundaries between corruption and actual participation in criminal activities are not clear-cut. Ceccarelli observes:

> Corruption in [certain] States goes far deeper than just paying off low level state employees and is present at far more elevated levels of sophistication. The criminal infiltration of an institution implies not only the passive acceptance of bribes and allowing crimes to take place but also the active facilitation of criminal businesses on the part of an institution or its leaders. In other words, corruption goes from being the simple acceptance of bribes to the direct involvement of the State in the supervision of organized crime.[22]

The extent of a state's subjection to corruption should not obscure the active role of corrupt officials in facilitating or supervising criminal activities. A UNODC report analysing the smuggling of migrants from West Africa to Europe observes that corrupt officials bribed to facilitate the passage of migrants may in fact be regarded as the heads of smuggling networks.[23] Senior state officials may themselves directly orchestrate criminal activities to further their own agenda. In such cases, the symbiotic paradigm no longer suffices to conceptualize the state's relationship to organized crime,[24] which can be more accurately defined as 'state organized crime'.

2. State organized crime and kleptocracy

The interplay between organized crime and government reaches a high degree of sophistication in kleptocratic regimes, and most notably in so-called 'weak states'.[25] In certain states, political power is exercised not only through the administrative structure of the state, but also and essentially through parallel networks that run deep into the economic and financial sectors. In the 'shadow state', control over economic resources is the key to political authority and legitimacy.

(a) The functioning of kleptocracy and the shadow state

Shadow states, as conceptualized by Reno, are characterized by '[t]he informal market role of rulers' construction of parallel political authority in the wake of the near total decay of formal state institutions'.[26] As resources augment political authority, power is exercised through control over informal markets.[27] Legitimacy rests

[22] Alessandra Ceccarelli, 'Clans, Politics and Organized Crime in Central Asia' (2007) 10 *Trends in Organized Crime* 19, at 33.

[23] UNODC, *Transnational Organized Crime in West Africa: A Threat Assessment* (United Nations, February 2013), at 29.

[24] See Alexander Kupatadze, *Organized Crime, Political Transitions and State Formation in Post-Soviet Eurasia* (Palgrave Macmillan, 2012), at 29–37 (analysing the political–criminal continuum and distinguishing between an 'underworld dominance' model, a 'symbiotic balance' model, and an 'elite dominance' model, where organized criminal activities are directly controlled by the state); Angela Veng Mei Leong, *The Disruption of International Organized Crime: An Analysis of Legal and Non-Legal Solutions* (Ashgate, 2007), at 13 (distinguishing between cases of symbiosis between organized crime and the state and cases where organized criminal activities are 'integrated into governmental activities').

[25] 'States are fragile when state structures lack political will and/or capacity to provide the basic functions needed for poverty reduction, development and to safeguard the security and human rights of their populations.' See OECD, *Principles for Good International Engagement in Fragile States and Situations* (April 2007), Principle 3.

[26] William Reno, *Corruption and State Politics in Sierra Leone* (Cambridge University Press, 1995), at 1.

[27] Ibid, at 1–3.

on the rulers' ability to redistribute resources to an influential clientele.[28] Patronage and clientelism are central to the functioning of shadow states. Clientelism can be defined as

> a pattern of social exchange between patrons, normally the holders of political administrative offices, and clients, who may be private citizens, businesses or more junior officials. The patron exercises power in favour of the client, who reciprocates by offering electoral support, political donations or personal gifts.[29]

Clientelism 'contributes to a political culture in which informal exchanges between state and non-state actors flourish'.[30] Shadow states are grounded in a neo-patrimonial system of government where kinship, patronage, and other forms of personal ties and networks are the keystone of governance. Political corruption—defined as 'the abuse of entrusted power by political leaders for private gain, with the objective of increasing power or wealth'[31]—is then generalized. Kleptocratic forms of governance are based on economic strategies of accumulation known as 'plunder economy' (*Raubwirtschaft*). Access to resources is the object of a constant struggle between rival groups aiming at securing their respective spheres of influence. In this context, the public and private sectors interpenetrate and can become almost indistinguishable as the accumulation of resources becomes the main focus of the rulers.[32] Control extends over clandestine markets in an effort to deprive rivals of potential sources of income.[33] In short, rent-seeking is institutionalized and becomes an operative goal of the state.[34] This mode of governance, aptly labelled by Bayart as the 'politics of the belly' (*la politique du ventre*),[35] is often predominant in states that lack the capacity to enforce government authority through administrative structures, but variations of Reno's model can also be observed in states with strong institutions.

Kleptocracy plays out in all economic and financial sectors,[36] often in a systematic and generalized fashion. Comparable patterns can be observed in all regions of the world. To begin with, the exploitation and marketing of natural resources often provides senior public officials with lucrative opportunities. In Cambodia, which has been described as a 'country for sale', Prime Minister Hun Sen and a small circle of power brokers control the exploitation of the country's natural resources, selling

[28] Patrick Chabal and Jean-Pascal Daloz, *Africa Works: Disorder as Political Instrument* (Indiana University Press, 1999), at 15–16.

[29] Penny Green and Tony Ward, *State Crime: Governments, Violence and Corruption* (Pluto Press, 2004), at 21.

[30] Ibid, at 187.

[31] Transparency International, *Global Corruption Report 2004* (Pluto Press, 2004), at 11.

[32] William Reno, *Warlord Politics and African States* (Lynne Rienner, 1999), at 22; Chabal and Daloz (n 28), at 9.

[33] William Reno, 'The Privatisation of Sovereignty and the Survival of Weak States' in Béatrice Hibou (ed), *Privatising the State* (C Hurst & Co, 2004) 95, at 103.

[34] Green and Ward (n 29), at 16–18.

[35] See Jean-François Bayart, *L'État en Afrique : La politique du ventre* (rev edn, Fayard, 2006), at 281–315.

[36] See e.g. the case of Armando Guebuza, former President of Mozambique, who together with his family was said to hold interests in the banking sector, the port industry, the transport and logistics sector, the construction sector, the power industry, the mining industry, the consulting industry, and the gaming industry. See US diplomatic cable, Embassy Maputo, 'Mozambican Businessman Talks of Corruption at the Highest Levels of Government' (28 January 2010) 10MAPUTO86.

private land to foreign companies and deriving personal profit from the timber industry.[37] In Equatorial Guinea, senior public officials and their relatives, operating as economic gatekeepers for foreign investment, have received payments from foreign oil companies.[38] In Nigeria, senior political figures are said to benefit from the trade in stolen crude oil (aka 'oil bunkering').[39] In Zimbabwe, high-ranking government officials have generated personal income from the diamond industry, including from the selling of undocumented diamonds[40] to foreign buyers who smuggled them out of the country.[41] Similarly, in the former Zaïre state officials were involved in the smuggling of the country's extracted natural resources.[42] Development aid can also be embezzled by state officials. Techniques for diverting project funds include the use by state officials of front companies operating as project contractors and overcharging for their services, or the more straightforward extortion of bribes.[43] The financial sector constitutes another major source of illicit revenue for kleptocrats. In Malaysia, more than US$ 3.5 billion belonging to 1Malaysia Development Berhad, a state-owned investment fund, were allegedly misappropriated by high-level government officials.[44] Another striking example is the Kabul Bank scandal in Afghanistan, a vast fraud that enabled nearly US$ 900 million worth of loans to be granted interest-free and without repayment date to members of the Afghan political and business elite, including Mahmoud Karzai, brother of former President Hamid Karzai.[45] Last but not least, state-owned companies can be used by state

[37] See Global Witness, *Country for Sale: How Cambodia's Elite Has Captured the Country's Extractive Industries* (February 2009).

[38] US Senate, Committee on Governmental Affairs, *Money Laundering and Foreign Corruption Enforcement and Effectiveness of the Patriot Act: Case Study involving Riggs Bank* (15 July 2004), at 98–108. See also Béatrice Hibou, 'The "Social Capital" of the State as an Agent of Deception, or the Ruses of Economic Intelligence' in Bayart, Ellis, and Hibou (n 17), at 84–85.

[39] Christina Katsouris and Aaron Sayne, *Nigeria's Criminal Crude, International Options to Combat the Export of Stolen Oil* (Chatham House, Royal Institute of International Affairs, September 2013), at 5.

[40] Rough diamonds must be certified in accordance with the Kimberley Process Certification Scheme, adopted at Interlaken on 5 November 2002. See generally Daniel L Feldman, 'Conflict Diamonds, International Trade Regulation, and the Nature of Law' (2003) 24 *University of Pennsylvania Journal of International Economic Law* 835.

[41] US diplomatic cable, Embassy Harare, 'Regime Elites Looting Deadly Diamond Field' (12 November 2008) 08HARARE1016. See also the report presented to the Zimbabwean Parliament by MP Edward Chindori-Chininga a few days before dying in a car crash: Parliament of Zimbabwe, 5th sess, 7th parliament, *First Report of the Portfolio Committee on Mines and Energy on Diamond Mining (with Special Reference to the Marange Diamond Fields), 2009–2013*, S.C.4, 2012 (presented June 2013), under section 4.2.1 (finding significant discrepancies between the level of revenue generated by the Zimbabwean diamond industry and the amount reportedly collected by the Treasury).

[42] See generally Janet MacGaffey, *The Real Economy of Zaire: The Contribution of Smuggling and Other Unofficial Activities to National Wealth* (University of Pennsylvania Press, 1991), at 36–39.

[43] W Michael Kramer, 'Summary of Fraud and Corruption Cases in International Development Projects', International Anti-Corruption Resource Center (6 February 2012), http://iacrc.org/fraud-and-corruption/summary-of-fraud-and-corruption-cases-in-international-development-projects/.

[44] See Randeep Ramesh, '1MDB: The inside story of the world's biggest financial scandal', *The Guardian* (28 July 2016). Money laundering charges were filed in the United States against several senior Malaysian government officials: see US Department of Justice, 'United States Seeks to Recover More Than $1 Billion Obtained from Corruption Involving Malaysian Sovereign Wealth Fund' (20 July 2016), https://www.justice.gov/opa/pr/united-states-seeks-recover-more-1-billion-obtained-corruption-involving-malaysian-sovereign.

[45] See Jon Boone, 'The financial scandal that broke Afghanistan's Kabul Bank', *The Guardian* (16 June 2011); Alissa J Rubin and Rod Nordland, 'Kabul Bank Is Portrayed as a Private A.T.M. for Afghanistan's Elite', *The New York Times* (29 March 2011).

officials for private gain or to finance political parties. The ongoing 'car wash' investigation (*operação lava jato*) in Brazil has uncovered a kickback scheme involving state-owned company Petrobras and a cartel of contractors, estimated to have funnelled at least US$ 2 billion to senior politicians and political parties, including former President Lula da Silva.[46]

Embezzlement of public funds can reach gargantuan proportions. The following table compares funds estimated to have been embezzled by certain heads of government, with the gross domestic product per capita of the state concerned:[47]

Head of government	Estimated funds embezzled (US$)	GDP per capita (2001) (US$)
Mohamed Suharto, President of Indonesia (1967–1998)	15 to 35 billion	695
Ferdinand Marcos, President of Philippines (1972–1986)	5 to 10 billion	912
Mobutu Sese Seko, President of Zaïre (1965–1997)	5 billion	99
Sani Abacha, President of Nigeria (1993–1998)	2 to 5 billion	319
Slobodan Milošević, President of Serbia/Yugoslavia (1989–2000)	1 billion	n/a
Jean-Claude Duvalier, President of Haiti (1971–1986)	300 to 800 million	460
Alberto Fujimori, President of Peru (1990–2000)	600 million	2,051
Pavlo Lazarenko, Prime Minister of Ukraine (1996–1997)	114 to 200 million	766
Arnoldo Alemán, President of Nicaragua (1997–2002)	100 million	490
Joseph Estrada, President of Philippines (1998–2001)	78 to 80 million	912

The resultant impoverishment of public resources drastically affects the state's budget and, coupled with poor remuneration for public servants, sustains in turn an environment conducive to political corruption. In Guinea, the average salary of civil servants in 1985 covered only 10 per cent of subsistence needs, barely

[46] Joe Leahy, 'What is the Petrobras scandal that is engulfing Brazil?', *The Financial Times* (1 April 2016); Ernesto Londoño, 'Ex-President of Brazil Sentenced to Nearly 10 Years in Prison for Corruption', *The New York Times* (12 July 2017).

[47] Source: Transparency International (n 31), at 13. For an updated compilation of cases, see Comité Catholique contre la Faim et pour le Développement, *Biens mal acquis … profitent trop souvent : la fortune des dictateurs et les complaisances occidentales* (March 2007) at 13–16. To this list should also be added proceedings initiated in the wake of the Arab Spring(s) against former Tunisian President Zine al-Abidine Ben Ali, former Egyptian President Hosni Mubarak, and former senior Libyan officials.

allowing recipients to feed their family for three days.[48] Such a climate encourages low-level officials to seek other sources of revenue, whether in the private sector or through bribery. Yet because corrupt bureaucracies involve additional costs for kleptocratic rulers, who need to share corrupt gains with lower-level officials, the former will usually reduce the size of the government and seek other means of controlling their subordinates.[49] Sustainability can be achieved only via parallel channels through which rulers exchange rent-seeking opportunities for political loyalty, replacing state administration with market control as a means of domination.[50] As observed by Mbembe, in a kleptocracy '[w]hat is therefore at stake is the possibility of new ways and means of subjecting and controlling people'.[51]

This mode of governance profoundly reshapes the structures of power:

> Alongside the traditional bureaucratic apparatus there is a real parallel administration: civil servants fulfil two roles, one public but not very active, the other private and often highly lucrative. [...] [C]ustoms officers' hierarchy can engage with impunity in rackets of all sorts (drugs, smuggling, etc.). Like business enterprises, the state has double bookkeeping.[52]

The result is a 'hybrid State' being 'simultaneously illusory and substantial'.[53] The state 'is no more than a décor, a pseudo-Western façade masking the realities of deeply personalized political relations',[54] where patronage, ethnic networks, and lineage play a central role.[55] The shadow state, being marked by a succession of conflicts and shifting coalitions between various actors, is not a harmonious structure,[56] but 'a fluid and contextual entity whose shape and internal configurations of power are constantly changing'.[57] The driving forces of the shadow state operate as 'dynamics of reterritorialization'.[58] They reshape the spatial and social

[48] Alain Morice, 'Guinée 1985 : État, corruption et trafics' (February 1987) *Les Temps Modernes*, no 487, 108, at 115–16.

[49] See Jacqueline Coolidge and Susan Rose-Ackerman, 'High-Level Rent Seeking and Corruption in African Regimes: Theory and Cases', World Bank Working Paper (1999), at 16–21.

[50] Reno (n 33), at 100.

[51] Achille Mbembe, *On the Postcolony* (University of California Press, 2001), at 85.

[52] Béatrice Hibou, 'From Privatising the Economy to Privatising the State: An Analysis of the Continual Formation of the State' in Hibou (n 33), at 7 (referring to Côte d'Ivoire). In some instances, state archives even keep records of private transactions carried out by public officials: see Reno (n 26), at 8.

[53] Chabal and Daloz (n 28), at 9.

[54] Ibid, at 16. See also Marat (n 6), at 68 (noting: 'interpersonal relationships and solidarity between state and non-state actors substituted for social and economic coherence, thus marginalizing the role of the state').

[55] Reno (n 26), at 3; Jean-François Bayart, 'The "Social Capital" of the Felonious State, or the Ruses of Political Intelligence' in Bayart, Ellis, and Hibou (n 17), at 34–41.

[56] Hibou (n 38), at 89–90.

[57] Michael G Schatzberg, *The Dialectics of Oppression in Zaïre* (Indiana University Press, 1988), at 142.

[58] Achille Mbembe, *On Private Indirect Government* (Council for the Development of Social Research in Africa, 2000), at 106.

organization of the state and fragment sovereignty,[59] 'displacing the material bases of power'.[60]

(b) *Endogenic and exogenic factors of state criminality*

The structure of power in shadow states can be explained by endogenic and exogenic factors combining to create a fertile environment for state organized crime.

(i) History of state construction

History is a key factor explaining the development of kleptocratic practices in certain states. To begin with, it has been argued that colonialism in Africa, whether in the form of direct or of indirect rule, has stimulated corruption and the plunder economy by promoting and relying on a small circle of local auxiliaries entrusted with significant authority over local communities, including the power to collect taxes on behalf of the colonial administration. Abuses were commonplace as members of the local elite took advantage of their privileged position to enrich themselves and consolidate their authority. This mode of governance both undermined the legitimacy of the formal state apparatus and established a connection between public office and access to wealth and prestige, sowing the seeds of contemporary kleptocracies.[61]

Different processes of state construction conducive to state organized crime can be observed in a number of former member and satellite states of the USSR. During the Soviet era, the monopoly exercised by the state over the economy and its occasional failure to meet the need for basic consumer goods gave birth to a flourishing black-market economy controlled by organized criminal groups in collusion with government officials. In parallel, the *nomenklatura* system established a cast of political and economic elite in control of the state's political apparatus and means of production, stimulating nepotism and patronage. The collapse of the Soviet Union, by displacing the centre of economic power towards a newly established private sector, had two major effects. First, it allowed the elite to take advantage of the process of privatization of state property to acquire and distribute capital. Secondly, and correlatively, it offered new economic opportunities for organized criminal groups and bolstered their ability to exercise influence over the political sphere.[62]

[59] See Achille Mbembe, 'At the Edge of the World: Boundaries, Territoriality, and Sovereignty in Africa' (2000) 12 *Public Culture* 259. Cf also Bertrand Badié, *La fin des territoires : Essai sur le désordre international et sur l'utilité sociale du respect* (Fayard, 1995), at 135 ('l'ordre des réseaux transperce et cisaille celui du territoire, l'affaiblit et lui fait perdre précisément cette cohésion et cette exceptionnalité qui fondaient sa nature essentiellement politique').

[60] Mbembe (n 51), at 86.

[61] See Giorgio Blundo, 'La corruption et l'État vus par les sciences sociales' in Giorgio Blundo and Jean-Pierre Olivier de Sardan (eds), *État et corruption en Afrique* (Karthala, 2007), at 48–58, and the authorities cited therein.

[62] See Louise I Shelley, 'Russia and Ukraine: Transition or Tragedy?' in Godson (n 5), at 200–205, 208–12; Janine R Wedel, 'Corruption and Organized Crime in Post-Communist States: New Ways of Manifesting Old Patterns' (2001) 7 *Trends in Organized Crime* 3, at 9–11, 13–15; Kupatadze (n 24), at 64–65, 182.

The case of Tajikistan illustrates a peculiar dynamic. The contemporary Tajik state is in part the product of the incorporation of organized crime into the state. The collapse of the Soviet Union triggered a civil war in Tajikistan. Members of local organized criminal groups were enlisted both by opposition forces and by the state, which lacked the necessary military resources to fight the opposition. All parties to the conflict were involved in the trafficking of drugs transiting through Tajikistan from Afghanistan. The peace accord reached in 1997 led to 'a far-reaching merger between the state and the drug economy' as pro-government paramilitaries and opposition members involved in drug trafficking were given key government positions. Prominent organized crime figures were subsequently eliminated from the political scene by President Emomali Rahmon, and government officials who had accumulated illicit financial capital during the conflict invested in the licit economy, consolidating the state's control over the private sector.[63]

(ii) Influence of social and cultural repertoires

The importance of social and cultural factors in the development of organized crime and political corruption should also be stressed. Organized crime 'may arise from adhesion to a certain code or norm within a particular community. These may be intensely social crimes, deeply collaborative at the subgroup level'.[64] In Central Asia, for example, a strong clan culture privileges nepotism and forms the backbone of local criminal groups.[65] Politicians connected to organized crime rely on extensive patronage networks and instrumentalize religious and cultural values to win election in traditionalist rural areas.[66] In certain regions of sub-Saharan Africa, where esotericism plays a role in structuring society (e.g. through secret societies),[67] members of criminal groups undergo oath-taking rituals to bind them to secrecy.[68] Furthermore, conceptions about crimes and wrongs sometimes do not coincide with the formal laws of the land. According to a UNODC report, 'respectable and honest people may engage in illegal activities without appearing to consider this as posing a moral problem. Some activities that are technically illegal may involve vast numbers of people who surely do not all consider themselves professional criminals'.[69] In this context, the distinction between the 'informal' and the 'criminal' does not depend on formal legal criteria, but rather on perceptions of legitimacy. Where legitimacy is based on a principle of clientelistic accountability, a patron's illicit activities will not be considered criminal as long as proceeds are redistributed fairly.[70]

Therefore, in many cases the idea that organized crime necessarily is the result of social and cultural deviance[71] must be rejected. Where the culture of

[63] Marat (n 6), at 105–108, 111–13.

[64] Mark A Drumbl, *Atrocity, Punishment, and International Law* (Cambridge University Press, 2007), at 32.

[65] See Ceccarelli (n 22), at 22–25; Marat (n 6), at 75.

[66] Marat (n 6), at 71–73.

[67] Bayart (n 35), at 34–38.

[68] See UNODC (n 21), at 16, 27.

[69] Ibid, at 32.

[70] Chabal and Daloz (n 28), at 79, 81.

[71] The influence of cultural factors on organized crime is often conceptualized through strain theory (see e.g. Leong (n 24), at 10–11), which posits that where the conventional and legitimate means to achieve the goals valued by society are unavailable or inaccessible, social pressure may lead individuals

neo-patrimonialism is profoundly anchored in society and promoted by representatives of the state, and where 'corruption creates its own "normative" patterns',[72] anomie is no longer a satisfying paradigm. On the contrary, criminal activities may be dictated by conformism to specific cultural expectations resting on patron–client relationships, ethnicity, kinship, or lineage.[73]

(iii) Integration into global networks

Shadow states are fully integrated into the networks of the global economy. 'Strategies of extraversion'[74] adopted by rulers and key players of shadow states have generated new opportunities for capital accumulation.[75] Transborder networks connect the domestic political and economic elite with foreign investors, financial institutions, government entities, politicians, law firms, lobbying firms, and a wide range of other individuals or entities able to deliver useful services in the global economy. Recent leaks of financial records and legal documents have revealed the capacity of senior state officials to use complex networks of front entities and intermediaries to move funds across borders anonymously in order to hide their assets in accounts held by offshore companies, or to funnel payments covertly to their intended recipients.[76] Elaborate schemes benefiting from financial secrecy laws greatly facilitate the laundering of the proceeds of embezzlement, corruption, and other criminal activities.[77] Senior government officials, '[p]ositioned at the juncture between local and global economies', use the prerogatives of sovereignty to protect and expand their clandestine activities.[78] In shadow states, the veil of sovereignty operates as an interface between criminal rulers and the global economy.

to have recourse to alternative, illegitimate means to achieve such goals. Accordingly, the argument goes, anomie is the result of innovation. See Robert K Merton, 'Social Structure and Anomie' (1938) 3 *American Sociological Review* 672.

[72] David Nelken and Michael Levi, 'The Corruption of Politics and the Politics of Corruption: An Overview' (1996) 23 *Journal of Law and Society* 1, at 3.

[73] See Reno (n 26), at 3; Bayart (n 55), at 34–41.

[74] See Jean-François Bayart, trans Stephen Ellis, 'Africa in the World: A History of Extraversion' (2000) 99 *African Affairs* 217.

[75] See e.g. the case-study of Belize in Rosaleen Duffy, 'Shadow States: Globalization, Criminalization, and Environmental Change' in Jean-Louis Briquet and Gilles Favarel-Garrigues (eds), *Organized Crime and States: The Hidden Face of Politics* (Palgrave Macmillan, 2010) 97 (discussing Belize's emergence as a key offshore financial center, money laundering and drug trafficking hub, and touristic destination).

[76] International Consortium of Investigative Journalists, 'Giant Leak of Offshore Financial Records Exposes Global Array of Crime and Corruption' (3 April 2016), https://panamapapers.icij.org/20160403-panama-papers-global-overview.html; International Consortium of Investigative Journalists, 'Leaked Records Reveal Offshore Holdings of China's Elite' (21 January 2014), https://www.icij.org/offshore/leaked-records-reveal-offshore-holdings-chinas-elite; Organized Crime and Corruption Reporting Project, 'The Azerbaijani Laundromat' (4 September 2017), https://www.occrp.org/en/azerbaijanilaundromat/.

[77] See e.g. the study of the US Senate on the laundering activities of former Gabonese President Omar Bongo, former Nigerian Vice-President Atiku Abubakar, and Teodoro Nguema Obiang Mangue, son of the incumbent President of Equatorial Guinea: US Senate, Committee on Homeland Security and Governmental Affairs, *Keeping Foreign Corruption out of the United States: Four Case Histories* (4 February 2010).

[78] Reno (n 33), at 97–98.

(iv) Privatization and economic liberalization

In certain cases, the intensification of foreign investment, combined with the weakening of state institutions hijacked by state officials for private ends, has progressively led to a privatization of sovereignty in all sectors, including domestic security and national defence.[79] It would be incorrect, however, to assume that the privatization of sovereignty goes hand in hand with an erosion of government power. As already noted in the case of former Soviet states,[80] privatization reforms have offered rulers new opportunities to expand their control over the private sector.[81] Structural adjustment programmes proposed by the World Bank are said to have worsened the situation of many African economies. The liberalization and privatization measures associated with these programmes have further blurred the boundaries between the public and private sectors and have encouraged nepotism, placing resources in the hands of the ruling circle and facilitating the plunder economy.[82] In particular, the deregulation of the banking sector has offered new financing opportunities for illicit activities, has facilitated fraud, embezzlement, and money laundering, and has provided domestic elites with new vehicles for rent-seeking activities.[83]

(c) The institutionalization of state organized crime

In states where all or some of these factors are present, state organized crime risks becoming a generalized practice. The goal of capital accumulation pursued by the state is a 'highly criminogenic force' likely to translate into organizational deviance.[84] Bayart, Ellis, and Hibou suggest six indicators of a 'felonious state': (i) the use by rulers of the coercive power of the state for the purpose of personal enrichment; (ii) the existence of a parallel structure of power intertwined with the organs of the state, benefiting from the privatization of sovereignty and able to have recourse to private violence; (iii) the involvement of this power structure in criminal activities; (iv) the integration of such activities in transnational organized crime networks; (v) a cultural osmosis between local economic practices and transnational globalization processes; and (vi) the economic and political predominance of kleptocratic practices in society.[85] In such political and social configuration, the 'government itself operates as an organized crime racket'.[86] Corruption ceases to be a mere 'environmental' factor of government criminality to become an institutionalized and

[79] Bayart, Ellis, and Hibou (n 17), at 116.

[80] Recall Section B.2(b)(i) of this chapter.

[81] Reno (n 33), at 105.

[82] Hibou (n 38), at 70–73; Adebayo O Olukoshi, 'The Elusive Prince of Denmark: Structural Adjustment and the Crisis of Governance in Africa' in Thandika Mkandawire and Charles C Soludo (eds), *African Voices on Structural Adjustment: A Companion to Our Continent, Our Future* (Council for the Development of Social Research in Africa, 2003) 229, at 258; Green and Ward (n 29), at 188.

[83] Hibou (n 38), at 74–76. On the impact of financial reforms recommended by the World Bank in Nigeria, see Peter Lewis and Howard Stein, 'Shifting Fortunes: The Political Economy of Financial Liberalization in Nigeria' (1997) 25 *World Development* 5 (arguing that 'financial liberalization was quickly captured by a clientelist state as a means of reallocating rents to strategic constituents').

[84] Green and Ward (n 29), at 89.

[85] Bayart, Ellis, and Hibou (n 17), at 25–26.

[86] UNODC, *Transnational Trafficking and the Rule of Law in West Africa: A Threat Assessment* (United Nations, July 2009), at 68.

systematized practice. Where 'it becomes difficult to disentangle purely personal and political objectives, [...] the state (or state agency) becomes a direct instrument of corruption'.[87]

3. State organized crime and armed conflict

State organized crime fuels armed conflicts, in particular in weak states where the propensity of rulers and private criminal groups to use violence for economic and political purposes may escalate into a full-blown armed conflict.[88] The dynamics of 'warlord capitalism' allow 'conflict entrepreneurs' to perpetuate war as a means of capital accumulation and political control.[89] The nexus between armed conflict and organized crime is evident in a number of situations, from the Kosovo war[90] to the ongoing conflicts in Syria and Iraq[91] and in the Sahel.[92] In a number of sub-Saharan African states, 'the linkage between the illegal exploitation of natural resources, including poaching and illegal trafficking of wildlife, illicit trade in such resources, and the proliferation and trafficking of arms as one of the major factors fuelling and exacerbating conflicts'.[93] As noted by UNODC:

> Transnational organized crime is, no doubt, putting bullets in guns. But [it is necessary to] prompt a rethink of what we understand as "conflict finance." The term should refer to more than just economic activity aimed at paying for bullets. It should also include money flows that provide an incentive to commit violence. The issue is not just criminal activity that

[87] David O Friedrichs (ed), *State Crime*, vol I: *Defining, Delineating and Explaining State Crime* (Ashgate, 1998), at xxv.

[88] See Chabal and Daloz (n 28), at 77–91.

[89] See Reno (n 32).

[90] See Council of Europe, Committee on Legal Affairs and Human Rights, *Inhuman Treatment of People and Illicit Trafficking in Human Organs in Kosovo* (7 January 2011), paras 37–92 (discussing the involvement of a branch of the former Kosovo Liberation Army in organized crime, notably implicating Hashim Thaçi, incumbent President of Kosovo).

[91] See Valérie Marcel, 'ISIS and the Dangers of Black Market Oil' (2014) 57 *Middle East Economic Survey* 19 (discussing the illicit exploitation and trafficking of Syrian and Iraqi crude oil by ISIL); UN Security Council Resolution 2347 (2017), 24 March 2017, UN Doc S/RES/2347 (2017), preamble, 5th recital (noting that 'the looting and smuggling of cultural property in the event of armed conflicts [...] can fuel and exacerbate conflict').

[92] See Wolfram Lacher, *Organized Crime and Conflict in the Sahel-Sahara Region* (Carnegie Endowment for International Peace, 2012), in particular at 11–14 (suggesting complicity between Malian public officials and members of al-Qaida in the Islamic Maghreb).

[93] UN Security Council Resolution 2136 (2014), 30 January 2014, UN Doc S/RES/2136 (2014), preamble, 10th recital. See also Resolution 1857 (2008), 22 December 2008, UN Doc S/RES/1857 (2008), at 2. Diamonds-for-arms deals between the Revolutionary United Front and former Liberian President Charles Taylor fuelled the conflict in Sierra Leone for years: see *Report of the Panel of Experts appointed pursuant to Security Council Resolution 1306 (2000), paragraph 19, in relation to Sierra Leone*, annexed to UN Doc S/2000/1195, 20 December 2000; *Prosecutor v Charles Ghankay Taylor*, Case no SCSL-03-01, Trial Judgment, 18 May 2012, paras 4624–6149. The existence of similar schemes has also been suspected in Côte d'Ivoire: see *Final report of the Group of Experts on Côte d'Ivoire pursuant to paragraph 19 of Security Council resolution 2101 (2013)*, annexed to UN Doc S/2014/266, 14 April 2014, para 172. See also generally Mamadou Aliou Barry, *Le commerce moderne des armes en Afrique : Données chiffrées, circuits et acteurs* (L'Harmattan, 2008).

finances armed groups. It is also the violence that emerges for the purpose of criminal financial activity.[94]

It is crucial to understand that armed violence is not simply a side-effect of tensions generated by organized crime. In certain cases, armed violence is a strategic instrument of organized crime used to generate or perpetuate a political and social climate favourable for illicit capital accumulation. Many exactions committed in the African Great Lakes region should accordingly be considered in the context of a struggle between various state and non-state actors for economic control over the exploitation of natural resources.[95] In the case of the Kosovo war, the Chief Prosecutor of the Special Investigative Task Force set up by the EU to investigate crimes committed during the conflict concluded: 'In the end, this was solely about certain individuals in the KLA [Kosovo Liberation Army] leadership using elements of that organization to perpetrate violence in order to obtain political power and personal wealth for themselves, not about any larger cause'.[96]

In this context, there can be a direct link between crimes committed in armed conflict and state organized crime. Military or paramilitary interventions constitutive of the crime of aggression may aim at gaining control over natural resources in a neighbouring state. Genocide, crimes against humanity, and war crimes may be committed by state actors not out of sheer bloodlust, but for the calculated purpose of eliminating economic competitors or fuelling a climate of chaos necessary to generate revenue.[97] It should be noted that, as a matter of law, genocidal intent and the discriminatory intent of persecution as a crime against humanity are compatible with ulterior motives, such as the purpose of obtaining a financial or other material benefit.[98]

C. The Motives of State Organized Crime

State organized crime is committed 'in order to obtain a financial or other material benefit'. Capital accumulation is the driving force of state organized crime, and is the key element that distinguishes it from other forms of state criminality. Although

[94] UNODC, *Organized Crime and Instability in Central Africa, A Threat Assessment* (United Nations, October 2011), at 101.

[95] See *Final Report of the Panel of Experts on the Illegal Exploitation of Natural Resources and Other Forms of Wealth of the Democratic Republic of the Congo*, annexed to UN Doc S/2002/1146, 16 October 2002.

[96] Statement of the Chief Prosecutor of the Special Investigative Task Force (29 July 2014), at 7.

[97] For an analysis of the profitability of crimes against humanity and war crimes, see Manuel Galvis Martínez, 'Forfeiture of Assets at the International Criminal Court: The Short Arm of International Criminal Justice' (2014) 12 *Journal of International Criminal Justice* 193, at 195–204 (discussing enslavement, sexual exploitation, taking of hostages, pillaging, unlawful appropriation, and seizure or destruction of property). For the argument that organized criminal groups may commit crimes against humanity and war crimes, see Pierre Hauck and Sven Peterke, 'Organized Crime and Gang Violence in National and International Law' (2010) 92 *International Review of the Red Cross* 407, at 434–36. The relationship between 'core' international crimes and the illicit exploitation of natural resources has recently become a matter of concern for the Office of the Prosecutor of the International Criminal Court: see Chapter 8, Section B.1(d).

[98] See Chapter 6, Section A.2(a).

perpetrators are usually motivated by the perspective of personal enrichment, financial or economic gain may not always be the only goal of state organized crime. In certain situations, perpetrators do not act for their personal benefit but in the pursuit of state policy or broader ideological objectives such as international terrorism. The cases discussed below illustrate the diversity of motives at play in state organized crime. Yet behind such apparent diversity of motives lies a commonality of intention: the intent to reap benefits from criminal activities.

1. Belly politics: state organized crime for profit

As discussed above, kleptocratic rulers and other corrupt officials may engage in organized criminal activities for purely private ends. The boundaries between private and public interests, however, are not always clear-cut. The accumulation of wealth and control over resources may in turn provide political capital and serve as the basis of a mode of governance.[99]

2. Dirty tricks politics: state organized crime for policy purposes

Because '[i]n certain circumstances the skills and operational resources of organized crime make it the best means to fulfil [state] goals',[100] state organized crime can also be driven by policy purposes,[101] whether domestic or foreign. This section discusses a selection of emblematic cases illustrating the political dimension of state organized crime.

(a) Domestic counter-insurgency

The decision on the part of state organs to team up with criminal organizations may be part of a domestic counter-insurgency strategy. This tactic was developed and used by the French military during the First Indochina War against the Viet Minh (1946–1954). The commanding officers of the *Groupement de commandos mixtes aéroportés* (Mixed Airborne Commando Group), placed under the authority of the French counter-espionage service, orchestrated a vast opium trafficking scheme to fund a counter-insurgency programme. Opium was purchased from local Hmong hill tribes in north-eastern Laos and western Tonkin and delivered to Bình Xuyên, the Saigon crime syndicate, for processing and local distribution or export. Bình Xuyên then paid a fixed percentage of their profits to the *deuxième bureau*, the French military intelligence services. The proceeds of this opium traffic fed into a secret fund used to train, equip, and pay paramilitary forces recruited amongst the local population. The alliance with local organized criminal groups, which also held key positions in the police, additionally allowed France to maintain control

[99] Recall Section B.2 of this chapter. [100] Green and Ward (n 29), at 94.
[101] According to Chambliss, state-organized crime is necessarily committed in furtherance of state policy. See William J Chambliss, 'State-Organized Crime – The American Society of Criminology, 1988 Presidential Address' (1989) 27 *Criminology* 183.

over Saigon. 'Operation X', as it was dubbed by the French military, stimulated the cultivation of opium poppy in the region, and generated strong hostility in certain communities who had been forced to sell their opium at a low price. Dissatisfied Hmong tribes eventually shifted allegiance and helped the Viet Minh position their artillery in the highlands surrounding the French defence lines at Dien Bien Phu, leading to the defeat of the French Far East Expeditionary Corps and precipitating the end of the war.[102]

In a similar vein, the 1996 'Susurluk scandal' in Turkey uncovered the existence of secret operations against the PKK and ties to organized crime at the highest level of government. Investigations established that the Turkish police and National Intelligence Organization (MİT), with sanction from former Prime Minister Tansu Çiller, cooperated with ultranationalist activists and other individuals involved in drug and arms trafficking, gambling, extortion, and money laundering, to conduct counter-guerrilla operations involving extra-judicial killings and kidnappings.[103] Mehmet Ağar, at the time successively General Director of the Turkish police and Minister of Interior Affairs, was convicted in 2011 in relation to the affair for 'establishing an armed organization for the purpose of committing crimes'.[104]

(b) *Covert operations in pursuance of foreign policy*

The state may also clandestinely engage in criminal activities in order to combat external enemies. This scenario can be illustrated by looking at the history of US covert operations[105] during the Cold War. A directive of the US National Security Council dated June 1948 defined 'covert operations' as

> all activities [...] which are conducted or sponsored by [the US] Government against hostile foreign states or groups or in support of friendly foreign states or groups but which are so planned and executed that any US Government responsibility for them is not evident to unauthorized persons and that if uncovered the US Government can plausibly disclaim any responsibility for them. Specifically, such operations shall include any covert activities related to: propaganda; economic warfare; preventive direct action, including sabotage, anti-sabotage, demolition and evacuation measures; subversion against hostile states, including assistance to underground resistance movements, guerrillas and refugee liberation groups, and support of indigenous anti-communist elements in threatened countries of the free world. Such operations shall not include armed conflict by recognized military forces, espionage, counter-espionage, and cover and deception for military operations.[106]

[102] McCoy (n 16), at 131–54. See also Jean-Marc Le Page, *Les services secrets en Indochine* (Nouveau Monde, 2012), at 107–11.

[103] See Human Rights Foundation of Turkey, *1996 Human Rights Report* (Ankara, 1998), at 135–53; Human Rights Foundation of Turkey, *1998 Human Rights Report* (Ankara, 2000), at 39–85 and Annex II (Republic of Turkey Prime Ministry, *3rd MİT Report*) at 564–87.

[104] 'High Court Upholds Five-Year Prison Sentence for Ex-Police Chief', *Today's Zaman* (15 April 2012). This newspaper was closed by decree in July 2016 further to the failed coup against President Recep Tayyip Erdoğan. All online articles have been removed.

[105] On US covert operations generally, see Roy Godson, *Dirty Tricks or Trump Cards: U.S. Covert Action and Counterintelligence* (3rd edn, Transaction Publishers, 2004).

[106] National Security Council Directive on Office of Special Projects, Washington, 18 June 1948, NSC 10/2, para 5.

In 1951, a note from the Executive Secretary of the National Security Council further approved the intensification of covert operations, placing emphasis on the necessity to '[d]evelop underground resistance and facilitate covert and guerrilla operations in strategic areas to the maximum practicable extent'.[107] It is within this legal framework that the Central Intelligence Agency (CIA) became involved in organized criminal activities in the name of the free world's fight against communism.

In France where the Communist Party was gaining increasing support after the end of the Second World War, the CIA allegedly paid and armed Corsican criminal groups in Marseille to break strikes organized by trade unions in 1947 and 1950.[108] A similar strategy was used in the late 1940s in post-war Japan, where the US occupation policy radically shifted after the defeat of the Guomindang in China. To oppose the spread of communism in Asia, the United States facilitated the expansion of Japanese far-right crime syndicates. The CIA notably worked in collaboration with Kodama Yoshio, an ultranationalist formerly arrested as a 'class A' war criminal and notorious *oyabun* who played a central role in the 1976 Lockheed corruption scandal.[109]

The US secret services were particularly active in South-east Asia throughout the Cold War. McCoy's solidly documented study[110] shows how the CIA, adapting the strategy of the French military against the Viet Minh in Indochina,[111] developed an intricate network of alliances with actors of the Golden Triangle narcotraffic to carry out covert operations against communism in the region. The CIA provided financial, logistical, and political support to local warlords and corrupt state officials involved in opium trafficking. It knowingly fostered, protected, and in some instances participated in drug trafficking operations. For instance, in the 1950s the CIA supplied weapons to the remnants of the Guomindang in Shan state in Burma, and provided the Thai national police with armoured vehicles, boats, and aircraft, knowing that the organizations it was supporting were playing central roles in the opium traffic and that they were being provided with the logistic capacity to carry out criminal activities. Opium grown in the mountains of Shan state and collected by the Guomindang to sustain its guerrilla activities was smuggled by the Thai police to Bangkok, the hub of South-east Asia's narcotics traffic, at the US government's expense.[112] In the same vein, General Vang Pao's Hmong guerrilla force in Laos, which relied heavily on opium for funding, was the pivotal instrument of the United States' 'secret war' against the Pathet Lao and the Vietnam People's Army from 1964 to 1973. CIA aircraft, which were indispensable in providing logistical and tactical

[107] Note from the Executive Secretary of the National Security Council (Lay) to the National Security Council, Scope and Pace of Covert Operations, Washington, 23 October 1951, NSC 10/5, para 1.c.

[108] Shortly afterwards, Corsican gangsters started operating heroin laboratories. For almost a quarter-century, the 'French Connection' supplied continuous flows of drugs to the United States: see McCoy (n 16), at 46–76.

[109] See David E Kaplan and Alec Dubro, *Yakuza: Japan's Criminal Underworld* (University of California Press, 2003), at 41–55, 83–93. On Kodama's role in the Lockheed scandal, see also Maruko (n 18), at 213.

[110] McCoy (n 16). [111] Recall Section C.2(a) of this chapter.

[112] McCoy (n 16), at 162–92.

support to Vang Pao's army in the mountainous regions of north-eastern Laos, were occasionally loaded with cargos of raw opium grown by the Hmong, to be delivered to the markets and heroin laboratories of the Golden Triangle.[113] McCoy demonstrates how 'a congruence of interests between the warlords, field operatives, and CIA headquarters [. . .] led to the agency's multi-faceted complicity in the Golden Triangle opium trade'.[114] The rationale for becoming involved in drug trafficking was very simple. Guomindang General Tuan Shi-Wen explained: 'We have to continue to fight the evil of communism, and to fight you must have an army, and an army must have guns, and to buy guns you must have money. In these mountains, the only money is opium'.[115]

A further example of state-sponsored criminal activities for US strategic purposes is commonly known as 'the Iran/*contra* affair'. Between 1985 and 1986, National Security Council staff, acting with the approval of the President of the United States and with the assistance of Israel, arranged for the sale to Iran of missiles from US army stocks, in violation of a domestic arms embargo. The proceeds were then diverted to finance covert operations in Nicaragua in support of the *contra* rebel groups fighting the Sandinista government.[116] These operations were carried out through a complex web of front companies, arms brokers, and financial institutions. It was allegedly financed, inter alia, via the Bank of Commerce and Credit International and its subsidiaries, which were suspected of having connections to organized crime and the intelligence services of several countries.[117] Several of the bank's executives had already been prosecuted and convicted in the United States for laundering of drug money in relation to other events.[118] An inquiry led by the Senate Sub-committee on Terrorism, Narcotics, and International Operations concluded that the effort of the US administration to support the *contras* was carried out with the knowledge that individuals associated with the *contras* were involved in drug trafficking and that the *contras* were receiving financial and logistical assistance from Colombian drug cartels.[119] The Senate Sub-committee also found that '[p]ayments [were made] to drug traffickers by the U.S. State Department [with] funds authorized by the

[113] Ibid, at 288–331. It is estimated that between 1967 and 1971 alone, 3,272 Hmong combatants were killed and 5,426 wounded. See US Senate, 92nd Congress, 1st sess, *Laos: April 1971 – A Staff Report prepared for the use of the Subcommittee on U.S. Security Agreements and Commitments Abroad of the Committee on Foreign Relations* (US Government Printing Office, 1971), at 16.

[114] McCoy (n 16), at 130. See also at 383–86.

[115] *Weekend Telegraph* (10 March 1967), at 25, cited in McCoy (n 16), at 129, 352.

[116] On the Iran/*contra* affair, see generally US Senate, 100th Congress, 1st sess, *Report of the Congressional Committees Investigating the Iran-Contra Affair—With Supplemental, Minority, and Additional Views*, S. Rept. 100-216 (US Government Printing Office, 1989); Peter Dale Scott and Jonathan Marshall, *Cocaine Politics: Drugs, Armies, and the CIA in Central America* (updated edn, University of California Press, 1998).

[117] For a detailed description of the relationships between the BCCI and the CIA, see US Senate, 102nd Congress, 2nd sess, *The BCCI Affair: A Report to the Committee on Foreign Relations, United States Senate, by Senator John Kerry and Senator Hank Brown*, S. Prt. 102-140 (US Government Printing Office, 1993), at 289–327.

[118] See *United States v Awan*, 966 F2d 1415 (11th Cir 1992). Charges brought against the bank itself were dropped following a plea bargain agreed in 1990.

[119] US Senate, 100th Congress, 2nd sess, *Drugs, Law Enforcement and Foreign Policy*, S. Prt. 100-165 (US Government Printing Office, 1989), at 136–37.

Congress for humanitarian assistance to the Contras, in some cases after the traffickers had been indicted by federal law enforcement agencies on drug charges, in others while traffickers were under active investigation by these same agencies'.[120] The Senate Sub-committee further noted that 'senior U.S. policy makers were not immune to the idea that drug money was a perfect solution to the Contra's funding problems'.[121] New light was shed on the affair on the occasion of the trial of Manuel Noriega, the former military ruler of Panama, on charges of drug trafficking.[122] Noriega claimed to have proof of the connivance of senior US politicians in drug trafficking for political purposes. Government documents submitted in pre-trial hearings in 1991–1992 revealed that Noriega received at least US$ 320,000 from the US government,[123] which the latter eventually admitted.[124] There is evidence that Noriega had ties to the CIA and that he was involved in providing funds and training to the *contras*.[125] An independent counsel was appointed to investigate and initiate prosecutions against individuals involved in the Iran/*contra* affair. The conclusions of the independent counsel, published in his 1993 final report, speak for themselves:

> Evidence obtained by Independent Counsel establishes that the Iran/contra affair was not an aberrational scheme carried out by a "cabal of zealots" on the National Security Council staff [...]. Instead, it was the product of two foreign policy directives by President Reagan which skirted the law and which were executed by the NSC staff with the knowledge and support of high officials in the CIA, State and Defense departments, and to a lesser extent, officials in other agencies.
>
> [...]
>
> Fundamentally, the Iran/contra affair was the first known criminal assault on the [...] rules governing the activities of national security officials. Reagan Administration officials rendered these rules ineffective by creating private operations, supported with privately generated funds that successfully evaded executive and legislative oversight and control.
>
> [...]
>
> The criminality in [the Iran/contra affair] did not arise primarily out of ordinary venality or greed, although some of those charged were driven by both. Instead, the crimes committed in Iran/contra were motivated by the desire of persons in high office to pursue controversial policies and goals [...].[126]

120 Ibid, at 36. 121 Ibid, at 41.

122 Noriega was convicted by a US court on drug charges (conviction affirmed on appeal: *United States v Noriega*, 117 F3d 1206 (11th Cir 1997)) and by a French court for money laundering (T corr Paris, 11ème ch, *Administration des Douanes et Droits Indirects c/ Noriega*, 7 July 2010, Case no 8935669013).

123 Simon Tisdall, 'Why Manuel Noriega became America's most wanted', *The Guardian* (28 April 2010); 'Ruling on Noriega Documents', *The New York Times* (8 August 1991), p A17.

124 David Johnston, 'U.S. Admits Payments to Noriega', *The New York Times* (19 January 1991).

125 Scott and Marshall (n 116), at 67, 70, 74, 157, and *passsim*; US Senate Report (n 119), at 92; Tisdall (n 123); Mark Tran, 'Senators are stunned by CIA "Panama connection"', *The Guardian* (11 February 1988), p 9.

126 US Court of Appeals (DC Cir), Division for the Purpose of Appointing Independent Counsel, Division no 86-6, *Final Report of the Independent Counsel for Iran/Contra Matters*, vol I: *Investigations and Prosecutions*, by Lawrence E Walsh, 4 August 1993, at 562–63, 565.

Covert operations were commonplace during the Cold War, and the United States itself was not spared destabilization attempts orchestrated by foreign governments. Senior Cuban officials allegedly supervised drug smuggling operations in partnership with Colombian narcotraffickers as part of a strategy to destabilize the United States. Cuban agents infiltrated the United States during the 1980 Mariel boatlift and facilitated the import and trafficking of drugs in the United States. In return for Cuba's assistance in smuggling drugs, Colombian drug traffickers supplied firearms to the *Movimiento 19 de Abril* (commonly called M-19), a Colombian guerrilla group supported by Cuba.[127]

The cases discussed in this section show that organized criminal activities may be carried out with the approval of the highest authorities of the state in furtherance of domestic or foreign policy goals. Profits generated by such activities are generally not intended to benefit state officials personally but to provide the means to further the policy of the state. In cases of mere collusion with organized criminal groups involving no financial benefit for the state, such collusion remains motivated by the expectation of some form of material benefit, such as territorial control.

3. Terror politics: state organized crime and international terrorism

State officials may use the proceeds of organized criminal activities for the purpose of supporting ideological causes that transcend national interests and policies, such as international terrorism. This was the case of the Taliban regime in Afghanistan. During the 1990s, Afghanistan had become the world's biggest opium producer[128] and most of the country's economy revolved around opium cultivation and production.[129] In 2000, the UN Security Council noted

> that the Taliban benefits directly from the cultivation of illicit opium by imposing a tax on its production and indirectly benefits from the processing and trafficking of such opium, and [...] that these substantial resources strengthen the Taliban's capacity to harbour terrorists.[130]

A report of the Committee of Experts established to monitor sanctions against the Taliban confirmed that '[f]unds raised from the production and trading of opium

[127] On the 'Cuban connection', see US Senate, Drug Enforcement Caucus, *Castro and the Narcotics Connection: The Cuban Government's Use of Narcotics Trafficking to Finance and Promote Terrorism*, October 1983 (published in 2007 by the Cuban American National Foundation); Emilio T González, 'The Cuban Connection: Drug Trafficking and the Castro Regime' (1997) 2 *Cuban Studies Association Occasional Paper Series*, paper no 7. Several Cuban officials involved in drug trafficking were convicted *in absentia* in the United States: see Richard D Gregorie, 'Extraterritorial Jurisdiction: Its Use, Its Roots and Its Viability' (1991) 15 *Nova Law Review* 625, at 636.

[128] Office for Drug Control and Crime Prevention, *Global Illicit Drug Trends 2001* (United Nations, 2001), at 33. Afghanistan owes its prominence in the world drug market in part to the United States. During the Cold War, the CIA worked in close collaboration with the Pakistani Inter-Services Intelligence to organize the Mujahedin resistance against the Soviet occupation in Afghanistan, providing support to local warlords involved in opium trafficking. See McCoy (n 16), at 470–87.

[129] See UNODC, *The Opium Economy in Afghanistan: An International Problem* (United Nations, 2003).

[130] Resolution 1333 (2000), 19 December 2000, UN Doc S/RES/1333 (2000), preamble, 9th recital.

and heroin are used by the Taliban to buy arms and other war materiel, and to finance the training of terrorists and support the actions of extremists in neighbouring countries and beyond'.[131] In 2001, the Taliban put a ban on opium poppy cultivation,[132] but suspicions about the sincerity of this measure were raised. According to the Committee of Experts, the Taliban had accumulated massive stocks of opium and ordered a stop in production in order to prevent a fall in prices.[133] An Iranian official speaking at a Security Council meeting in 2001 noted that 'the order d[id] not cover the stockpiling, transit and processing of and trade in opium and heroin' and that 'the stockpiles of drugs in Afghanistan [were] huge enough to feed the market at a steady rate for about 10 years'.[134]

D. The Actors of State Organized Crime

State organized crime is defined by an abuse of power on the part of individuals entrusted with governmental authority. Perpetrators must therefore, by definition, be public officials 'in a position to shape or influence the actions of a state'. Documented instances of senior public officials involved in organized criminal activities include heads of state,[135] members of government,[136] military

[131] *Report of the Committee of Experts established pursuant to Resolution 1333 (2000), paragraph 15(a), regarding monitoring of the arms embargo against the Taliban and the closure of terrorist camps in Taliban-held areas of Afghanistan*, annexed to UN Doc S/2001/511, 22 May 2001, para 55.

[132] The production of Afghani opium fell by 94% within a year: see Office for Drug Control and Crime Prevention, *Global Illicit Drug Trends 2002* (United Nations, 2002), at 45.

[133] Report of the Committee of Experts on Afghanistan (n 131), para 58. See also US State Department, Bureau for International Narcotics and Law Enforcement Affairs, *International Narcotics Control Strategy Report*, 1 March 2002, at VII-4. The effect of the ban was in fact to increase the price of dry opium in Afghanistan's main cultivation provinces more than fourteenfold within a year: see UNODC (n 129), at 217.

[134] Security Council, 4325th meeting, 5 June 2001, UN Doc S/PV.4325 (Resumption 1), at 3.

[135] See e.g. the cases of Manuel Noriega, former commander of the Panamanian Defence Forces and ruler of Panama, discussed in n 122; Desi Bouterse, former chairman of the National Military Council and incumbent President of Suriname, convicted *in absentia* by a Dutch court on drug charges (Rb. 's-Gravenhage, 16 July 1999; conviction partly overturned on appeal: Hof 's-Gravenhage, 30 June 2000, *LJN* AA6305); Armando Guebuza, former President of Mozambique, alleged to 'exercise complete control over the [...] illicit economy of Mozambique' (US diplomatic cable, Embassy Maputo, 'Important Drug Trafficking Transit Point for East Africa' (19 November 2009) 09MAPUTO1309; see also US diplomatic cable (n 36)); and Tareck El Aissami, incumbent Vice-President of Venezuela, included on the list of 'specifically designated drug traffickers' by the US Department of the Treasury's Office of Foreign Assets Control (US Department of the Treasury, 'Treasury Sanctions Prominent Venezuelan Drug Trafficker Tareck El Aissami and His Primary Frontman Samark Lopez Bello', 13 February 2017).

[136] See e.g. the cases of Luis Arce Gómez, former Minister of Interior of Bolivia, convicted by a US court on drug charges (conviction affirmed on appeal: *United States v Gomez*, 979 F2d 212 (11th Cir 1992)); Boris Shikhmuradov, former Vice-Prime Minister and Minister of Foreign Affairs of Turkmenistan, charged with illegal arms sales (UNODC, *An Assessment of Transnational Organized Crime in Central Asia* (United Nations, 2007), at 50); Eligio Briceño, former Minister of Energy and Communications of Belize, convicted by a US court on drug charges ('Ex-Cabinet Minister of Belize Is Guilty of Drug Conspiracy', *The New York Times* (6 August 1985), p B8); Norman Saunders, former chief minister of the Turks and Caicos Islands, convicted by a US court on drug charges ('Ex-Caribbean Official Guilty of Six Drug-Related Counts', *The New York Times* (20 July 1985), p 28); Etienne Boerenveen, former number two of Desi Bouterse's military government and President-Commissioner for State Oil in Suriname, convicted by a US court on drug charges (conviction affirmed on appeal: *United States v Boerenveen*, 830 F2d 1130 (11th Cir 1987)).

officials,[137] top law-enforcement officials,[138] diplomats,[139] intelligence officials,[140] and members of parliament.[141]

Perpetrators of state organized crime do not act alone, but 'in concert with a structured group'. A 'structured group' may be formed by non-state actors or other public officials, or a combination of both. In most cases, the perpetrator, either directly or through *de facto* agents of the state, will act in concert with private criminals, such as members of drug cartels, warlords, and the like. A group of public officials may also conspire together, for example to embezzle public funds.

State organized crime involves a range of peripheral actors, both in the public and the private sectors, who contribute to the commission of the underlying offences. Such actors include private and state-owned corporations, banks and financial institutions, lawyers, business people, rebel groups, and other entities involved in organized criminal activities.

E. The Means of State Organized Crime

State organized crime involves the 'use of the resources of the state'. It goes beyond passive collusion to require an active contribution on the part of state officials abusing their authority to mobilize the state's material, financial, and human resources.

[137] See e.g. the cases of Aldo Santamaría Cuadrado, former Vice Admiral of the Cuban Navy, convicted *in absentia* by a US court on drug charges along with several Cuban officials and narcotraffickers (see Gregorie (n 127); *United States v Cortez*, 757 F2d 1204 (11th Cir 1985)); Bubo Na Tchuto, former chief of staff of the Guinea-Bissau Navy, convicted by a US court on drug charges after a guilty plea (indictment: District Court (SD New York), *United States v Na Tchuto*, S1 12 Cr. 972)); Bento dos Santos Kangamba, General of the Angolan armed forces, charged in Brazil with trafficking women for the purpose of sexual exploitation (for extracts of the indictment, see TRF 3a região, HC 0031957-43.2013.4.03.0000/SP, Relator Desembargador Federal Paulo Fontes, Decision of 12 December 2013, e-DJF3 (18 December 2013), p 334); and Issiaka Ouattara (aka Wattao), Vice Commander of the Ivorian Presidential Guard, suspected of being involved in illicit gold mining and illicit trade in rough diamonds (see Final report of the Group of Experts on Côte d'Ivoire (n 93), paras 94–100, 172, 258, 272).

[138] See e.g. the case of Mehmet Ağar, former General Director of the Turkish police, convicted for his participation in a criminal organization, discussed in Section C.2(a) of this chapter.

[139] See e.g. the cases of Fernando Ravelo Renado, former Cuban ambassador to Colombia, and Gonzalo Bassols Suárez, former Minister-Counsellor of the Cuban embassy in Colombia, convicted *in absentia* by a US court on drug charges (Gregorie (n 127)); Domingo S Canieso, former attaché for administration at the Philippine embassy in Laos (Morris Kaplan, 'Philippine Diplomat Seized Here as Heroin Smuggler' *The New York Times* (12 November 1971), p 93); Mauricio Rosal, former Guatemalan ambassador to Belgium ('Ambassador on drug charge', *The Guardian* (4 October 1960), p 1); Prince Sopsaisana, former ambassador of Laos to France (McCoy (n 16), at 283–84, 379–80). See also UNODC (n 136), at 50 (mentioning the case of the Tajik ambassador to Kazakhstan).

[140] Recall the cases discussed in Section C.2 of this chapter.

[141] See e.g. the case concerning Yusuf Emir Faishal, Sarjan Taher, and Al Amin Nur Nasution, all members of the Indonesian House of Representatives' Commission on forestry, agriculture, and fisheries, convicted for having taken bribes to help strip forest land of its protected status and convert it into constructible land. Three other members of the House of Representatives, Azwar Chesputra, Fahri Andi Leluasa, and Hilman Indra, were also named as suspects in the case ('Prison term for former governor extended', *The Jakarta Post* (23 April 2010)).

State organized crime is first characterized where state facilities are used as instrumentalities by state officials to commit a crime. This condition is fulfilled, for example, where a government agency is tasked with engaging in organized crime. In North Korea, criminal activities have been planned, coordinated, and directed through a secret branch of the Workers' Party Central Committee known as 'Office 39'.[142] Observers have noted that in order '[t]o commit its criminal acts, Office #39 uses the powers and resources of a nation-state—merchant and military vessels, diplomatic and embassy posts, as well as state run companies and collective farms—that nonstate groups do not possess'.[143] Similarly, in Guinea airport facilities were used to negotiate drug deals and receive drug shipments under the supervision of the presidential guard, and diplomatic pouches were used to smuggle drugs out of the country.[144] In the case of the Iran/*contra* affair, a CIA airplane was used to ship missiles from Israel to Iran.[145] The judicial system and the authority of the courts may also be used for criminal purposes. Between 2011 and 2014, over US$ 20 billion worth of criminal proceeds from Russia were laundered through court orders rendered by judges in Moldova. Fictitious loans were concluded between shell companies, and guaranteed by Russian entities seeking to launder money. The debtor would purport to default, and the creditor would then call on the guarantor to repay the loan. Complicit judges would authenticate the 'debt' and order the guarantor to repay it, thereby allowing illicitly obtained funds to be transferred out of Russia under the guise of legitimacy.[146] Lastly, state-owned corporations and their personnel may also contribute to organized criminal activities. For example, in Laos illicit logging operations are allegedly conducted by a company owned by

[142] Evidence suggests that the Democratic Republic of North Korea, in an effort to finance its trade deficit, is directly involved in organized criminal activities. These include, most notably, the counterfeiting of US 'supernotes' and production of heroin and methamphetamines for trafficking, but also a range of other criminal activities such as trafficking in counterfeit cigarettes, illegal sales of military equipment, insurance fraud, and money laundering: see Dick K Nanto, *North Korean Counterfeiting of US Currency* (Congressional Research Service, 12 June 2009); Raphael Perl and Dick K Nanto, *North Korean Crime-for-Profit Activities* (Congressional Research Service, 16 February 2007); Paul Rexton Kan, Bruce E Bechtol, Jr, and Robert M Collins, *Criminal Sovereignty: Understanding North Korea's Illicit International Activities* (Strategic Studies Institute, US Army War College, March 2010); US diplomatic cable, Embassy Tokyo, 'DPRK Flags of Convenience' (17 March 2006) 06TOKYO1446; US diplomatic cable, Secretary of State, 'DPRK Financial Activities in Switzerland' (5 September 2007) 07STATE124655.

[143] Kan, Bechtol, and Collins (n 142), at 2–3 (noting further: 'Unlike [...] ordinary corrupt autocratic regimes, or criminally linked warlords and insurgent groups, North Korea practices a form of "criminal sovereignty" that is unique in the contemporary international security arena. North Korea uses state sovereignty to protect itself from external interference in its domestic affairs while dedicating a portion of its government and the KWP to carrying out illicit international activities in defiance of international law and the domestic laws of numerous other nations. [...] [T]he state, in the case of North Korea, maintains the monopoly on the conduct of illicit activities').

[144] Recall the Introduction.

[145] US Senate Report (n 116), at 181–82, 184–85.

[146] See Organized Crime and Corruption Reporting Project, 'The Russian Laundromat Exposed' (20 March 2017) at https://www.occrp.org/en/laundromat/the-russian-laundromat-exposed/; Luke Harding, 'The Global Laundromat: how did it work and who benefited?', *The Guardian* (20 March 2017).

the Vietnamese Ministry of Defence, which provides the logistics and manpower needed to process the logs and transport them across the border.[147]

In the case of mere collusion between state officials and organized criminal groups, the former may facilitate the commission of crimes by providing the latter with equipment belonging to the state or otherwise obtained with state funds. For instance, the Turkish police provided members of the 'Susurluk gang' with police identification and passports.[148] Similarly, US covert operations in South-east Asia, involving the supply of military equipment to drug traffickers, were financed with special funds dedicated to covert operations.[149]

In some cases, state property may itself be the object of the crime. This is the case where public funds are embezzled by state officials, or where a state is involved in the trafficking of its own arms stocks, such as in the Iran/*contra* affair.[150]

The case of corruption must be nuanced. The mere receiving or solicitation of a bribe by a public official does not in itself satisfy the requirements of state organized crime. State organized crime is characterized where state officials acting in concert abuse their authority and the resources of the state to extort bribes. This can mean having recourse to the state's means of coercion, for example instructing military or police staff to intimidate businesses into paying bribes. It can also take the form of a pyramidal corruption scheme involving several echelons in the organization of the state, whereby senior state officials collect a share of the bribes received by their subordinates. Corruption can only be considered to amount to state organized crime where it occurs in the framework of an institutionalized system of extortion established and controlled by senior state officials.

The examples analysed here show that state organized crime relies both on the use of the material means and facilities of the state, and on the mobilization of its human resources. Rank-and-file officials, military and police staff, employees of state-owned corporations, and secret services agents fulfil tasks indispensable to implement criminal schemes designed by more senior officials. Although the role of these agents remains secondary, the prerogatives they enjoy on account of their official authority greatly facilitate the commission of organized criminal activities.

F. Conclusion

This chapter has shown how senior public officials abuse their authority to facilitate or directly engage in organized criminal activities, whether in the form of partnerships with organized criminal groups involved in drug or arms trafficking, of the plundering of a country's resources by kleptocratic rulers, or of high-level corruption schemes. In a number of cases, the convergence of economic and political interests

[147] See Environmental Investigation Agency, *Crossroads: The Illicit Timber Trade Between Laos and Vietnam* (July 2011), at 8–12. Whether the resources of a state-owned corporation may be considered the resources of the state depends on a number of considerations: see Chapter 2, Section B.3.

[148] See 3rd MİT Report (n 103), at 545, 553.

[149] Recall Section C.2(b) of this chapter.

[150] See US Senate Report (n 116), at 213–33.

tends to blur the frontier between crime committed by public officials for private ends and crime committed in pursuance of state policy. Examples drawn from a range of different states indicate that patterns of state organized crime vary depending on the political, economic, and institutional configuration in each state.[151] Interesting as they are from the perspective of criminology, these differences do not call into question the unicity of the concept of state organized crime from a legal perspective.[152] Regardless of its underlying motives or manifestations in a particular case, state organized crime always entails an abuse of state authority on the part of senior public officials using the state's resources with a view to obtaining a financial or other material benefit. The analysis performed in this chapter suggests that state criminality—including 'core' international crimes such as aggression or crimes against humanity—often plainly boils down to the pursuit of financial interests. State organized crime is about the accumulation or maintenance of economic, political, or social capital.[153]

[151] See Green and Ward (n 29), at 185–90; Gregg Barak (ed), *Crimes by the Capitalist State: An Introduction to State Criminality* (State University of New York Press, 1991), at x (arguing that 'the nature, patterns, or seriousness of state crime will not necessarily be the same for all types of state formation. In fact, [...] crimes by the state would vary according to the changing interaction between a particular state formation and the developing worldwide political economy').

[152] To qualify as 'organized crime', it is sufficient that criminal acts be committed by a structured group in order to obtain, directly or indirectly, a financial or other material benefit, irrespective of whether the final purpose is to further political objectives: see Chapter 3, Section A.7.

[153] Dawn L Rothe, *State Criminality: The Crime of All Crimes* (Lexington Books, 2009), at 223.

PART II

THE LIMITS OF APPLICABLE INTERNATIONAL LAW

2

State Responsibility for State Organized Crime

Our examination of the rules and mechanisms of international law relevant to the suppression of state organized crime begins in this chapter with an analysis of the law of state responsibility. Conduct so far described as 'state organized crime' from the perspective of criminology will be analysed from a legal perspective, with a view to determining whether the participation of state officials in organized crime may give rise to the international responsibility of the state. Following the classical structure of the law of state responsibility as codified by the International Law Commission (ILC) in the Articles on Responsibility of States for Internationally Wrongful Acts (ARSIWA),[1] the chapter will discuss in turn whether the conduct of public officials or of non-state actors involved in organized crime may be attributed to the state, whether the participation of the organs or agents of a state in organized crime may constitute a breach of an international obligation of the state, and, in the affirmative, whether other states may be entitled to invoke the responsibility of a state having committed an internationally wrongful act by participating in organized crime. By means of introduction, this chapter opens with general considerations concerning the nature of state responsibility for criminal acts committed by individuals acting as organs or agents of the state.

A. State Responsibility for Criminal Conduct of Individuals Acting as Organs or Agents of the State

State organized crime involves the commission of criminal offences by state officials acting in the performance of their official duties or abusing their authority for private ends. Such conduct is likely to give rise to the individual criminal responsibility of the perpetrators under domestic law. The purpose of the present chapter is to determine whether it may also entail legal consequences for the state under international law. As noted by Anzilotti, under international law the conduct of the state is nothing more than the conduct of individuals which are attributed to the state by law.[2] That is not to say, however, that a crime committed by an individual may be

[1] Annexed to UN General Assembly Resolution 56/83, 12 December 2001, UN Doc A/RES/56/83.

[2] Dionisio Anzilotti, *Cours de droit international*, vol I: *Introduction, Théories générales*, trans Gilbert Gidel (Librairie du Recueil Sirey, 1929), at 469.

imputed to the state so that the state itself may be considered to have committed a crime. As the Nuremberg Tribunal put it, '[c]rimes against international law are committed by men, not by abstract entities'.[3] As a matter of international law, the responsibility of a state for criminal acts committed by its organs or agents is not of a criminal nature.[4] In its work on the law of state responsibility, the ILC rejected the concept of 'international crime'[5] in view of the conceptual difficulties of using criminal terminology for the purposes of state responsibility.[6] Nevertheless, the conduct of a public official constitutive of a criminal offence giving rise to individual criminal responsibility under domestic law may at the same time constitute an internationally wrongful act of the state under international law,[7] if the conduct in question is attributable to the state and if it constitutes a breach of a distinct obligation binding on the state itself under international law.[8] This chapter will accordingly consider the general *corpus* of primary norms of international law to identify relevant international obligations potentially applicable to state conduct amounting to state organized crime.

On a side note, it should be pointed out that the international responsibility of a state may be incurred not only as a result of acts committed by its organs or agents, but also when the state has breached its due diligence obligation to prevent or punish certain acts committed by non-state actors that have caused injury to another state.[9] In such cases, crimes committed by non-state actors operate as a 'catalyst' causing the wrongfulness of the conduct of the state.[10]

[3] *Trial of the Major War Criminals before the International Military Tribunal, Nuremberg*, vol XXII: *Proceedings, 27 August – 1 October 1946* (Nuremberg, 1948), at 466.

[4] *Application of the Convention on the Prevention and Punishment of the Crime of Genocide (Bosnia and Herzegovina v Serbia and Montenegro)*, Judgment, ICJ Rep 2007, p 43, at 114, para 167, and 115, para 170.

[5] See *Report of the International Law Commission* (50th sess), UN Doc A/53/10 in *Yearbook of the International Law Commission* (1998), vol II(2), at 77, para 331.

[6] See *First report on State responsibility, by Mr. James Crawford, Special Rapporteur, Addendum*, 1 May 1998, UN Doc A/CN.4/490/Add.1; *First report on State responsibility, by Mr. James Crawford, Special Rapporteur, Addendum*, 11 May 1998, UN Doc A/CN.4/490/Add.3 both in *Yearbook of the International Law Commission* (1998), vol II(1), at 9–23.

[7] See *Application of the Convention on the Prevention and Punishment of the Crime of Genocide* (n 4), at 115–17, paras 172–74 (noting that 'duality of responsibility [is] a constant feature of international law' and that certain provisions of the Genocide Convention 'impose obligations on States distinct from the obligations which the Convention requires them to place on individuals'); Draft Code of Crimes against the Peace and Security of Mankind, Art 4, in *Report of the International Law Commission* (48th sess), UN Doc A/51/10 in *Yearbook of the International Law Commission* (1996), vol II(2), at 23 (providing that the individual criminal responsibility of individuals is without prejudice to the responsibility of the state under international law).

[8] ARSIWA, Art 2.

[9] See generally Joanna Kulesza, *Due Diligence in International Law* (Brill Nijhoff, 2016). For an analysis of the obligation of states to prevent acts contrary to the rights of other states within their territory, see Section C.3 of this chapter.

[10] See *Fourth Report on State Responsibility, by Mr. Roberto Ago, Special Rapporteur*, 30 June 1972 and 9 April 1973, UN Doc A/CN.4/264 and Add.1 in *Yearbook of the International Law Commission* (1972), vol II, at 97, para 65 and n 120 ('The act of the individual could not be considered as an act of the State, either in itself or because of the alleged participation or complicity of organs of the State. It would merely be an external event distinct from the act of the State. This does not mean that such an event would not affect the determination of the State's responsibility. On the contrary, it could be a condition for the existence of such responsibility acting externally as a catalyst on the wrongfulness of the conduct of the State organs in this particular case.'). See also at 123, para 140.

B. Attribution of Conduct to the State

The first condition of an internationally wrongful act of a state is that the conduct under consideration be attributable to the state under international law.[11] As 'States can act only by and through their agents and representatives',[12] in most cases the responsibility of the state is determined by the conduct of its organs and agents. This section reviews the conditions under which the conduct of organs and agents of a state may be attributed to that state under the law of state responsibility, and discusses their relevance for the purposes of determining the existence of an internationally wrongful act in cases of state organized crime.

1. Conduct of state officials acting in an official capacity

It is an established principle of international law that '[t]he conduct of any State organ shall be considered an act of that State under international law, whether the organ exercises legislative, executive, judicial or any other functions, whatever position it holds in the organization of the State'.[13] This does not mean, however, that any conduct of a person who is an organ of the state may be attributable to the state. It is necessary that the individual in question act in his capacity as an organ of the state, and not in a purely private capacity.[14] This point is central in cases of state organized crime, where it may be questioned whether criminal acts committed by state officials for profit purposes may be considered to have been committed in an official capacity.

(a) Ultra vires and criminal conduct

Under the law of state responsibility, 'the conduct of an organ of a State or of a person or entity empowered to exercise elements of the governmental authority shall be considered an act of the State under international law if the organ, person or entity acts in that capacity, even if it exceeds its authority or contravenes instructions'.[15] As a result, acts that do not fall within the delineated sphere of competence

[11] ARSIWA, Art 2(a).

[12] *German Settlers in Poland*, Advisory Opinion, PCIJ Series B no 6 (1923), at 22.

[13] ARSIWA, Art 4(1); *Application of the Convention on the Prevention and Punishment of the Crime of Genocide* (n 4), at 163, para 385.

[14] See *Claim of the Salvador Commercial Company (El Salvador v United States)*, 8 May 1902, 15 RIAA 467, at 477 ('a State is responsible for the acts of its rulers, whether they belong to the legislative, executive, or judicial department of the Government, so far as the acts are done in their official capacity'). Draft Art 10 of ARSIWA presented by Special Rapporteur Ago provided that 'conduct is not considered to be an act of the State if, by its very nature, it was wholly foreign to the specific functions of the organ or if, even from other aspects, the organ's lack of competence was manifest' (Fourth Report on State Responsibility (n 10), at 95, para 60). This provision was later abandoned, but the general idea is still reflected in the wording of ARSIWA, Arts 5 and 7, which require that the person, organ, or entity empowered to exercise elements of the governmental authority 'act in that capacity'.

[15] ARSIWA, Art 7. See also *Armed Activities on the Territory of the Congo (Democratic Republic of the Congo v Uganda)*, Judgment, ICJ Rep 2005, p 168, at 242, para 214.

of an organ of the state, including acts considered criminal under the law of that state, may be attributed to the state provided that it can be established that the organ in question acted in his capacity as an organ of the state.[16]

The determining question to draw the line between conduct attributable to the state and private acts is whether the conduct in question is performed by a person vested with governmental authority who appears or purports to carry out his official functions.[17] Conduct attributable to the state includes all acts of state officials 'cloaked with governmental authority'.[18] In the words of the US Supreme Court, '[m]isuse of power, possessed by virtue of state law and made possible only because the wrongdoer is clothed with the authority of state law, is action taken "under color of" state law'.[19] In short, attribution of conduct to the state is determined by the appearance of official authority.[20] For example, in *Caire* the French–Mexican Claims Commission held Mexico responsible for the murder of a French national committed by members of the Mexican armed forces who 'acted under cover of their official status as officers and used means placed at their disposal on account of that status'.[21]

Specifically in cases of state organized crime, it would seem that criminal acts carried out by states officials on behalf of the state and through the means and resources available to them by virtue of their official authority are attributable to the state. Where, for example, a secret state organ is tasked by the highest authorities of the state with overseeing the production of counterfeit foreign banknotes and of heroin and methamphetamines, such as in North Korea,[22] it is beyond dispute that the activities of this entity are carried out in an official capacity. Paradoxically, in this particular case criminal conduct is not *ultra vires*, as it seems to conform to the instructions issued to the organ and to remain within the confines of the authority granted to it.

In the case of undercover secret services agents operating in the territory of another state, the criterion of appearance of governmental authority cannot be fulfilled. The question of attribution is problematic, even though the agents are officials of the state acting under the instructions of their government. The issue arose in the case concerning the destruction of the *Rainbow Warrior* by French secret services agents in New Zealand. The perpetrators were acting undercover, posing as tourists and carrying Swiss passports. Despite denying at first any official connection to the French government, France eventually acknowledged that its agents had been acting in their official capacity,[23] and after the dispute was referred to the

[16] *Velásquez Rodríguez v Honduras*, Judgment, 29 July 1988, Series C no 4, para 170.

[17] ARSIWA Commentary in *Report of the International Law Commission* (53rd sess), UN Doc A/56/10 in *Yearbook of the International Law Commission* (2001), vol II(2), at 42, para 13, and 46, para 7.

[18] *Petrolane, Inc v Islamic Republic of Iran,* (1991) 27 Iran–US CTR 64, at 92.

[19] *United States v Classic*, 313 US 299 (1941), at 326.

[20] On the function of the 'theory of appearance' (*théorie de l'apparence*) for the purposes of attribution in the law of state responsibility, see Olivier de Frouville, 'Attribution of Conduct to the State: Private Individuals' in James Crawford, Alain Pellet, and Simon Olleson (eds), *The Law of International Responsibility* (Oxford University Press, 2010) 257, at 263–64.

[21] *Estate of Jean-Baptiste Caire (France) v United Mexican States*, 7 June 1929, 5 RIAA 516, at 531.

[22] Recall Chapter 1, Section E.

[23] Communiqué from the Prime Minister of France, 22 September 1985, 74 ILR 261.

UN Secretary-General for binding arbitration, France was found responsible for the conduct of its agents.[24] This case suggests that the conduct of secret services agents posing as private individuals may be attributed to the state, on the assumption that criminal acts could be considered to fall within the official functions of an organ of the state. This assumption seems to be accepted in the literature, although in practice it may be challenging for an international court or tribunal to make such a determination.[25] In cases of state organized crime where, for example, secret services operatives use proceeds of drug trafficking to purchase military equipment and train paramilitary forces,[26] the conclusion to be drawn is that they do so in their capacity as representatives of the state and in furtherance of state policy, despite the fact that they attempt to conceal their affiliation to the state.[27]

In conclusion, where it can be established that the criminal conduct of state officials was performed in furtherance of state policy, attribution to the state is possible. The case of criminal conduct motivated by apparently purely private motives, such as corruption and embezzlement of public funds, is less clear-cut.

(b) *Conduct motivated by personal motives*

It is open to question whether acts committed by state officials for the satisfaction of purely private motives may be considered to be carried out in an official capacity. As noted by the ILC, '[c]ases where officials acted in their capacity as such, albeit unlawfully or contrary to instructions, must be distinguished from cases where the conduct is so removed from the scope of their official functions that it should be assimilated to that of private individuals, not attributable to the State'.[28] Whether conduct may be assimilated to that of a private individual and not to state conduct does not depend on the underlying motives of the organ or agent.[29] In *Mallén*, for instance, an arrest carried out by a police officer as 'a mere pretext for taking private vengeance' was considered attributable to the state.[30] Accordingly, the conduct of public officials motivated by personal profit is eligible for attribution to the state, provided that the conditions for attribution under international law are met.

The arbitral tribunal in *Mallén* also noted that the officer 'could not have taken the [victim] to jail if he had not been acting as a police officer'.[31] This latter element is particularly relevant in cases of state organized crime, where the ability of state

[24] *Rainbow Warrior (New Zealand v France)*, 6 July 1986, 74 ILR 241.

[25] See James Crawford, *State Responsibility: The General Part* (Cambridge University Press, 2013), at 140; Kimberley N Trapp, *State Responsibility for International Terrorism* (Oxford University Press, 2011), at 36.

[26] Recall Chapter 1, Section C.2(a).

[27] The status of covert agents operating in the territory of a foreign state also presents difficulties from the perspective of the law of jurisdictional immunities: see Chapter 4, Section B.4(a)(i).

[28] ARSIWA Commentary (n 17), at 46, para 7.

[29] Ibid, at 42, para 13 (noting that '[i]t is irrelevant for [the] purpose [of attribution] that the person concerned may have had ulterior or improper motives').

[30] *Francisco Mallén (United Mexican States) v United States of America*, 7 April 1927, 4 RIAA 173, at 177, paras 7–9.

[31] Ibid.

officials to commit crimes is greatly increased by the possibility of taking advantage of their official position. For example, where diplomats use diplomatic pouches to smuggle drugs,[32] their conduct is rendered possible by the prerogatives they enjoy by virtue of their official position. Without it, they would not be able to bypass customs inspection.

It would seem that the same reasoning could apply in cases of corruption and other cases of abuse of functions, which involve public officials in a position to extort bribes or embezzle public funds precisely because of their functions. This is reflected in the definitions of the offences of corruption and abuse of functions in the United Nations Convention against Corruption (UNCAC),[33] which respectively require that a public official act 'in the exercise of his or her official duties' and 'in the discharge of his or her functions'.[34] For instance, where members of the Indonesian parliamentary commission on forestry are bribed to strip forest land of protected status and convert it into constructible land,[35] their criminal conduct is rendered possible by the official prerogatives they enjoy on account of their membership in the commission. The issue of corruption was addressed by the Iran–US Claims Tribunal in *Yeager*, a case in which the claimant was seeking compensation for a bribe he had to pay to an agent of Iran Air. The Commission held:

> Acts which an organ commits in a purely private capacity, even if it has used the means placed at its disposal by the State for the exercise of its function, are not attributable to the State. [...] The critical question here, then, is whether the Iran Air agent was acting in his official capacity as an organ of Iran Air when he demanded the extra payment. There is no indication in this case that the Iran Air agent was acting for any other reason than personal profit, or that he had passed on the payment to Iran Air. He evidently did not act on behalf or in the interests of Iran Air. The Tribunal finds, therefore, that this agent acted in a private capacity and not in his official capacity as an organ for Iran Air.[36]

The key element distinguishing this case from other cases where criminal conduct of state officials was considered attributable to the state is that 'the Iran Air agent [...], although he was able to extract a bribe by virtue of his position, did not hold himself out as acting on behalf of the state'.[37] By contrast, in the same case Iran was found responsible for the actions of Revolutionary Guards who had arbitrarily seized cash carried by the claimant. While this latter act may also have been motivated by greed, the fact that the guards 'were performing the functions of customs, immigration and security officers' was sufficient to render their conduct attributable to the state.[38] This goes to show that the existence of private motives, even in cases of corruption, does not *ipso facto* exclude attribution of criminal conduct to the state. The determining condition is that the person or organ appears to represent the state. The ILC

[32] Recall Chapter 1, Section E.

[33] United Nations Convention against Corruption, 31 October 2003, entered into force on 14 December 2005, 2349 UNTS 41.

[34] See Chapter 3, Sections A.4 and 5.

[35] See 'Prison term for former governor extended', *The Jakarta Post* (23 April 2010).

[36] *Yeager v Islamic Republic of Iran,* (1987) 17 Iran–US CTR 92, at 111, para 65.

[37] Crawford (n 25), at 138.

[38] *Yeager* (n 36), at 110, para 61.

has taken the view that the acceptance by a state official of a bribe to perform an act in the exercise of his official duties could be attributable to the state, although the Commission did not provide any guidance on the issue.[39]

The line between private and official acts is not easy to draw, and the attribution of conduct to the state will depend on the facts of each particular case. An interesting question is whether established socio-political practices of the government may impact on the characterization of certain acts as acts of the state. In kleptocratic regimes where state organized crime is part of a mode of governance based on socially embedded mechanics of neo-patrimonialism, it would be artificial to make a neat separation between the private and public spheres.[40] In this context, criminal acts perhaps more commonly considered to further private interests could, from the perspective of political sociology, be regarded as acts of government. Whether they could, as a matter of international law, be considered to have been carried out in an official capacity, with the consequence that they would be attributable to the state, is open to question.[41]

2. Conduct of *de facto* agents acting under the direction or control of the state

Under customary international law, a state may also be held responsible for acts carried out by non-state actors 'acting on the instructions of, or under the direction or control of, that State'.[42] This scenario is relevant for the purposes of an analysis of state responsibility for state organized crime in cases where the organs of the state, while not engaging themselves directly in organized crime, team up with organized criminal groups to further a personal or governmental agenda.

The test to determine whether non-state actors act 'under the direction or control' of the state, expounded by the International Court of Justice (ICJ) in the case of the *Military and Paramilitary Activities in Nicaragua*, is a stringent one. The Court found that 'agents of the United States participated in the planning, direction, support and execution of the operations' of the *contras* in Nicaraguan territory.[43] However, it rejected Nicaragua's claim that the acts of the *contras* were attributable to the United States on that basis. The Court held:

> United States participation, even if preponderant or decisive, in the financing, organizing, training, supplying and equipping of the *contras*, the selection of its military or paramilitary targets, and the planning of the whole of its operation, is still insufficient in itself, on the basis of the evidence in the possession of the Court, for the purpose of attributing to the United States the acts committed by the *contras* in the course of their military or paramilitary

[39] ARSIWA Commentary (n 17), at 46, n 150.

[40] Recall Chapter 1, Section B.2.

[41] This proposition would also entail major consequences for the law of jurisdictional immunities: see Chapter 4, Section B.4(a)(i).

[42] ARSIWA, Art 8; *Application of the Convention on the Prevention and Punishment of the Crime of Genocide* (n 4), at 207, para 398.

[43] *Military and Paramilitary Activities in and against Nicaragua (Nicaragua v United States of America)*, Merits, Judgment, ICJ Rep 1986, p 14, at 51, para 86.

operations in Nicaragua. [...] For this conduct to give rise to legal responsibility of the United States, it would in principle have to be proved that that State had effective control of the military or paramilitary operations in the course of which the alleged violations were committed.[44]

To attribute to a state the conduct of a non-state actor acting under the 'effective control' of that state, 'it must [...] be shown that this "effective control" was exercised, or that the State's instructions were given, in respect of each operation in which the alleged violations occurred, not generally in respect of the overall actions taken by the persons or groups of persons having committed the violations'.[45]

The ILC did not explicitly endorse the 'effective control' test, opting for the more general and flexible formulation of Article 8 ARSIWA.[46] The Appeals Chamber of the International Criminal Tribunal for the former Yugoslavia (ICTY), for its part, departed from the ICJ's 'effective control' test and adopted a more flexible test requiring 'overall control going beyond the mere financing and equipping of such forces and involving also participation in the planning and supervision of military operations'.[47] In subsequent cases, however, the ICJ reiterated its previous ruling in *Nicaragua*, holding that the correct test to determine the degree of control required under Article 8 ARSIWA was the 'effective control' test.[48]

The instances of state organized crime discussed in Chapter 1 indicate that a close *de facto* relationship may exist between state organs and organized criminal groups, including where the former supply military equipment and provide logistical support to the latter.[49] However, the research for this book has not uncovered evidence of a degree of control, on the part of a state over a criminal group comprised of non-state actors, sufficient to satisfy the 'effective control' test. In any event, the question whether a non-state actor may be considered to act 'under the direction or control' of a state is a matter of fact which depends on the circumstances of each particular case.[50] As a matter of law, it would seem that the conduct of an organized criminal group could be attributable to a state exercising control over the group's activities.

3. Conduct of state-owned corporations

A few words should finally be said about the attribution to the state of the conduct of state-owned or state-controlled corporations, entities which occasionally play a role in cases of state organized crime.[51] In the eyes of international law, corporate

44 Ibid, at 64–65, para 115.

45 *Application of the Convention on the Prevention and Punishment of the Crime of Genocide* (n 4), at 208, para 400. See also ARSIWA Commentary (n 17), at 47, para 3, and 48, para 7.

46 See ILC Report (50th sess) (n 5), at 83, para 395 (indicating that '[s]upport was expressed for the Special Rapporteur's proposal to amend art 8, subparagraph (a), to reflect the control test, with attention being drawn to the varying degree of sufficient control required in different specific legal contexts').

47 *Prosecutor v Duško Tadić*, Case no IT-94-1, Appeals Judgment, 15 July 1999, paras 98–145.

48 *Armed Activities on the Territory of the Congo* (n 15), at 226, para 160; *Application of the Convention on the Prevention and Punishment of the Crime of Genocide* (n 4), at 207–208, paras 398–99.

49 Recall Chapter 1, Section C.2.

50 ARSIWA Commentary (n 17), at 48, paras 5 and 7.

51 Recall Chapter 1, Section E (mentioning the case of illicit logging carried out by COECCO, a company held by the Vietnamese Ministry of Defence).

entities established under domestic law are acknowledged as self-standing legal persons,[52] and state-owned corporations are recognized as having a legal personality distinct from the state.[53] As a result, '*prima facie* their conduct in carrying out their activities is not attributable to the State unless they are exercising elements of governmental authority within the meaning of article 5 [ARSIWA]',[54] or unless they can be deemed to act on the instructions or under the direction or control of the state within the meaning of Article 8.[55] The concept of 'governmental authority' is not defined by Article 5. The ILC notes in its commentary that

> what is regarded as "governmental" depends on the particular society, its history and traditions. Of particular importance will be not just the content of the powers, but the way they are conferred on an entity, the purposes for which they are to be exercised and the extent to which the entity is accountable to government for their exercise.[56]

Relevant criteria to determine whether a state-owned corporation acts 'on the instructions or under the direction or control' of the state include the share of capital held by the state, the presence of state officials in the board of directors, and the interference of state officials in corporate decision-making.[57] Since as a general rule the conduct of a state-owned corporation is presumed not to be attributable to the state, the weight to be afforded to the above functional and structural criteria has to be significant to lift the corporate veil.[58] Whether the conduct of a state-owned corporation in a particular case may be attributed to the state will ultimately depend on the facts of the case.

4. Conclusion

The criminal conduct of public officials may be attributed to the state, provided that it can be established that they acted in an official capacity. Cases involving criminal acts overtly committed by public officials in furtherance of state policy would

[52] *Ahmadou Sadio Diallo (Republic of Guinea v Democratic Republic of the Congo)*, Preliminary Objections, Judgment, ICJ Rep 2007, p 582, at 605, para 61; *Barcelona Traction, Light and Power Company, Limited*, Judgment, ICJ Rep 1970, p 3, at 33, para 38.

[53] See e.g. *EDF (Services) Ltd v Romania*, ICSID Case no ARB/05/13, 8 October 2009, para 190.

[54] ARSIWA Commentary (n 17), at 48, para 6. Art 5 ARSIWA provides: 'The conduct of a person or entity which is not an organ of the State under article 4 but which is empowered by the law of that State to exercise elements of the governmental authority shall be considered an act of the State under international law, provided the person or entity is acting in that capacity in the particular instance'.

[55] See e.g. *EDF (Services) Ltd v Romania* (n 53), paras 200–209.

[56] ARSIWA Commentary (n 17), at 43, para 6.

[57] *Salini Costruttori SpA and Italstrade SpA v Morocco*, Decision on Jurisdiction, ICSID Case no ARB/00/4, 23 July 2001, paras 31–35; *Hyatt International Corporation v Islamic Republic of Iran*, (1985) 9 Iran–US CTR 72, at 88–94, para 4.

[58] *La Générale des Carrières et des Mines v F.G. Hemisphere Associates LLC*, [2012] UKPC 27, para 29 (holding that 'constitutional and factual control and the exercise of sovereign functions do not without more convert a separate entity into an organ of the state. Especially where a separate juridical entity is formed by the state for what are on the face of it commercial or industrial purposes, with its own management and budget, the strong presumption is that its separate corporate status should be respected, and that it and the state forming it should not have to bear each other's liabilities. It will [...] take quite extreme circumstances to displace this presumption').

pose little difficulty, but the more common situation involving state agents acting covertly would be potentially problematic, as it would require a determination that criminal acts may fall within the legitimate sphere of competence of a state organ. In cases where public officials act purely for personal profit (typically in cases of corruption or abuse of functions), the attribution of conduct to the state will depend on whether the officials in question appeared or purported to act on behalf of the state. In kleptocratic regimes where mechanisms of governance rest on neo-patrimonialism, it is suggested that acts commonly considered to be carried out for private motives may in certain circumstances be considered as acts of government attributable to the state. In cases where state organs do not themselves directly engage in organized crime, but act in concert with and provide support to organized criminal groups, the conduct of the groups in question could be attributed to the state where it can be established that they acted on the instructions or under the direction or control of the state. Finally, the conduct of a state-owned corporation could in certain circumstances be attributed to the state where the former can be considered as an instrumentality of the state. Despite undeniable conceptual and evidentiary difficulties, on balance and in most cases it would seem that the conduct of public officials using the resources of the state to commit or facilitate the commission of organized criminal activities may be considered attributable to the state under the law of state responsibility.

C. Difficulties Relating to the Establishment of a Breach of an International Obligation

The second condition of an internationally wrongful act of a state is that the conduct of the state 'constitutes a breach of an international obligation of the State'.[59] This section discusses whether the involvement of the organs or agents of a state in organized crime may constitute, as a matter of international law, a breach of an international obligation binding on the state concerned. It reviews primary norms of international law potentially relevant to the phenomenon of state organized crime with a view to determining the applicable substantive law and the existence of a breach.

1. Absence of a general prohibition on state participation in organized crime

To begin with the obvious: no treaty contemplates the involvement of state organs or agents in organized crime, and no treaty contains a provision expressly prohibiting states parties acting through their organs or agents from participating in or facilitating organized crime. Nonetheless, one should examine the possibility of inferring the existence of such a prohibition from existing treaty provisions as well as from state practice and *opinio juris*.

[59] ARSIWA, Art 2(b).

(a) *Impossibility of inferring a general prohibition on state participation in organized crime from existing treaty provisions*

In the absence of an express treaty provision prohibiting states parties from participating in or facilitating organized crime, such a treaty-based prohibition could potentially be inferred from other obligations imposed on states parties by international instruments pertaining to organized crime and corruption.

(i) **Obligations of states parties under crime-suppression conventions pertaining to organized crime and corruption**

The international obligations of states with respect to organized crime and corruption are for the most part enshrined in a number of multilateral treaties designed to establish common minimum standards across domestic laws and to strengthen international cooperation for the purpose of preventing and punishing crime. The obligations of states parties under such 'crime-suppression conventions' cover aspects of criminal law, both substantive and procedural, pertaining to the criminalization of conduct, the establishment of jurisdiction over crimes, the duty to extradite or prosecute suspected offenders, international cooperation in criminal matters, and the seizure and confiscation of proceeds of crime. These will be analysed in detail in the next chapter. The concern of the present analysis is to focus on the preventive measures provided for in existing treaties pertaining to organized crime and corruption, to determine, first, whether a general obligation to prevent crime may be identified in these instruments, and secondly, whether a treaty-based prohibition on participation in organized crime may be inferred from the provisions pertaining to preventive measures.

The cornerstone of the international crime-suppression regime against organized crime is UNCTOC. Article 1 provides that '[t]he purpose of this Convention is to promote cooperation to prevent and combat transnational organized crime more effectively'. Article 31 lays down obligations for the prevention of transnational organized crime, requiring states parties inter alia to 'endeavour [...] to establish and promote best practices and policies aimed at the prevention of transnational organized crime'. Article 9 also requires states parties, consistent with their legal systems, to adopt measures to prevent the corruption of public officials. Similarly, the stated purpose of UNCAC is '[t]o promote and strengthen measures to prevent and combat corruption more efficiently and effectively'.[60] Chapter II of the Convention requires states parties to adopt a range of preventive measures against corruption and money laundering, including a general obligation to 'endeavour to establish and promote effective practices aimed at the prevention of corruption'.[61] The United Nations Convention against Illicit Traffic in Narcotic Drugs and Psychotropic Substances[62] (UN Drug Convention) also provides for preventive measures, requiring states parties inter alia to take measures to prevent the diversion

[60] UNCAC, Art 1(a). [61] Ibid, Art 5(2). See also UNCTOC, Art 9.

[62] United Nations Convention against Illicit Traffic in Narcotic Drugs and Psychotropic Substances, 20 December 1988, entered into force on 11 November 1990, 1582 UNTS 95.

of certain substances or equipment used for the purpose of illicit drug manufacturing[63] and to prevent illicit cultivation of narcotic plants.[64] Similar provisions requiring states parties to take measures for the prevention of offences related to organized crime and corruption may be found in a number of crime-suppression conventions, with varying degrees of specificity and obligation.[65] The Arab Convention against Transnational Organized Crime stands out, as it specifically requires states parties to ensure that their territory is not used for planning, carrying out, initiating, or participating in any of the crimes listed in the Convention.[66]

This latter provision notwithstanding, existing crime-suppression conventions do not establish actual obligations of prevention in the form of obligations of due diligence requiring states parties to employ all possible means to prevent the occurrence of crime.[67] At best, they establish positive obligations of result that simply require states parties to adopt certain measures in their domestic law.[68] Such obligations are typically phrased in very general terms, and often remain subject to the principles of the domestic legal system of the states parties. As a result, states parties can often choose at their discretion the means to be employed to achieve the specified result, and their treaty obligations will be discharged merely by adopting the prescribed measures under their domestic law.[69] Nevertheless, considering that the object and purpose of crime-suppression conventions is to prevent and punish conduct considered as criminal in the eyes of international law, it would seem logical to infer from the provisions and overall structure of these instruments an obligation for states parties not to participate in or facilitate the commission of offences that they are expected to prevent and punish in their domestic law. Logic and common sense, however, do not necessarily translate into binding obligations for states under international law. As the Permanent Court of International Justice famously stated,

[63] Ibid, Arts 12(1) and 13. [64] Ibid, Art 14(2).

[65] See e.g. Protocol to Prevent, Suppress and Punish Trafficking in Persons, Especially Women and Children, Supplementing the United Nations Convention against Transnational Organized Crime, 15 November 2000, entered into force on 25 December 2003, 2237 UNTS 319, Art 9(1)(a); Optional Protocol to the Convention on the Rights of the Child on the Sale of Children, Child Prostitution and Child Pornography, 25 May 2000, entered into force on 18 January 2002, 2171 UNTS 247, Art 9(1); Protocol against the Illicit Manufacturing of and Trafficking in Firearms, Their Parts and Components and Ammunition, Supplementing the United Nations Convention against Transnational Organized Crime, 31 May 2001, entered into force on 3 July 2005, 2326 UNTS 208, Arts 7–15; Convention on the Control of Transboundary Movements of Hazardous Wastes and their Disposal, 22 March 1989, entered into force on 5 May 1992, 1673 UNTS 57, Art 4(4).

[66] Arab Convention against Transnational Organized Crime, 21 December 2010, entered into force on 5 October 2013, Art 37(1).

[67] Such an obligation of prevention may be found in the Genocide Convention: see *Application of the Convention on the Prevention and Punishment of the Crime of Genocide* (n 4), at 221, para 430 (defining the obligation to prevent genocide as an obligation 'to employ all means reasonably available [...] so as to prevent genocide so far as possible').

[68] Cf *Immunities and Criminal Proceedings (Equatorial Guinea v France)*, Request for the Indication of Provisional Measures, Order of 7 December 2016, para 48 (summarizing the obligations of states parties to UNCTOC as follows: 'Under the terms of the Convention, the States parties must, if they have not already done so, legislate against the transnational offences set out in the said instrument and participate in the international co-operation mechanism referred to therein').

[69] See generally Constantin P Economides, 'Content of the Obligations: Obligations of Means and Obligations of Result' in Crawford, Pellet, and Olleson (n 20), at 378.

'[t]he rules of law binding upon States [...] emanate from their own free will as expressed in conventions or by usages generally accepted as expressing principles of law [...]. Restrictions upon the independence of States cannot therefore be presumed'.[70]

(ii) Obligation of prevention and inferred obligation not to commit crime in the *Bosnian Genocide* case

The possibility of inferring the existence of a treaty-based obligation prohibiting states parties from committing a particular crime, from an obligation to prevent the commission of the crime in question, was posited by the ICJ in the *Bosnian Genocide* case. The issue before the Court concerned the interpretation of Article I of the Convention on the Prevention and Punishment of the Crime of Genocide (Genocide Convention),[71] which provides: 'The Contracting Parties confirm that genocide, whether committed in time of peace or in time of war, is a crime under international law which they undertake to prevent and to punish'. Noting that this provision 'does not *expressis verbis* require States to refrain from themselves committing genocide', the Court nevertheless held that 'taking into account the established purpose of the Convention, the effect of Article I is to prohibit States from themselves committing genocide'.[72] The Court's reasoning was as follows:

> Such a prohibition follows, first, from the fact that the Article categorizes genocide as "a crime under international law": by agreeing to such a categorization, the States parties must logically be undertaking not to commit the act so described. Secondly, it follows from the expressly stated obligation to prevent the commission of acts of genocide. That obligation requires the States parties, *inter alia*, to employ the means at their disposal, in circumstances to be described more specifically later in this Judgment, to prevent persons or groups not directly under their authority from committing an act of genocide or any of the other acts mentioned in Article III. It would be paradoxical if States were thus under an obligation to prevent, so far as within their power, commission of genocide by persons over whom they have a certain influence, but were not forbidden to commit such acts through their own organs, or persons over whom they have such firm control that their conduct is attributable to the State concerned under international law. In short, the obligation to prevent genocide necessarily implies the prohibition of the commission of genocide.[73]

The Court's interpretation of Article I of the Convention was far from unanimous. It was rejected by almost half of the judges in the majority for disregarding the ordinary meaning of the text of the Convention as well as its object and purpose.[74] For

[70] *The Case of the S.S. 'Lotus' (France v Turkey)*, PCIJ Series A no 10 (1927), at 18.

[71] Convention on the Prevention and Punishment of the Crime of Genocide, 9 December 1948, entered into force on 12 January 1951, 78 UNTS 277.

[72] *Application of the Convention on the Prevention and Punishment of the Crime of Genocide* (n 4), at 74, para 166.

[73] Ibid.

[74] *Application of the Convention on the Prevention and Punishment of the Crime of Genocide*, Joint Declaration of Judges Shi and Koroma, ICJ Rep 2007, p 279, at 279–82, paras 1–4; Separate Opinion of Judge Owada, ICJ Rep 2007, p 285, at 297–301, paras 38–53; Separate Opinion of Judge Tomka, ICJ Rep 2007, p 310, at 332–335, 344, paras 40–45, 61; Declaration of Judge Skotnikov, ICJ Rep 2007, p 366, at 370–372; Separate Opinion of Judge ad hoc Kreca, ICJ Rep 2007, p 457, at 551–52, paras 126–27.

the same reasons, the Court's approach was also met with significant scepticism by commentators in the literature. Relying notably on the *travaux préparatoires*, critics of the Court's interpretation have argued that the Genocide Convention is a crime-suppression convention requiring states parties to take measures in their domestic law to criminalize acts of genocide and punish individual perpetrators, and not an instrument intended to provide for the international responsibility of states parties for the criminal conduct of their organs or agents. While it is undisputed that states are under an international obligation not to commit genocide, the source of this obligation is generally believed to be found in customary international law, and not in the Convention itself.[75]

(iii) Discussion

Notwithstanding the controversy as to the validity under the law of treaties of the Court's interpretation of the Genocide Convention, it is not certain that the Court's reasoning may be adopted, *mutatis mutandis*, to infer from existing treaty provisions pertaining to organized crime and corruption a general prohibition on the participation of states parties in organized crime. The Court itself pointed out that it did 'not, in [the *Bosnian Genocide*] case, purport to establish a general jurisprudence applicable to all cases where a treaty instrument, or other binding legal norm, includes an obligation for States to prevent certain acts'.[76] There are indeed significant differences between the Genocide Convention and crime-suppression conventions pertaining to organized crime and corruption. First, whereas in the Genocide Convention genocide is recognized as 'a crime under international law', a similar characterization is absent from instruments pertaining to organized crime or corruption. Although the distinction between 'crimes under international law' and other international crimes may be disputed,[77] it is difficult not to acknowledge the rather unique position occupied by genocide in international criminal law, which is reflected in the wording of the Genocide Convention. Secondly, the formulation of the obligations to prevent crime in the respective instruments differs markedly. In the crime-suppression conventions pertaining to organized crime and corruption, obligations to take preventive measures are often qualified and phrased in much more equivocal terms[78] than the undertaking to prevent genocide in the Genocide

[75] See Paola Gaeta, 'On What Conditions Can a State Be Held Responsible for Genocide?' (2007) 18 *European Journal of International Law* 631, at 632–40; Olivier Corten, 'L'arrêt rendu par la CIJ dans l'affaire du *Crime de génocide (Bosnie-Herzégovine c. Serbie)* : vers un assouplissement des conditions permettant d'engager la responsabilité d'un État pour génocide ?' (2007) 53 *Annuaire français de droit international* 249, at 270; Pierre-Marie Dupuy, 'A Crime without Punishment' (2016) 14 *Journal of International Criminal Justice* 879, at 882. See also Antonio Cassese, 'On the Use of Criminal Law Notions in Determining State Responsibility for Genocide' (2007) 5 *Journal of International Criminal Justice* 875, at 878.

[76] *Application of the Convention on the Prevention and Punishment of the Crime of Genocide* (n 4), at 220, para 429.

[77] See Chapter 5, Section B.1.

[78] See e.g. UNCTOC, Art 31(1): 'States Parties shall endeavour [...] to establish and promote best practices and policies aimed at the prevention of transnational organized crime'; UNCAC, Art 5(2): 'Each State Party shall endeavour to establish and promote effective practices aimed at the prevention of corruption'.

Convention. Thirdly, the drafting history of the respective instruments evidences different approaches. At the time of the drafting of the Genocide Convention there was an understanding that state organs could be involved in genocide, and a number of states expressed the view that a state could incur responsibility for genocide under international law.[79] There was clearly no such understanding regarding state responsibility for organized crime during the negotiation of UNCTOC.[80] When considering whether the Court's reasoning in *Bosnian Genocide* would potentially be applicable to other crime-suppression conventions such as the Convention for the Suppression of the Traffic in Persons and of the Exploitation of the Prostitution of Others, Gaeta rejected this possibility as absurd and contrary to the object and purpose of crime-suppression conventions.[81] It would seem that a teleological interpretation of the provisions of relevant crime-suppression conventions cannot establish the existence of a treaty-based prohibition on state participation in organized crime.

An isolated passage from the judgment of the International Military Tribunal for the Far East appears to lend credence to the view that a state party to a crime-suppression convention may be considered in breach of its treaty obligations when its organs or agents directly participate in the crimes forming the object of the convention. The tribunal began by reviewing the obligations assumed by Japan pursuant to a number of international agreements, including the 1912 and 1925 International Opium Conventions and the 1931 Convention for Limiting the Manufacture and Regulating the Distribution of Narcotic Drugs.[82] The tribunal noted:

> In order to finance her operations in Manchuria and also in order to weaken the power of resistance of the Chinese, Japan sanctioned and developed the traffic in opium and narcotics [...]. Japan as a signatory to the above opium conventions was obligated to assist the Chinese Government in the eradication of the drug habit by limiting the manufacture and sale of the drugs within her territory and by preventing smuggling of the drugs into China.[83]

The tribunal concluded by holding that 'Japan having signed and ratified the Opium Conventions was bound not to engage in the drug traffic'.[84] While the tribunal's ruling is directly in point and unequivocal, it is dubious that it may constitute a persuasive precedent for the purposes of determining the responsibility of a state for an internationally wrongful act. The task of the tribunal was not to adjudicate the

[79] *Application of the Convention on the Prevention and Punishment of the Crime of Genocide* (n 4), at 117–18, paras 176–78; Anja Seibert-Fohr, 'State Responsibility for Genocide under the Genocide Convention' in Paola Gaeta (ed), *The UN Genocide Convention: A Commentary* (Oxford University Press, 2009) 349, at 354–56.

[80] See UNODC, *Travaux préparatoires of the Negotiations for the Elaboration of the United Nations Convention against Transnational Organized Crime and the Protocols thereto* (United Nations, 2006).

[81] See Gaeta (n 75), at 640.

[82] International Opium Convention, 23 January 1912, entered into force on 28 June 1919, 8 LNTS 187; International Opium Convention, 19 February 1925, entered into force on 25 September 1928, 81 LNTS 317; Convention for Limiting the Manufacture and Regulating the Distribution of Narcotic Drugs, 13 July 1931, entered into force on 9 July 1933, 139 LNTS 301.

[83] See 'Majority Judgment' in Neil Boister and Robert Cryer (eds), *Documents on the Tokyo International Military Tribunal: Charter, Indictment, and Judgments* (Oxford University Press, 2008) 71, at 364–65.

[84] Ibid, at 366.

responsibility of Japan under the law of state responsibility, but to determine the individual criminal responsibility of the persons named in the indictment for the crimes included within its jurisdiction—which did not include drug trafficking or any other offence related to organized crime. In his dissenting judgment, Justice Pal wrote that he did 'not see any bearing of these treaties on the question before [the tribunal]', noting that a potential breach by Japan of its treaty obligations would be a matter of state responsibility.[85] Moreover, assuming that state responsibility could have been incurred for a breach of the Opium Conventions, such responsibility could hardly be considered as arising on account of the involvement of state officials in criminal conduct. The regime established by the Opium Conventions to limit the manufacturing and distribution of narcotic drugs, relying as it did essentially on administrative and other regulatory mechanisms, did not approach drug control from a criminal-law perspective. The 1931 Convention does not contain any criminal-law provisions. The 1912 Opium Convention, for its part, merely required states parties to 'examine the possibility of' criminalizing illicit drug possession.[86] Only the 1925 Opium Convention required states parties to provide for 'adequate penalties' to enforce the provisions of the Convention[87] and to 'examine in the most favourable spirit the possibility of' establishing their jurisdiction over aiding and abetting drug offences committed abroad.[88] In the absence of any analysis in the tribunal's judgment involving a detailed application of general principles of treaty interpretation, it would be imprudent to afford too much weight to it.

In view of these considerations, the possibility of inferring, from the obligations of states parties under relevant crime-suppression conventions, a general, treaty-based prohibition on the participation of state organs or agents in organized crime is uncertain at best under international law.

(b) *Impossibility of identifying a general prohibition on state participation in organized crime under customary international law*

A customary obligation, independent of any treaty obligation, prohibiting states acting through their organs or agents from participating in or facilitating organized crime, would have to be inferred from the practice and *opinio juris* of states.[89] When it comes to assessing the existence of a prohibition (as opposed to a prescription or a permissive rule), evidence of the elements of custom has to be sought in positive expressions of *opinio juris* reflecting the views of states regarding the illegality of the considered conduct.[90] In this case, state practice is conflated with

[85] *International Tribunal for the Far East: Dissenting Judgment of Justice Pal* (Kokusho-Kankokai, 1999), at 131–33.

[86] International Opium Convention 1912, Art 20.

[87] International Opium Convention 1925, Art 28.

[88] Ibid, Art 29.

[89] *Continental Shelf (Libyan Arab Jamahiriya v Malta)*, Judgment, ICJ Rep 1985, p 13, at 29, para 27; Draft conclusions on identification of customary international law, in *Report of the International Law Commission* (68th sess), UN Doc A/71/10 in *Yearbook of the International Law Commission* (2016), vol II(2), para 62, Conclusion 2.

[90] See Luigi Ferrari Bravo, 'Méthodes de recherche de la coutume internationale dans la pratique des États' (1985) 192 *Recueil des cours de l'Académie de droit international* 233, at 253 (noting that the

opinio juris,[91] and the ascertainment of a customary rule relies not only on an inductive method examining the reactions of states in particular cases, but also on a deductive interpretation of general principles affirmed by states.[92]

The challenge inherent in the exercise of ascertaining the existence of customary rules is particularly acute with respect to state conduct that often occurs covertly and therefore rarely attracts international attention. If a state takes issue with another state's involvement in organized crime, such matters are probably discussed through diplomatic backchannels and not on the record. However, a paucity of state practice may not necessarily be an obstacle to the recognition of a rule of customary international law, provided that the existing practice is sufficiently 'constant and uniform'.[93] Modern theories of customary international law posit that strong evidence of *opinio juris* can offset a paucity of state practice.[94]

States have rarely expressed their views publicly in reaction to another state's participation in organized crime. The few relevant instances of state practice include the discussion of Japan's alleged involvement in drug manufacturing and trafficking in East Asia at meetings of the League of Nations Advisory Committee on the Traffic in Opium and Other Dangerous Drugs. The representative of China accused Japan of 'deliberately encourag[ing]' the illicit traffic in China to generate revenue.[95] The United States representative called upon Japan to 'exercise the restraining influence which it is in a position to bring to bear upon its nationals in the occupied areas of China and upon the regimes which have been established therein to prevent [drug manufacturing and trafficking]'.[96] The representative of Egypt denounced the

subjective element of customary international law may manifest itself in statements made by states regarding the conduct of other states); Andrew T Guzman, 'Saving Customary International Law' (2005) 27 *Michigan Journal of International Law* 115, at 146 (defining *opinio juris* as 'the beliefs of states that interact with a potential violator'). In the particular domain of the law of armed conflict, which essentially comprises prohibitions, '[p]ractice establishing the existence of a prohibition [...] includes [...] statements that such behaviour is prohibited and condemnations of instances where the prohibited behaviour did take place' (Jean-Marie Henckaerts and Louise Doswald-Beck, International Committee of the Red Cross, *Customary International Humanitarian Law*, vol I: *Rules* (3rd edn, Cambridge University Press, 2009), at xlv). The abstention of states, refraining from engaging in particular conduct, may also be analysed as state practice in support of the existence of a customary prohibition regarding said conduct, but reliance on such 'practice' is not particularly conclusive.

[91] See Jean-Marie Henckaerts and Els Debuf, 'The ICRC and the Clarification of Customary International Humanitarian Law' in Brian D Lepard (ed), *Reexamining Customary International Law* (Cambridge University Press, 2017) 161, at 181 (pointing out that verbal acts of reaction to violations of a putative customary prohibition 'are evidence of both practice and *opinio juris*').

[92] Jean d'Aspremont, *Formalism and the Sources of International Law: A Theory of the Ascertainment of Legal Rules* (Oxford University Press, 2011), at 169.

[93] *Colombian-Peruvian Asylum Case (Colombia v Peru)*, Judgment, ICJ Rep 1950, p 266, at 276–77.

[94] See Frederic L Kirgis, 'Custom on a Sliding Scale' (1987) 81 *American Journal of International Law* 146, at 149; Michael P Scharf, 'Seizing the "Grotian Moment": Accelerated Formation of Customary International Law in Times of Fundamental Change' (2010) 43 *Cornell International Law Journal* 439. On the increasing reliance on *opinio juris* as a method for the ascertainment of rules of customary international law, see generally Niels Petersen, 'Customary Law without Custom: Rules, Principles, and the Role of State Practice in International Norm Creation' (2008) 23 *American University International Law Review* 275, at 278–84, and the authorities cited therein.

[95] Advisory Committee on the Traffic in Opium and Other Dangerous Drugs, *Report to the Council* (24th sess), 30 June 1939, Doc no C.202.M.131.1939.XI, at 8–9.

[96] Ibid, at 12.

'serious character of the conditions in the territories under Japanese occupation',[97] and the representative of India invited the Committee 'to throw light on this state of affairs'.[98] However, none of these states has taken a stance as to the legality of Japan's conduct under international law, and even if one were to consider that legal considerations were implicitly underpinning the above statements, such considerations would have been more likely to relate to Japan's obligations under the Opium Conventions rather than to the existence of a general rule of customary international law. These statements are therefore inconclusive for the purpose of establishing the existence of a customary norm.

The case of North Korea presents a noteworthy and more recent instance of a state being officially condemned by other states for its participation in organized crime. The involvement of the government of North Korea in criminal activities, such as the counterfeiting of US currency, drug trafficking, and money laundering, was one of the grounds cited by the US Congress for the adoption of sanctions against North Korea.[99] Whether such sanctions ought to be considered as countermeasures or measures of retortion is debatable. In any event, the fact that they also refer to North Korea's violation of UN Security Council resolutions, sponsoring of terrorist groups, and violation of internationally guaranteed human rights[100] suggests that they are intended to respond to conduct considered unlawful under international law. South Korea's ambassador to the United States, referring to North Korea's counterfeiting of US currency, declared that 'such illicit activities are not acceptable and that Pyongyang should unequivocally turn away from such illicit behavior once and for all'. There is a degree of ambiguity as to whether South Korea's condemnation was expressed in response to North Korea's direct participation in organized crime, considered as an internationally wrongful act of the state, or to North Korea's condonation of the criminal conduct of individual North Korean firms.[101] This ambiguity notwithstanding, the position of the United States and of South Korea arguably provides evidence of *opinio juris* regarding the unlawfulness of state organized crime under international law.

Evidence of *opinio juris* regarding the existence of a rule of customary international law prohibiting states from participating in organized crime may also be sought in the reaction of states to the Taliban's involvement in drug trafficking. Several resolutions of the UN General Assembly adopted by consensus[102] have called upon the Taliban 'to halt all illegal drug activities'.[103] Although General Assembly resolutions

[97] Ibid, at 13. [98] Ibid.

[99] See North Korea Sanctions and Policy Enhancement Act of 2016, Public Law no 114-122, 22 USC § 9201(a)(3).

[100] Ibid, § 9201(a)(1)(B), (10), and (4), respectively.

[101] See Dick K Nanto, *North Korean Counterfeiting of US Currency* (Congressional Research Service, 12 June 2009), at 13, and the sources cited therein.

[102] Official records of the plenary meetings of the General Assembly, 53rd sess, 18 December 1998, UN Doc A/53/PV.93, at 1; 54th sess, 17 December 1999, UN Doc A/54/PV.84, at 1; 55th sess, 19 December 2000, UN Doc A/55/PV.86, at 21.

[103] UN General Assembly Resolution 53/203 A, 18 December 1998, UN Doc A/RES/53/203 A, para 20; Resolution 54/189 A, 17 December 1999, UN Doc A/RES/54/189 A, para 27; Resolution 55/174 A, 19 December 2000, UN Doc A/RES/55/174 A, para 25.

may be used as a valid indicator of *opinio juris*, caution must be exercised when referring to them to ascertain the existence of customary rules, as they do not necessarily have a normative character.[104] In the resolutions concerning Afghanistan, the express characterization of the Taliban's activities as 'illegal' does not seem to amount to the assertion of a breach on the part of Afghanistan of its international obligations, as it may simply be taken to refer to the criminal conduct of individuals belonging to an organization that was not recognized as the legitimate government of Afghanistan. Those resolutions therefore cannot be considered to constitute conclusive evidence of *opinio juris* regarding the legality under international law of the participation of a state's organs or agents in organized crime.

Formal declarations of principles concerning the fight against transnational organized crime adopted by states do not provide any more evidence of the existence under customary international law of a potential prohibition on state participation in organized crime. The Naples Political Declaration and Global Action Plan against Organized Transnational Crime[105] and the Declaration on Crime and Public Security[106] adopted by the General Assembly, the Buenos Aires Declaration on Prevention and Control of Organized Transnational Crime[107] adopted by Latin-American and Caribbean states, and the Dakar Declaration on the Prevention and Control of Organized Transnational Crime and Corruption[108] adopted by African states do not have anything to say about the involvement of state organs in organized crime.

In conclusion, state practice and *opinio juris* are largely insufficient to support the proposition that customary international law prohibits the participation of state organs or agents in organized crime as such.

Nevertheless, the absence of such a prohibition does not mean, as the well-known *dictum* of the *Lotus* case might be taken to suggest,[109] that such conduct is necessarily permissible under international law. State conduct amounting to state organized crime may remain subject to more general obligations under customary international law or general principles of law, and certain particular aspects of state organized crime, such as the illicit exploitation of another state's natural resources or state-sponsored human trafficking, may fall within the ambit of prohibitions provided by specific branches of international law.

[104] *Military and Paramilitary Activities in Nicaragua* (n 43), at 99–100, para 188; *Legality of the Threat or Use of Nuclear Weapons*, Advisory Opinion, ICJ Rep 1996, p 226, at 254–55, para 70. See also Draft conclusions on identification of customary international law (n 89), Conclusion 12(2).

[105] In *Report of the World Ministerial Conference on Organized Transnational Crime*, annexed to UN Doc A/49/748, at 5, and adopted by Resolution 49/159.

[106] Annexed to Resolution 51/60, 28 January 1997, UN Doc A/RES/51/60.

[107] 30 November 1995, annexed to UN Doc E/CN.15/1996/2/Add.1.

[108] 23 July 1997, in UN Doc E/CN.15/1998/6/Add.1.

[109] See *Lotus* (n 70). This passage of the Court's judgment is often understood to imply that 'under international law everything which is not prohibited is permitted' and that 'under international law, every door is open unless it is closed by treaty or by established custom' (Dissenting Opinion of Judge Loder, at 34).

2. Obligation to perform treaty obligations in good faith

In the absence of a primary norm prohibiting state participation in organized crime as such, a determination that a state has violated particular provisions of relevant crime-suppression conventions—for example, by failing to adopt the preventive measures provided for by the treaty, or by failing to initiate proceedings for the purposes of prosecuting a suspect it refuses to extradite—remains possible. The problem in this case is that the wrongfulness of the state's conduct would have nothing to do with the participation of its organs or agents in organized crime. Moreover, in many instances of state organized crime it may well be the case that the state concerned has fulfilled its treaty obligations by adopting adequate measures under its domestic law. In formal terms, most of the obligations imposed by the relevant crime-suppression conventions can be discharged by enacting a comprehensive legal framework for the prevention and suppression of organized crime and corruption,[110] even though in practice the state may not make any genuine effort to investigate, prosecute, and punish perpetrators. It has been suggested that a state having formally fulfilled its treaty obligations under a crime-suppression convention while trying to shield offenders from effective punishment would be in breach of its obligation to perform treaty obligations in good faith and in particular to refrain from acts that would defeat the object and purpose of the treaty.[111] In a similar vein, one ought to consider whether the involvement in organized crime of a state party to a crime-suppression convention pertaining to organized crime or corruption may constitute a breach of the obligation to perform treaty obligations in good faith.

Good faith (*bona fides*) is '[o]ne of the basic principles governing the creation and performance of legal obligations',[112] endorsed by the UN General Assembly[113] and considered to be a fundamental principle of international law. Under the international law of treaties, this general principle translates into a legal obligation[114] to perform treaty obligations in good faith (*pacta sunt servanda*).[115] Good faith operates as a substantive principle, not only by influencing the determination of the content of treaty obligations, but also as a self-standing source of obligation,[116] the violation of which may entail the international responsibility of the state.[117] It

[110] Recall Section C.1(a)(i) of this chapter.

[111] Robert Kolb, 'La bonne foi en droit international public' (1998) 31 *Revue belge de droit international* 661, at 712.

[112] *Nuclear Tests (New Zealand v France)*, Judgment, ICJ Rep 1974, p 457, at 473, para 49.

[113] *Declaration on Principles of International Law Concerning Friendly Relations and Cooperation among States in accordance with the Charter of the United Nations*, annexed to UN General Assembly Resolution 2625 (XXV), 24 October 1970, UN Doc A/RES/2625 (XXV).

[114] Record of the 724th meeting of the ILC, 20 May 1964 in *Yearbook of the International Law Commission* (1964), vol I, at 29, para 31.

[115] Vienna Convention on the Law of Treaties (VCLT), 23 May 1969, entered into force on 27 January 1980, 1155 UNTS 331, Art 26.

[116] Kolb (n 111), at 676, 682–84.

[117] See e.g. *Westland Helicopters Ltd v Arab Organization for Industrialisation and others*, International Chamber of Commerce Case no 3879/AS, English translation reproduced in (1984) 23 ILM 1071, at 1084 (holding that in the absence of any rule of applicable law, the responsibility of the respondent states subsists on the basis of general principles of law and good faith).

notably requires states parties to a treaty to abstain from acts which would frustrate the object and purpose of the treaty.[118]

A state cannot pretend to do with the one hand what it undoes with the other. Where a state party to a crime-suppression convention acting through its organs or agents participates in or facilitates the commission of crimes that it is bound by treaty to prevent and punish, its conduct would arguably be 'such as to undermine the whole spirit' of the treaty.[119] Although such a determination is closely linked to an interpretation of relevant treaty provisions, the internationally wrongful act of the state in this case is best characterized as a violation of a general principle of law rather than as a breach of an obligation imposed by the treaty itself.[120] Considering its flexibility and intrinsically normative dimension, the principle of bona fide performance of treaty obligations arguably constitutes a promising candidate for establishing the existence of a breach of an international obligation in cases of state organized crime, with the caveat that it would only come into play with respect to states parties to the relevant crime-suppression conventions.[121] It should finally be emphasized that any allegation that a state has breached its obligation to act in good faith would have to overcome a strong legal presumption.[122]

3. Obligation to prevent acts contrary to the rights of other states

It is a well-established principle of general international law that 'every State [has an] obligation not to allow knowingly its territory to be used for acts contrary to the rights of other States'.[123] This obligation is a corollary of territorial sovereignty, which entails 'the obligation to protect within the territory the rights of other States'.[124] The obligation incumbent on states to prevent acts contrary to the rights of other states within their territory involves in particular more specific obligations to prevent criminal conduct potentially harmful to other states: the obligation to prevent crimes committed against diplomatic agents and other internationally

[118] *Report of the International Law Commission* (18th sess), UN Doc A/6309/Rev.l (A/21/9) in *Yearbook of the International Law Commission* (1966), vol II, at 211, para 4; *Military and Paramilitary Activities in Nicaragua* (n 43), at 135–38, paras 270–76.

[119] *Military and Paramilitary Activities in Nicaragua* (n 43), at 138, para 275.

[120] Ibid, at 138, para 270 ('if there is a duty of a State not to impede the due performance of a treaty to which it is a Party, that is not a duty imposed by the treaty itself. [Nicaragua's] claim therefore does not in fact fall under the heading of possible breach by the United States of the provisions of the 1956 Treaty, though it may involve the interpretation or application thereof').

[121] For a discussion of the conditions under which the responsibility of the culpable state may be invoked by other states parties, see Section D of this chapter.

[122] See *Case concerning certain German interests in Polish Upper Silesia (Germany v Poland)*, Merits, PCIJ Series A no 7 (1926), at 30 (noting that a breach of good faith 'cannot be presumed' and that 'it rests with the party who states that there has been such [breach] to prove his statement').

[123] *Corfu Channel Case (United Kingdom v Albania)*, ICJ Rep 1949, p 4, at 22. See also *Trail Smelter Case (United States of America v Canada)*, 11 March 1941, 3 RIAA 1905, at 1965 (holding that 'no State has the right to use or permit the use of its territory in such a manner as to cause injury [in this case, by fumes] in or to the territory of another').

[124] *Island of Palmas Case (United States of America v Netherlands)*, 4 April 1928, 2 RIAA 829, at 839.

protected persons,[125] the obligation to prevent and punish crimes committed against aliens,[126] and the obligation to prevent acts of international terrorism, which entails in particular an obligation for states to refrain from 'acquiescing in or encouraging' activities within their territory directed towards the commission of terrorist acts in the territory of other states.[127] These particular instantiations of the obligation to prevent acts contrary to the rights of other states point to the existence under international law of a more general derivative of that obligation, requiring states to prevent within their territory any form of criminal conduct adversely affecting the rights of other states. This latter proposition is supported by the work of the ILC on the Draft Articles on the Prevention and Punishment of Crimes against Diplomatic Agents and Other Internationally Protected Persons. In its commentary, the Commission noted the existence of a 'well established principle of international law that every State must ensure that its territory is not used for the preparation of crimes to be committed in other States'.[128] This principle has also been recognized in the literature.[129] It should finally be noted that while the obligation to prevent acts contrary to the rights of other states is commonly regarded as a due diligence obligation of the state to prevent harmful acts committed within its territory by a third party, it is accepted that a breach may also occur *a fortiori* in case of direct participation of the organs or agents of the state in the harmful conduct.[130] In this case, the obligation to prevent acts contrary to the rights of other states may overlap with the obligation not to intervene in the affairs of another state, discussed separately below.[131]

The parallel with state organized crime is evident where the participation of state organs or agents in organized crime may adversely affect the rights of other states, for

[125] This principle is codified in the Convention on the Prevention and Punishment of Crimes against Internationally Protected Persons, Including Diplomatic Agents, 14 December 1973, entered into force on 20 February 1977, 1035 UNTS 167, Art 4(a).

[126] *British Property in Spanish Morocco (Spain v United Kingdom)*, 1 May 1925, 2 RIAA 615, at 640–47.

[127] *Declaration on Measures to Eliminate International Terrorism*, annexed to General Assembly Resolution 49/60, 17 February 1995, UN Doc A/RES/49/60, paras 4 and 5(a); Resolution 2625 (XXV); Security Council Resolution 1189 (1998), 13 August 1998, UN Doc S/RES/1189 (1998), preamble, 5th recital; Resolution 1373 (2001), 28 September 2001, UN Doc S/RES/1373 (2001), preamble, 9th recital.

[128] *Report of the International Law Commission* (24th sess) in *Yearbook of the International Law Commission* (1972), vol II, at 317, para 2.

[129] See Franciszek Przetacznik, *Protection of Officials of Foreign States According to International Law* (Martinus Nijhoff, 1983), at 95; Trapp (n 25), at 64, 66 (arguing with respect to the obligation to prevent acts of international terrorism that 'States did not consider themselves to be formulating a new obligation, but rather to be applying existing international law to the specific offences defined in the [terrorism suppression conventions]').

[130] See in particular, regarding state-sponsored terrorism: Trapp (n 25), at 80–82; Pierre-Marie Dupuy and Cristina Hoss, '*Trail Smelter* and Terrorism: International Mechanisms to Combat Transboundary Harm' in Rebecca M Bratspies and Russell A Miller (eds), *Transboundary Harm in International Law: Lessons from the Trail Smelter Arbitration* (Cambridge University Press, 2006) 225, at 235–38. See also generally Louis Delbez, 'La responsabilité internationale pour crimes commis sur le territoire d'un État et dirigés contre la sûreté d'un État étranger' (1930) 4 *Revue générale de droit international public* 461, at 464.

[131] See Section C.4 of this chapter.

instance in cases of state-sponsored drug or arms trafficking designed to destabilize a foreign government,[132] but perhaps also more generally in any case involving transnational criminal activities involving a potential harmful impact in other states. The problem is that not every type of criminal activity may, by its nature, be considered to be committed 'against' another state. State organized crime typically involves economic crimes that are usually not classified as offences against the state, national security, public safety, or public order. For instance, in the case of drug trafficking, the determination of the harm potentially caused in consumer states on account of a deleterious impact on public health and safety is a difficult exercise.[133] By contrast, one could consider that the large-scale counterfeiting and trafficking of US currency by North Korea[134] adversely affects vital interests of the United States.[135] The characterization of particular crimes as 'acts contrary to the rights of other states' will ultimately depend not only on the nature of the acts, but also on the purpose and circumstances of their commission.

In view of the above, it seems reasonable to conclude that a state acting through its organs or agents to support within its territory organized criminal activities having an actual or potential harmful impact on other states would be in breach of its obligation under international law to prevent acts contrary to the rights of other states within its territory. The determination of the responsibility of the state on this basis would essentially turn on an analysis of what may considered to constitute an act 'contrary to the rights' of another state, and notably on the extent to which the latter state may be considered to have been injured by the conduct of the former state.

4. Obligation not to intervene in the affairs of another state

Under customary international law, the principle of non-intervention prohibits states from intervening, directly or indirectly, in the internal or external affairs of another state.[136] An intervention in the affairs of another state is wrongful when it involves methods of coercion used by the intervening state with a view to preventing

[132] Recall the case of the 'Cuban connection' discussed in Chapter 1, Section C.2(b).

[133] See Judith Wise and Eric L Jensen, 'International Drug Pollution? Reflections on *Trail Smelter* and Latin American Drug Trafficking' in Bratspies and Miller (n 130), at 281 ff.

[134] Recall Chapter 1, Section E.

[135] See Nanto (n 101), at 1. Under UNCTOC, the counterfeiting in a state party of another state party's currency and its putting into global circulation is considered to have 'a substantial consequential adverse effect' on the latter state. See Ad Hoc Committee on the Elaboration of a Convention against Transnational Organized Crime, *Interpretative Notes for the Official Records (travaux préparatoires) of the Negotiation of the United Nations Convention against Transnational Organized Crime and the Protocols Thereto*, 3 November 2000, UN Doc A/55/383/Add.1.

[136] UN General Assembly Resolution 2131 (XX), *Declaration on the Inadmissibility of Intervention in the Domestic Affairs of States and the Protection of Their Independence and Sovereignty*, 21 December 1965, UN Doc A/RES/20/2131; Resolution 2625 (XXV); Conference on Security and Co-operation in Europe, Final Act, Helsinki, 1 August 1975, *Declaration on Principles Guiding Relations between Participating States*, Principle VI; *Military and Paramilitary Activities in Nicaragua* (n 43), at 106–108, paras 202–205. See also *Declaration on the Inadmissibility of Intervention and Interference in the Internal Affairs of States*, annexed to General Assembly Resolution 36/103, 9 December 1981, UN Doc A/RES/36/103 (adopted despite the opposition of a significant number of states).

the affected state from exercising its sovereign rights.[137] Prohibited measures include the use or threat of force, as well as 'economic, political or any other type' of coercive measures.[138] In particular, states must not 'organize, assist, foment, finance, incite or tolerate subversive, terrorist or armed activities directed towards the violent overthrow of the régime of another State'.[139]

The analysis of the motives of state organized crime in Chapter 1 has shown that state organs or agents may participate in organized crime with a view to destabilizing a foreign government. State organized crime may notably involve covert operations carried out in the territory of a foreign state by secret services agents acting in concert with organized criminal groups.[140] In such cases, the support provided by a state to an organized criminal group may amount to a violation of the principle of non-intervention. In the case of the *Military and Paramilitary Activities in Nicaragua*, the United States was held responsible for 'training, arming, equipping, financing and supplying the *contra* forces or otherwise encouraging, supporting and aiding military and paramilitary activities in and against Nicaragua'.[141] However, the fact that proceeds of crime had been used by the United States to fund the *contras* was irrelevant to the determination of the breach and remained outside the scope of the dispute.

The participation of a state's organs or agents in organized criminal activities involving a cross-border element would probably not in itself amount to a breach of the obligation not to intervene in the affairs of another state, unless it can be established that such activities aim at restraining the affected state's ability to exercise its sovereign rights. Given the paucity of relevant state practice and *opinio juris*, one can only speculate as to the circumstances that may be taken into consideration to characterize a breach in cases of state organized crime. A distinction can be drawn between cases where a state participates in or supports transnational organized criminal activities in its own territory, and cases where organs or agents of a state operate in the territory of another state without its consent. In the former case, the responsibility of the state would be more likely to be incurred on the basis of the territorial obligation to prevent activities contrary to the rights of other states, whereas in the latter case international responsibility might be incurred on the basis of the principle of non-intervention. The existence of a breach of the obligation not to intervene in the affairs of another state would have to be determined *in concreto*, taking into

[137] *Military and Paramilitary Activities in Nicaragua* (n 43), at 108, para 205 (noting that '[t]he element of coercion [...] defines, and indeed forms the very essence of, prohibited intervention'). But see Éric David, 'Portée et limites du principe de non-intervention' (1990) 23 *Revue belge de droit international* 350, at 351–53 (arguing that coercion is not a necessary element of prohibited intervention, and insisting instead on the objective pursued by the intervening state to infringe the rights of another state).

[138] Resolution 2131 (XX), para 2; Final Act of the Conference on Security and Co-operation in Europe, Principle VI.

[139] Resolution 2131 (XX), para 2; Resolution 2625 (XXV).

[140] Recall Chapter 1, Section C.2(b).

[141] *Military and Paramilitary Activities in Nicaragua* (n 43), at 146, para 292(3).

account the nature and impact of the criminal activities involved, as well as the motivation and *modus operandi* of the intervening state.

5. Obligation not to infringe another state's permanent sovereignty over its natural resources

Cases of state organized crime involving criminal activities carried out in the territory of another state without its consent include in particular the illicit exploitation of natural resources, notably but not exclusively in the context of an armed conflict.[142] Such conduct contravenes the principle of permanent sovereignty over natural resources proclaimed by the UN General Assembly[143] and may constitute a violation of a corresponding rule of customary international law.

In its contemporary meaning, permanent sovereignty over natural resources denotes the sovereign right of every state to dispose freely of the natural resources present in its territory, and to exercise control over the prospecting, exploration, development, exploitation, use, and marketing of such resources.[144] The rights inherent in the principle of permanent sovereignty over natural resources entail as a corollary a duty for other states to 'refrain from acts, direct or indirect, designed to impede the exercise of the sovereignty of any State over its natural resources'.[145] The principle of permanent sovereignty over natural resources has long been considered as a political principle devoid of legal force.[146] The contours of the specific rights and obligations that this principle entails for states as a matter of international law remain indistinct, but despite—or perhaps because of—its somewhat abstract quality it has come to be considered as part and parcel of customary international law.[147] The legal character of the principle of permanent sovereignty over natural resources has notably been recognized by the ICJ in the case of the *Armed Activities on the Territory of the Congo*. The Democratic Republic of the Congo argued that its sovereignty over its natural resources had been infringed by Uganda on account of the involvement of the Ugandan armed forces in the plundering of natural resources

[142] Recall Chapter 1, Section B.3.

[143] Resolution 626 (VII), 21 December 1952, UN Doc A/RES/626 (VII); Resolution 1803 (XVII), 14 December 1962, UN Doc A/RES/1803 (XVII); Resolution 2158 (XXI), 25 November 1966, UN Doc A/RES/2158 (XXI); Resolution 3201 (S-VI), *Declaration on the Establishment of a New International Economic Order*, 1 May 1974, UN Doc A/RES/3201 (S-VI), Principle 4(e); *Charter of Economic Rights and Duties of States*, Art 2(1), in Resolution 3281 (XXIX), 12 December 1974, UN Doc A/RES/3281 (XXIX).

[144] See generally Nico Schrijver, *Sovereignty over Natural Resources: Balancing Rights and Duties* (Cambridge University Press, 1997), at 260–66.

[145] Resolution 626 (VII), para 2. See also Resolution 3201 (S-VI) ('No State may be subjected to economic, political or any other type of coercion to prevent the free and full exercise of this inalienable right').

[146] See e.g. Georges Fischer, 'La souveraineté sur les ressources naturelles' (1962) 8 *Annuaire français de droit international* 516.

[147] See *Texaco Overseas Petroleum Co and California Asiatic Oil Co v Government of Libyan Arab Republic*, 19 January 1977, 53 ILR 389, at 491–92, para 87 (holding that Resolution 1803 (XVII) reflects *opinio juris*); Schrijver (n 144), at 375; Stephan Hobe, 'Evolution of the Principle on Permanent Sovereignty over Natural Resources: From Soft Law to a Customary Law Principle?' in Marc Bungenberg and Stephan Hobe (eds), *Permanent Sovereignty over Natural Resources* (Springer, 2015) 1, at 10.

in the territory of the Congo.[148] The Court held that the principle of permanent sovereignty over natural resources declared by the UN General Assembly was a principle of customary international law,[149] but it rejected the DRC's argument on the ground that this principle was not 'applicable to the specific situation of looting, pillage and exploitation of certain natural resources by members of the army of a State militarily intervening in another State'.[150] It is not stated whether the principle would have been considered applicable in the absence of an armed conflict. Some judges and commentators have lamented the Court's decision not to uphold the principle of permanent sovereignty over natural resources, arguing that this principle should be recognized as of full legal effect regardless of the existence of an armed conflict, and that Uganda's conduct constituted an internationally wrongful act.[151] Given the indeterminate and controversial character of the principle of permanent sovereignty over natural resources under international law, it remains open to question whether the exploitation, by the organs or agents of a state, of the natural resources of another state without its consent may constitute a breach of a customary obligation arising from this principle.

6. Prohibition of pillage under the law of armed conflict

The exploitation, by the organs or agents of a state, of the natural resources of another state in the context of an armed conflict[152] may also fall within the ambit of the prohibition of pillage under the law of armed conflict.[153] The prohibition of pillage in both international and non-international armed conflicts is part of customary international law.[154] Pillage is defined as unlawful appropriation, 'for private or personal use',[155] of any type of property, whether private or public, movable or immovable.[156] While the prohibition of pillage traditionally applies to the unlawful taking of property from protected persons, it may also encompass cases of

[148] *Armed Activities on the Territory of the Congo* (n 15), at 246, para 226.

[149] Ibid, at 251, para 244.

[150] Ibid.

[151] See *Armed Activities on the Territory of the Congo (Democratic Republic of the Congo v Uganda)*, Declaration by Judge Koroma, ICJ Rep 2005, p 284, at 289, para 11; María José Cervell Hortal, 'La explotación ilegal de los recursos naturales de un estado a la luz de la sentencia del Tribunal Internacional de Justicia sobre las actividades armadas en el territorio de Congo (2005)' (2006) 22 *Anuario Español de Derecho Internacional* 559, at 571–72.

[152] Recall Chapter 1, Section B.3.

[153] Regulations Respecting the Laws and Customs of War on Land, annexed to Convention Respecting the Laws and Customs of War on Land, 18 October 1907, entered into force on 21 January 1910, Arts 28 and 47; Geneva Convention Relative to the Protection of Civilian Persons in Time of War, 12 August 1949, entered into force on 21 October 1950, 75 UNTS 287, Art 33, 2nd paragraph; Additional Protocol to the Geneva Conventions of 12 August 1949, and Relating to the Protection of Victims of Non-International Armed Conflicts, 8 June 1977, entered into force on 7 December 1978, 1125 UNTS 609, Art 4(2)(g).

[154] Henckaerts and Doswald-Beck, ICRC (n 90), Rule 52, at 182 ff.

[155] Ibid, at 185 (endorsing the definition of the war crime of pillaging in the ICC Elements of Crimes).

[156] *Prosecutor v Jean-Pierre Bemba Gombo*, Case no ICC-01/05-01/08, Trial Judgment, 21 March 2016, para 115 (discussing the constitutive elements of pillaging as a war crime).

illicit exploitation of a state's natural resources.[157] This proposition is supported by Article 55 of the Hague Regulations, which requires an occupying power to 'safeguard the capital of public buildings, real estate, forests, and agricultural estates' in occupied territory. This provision is considered to apply to natural resources such as oil and gas deposits.[158] In the case of the *Armed Activities on the Territory of the Congo*, the ICJ held that 'looting, plundering and exploitation of natural resources' by a foreign army are prohibited under the law of armed conflict.[159] While the Court did not provide much explanation in support of this finding, it did refer specifically to the prohibition of pillage in the Hague Regulations and the fourth Geneva Convention.[160] In this case, Uganda was found responsible not only for failing to prevent acts of looting and plundering committed by members of its armed forces, but also directly for the illicit exploitation of natural resources conducted by its organs in the territory of the Congo.[161] The plundering, by the organs or agents of a state, of another state's natural resources in the context of an armed conflict may therefore constitute a breach of treaty and customary obligations under the law of armed conflict.

7. Prohibition of slavery, servitude, and forced labour in international human rights law

Finally, in cases where the organs or agents of a state take part in human trafficking, for example where military officials are involved in the trafficking of women for the purpose of sexual exploitation,[162] the state may be in breach of its obligations under international human rights law. Trafficking of women and girls for sexual exploitation falls within the ambit of the protection against slavery, servitude, and forced labour[163] enshrined in international human rights instruments.[164] States' human rights obligations with respect to human trafficking are conceptualized essentially as

[157] See Michael A Lundberg, 'The Plunder of Natural Resources during War: A War Crime?' (2008) 39 *Georgetown Journal of International Law* 495, at 515–17.

[158] Brice M Clagett and O Thomas Johnson, Jr, 'May Israel as a Belligerent Occupant Lawfully Exploit Previously Unexploited Oil Resources of the Gulf of Suez?' (1978) 72 *American Journal of International Law* 558, at 563–64, and the authorities cited therein. See also Lundberg (n 157), at 514–15.

[159] *Armed Activities on the Territory of the Congo* (n 15), at 252, para 245.

[160] Ibid.

[161] Ibid, at 252–53, para 246.

[162] Recall the case of Bento dos Santos Kangamba, General of the Angolan armed forces, charged in Brazil with human trafficking. For extracts of the indictment, see TRF 3a região, HC 0031957-43.2013.4.03.0000/SP, Relator Desembargador Federal Paulo Fontes, Decision of 12 December 2013, e-DJF3 (18 December 2013), p 334.

[163] See the judgments of the European Court of Human Rights in *Rantsev v Cyprus and Russia*, App no 25965/04, ECHR 2010, paras 272–82; *L.E. v Greece*, App no 71545/12, 21 January 2016, para 58.

[164] International Covenant on Civil and Political Rights (ICCPR), 16 December 1966, entered into force on 23 March 1976, 999 UNTS 171, Art 8; Universal Declaration of Human Rights, annexed to General Assembly Resolution 217 (III), 10 December 1948, UN Doc A/RES/217 (III), Art 4; Convention for the Protection of Human Rights and Fundamental Freedoms, 4 November 1950, entered into force on 3 September 1953, 213 UNTS 221, Art 4; American Convention on Human Rights, 22 November 1969, entered into force on 18 July 1978, 1144 UNTS 143, Art 6(1); African Charter on Human and Peoples' Rights, 27 June 1981, entered into force on 21 October 1986, 1520 UNTS 217, Art 5.

positive obligations, including an obligation to criminalize, investigate, and punish acts of trafficking, and an obligation to take measures to protect victims of trafficking.[165] However, the general protection against slavery, servitude, and forced labour also encompasses situations where individuals are directly subjected to the state's coercive power.[166] In such cases, states are under a negative obligation to refrain from subjecting individuals within their jurisdiction to slavery, servitude, or forced labour.[167] Where acts of human trafficking are directly attributable to a state, such conduct would clearly constitute a breach of international human rights obligations related to the prohibition of slavery, servitude, and forced labour.

D. Invocation of State Responsibility

A few words should finally be said about the conditions under which the responsibility of a state involved in state organized crime may, if established, be invoked by other states. Although 'State responsibility arises under international law independently of its invocation by another State',[168] in practical terms state responsibility can only entail consequences for the responsible state when other states are entitled to react to the commission of the internationally wrongful act. Depending on the nature and scope of the international obligation breached, some states may be entitled to invoke the responsibility of the culpable state.

The analysis conducted in this chapter has suggested that state organized crime does not as such breach any treaty obligation under relevant crime-suppression conventions. It may, however, constitute a breach of the obligation to perform treaty obligations in good faith and in particular not to defeat the object and purpose of the treaty. Obligations under crime-suppression conventions are *erga omnes partes*, thereby entitling all states parties to invoke the responsibility of another state party,[169] irrespective of injury.[170] Yet since the obligation to perform treaty obligations in good faith does not find its source in any particular treaty, but derives from a general principle of law, it is not self-evident that the responsibility of a state party to a crime-suppression convention having failed to perform its treaty obligations in good faith may be invoked under the same conditions. It would seem, however, that the obligation to perform treaty obligations in good faith, irrespective of its source,

[165] *Rantsev v Cyprus and Russia* (n 163), paras 283 ff.

[166] See *Siliadin v France*, App no 73316/01, ECHR 2005-VII, para 89 (holding that the protection against slavery, servitude, and forced labour is not limited 'only to direct action by the State authorities').

[167] Interpretative limitations apply, allowing work performed in detention as well as military service (ICCPR, Art 8(3)(b) and (c)).

[168] ARSIWA Commentary (n 17), at 116.

[169] See, *mutatis mutandis*, regarding the Convention against Torture: *Questions relating to the Obligation to Prosecute or Extradite (Belgium v Senegal)*, Judgment, ICJ Rep 2012, p 422, at 449–50, paras 68–69. See also, regarding the Genocide Convention: *Reservations to the Convention on the Prevention and Punishment of the Crime of Genocide*, Advisory Opinion, ICJ Rep 1951, p 15, at 23. See also generally Kamen Sachariew, 'State Responsibility for Multilateral Treaty Violations: Identifying the "Injured State" and Its Legal Status' (1988) 35 *Netherlands International Law Review* 273, at 281–82.

[170] *Questions relating to the Obligation to Prosecute or Extradite* (n 169), at 450, para 70; ARSIWA, Art 48(1)(a); ARSIWA Commentary (n 17), at 36, para 9, and 126, para 1.

may be considered to be owed to all states parties to a treaty, and that all parties have a common interest in ensuring that treaty obligations are performed in good faith.[171] Accordingly, any state party to a crime-suppression convention would arguably be entitled to invoke the responsibility of the culpable state without having to demonstrate how it has been specially affected by the breach.[172] In the absence of any injury, the range of remedies available to the state denouncing the breach will be limited.[173]

The right of a state to invoke the responsibility of another state involved in state organized crime would be easier to establish in cases where the former state suffers an injury as a result of the conduct of the responsible state, for instance in the case of a violation by that latter state of its obligation to prevent acts contrary to the rights of other states within its territory, of the principle of non-intervention, or of the principle of permanent sovereignty over natural resources. In general terms, whether a state may be considered to be injured by an internationally wrongful act committed by another state 'ha[s] to be assessed on a case-by-case basis, having regard to the object and purpose of the obligation breached and the facts of each case'.[174] The injured state would be entitled to take countermeasures in order to induce the responsible state to comply with its obligations,[175] and to claim reparations from the responsible state for the injury caused by the internationally wrongful act.[176]

In the particular case of a state participating, through its organs or agents, in human trafficking, any state would be entitled to invoke the responsibility of the culpable state,[177] as the obligation to uphold basic human rights such as the protection from slavery is an obligation considered to be owed to the international community as a whole (*erga omnes*).[178]

In summary, if and to the extent that a state party to a crime-suppression convention involved in state organized crime may be considered to have committed an internationally wrongful act by breaching its obligation to perform treaty obligations in good faith, any state party to the relevant treaty may be entitled to invoke the responsibility of the culpable state without having to demonstrate injury. In addition, where the conduct of the responsible state causes an injury to another state, the injured state may also be entitled to invoke the responsibility of the culpable state.

E. Conclusion

The analysis performed in this chapter has shed light on the conceptual, legal, and factual difficulties of establishing the international responsibility of a state involved

[171] See D N Hutchinson, 'Solidarity and Breaches of Multilateral Treaties' (1988) 59 *British Yearbook of International Law* 151, at 191–92 (arguing that 'the performance of acts tending to thwart the accomplishment of the object and purpose of a treaty should be prevented by placing the legal means to avert them in the hands of each of the parties to the treaty').

[172] As would otherwise be required under ARSIWA, Art 42(b)(i).

[173] Ibid, Art 48(2).

[174] ARSIWA Commentary (n 17), at 119, para 12.

[175] ARSIWA, Arts 49 ff.

[176] Ibid, Arts 31 and 34 ff.

[177] Ibid, Art 48(1)(b).

[178] *Barcelona Traction* (n 52), at 32, para 34.

in state organized crime. While in most cases of state organized crime the conduct of public officials may be considered attributable to the state, state participation in organized crime is not prohibited as such under international law, whether pursuant to the provisions of crime-suppression conventions pertaining to organized crime and corruption, or pursuant to customary international law. The international responsibility of a state involved in state organized crime may therefore only arise incidentally where the conduct of the state happens to violate specific international obligations deriving from general principles of international law or from prohibitions established by particular branches of international law. Such obligations include the obligation to perform treaty obligations in good faith, the obligation of states to prevent acts contrary to the rights of other states within their territory, the obligation not to intervene in the internal affairs of another state, the obligation not to infringe another state's sovereignty over its natural resources, the obligation not to commit pillage in the context of an armed conflict, and the obligation under international human rights law to uphold the protection from slavery, servitude, and forced labour. If and to the extent that a state involved in state organized crime may be considered to have committed an internationally wrongful act by breaching any of the above obligations, a number of states may be entitled to invoke the responsibility of the culpable state.

In the absence of a primary norm prohibiting state participation in organized crime, the possibility of establishing a breach of an international obligation in cases of state organized crime depends either on the existence of a transnational element involving some form of prohibited adverse impact on another state—in which case only the injured state may be entitled to invoke the responsibility of the culpable state—or, where the responsible state is a party to a crime-suppression convention pertaining to organized crime and corruption, on the exercise of a form of *actio popularis* by another state party acting to vindicate the common interest of all states parties in the bona fide performance of treaty obligations. In cases of state organized crime that do not adversely affect the rights of another state, or in cases involving a state that is not a party to UNCTOC or to any other relevant crime-suppression convention, the conclusion to be drawn is that no breach of an international obligation can be established.

It is apparent from the above findings that the responsibility of a state involved in state organized crime could only be established on the basis of a breach essentially peripheral to the wrong inherent in state organized crime, and that available remedies would be inadequate to address that wrong as such. The apparent failure of the primary and secondary rules of state responsibility to regulate and attach legal consequences to the involvement of states in organized crime constitutes a major problem from the perspective of expressivist theories of law. A key function of legal rules is to establish normative standards that shape and nurture social norms and values. Expressivist theories accordingly posit that a legal norm should 'be evaluated in terms of what it "symbolizes," "expresses," or "means"'.[179] The silence of

[179] Matthew D Adler, 'Expressive Theories of Law: A Skeptical Overview' (2000) 148 *University of Pennsylvania Law Review* 1363, at 1364 (emphasis removed). For a discussion of expressivist theories of law and of their relevance to my argument, see Chapter 4, Section C, and Chapter 5, Section A.2.

international law in the face of state organized crime does not merely constitute a normative void within which wrongful conduct may occur without appropriate legal consequences; it also undermines the perception, recognition, comprehension, and conceptualization of this phenomenon in normative terms.

Irrespective of any particular conceptual or practical difficulty, as a matter of legal policy it is doubtful whether classical mechanisms of international law designating the state as the primary subject of obligations and the primary vehicle for responsibility are appropriate for the purposes of addressing state organized crime. Although state organized crime may be considered state conduct from the perspective of the law of state responsibility, it involves in the first place criminal acts committed by individuals, and it is principally through the criminal law, as a means to punish individuals for reprehensible conduct, that endeavours to address organized crime and corruption at the international level have been channelled. The examination of international law's potential for addressing state organized crime continues in the next part of the book with an analysis of the rules and mechanisms of international criminal law for the suppression of organized crime and corruption.

3

International Criminal Law Instruments for the Suppression of Organized Crime and Corruption

In most states, domestic laws contain provisions criminalizing in some form or another the participation of individuals in organized crime and corruption. Crime-suppression conventions pertaining to organized crime and corruption such as UNCTOC or UNCAC—which are among the most widely ratified universal treaties with 189 and 183 states parties respectively—subject states parties to a number of obligations designed to establish common minimum standards across domestic laws and to strengthen international cooperation in criminal matters. The obligations of states pursuant to these instruments consist in adopting legislative or other regulatory measures in their domestic law, principally measures falling within the realm of the criminal law. This chapter examines the source, scope, and, where relevant, implementation of obligations pertaining respectively to the criminalization of conduct, the establishment of jurisdiction over crimes, the obligation to extradite or prosecute, international cooperation in criminal matters, and the seizure and confiscation of proceeds of crime. While universal and regional treaties constitute the main relevant sources, the secondary law of the European Union is also mentioned as appropriate. This chapter does not provide an exhaustive study of the positive law. Rather, the object of the present chapter is to focus on certain aspects relevant to the suppression of state organized crime.

A. Criminalization under Domestic Law

Efforts to combat transnational organized crime and corruption focus to a significant extent on ensuring that certain types of criminal conduct are established as criminal offences under domestic laws. This section reviews the definition under relevant international instruments of offences most typically found in instances of state organized crime, namely: drug trafficking and manufacturing; human trafficking and smuggling of migrants; trafficking in firearms; corruption and trading in influence; embezzlement of public funds, abuse of functions, and illicit enrichment; money laundering; and participation in an organized criminal group. Other relevant offences linked to organized crime, as defined under applicable treaties, are also mentioned.

From the perspective of the domestic law of states parties, the prohibitions set forth in the relevant treaties are not self-executing. The treaties themselves make it clear that to be given effect their provisions have to be implemented in the domestic law of states parties, and that the description of offences remains 'reserved to the domestic law' of states parties.[1] While implementation is mandatory when the language of the treaty so indicates, states parties are generally left with a significant degree of flexibility in determining how to implement the provisions of the treaties. As a result, 'it is not necessary for relevant domestic criminal laws to make specific mention of each distinct category and element mentioned in [the definition of the offence]'.[2] The definition of the offence, however, must cover all the constitutive elements defined in the treaty.

1. Drug manufacturing and trafficking

A plethora of international instruments have been adopted over the course of the twentieth century with a view to regulating and controlling the production, use, and distribution of narcotic drugs, including increasingly developed penal provisions requiring states parties to prohibit and punish certain activities related to drug manufacturing and trafficking.[3] With the emergence and acknowledgement of the organized crime threat, the international approach to drug control shifted to a model with enhanced focus on the suppression and punishment of illicit

[1] See e.g. UN Drug Convention, Art 3(11); UNCTOC, Art 11(6); UNCAC, Art 30(9). See also Neil Boister, *An Introduction to Transnational Criminal Law* (Oxford University Press, 2012), at 14; William C Gilmore and David McClean, *Commentary on the United Nations Convention against Illicit Traffic in Narcotic Drugs and Psychotropic Substances, 1988* (United Nations, 1998), para 3.131. Even partially monist legal systems need a legislative act to implement the relevant treaties. In the United States, for example, a treaty cannot be self-executing if it does not 'operate[. . .] of itself, without the aid of any legislative provision' (*Foster and Elam v Neilson*, 27 US 253 (1829), at 314).

[2] Gilmore and McClean (n 1), para 3.37.

[3] See in chronological order: International Opium Convention 1912, Art 20; International Opium Convention 1925, Arts 28 and 29; Convention for Limiting the Manufacture and Regulating the Distribution of Narcotic Drugs; Convention for the Suppression of the Illicit Traffic in Dangerous Drugs, 26 June 1936, entered into force on 26 October 1939, 198 LNTS 299, Art 2; Protocol amending the Agreements, Conventions and Protocols on Narcotic Drugs, concluded at The Hague on 23 January 1912, at Geneva on 11 February 1925 and 19 February 1925, and 13 July 1931, at Bangkok on 27 November 1931 and at Geneva on 26 June 1936, 11 December 1946, entered into force on 11 December 1946, 12 UNTS 179; Protocol Bringing under International Control Drugs Outside the Scope of the Convention of 13 July 1931 for Limiting the Manufacture and Regulating the Distribution of Narcotic Drugs, as amended by the Protocol signed at Lake Success, New York, on 11 December 1946, 19 November 1948, entered into force on 1 December 1949, 44 UNTS 277; Protocol for Limiting and Regulating the Cultivation of the Poppy Plant, the Production of, International and Wholesale Trade in, and Use of Opium, 23 June 1953, entered into force on 8 March 1963, 456 UNTS 3; Single Convention on Narcotic Drugs, 30 March 1961, entered into force on 13 December 1964, 520 UNTS 151, Art 36; Protocol amending the Single Convention on Narcotic Drugs, 25 March 1972, entered into force on 8 August 1975, 976 UNTS 3; Convention on Psychotropic Substances, 21 February 1971, entered into force on 16 August 1976, 1019 UNTS 175, Art 22.

trafficking, culminating with the adoption of the 1988 UN Drug Convention.[4] The preamble to the Convention notes 'that illicit traffic generates large financial profits and wealth enabling transnational criminal organizations to penetrate, contaminate and corrupt the structures of government'.[5] Article 3(1)(a) of the Convention requires states parties to establish the following as criminal offences under their domestic law:

(i) The production, manufacture, extraction, preparation, offering, offering for sale, distribution, sale, delivery on any terms whatsoever, brokerage, dispatch, dispatch in transit, transport, importation or exportation of any narcotic drug or any psychotropic substance [...];

(ii) The cultivation of opium poppy, coca bush or cannabis plant for the purpose of the production of narcotic drugs [...];

(iii) The possession or purchase of any narcotic drug or psychotropic substance for the purpose of any of the activities enumerated in (i) above;

(iv) The manufacture, transport or distribution of equipment, materials or of substances listed in [annexed tables], knowing that they are to be used in or for the illicit cultivation, production or manufacture of narcotic drugs and psychotropic substances;

(v) The organization, management or financing of any of the offences enumerated in (i), (ii), (iii) or (iv) above.

This definition covers a wide range of activities related to drug trafficking, impacting on numerous potential actors of the drug trade. In particular, sub-paragraph (v) targets the leadership of organized criminal groups.[6] Only intentional conduct is to be prohibited. In addition to direct perpetration of the crimes, attempting, as well as aiding and abetting the commission of such offences must be criminalized, although states parties are given some leeway in implementing this obligation in accordance with the principles of their legal system.[7] Most importantly, the Convention also requires states parties to ensure that their domestic courts will regard as an aggravating circumstance 'the fact that the offender holds a public office and that the offence is connected with the office in question'.[8]

[4] This model has been criticized for its failure to curb drug addiction and its perverse effects boosting illicit trafficking globally. Commentators suggest that the regime established by the UN Drug Convention provides a justification for many states to 'interven[e] in neighbouring states' and 'maintain [...] extensive military, police, and security agencies and networks of surveillance'. See Richard Vogler and Shahrzad Fouladvand, 'The Convention against Illicit Traffic in Narcotic Drugs and Psychotropic Substances 1988 and the Global War on Drugs' in Pierre Hauck and Sven Peterke (eds), *International Law and Transnational Organized Crime* (Oxford University Press, 2016) 107, at 120–25.

[5] UN Drug Convention, preamble, 5th recital.

[6] Gilmore and McClean (n 1), para 3.32.

[7] UN Drug Convention, Art 3(1)(c)(iv). The responsibility of secondary parties to a crime may be determined differently in common-law and civil-law countries. For example, in England and Wales they may be punished both as accessories at common law and on the basis of a distinct statutory offence (ancillary offences: see Serious Crime Act 2007, s 44–46). By contrast, in continental legal systems accessorial liability for secondary participation to the principal offence remains the norm (see e.g. in Germany: Strafgesetzbuch, §§ 26, 27).

[8] UN Drug Convention, Art 3(5)(e).

In the EU, the 2004 Council Framework Decision laying down minimum provisions on the constituent elements of criminal acts and penalties in the field of illicit drug trafficking also requires member states to establish drug-related offences under their domestic law.[9] The definition of the crimes under Article 2 of the Framework Decision is almost identical to that provided under the UN Drug Convention, to ensure consistency in the implementation of international obligations regarding illicit drug trafficking. In addition, attempting, inciting, as well as aiding and abetting the commission of the defined offences also have to be criminalized.[10] As regards sentencing, the Framework Decision fixes a minimum threshold for the maximum sentence applicable to drug offences.[11] Finally, the Framework Decision provides for the liability of legal persons and for the definition of particular sanctions to be taken against them, such as temporary or permanent disqualification from the pursuit of commercial activities or the closure of establishments used for committing the offence.[12]

At the regional level, the League of Arab States adopted the Arab Convention against Illicit Traffic in Narcotic Drugs and Psychotropic Substances to transpose the provisions of the UN Drug Convention. The Convention requires states parties to criminalize drug trafficking offences in their domestic law.[13]

2. Human trafficking and smuggling of migrants

Numerous instruments have been adopted to tackle trafficking in persons. Most of them require states parties to criminalize certain acts, such as conveying or attempting to convey slaves from one country to another,[14] enslaving another person,[15] procuring or exploiting another person for the purpose of prostitution,[16] and procuring or accepting children for the purpose of sexual exploitation, organ trafficking, or forced labour.[17] The Protocol to Prevent, Suppress and Punish

[9] Council Framework Decision 2004/757/JHA laying down minimum provisions on the constituent elements of criminal acts and penalties in the field of illicit drug trafficking, 25 October 2004, OJ L335 (11 November 2004) 8.

[10] Ibid, Art 3. [11] Ibid, Art 4.

[12] Ibid, Arts 6 and 7. Note that the responsibility of legal persons need not be of a criminal nature. In several legal systems where the concept of corporate criminal liability is not recognized, corporations may be subject to administrative sanctions. This is, for example, the case in Germany. See Thomas Weigend, '*Societas delinquere non potest*? A German Perspective' (2008) 6 *Journal of International Criminal Justice* 927.

[13] Arab Convention against Illicit Traffic in Narcotic Drugs and Psychotropic Substances, 15 January 1994, entered into force on 30 June 1996, Art 2(1)(a).

[14] Supplementary Convention on the Abolition of Slavery, the Slave Trade, and Institutions and Practices Similar to Slavery, 7 September 1956, entered into force on 30 April 1957, 226 UNTS 3, Art 3(1).

[15] Ibid, Art 6(1).

[16] Convention for the Suppression of the Traffic in Persons and of the Exploitation of the Prostitution of Others, 21 March 1950, entered into force on 25 July 1951, 96 UNTS 271, Art 1; International Convention for the Suppression of the Traffic in Women of Full Age, 11 October 1933, entered into force on 24 August 1934, 150 LNTS 431, Art 1; International Convention for the Suppression of the 'White Slave Traffic', 4 May 1910, entered into force on 14 August 1951, 98 UNTS 101, Art 1.

[17] Optional Protocol to the Convention on the Rights of the Child on the Sale of Children, Child Prostitution and Child Pornography, Art 3(1)(a) and (b).

Trafficking in Persons, Especially Women and Children, supplementing UNCTOC (UNCTOC Human Trafficking Protocol) was adopted in 2000 to provide a comprehensive legal framework for combating human trafficking by organized criminal groups. Article 5 requires states parties to establish trafficking in persons as a criminal offence. Trafficking in persons in defined as

> the recruitment, transportation, transfer, harbouring or receipt of persons, by means of the threat or use of force or other forms of coercion, of abduction, of fraud, of deception, of the abuse of power or of a position of vulnerability or of the giving or receiving of payments or benefits to achieve the consent of a person having control over another person, for the purpose of exploitation. Exploitation shall include, at a minimum, the exploitation of the prostitution of others or other forms of sexual exploitation, forced labour or services, slavery or practices similar to slavery, servitude or the removal of organs.[18]

Human trafficking offences as defined in the Protocol require the use of specific means of coercion or deception, in the pursuit of a defined purpose, namely the exploitation of the victim. However, if the victim is a child (that is, under the age of 18), it is not required that the acts be undertaken through the means listed in this definition.[19] It should be noted that the victim's lack of consent is not a constitutive element of the crime.[20] States parties must also enact legislation criminalizing participating as an accomplice, organizing or directing others to commit the offence, and, subject to the principles of their legal system, attempting to commit the offence.[21] Furthermore, certain general provisions of UNCTOC are also applicable, *mutatis mutandis*, to the crimes defined in the Protocol.[22] As a result, a cross-border element or the involvement of an organized criminal group is not a prerequisite for criminalizing human trafficking.[23] Moreover, states parties are required to enact legislation providing for the liability of legal persons participating in human trafficking, although the nature and modalities of such liability are left to the discretion of each state party.[24]

Regional instruments also impose obligations on states regarding the criminalization of human trafficking. The 1994 Inter-American Convention on International Traffic in Minors requires states parties to criminalize 'the abduction, removal or retention, or attempted abduction, removal or retention, of a minor for unlawful purposes or by unlawful means'.[25] The Arab Convention against Transnational

[18] UNCTOC Human Trafficking Protocol, Art 3(a).

[19] Ibid, Art 3(c).

[20] Ibid, Art 3(b).

[21] Ibid, Art 5(2). In order to assist states and achieve coherent standards in implementing the Protocol, the UNODC has drafted a model law with detailed guidance for different legal systems: see UNODC, *Model Law against Trafficking in Persons* (United Nations, 2009).

[22] UNCTOC Human Trafficking Protocol, Art 1(2) and (3); Ad Hoc Committee on the Elaboration of a Convention against Transnational Organized Crime, *Interpretative Notes for the Official Records (travaux préparatoires) of the Negotiation of the United Nations Convention against Transnational Organized Crime and the Protocols Thereto*, 3 November 2000, UN Doc A/55/383/Add.1, para 62.

[23] David McClean, *Transnational Organized Crime: A Commentary on the UN Convention and its Protocols* (Oxford University Press, 2007), at 330. See UNCTOC, Art 34(2); Interpretative Notes for UNCTOC (n 22), para 59.

[24] UNCTOC, Art 10.

[25] Inter-American Convention on International Traffic in Minors, 18 March 1994, entered into force on 15 August 1997, OASTS no 79, Arts 2(b) and 7.

Organized Crime, adopted by the League of Arab States to transpose UNCTOC and its Protocols, also requires states parties to criminalize trafficking in human beings, notably women and children, as well as organ trafficking.[26] Within the EU, the 2011 Directive on preventing and combating trafficking in human beings[27] also provides for the criminalization of trafficking in persons. The definition provided in the Directive is the same as that of the UNCTOC Human Trafficking Protocol, with the added definition of the concept of 'position of vulnerability'.[28] The Directive requires member states to take into consideration aggravating circumstances, such as the involvement of a criminal organization and, most notably, of a public official acting in the performance of his duties.[29] The Directive also contains provisions on corporate liability.[30] Similar provisions may be found in the 2005 Council of Europe Convention on Action against Trafficking in Human Beings.[31]

The Protocol against the Smuggling of Migrants by Land, Sea and Air, supplementing UNCTOC (UNCTOC Migrants Smuggling Protocol)[32] obliges states parties to criminalize the smuggling of migrants.[33] Smuggling of migrants constitutes a phenomenon distinct from human trafficking. It is defined under Article 3(a) as 'the procurement, in order to obtain, directly or indirectly, a financial or other material benefit, of the illegal entry of a person into a State Party of which the person is not a national or a permanent resident'. Smuggling of migrants is by nature a transnational crime. Contrary to most cases of human trafficking, victims of migrant smuggling generally consent to being smuggled. Under Article 6(2) of the Protocol, states parties must also criminalize participating as an accomplice, organizing or directing other persons to commit the offence, and, subject to the principles of their legal systems, the attempt to commit the offence.[34] Certain general provisions of UNCTOC are also applicable, *mutatis mutandis*, to the crimes defined in the Protocol.[35] At the regional level, the Arab Convention against Transnational Organized Crime also requires states parties to criminalize the smuggling of migrants.[36]

[26] Arab Convention against Transnational Organized Crime, Arts 11 and 12.

[27] Directive 2011/36/EU on preventing and combating trafficking in human beings and protecting its victims, 5 April 2011, OJ L101 (15 April 2011) 1.

[28] Ibid, Art 1. [29] Ibid, Art 4(2)(b) and (3). [30] Ibid, Art 5.

[31] Council of Europe Convention on Action against Trafficking in Human Beings, 16 May 2005, entered into force on 1 February 2008, ETS no 197.

[32] Protocol against the Smuggling of Migrants by Land, Sea and Air, Supplementing the United Nations Convention against Transnational Organized Crime, 15 November 2000, entered into force on 28 January 2004, 2241 UNTS 507.

[33] Ibid, Art 6(1).

[34] In order to assist states and achieve coherent standards in implementing the Protocol, the UNODC has drafted a model law with detailed guidance for different legal systems: see UNODC, *Model Law against the Smuggling of Migrants* (United Nations, 2010).

[35] UNCTOC Migrants Smuggling Protocol, Art 1(2) and (3); Interpretative Notes for UNCTOC (n 22), para. 87.

[36] Arab Convention against Transnational Organized Crime, Art 13.

3. Trafficking in firearms

Trafficking in firearms, especially small arms and light weapons, has a particularly deleterious impact 'on the security of each state, region and the world as a whole, endangering the well-being of peoples, their social and economic development and their right to live in peace'.[37] The Protocol against the Illicit Manufacturing of and Trafficking in Firearms, Their Parts and Components and Ammunition, supplementing UNCTOC (UNCTOC Firearms Protocol) requires states parties to establish as criminal offences 'the illicit manufacturing and trafficking of firearms, their parts and components and ammunition'.[38] Illicit trafficking is defined as

> the import, export, acquisition, sale, delivery, movement or transfer of firearms, their parts and components and ammunition from or across the territory of one State Party to that of another State Party if any one of the States Parties concerned does not authorize it [...] or if the firearms are not marked [...].[39]

Trafficking in firearms is necessarily a transnational crime. The scope of prohibited conduct extends to organizing, directing, aiding, abetting, facilitating, or counseling the commission of the crimes defined under the Protocol and, subject to the principles of the legal system of each state party, to the attempt to commit such crimes.[40] Certain general provisions of UNCTOC are also applicable, *mutatis mutandis*, to the crimes defined in the Protocol.[41]

The UNCTOC Firearms Protocol does not apply to state-to-state transactions or transfers[42]—that is, 'transactions by states in a sovereign capacity'.[43] Such transactions fall within the ambit of the Arms Trade Treaty adopted in April 2013 by the UN General Assembly,[44] which regulates the export, import, transit, transshipment, and brokering of conventional arms by states parties.[45] Some provisions of the Arms Trade Treaty are relevant to the suppression of illicit trafficking in firearms and transnational organized crime. First, states parties must refrain from authorizing a transfer which would violate their obligations under international agreements relating to illicit arms trafficking.[46] In addition, states parties are under the obligation to conduct a risk assessment prior to authorizing the export of arms and to consider, inter alia, the possibility that the arms be used to 'commit or facilitate an act constituting an offence under international conventions or protocols relating to transnational organized crime'.[47]

[37] UNCTOC Firearms Protocol, preamble, 1st recital.
[38] Ibid, Art 5(1)(a) and (b).
[39] Ibid, Art 3(e).
[40] Ibid, Art 5(2).
[41] Ibid, Art 1(2) and (3).
[42] Ibid, Art 4(2).
[43] Ad Hoc Committee on the Elaboration of a Convention against Transnational Organized Crime, *Interpretative Notes for the Official Records (travaux préparatoires) of the Negotiation of the Protocol against the Illicit Manufacturing of and Trafficking in Firearms, Their Parts and Components and Ammunition, Supplementing the United Nations Convention against Transnational Organized Crime*, 21 March 2001, UN Doc A/55/383/Add.3, para 4.
[44] Arms Trade Treaty, 2 April 2013, entered into force on 24 December 2014, annexed to UN General Assembly Resolution 67/234 B, UN Doc A/RES/67/234 B.
[45] Ibid, Art 2.
[46] Ibid, Art 6(2).
[47] Ibid, Art 7(1)(b)(iv).

Regional instruments also provide for the criminalization of illicit arms trafficking by non-state actors. Article IV of the Inter-American Convention against the Illicit Manufacturing of and Trafficking in Firearms, Ammunition, Explosives, and Other Related Materials (Inter-American Convention against Arms Trafficking)[48] requires states parties to criminalize 'the illicit manufacturing of and trafficking in firearms, ammunition, explosives, and other related materials' and other forms of participation. The Arab Convention against Transnational Organized Crime also requires states parties to criminalize illicit arms trafficking.[49]

4. Corruption and trading in influence

Acts of corruption may be considered a form of organized crime in situations where they amount to a collective, coordinated, and systematized practice. A number of multilateral treaties provide for the criminalization of corruption and related conduct.

One of the first international instruments to address corruption is the Convention on Combating Bribery of Foreign Public Officials in International Business Transactions of the Organization for Economic Cooperation and Development (OECD Convention on Bribery).[50] States parties are required to establish as a criminal offence the fact for a person

> intentionally to offer, promise or give any undue pecuniary or other advantage, whether directly or through intermediaries, to a foreign public official, for that official or for a third party, in order that the official act or refrain from acting in relation to the performance of official duties, in order to obtain or retain business or other improper advantage in the conduct of international business.[51]

In this definition the term 'in relation to the performance of official duties' includes 'any use of the public official's position, whether or not within the official's authorized competence'.[52] States parties to the OECD Convention on Bribery are also obliged to criminalize complicity in an act of bribery. Attempt and conspiracy to commit the offence must be criminalized by a state party only 'to the same extent' as attempt and conspiracy to bribe an official of that state party.[53] This latter provision merely aims at assimilating the regime of transnational bribery with that of domestic bribery,[54] as the obligation to extend criminal responsibility to attempt

48 Inter-American Convention against the Illicit Manufacturing of and Trafficking in Firearms, Ammunition, Explosives, and Other Related Materials, 14 November 1997, entered into force on 1 July 1998, 2029 UNTS 55.

49 Arab Convention against Transnational Organized Crime, Art 19.

50 Convention on Combating Bribery of Foreign Public Officials in International Business Transactions, 21 November 1997, entered into force on 15 February 1999, (1998) 37 ILM 1.

51 Ibid, Art 1(1).

52 Ibid, Art 1(4)(c). Yet the public official must still act in his official capacity, and not merely use the practical advantages of his office. See Ingeborg Zerbes, 'Article 1. The Offence of Bribery of Foreign Public Officials' in Mark Pieth, Lucinda A Low, and Peter J Cullen (eds), *The OECD Convention on Bribery: A Commentary* (Cambridge University Press, 2007) 45, at 136–37.

53 OECD Convention on Bribery, Art 1(2).

54 Zerbes (n 52), at 166, 169.

and conspiracy remains subject to the domestic law of the states parties. The OECD Convention also provides for the liability of legal persons.[55] It should be noted that the Convention only addresses bribery, which is commonly assimilated to the active form of corruption. The Convention says nothing about passive corruption,[56] that is, the solicitation or acceptance of an undue advantage by a public official.

The gap left by the OECD Convention on Bribery was partially filled by UNCTOC, which provides for the criminalization of both active and passive corruption of public officials.[57] However, UNCTOC does not require states parties to extend this prohibition to acts involving foreign public officials.[58]

The adoption of UNCAC marked a major development. UNCAC lays down comprehensive obligations for states parties regarding the criminalization of corruption and related offences. Article 15 requires states parties to establish as criminal offences under their domestic law both active and passive corruption, respectively defined as follows:

(a) The promise, offering or giving, to a public official, directly or indirectly, of an undue advantage, for the official himself or herself or another person or entity, in order that the official act or refrain from acting in the exercise of his or her official duties;
(b) The solicitation or acceptance by a public official, directly or indirectly, of an undue advantage, for the official himself or herself or another person or entity, in order that the official act or refrain from acting in the exercise of his or her official duties.

States parties also have to criminalize the act of bribing a foreign public official or an official of an international organization, notably for the purpose of 'obtain[ing] or retain[ing] business or other undue advantage in relation to the conduct of international business'—which includes the provision of international aid.[59] Lastly, UNCAC contains non-mandatory provisions encouraging states parties to criminalize the solicitation or acceptance of an undue advantage by a foreign official.[60]

A 'public official' is defined in Article 2(a) of UNCAC as

(i) any person holding a legislative, executive, administrative or judicial office of a State Party, whether appointed or elected, whether permanent or temporary, whether paid or unpaid, irrespective of that person's seniority; (ii) any other person who performs a public function, including for a public agency or public enterprise, or provides a public service, as defined in the domestic law of the State Party and as applied in the pertinent area of law of that State Party; (iii) any other person defined as a "public official" in the domestic law of a State Party [...].

[55] OECD Convention on Bribery, Art 2.

[56] The term 'passive' corruption is traditionally used in contrast to active corruption to distinguish between the acts of receiving and offering a bribe. It does not mean that the criminal responsibility of the offender who solicits or accepts a bribe is a liability by omission, nor does it suggest any degree of 'passivity' in the offender's conduct.

[57] UNCTOC, Art 8(1).

[58] Ibid, Art 8(2).

[59] Ad Hoc Committee for the Negotiation of a Convention against Corruption, *Interpretative Notes for the Official Records (travaux préparatoires) of the Negotiation of the United Nations Convention against Corruption*, 7 October 2003, UN Doc A/58/422/Add.1, para 25.

[60] UNCAC, Art 16(2).

This definition covers both holders of public office, as well as any individual formally entrusted with the authority to perform activities in the public interest.[61] It is much more precise and comprehensive than the tautological and 'tentative'[62] one contained in UNCTOC, which reads as follows:

"public official" shall mean a public official or a person who provides a public service as defined in the domestic law and as applied in the criminal law of the State Party in which the person in question performs that function.[63]

A 'foreign public official' is further defined in UNCAC as

any person holding a legislative, executive, administrative or judicial office of a foreign country, whether appointed or elected; and any person exercising a public function for a foreign country, including for a public agency or public enterprise.[64]

This latter provision provides an autonomous definition of a foreign public official, irrespective of the domestic legislation of the state in which the individual in question exercises his functions.[65]

Although UNCAC does not define what is to be understood by an 'undue advantage', it is generally accepted that this term includes both tangible and intangible, pecuniary and non-pecuniary advantages.[66] Intangible advantages include, for instance, the rewarding of a public official with a position or a career prospect.[67] Any advantage granted by a private person or entity to a public official *ad personam* is presumed to be 'undue', unless it falls within a category of advantages or gifts whose acceptance is permitted under domestic law.[68] The advantage does not have to benefit the corrupt official himself. It may also be granted to any other person or entity, including entities that may not be recognized as legal persons under domestic law, such as political parties or charities.[69] It is important to note that acts of active corruption entail an intentional element: it is required to prove that 'the accused intended not only to offer the bribe, but also to influence the conduct of the recipient, regardless of whether or not this actually took place'.[70] The material elements of corruption therefore do not require proof that the act or omission for which the public official received or solicited a bribe actually occurred.[71] Contrary to the provisions of the OECD Convention on Bribery, the provisions of UNCAC requiring states parties to criminalize corruption apply only to acts performed 'in the exercise of [a

61 Michael Kubiciel, 'Core Criminal Law Provisions in the United Nations Convention against Corruption' (2009) 9 *International Criminal Law Review* 139, at 143.

62 McClean (n 23), at 121. 63 UNCTOC, Art 8(4). 64 UNCAC, Art 2(b).

65 Kubiciel (n 61), at 152.

66 UNODC, *Legislative Guide for the Implementation of the United Nations Convention against Corruption* (United Nations, 2006), para 196; Kubiciel (n 61), at 144.

67 Kubiciel (n 61), at 144.

68 Ibid, at 145. For instance, 'socially acceptable gifts' may be excluded from the definition of 'undue advantage'. See Council of Europe, *Explanatory Report to the Criminal Law Convention on Corruption* (27 January 1999), para 38.

69 Kubiciel (n 61), at 148.

70 Legislative Guide for the Implementation of UNCAC (n 66), para 198.

71 Kubiciel (n 61), at 149.

public official's] official duties', which does not include acts performed *ultra vires*.[72] Finally, it should be stressed that defences and 'other legal principles controlling the lawfulness of conduct' remain regulated by the domestic law of states parties.[73]

Under UNCAC, in addition to direct perpetration states parties must criminalize 'participation in any capacity such as an accomplice, assistant or instigator'.[74] There is, however, no obligation to criminalize attempt or preparatory acts.[75] States parties are also required to take legislative measures providing for the liability of legal persons, in accordance with the principles of their legal systems.[76]

The establishment of both active and passive corruption as criminal offences under domestic law is also provided for by regional instruments, namely the Inter-American Convention against Corruption[77] (which also includes within the material elements of corruption 'any act or omission in the discharge of his duties by a government official or a person who performs public functions for the purpose of illicitly obtaining benefits for himself or for a third party'[78]), the Council of Europe Criminal Law Convention on Corruption,[79] the Convention on the fight against corruption involving officials of the European Communities or officials of Member States of the European Union,[80] the African Union Convention on Preventing and Combating Corruption (AU Convention on Corruption),[81] and the Arab Convention against Corruption.[82]

Trading in influence is in many respects similar to corruption. Its active and passive forms are defined in Article 18 of UNCAC, respectively, as follows:

(a) The promise, offering or giving to a public official or any other person, directly or indirectly, of an undue advantage in order that the public official or the person abuse his or her real or supposed influence with a view to obtaining from an administration or public authority of the State Party an undue advantage for the original instigator of the act or for any other person;
(b) The solicitation or acceptance by a public official or any other person, directly or indirectly, of an undue advantage for himself or herself or for another person in order that the public official or the person abuse his or her real or supposed influence with a view

[72] Legislative Guide for the Implementation of UNCAC (n 66), at 87, n 41. See *contra* Kubiciel (n 61), at 150.

[73] UNCAC, Art 30(9).

[74] Ibid, Art 27(1).

[75] Ibid, Art 27(2) and (3).

[76] Ibid, Art 26.

[77] Inter-American Convention against Corruption, 29 March 1996, entered into force on 6 March 1997, (1996) 35 ILM 724, Art VI(1)(a) and (b). Art VIII further requires states parties to criminalize transnational bribery of foreign public officials, but this obligation remains subject to the domestic law of each state party.

[78] Ibid, Art VI(1)(c).

[79] Criminal Law Convention on Corruption, 27 January 1999, entered into force on 1 July 2002, ETS no 173, Arts 2, 3, and 5.

[80] Convention drawn up on the basis of Article K.3 (2) (c) of the Treaty on European Union on the fight against corruption involving officials of the European Communities or officials of Member States of the European Union, 26 May 1997, OJ C195 (25 June 1997) 2, Arts 2 and 3.

[81] African Union Convention on Preventing and Combating Corruption, 11 July 2003, entered into force on 5 August 2006, (2004) 43 ILM 5, Art 5(1) in conjunction with Art 4(1)(a) and (b).

[82] Arab Convention against Corruption, 21 December 2010, entered into force on 29 June 2013, Art 4(1) and (4). The Convention requires states parties to criminalize 'bribery of a public official', but it is unclear from the English text whether this covers both active and passive corruption.

to obtaining from an administration or public authority of the State Party an undue advantage.

Whether the real or supposed influence is in fact exerted by the public official, or leads to the intended obtainment of an undue advantage, is irrelevant.[83]

Under UNCAC, the prohibition of trading in influence is not mandatory. This may be because the sort of conduct it encompasses is to some extent already covered by the definition of corruption. There are, however, important differences between corruption and trading in influence. Most importantly, in contrast to the offence of corruption, the offence of trading in influence does not require that the public official act in the exercise of his official duties or in any official capacity.

The criminalization of trading in influence is made mandatory in several regional instruments, namely the Council of Europe Criminal Law Convention on Corruption,[84] the Arab Convention against Corruption,[85] and the AU Convention on Corruption. In the latter, the definition of trading in influence encompasses in particular the offering of an undue advantage for the exercise of improper influence over persons in the private sector.[86]

5. Embezzlement of public funds, abuse of functions, and illicit enrichment

Like other corruption offences, embezzlement of public funds, abuse of functions, and illicit enrichment may amount to organized crime in situations where they form part of a collective and coordinated criminal enterprise, notably but not exclusively in kleptocratic regimes. UNCAC contains provisions requiring or encouraging states parties to establish such conduct as criminal offences in their domestic law.[87] States parties are first required to criminalize

> the embezzlement, misappropriation or other diversion by a public official for his or her benefit or for the benefit of another person or entity, of any property, public or private funds or securities or any other thing of value entrusted to the public official by virtue of his or her position.[88]

[83] Michael Kubiciel and Anna Cornelia Rink, 'The United Nations Convention against Corruption and Its Criminal Law Provisions' in Hauck and Peterke (n 4), at 233–34.

[84] Criminal Law Convention on Corruption, Art 12.

[85] Arab Convention against Corruption, Art 4(5).

[86] AU Convention on Corruption, Art 4(1)(f).

[87] Interestingly, during the negotiations of UNCAC in Vienna, a proposal was also made to criminalize, along with the misappropriation of state property, '[a]ny other serious misconduct in office by a public official designed to secure a benefit for himself or herself or for another person or entity'. See Ad Hoc Committee for the Negotiation of a Convention against Corruption, 3rd sess (Vienna, 30 September – 11 October 2002), *Proposals and contributions received from Governments—Australia, Botswana, Cameroon, Canada, New Zealand and the United Kingdom of Great Britain and Northern Ireland: amendments to Articles 19–32 and proposal of a new art on knowledge, intent or purpose as elements of an offence*, 8 October 2002, UN Doc A/AC.261/L.137, para 5.

[88] UNCAC, Art 17.

This provision covers not only acts of misappropriation of public or private funds for the personal benefit of a state official, but also the diversion of public funds for the benefit of another person or entity, for example the unlawful use of state subsidies to fund a political party.[89] UNCAC also contains non-mandatory criminal-law provisions requiring states parties to 'consider' establishing abuse of functions and illicit enrichment as criminal offences. Abuse of functions is defined as

> the performance of or failure to perform an act, in violation of laws, by a public official in the discharge of his or her functions, for the purpose of obtaining an undue advantage for himself or herself or for another person or entity.[90]

Contrary to other corruption offences, abuse of functions requires a breach of a duty imposed on the public official by law in connection to the exercise of his official functions.[91]

Illicit enrichment is defined as 'a significant increase in the assets of a public official that he or she cannot reasonably explain in relation to his or her lawful income'.[92] The definition of illicit enrichment may pose difficulties in certain legal systems with respect to the presumption of innocence,[93] although it is commonly accepted that 'the burden of proof remains on the prosecution, as it has to demonstrate that the enrichment is beyond one's lawful income. It may thus be viewed as a rebuttable presumption. Once such a case is made, the defendant can then offer a reasonable or credible explanation'.[94]

At the regional level, the AU Convention on Corruption requires states parties to adopt legislative measures to criminalize abuse of functions, embezzlement of public funds and illicit enrichment.[95] The Arab Convention against Corruption requires states parties to criminalize 'abuse of public office', 'illicit enrichment', and 'misappropriation of public property'.[96] The Inter-American Convention against Corruption, for its part, provides for the criminalization of abuse of functions and illicit enrichment.[97] The Inter-American Convention also contains provisions on progressive development requiring states parties to consider criminalizing other forms of corrupt practices, such as

> [t]he improper use by a government official or a person who performs public functions, for his own benefit or that of a third party, of any kind of property belonging to the State or to

[89] Kubiciel and Rink (n 83), at 230. [90] UNCAC, Art 19.

[91] Kubiciel and Rink (n 83), at 234–35. [92] UNCAC, Art 20.

[93] For a discussion of the standard of proof of the offence of illicit enrichment from the perspective of the right to a fair trial under human rights law, see Ndiva Kofele-Kale, *Combating Economic Crimes: Balancing Competing Rights and Interests in Prosecuting the Crime of Illicit Enrichment* (Routledge, 2012); Dan Wilsher, 'Inexplicable Wealth and Illicit Enrichment of Public Officials: A Model Draft That Respects Human Rights in Corruption Cases' (2006) 45 *Crime, Law & Social Change* 27.

[94] Legislative Guide for the Implementation of UNCAC (n 66), para 297.

[95] AU Convention on Corruption, Arts 5(1) and 8. The offences of abuse of functions, embezzlement of public funds, and illicit enrichment are respectively defined under Art 4(1)(c), Art 4(1)(d), and Arts 4(1)(g) and 1(1) of the Convention.

[96] Arab Convention against Corruption, Art 4(6), (7), and (11). The Convention, however, does not define the constitutive elements of these offences.

[97] Inter-American Convention against Corruption, Arts VI(1)(c) and IX.

any firm or institution in which the State has a proprietary interest, to which that official or person who performs public functions has access because of, or in the performance of, his functions.[98]

This provision covers a central feature of state organized crime, namely the abuse of state resources and facilities by a state official abusing his authority for criminal purposes.

6. Laundering of proceeds of crime

Mirroring innovative crime-control strategies implemented in the domestic criminal law of several states, the criminalization of money laundering[99] was gradually integrated in crime-suppression conventions pertaining to organized crime and corruption, starting with the UN Drug Convention, which requires states parties to criminalize the laundering of the proceeds of drug-related offences.[100] Building on the UN Drug Convention, UNCTOC and UNCAC have established a general regime for the criminalization of money laundering. States parties to UNCTOC and UNCAC must establish the following as criminal offences under their domestic law:

(a) (i) The conversion or transfer of property, knowing that such property is the proceeds of crime, for the purpose of concealing or disguising the illicit origin of the property or of helping any person who is involved in the commission of the predicate offence to evade the legal consequences of his or her action;
(ii) The concealment or disguise of the true nature, source, location, disposition, movement or ownership of or rights with respect to property, knowing that such property is the proceeds of crime;
(b) Subject to the basic concepts of its legal system:
(i) The acquisition, possession or use of property, knowing, at the time of receipt, that such property is the proceeds of crime; [...][101]

Proceeds of crime are defined as 'any property derived from or obtained, directly or indirectly, through the commission of an offence'.[102] Sub-paragraphs (a)(i), (a)(ii), and (b)(i) above apply, respectively, to the three traditional stages of money laundering, namely placement, layering, and integration.[103] The offence must be committed with knowledge of the illicit origin of the assets and, in the case of sub-paragraph (a)(i), for the specific purpose of concealing that origin. Under UNCTOC and UNCAC, criminal responsibility for negligence or failure to perform due diligence is therefore not incurred. These requirements aim at protecting

[98] Ibid, Art XI(1)(b).

[99] The expression 'money laundering' must be understood as an equivalent of the technical term 'laundering of the proceeds of crime': see Interpretative Notes for UNCTOC (n 22), para 10.

[100] UN Drug Convention, Art 3(1)(b).

[101] UNCTOC, Art 6; UNCAC, Art 23.

[102] UNCTOC, Art 2(e); UNCAC, Art 2(e).

[103] For a description of the different stages of the money laundering process, see William C Gilmore, *Dirty Money: The Evolution of International Measures to Counter Money Laundering and the Financing of Terrorism* (4th edn, Council of Europe, 2011), at 34.

ignorant participants in the laundering process.[104] However, as commentators point out, it is not required that the offender know the exact nature of the offence from which the property in question has been derived.[105] The obligation to enact legislation criminalizing aiding and abetting, facilitating and counseling the commission of the crimes, as well as the attempt and conspiracy to commit the crime, is made subject to the basic principles of the legal system of each state party.[106]

In line with the recommendations of the Financial Action Task Force (FATF), an intergovernmental group established to set legal and regulatory standards for combating money laundering, terrorist financing, and other related threats to the integrity of the international financial system,[107] UNCTOC and UNCAC both encourage states parties to apply the definition of money laundering to 'the widest range of predicate offences', and require that the list of predicate offences include at least the crimes defined in each Convention and examined above.[108] Nevertheless, a crime committed outside the jurisdiction of a state party may be included as a predicate offence only when the relevant conduct also constitutes a criminal offence under its laws as well as under the *lex loci delicti*.[109] Where required by the fundamental principles of the domestic law of a state party, it may also be provided that money-laundering offences shall not apply to individuals having committed the predicate offence.[110] In other words, 'self-laundering', that

[104] Neil Boister, 'The UN Convention against Transnational Organized Crime 2000' in Hauck and Peterke (n 4), at 142–43. Note that certain states punish negligence regardless: see e.g. in South Africa, Prevention of Organized Crime Act no 121 of 1998, as amended, s 4.

[105] McClean (n 23), at 79; Guy Stessens, *Money Laundering: A New International Law Enforcement Model* (Cambridge University Press, 2000), at 230.

[106] UNCTOC, Art 6(1)(b)(ii); UNCAC, Art 23(1)(b)(ii).

[107] Following the adoption of the UN Drug Convention, the FATF recommended that '[e]ach country should consider extending the offense of drug money laundering to any other crimes for which there is a link to narcotics; an alternative approach is to criminalize money laundering based on all serious offenses, and/or on all offenses that generate a significant amount of proceeds, or on certain serious offenses' (*The Forty Recommendations of the Financial Action Task Force on Money Laundering* (1990), Recommendation 5).

[108] UNCTOC, Art 6(1)(2)(a) and (b) (also including all 'serious crimes' as defined under Art 2(b)); UNCAC, Art 23(2)(a) and (b).

[109] UNCTOC, Art 6(1)(2)(c); UNCAC, Art 23(2)(c). This requirement flows from the principle of legality: see Stessens (n 105), at 227.

[110] UNCTOC, Art 6(2)(e); UNCAC, Art 23(2)(e). Commentators suggest that this clause was included on account of the fact that in certain jurisdictions the principle of double jeopardy would make it unlawful for the same conduct to give rise to criminal responsibility under two separate offences (McClean (n 23), at 85–86). For Sweden, however, the reason for barring the prosecution of self-laundering appears to be different. The Swedish authorities have argued that the offence of 'receiving of stolen property', which corresponds to a form of money laundering, 'is "co-punished" with the predicate offence, since the receiving offence is a necessary and evident subsequent action following the predicate offence' and that 'introduc[ing] separate criminal liability for concealing a person's own crime could also come into conflict with the fundamental principle that no one should be forced to testify against himself' (Financial Action Task Force, *Third Mutual Evaluation / Detailed Assessment Report, Anti-Money Laundering and Combating the Financing of Terrorism: Sweden*, 17 February 2006, para 104). Notwithstanding the Swedish position, it is sometimes easier or preferable for law enforcement authorities to prosecute offenders on the basis of the predicate offence. For example, out of 16 money laundering investigations conducted between 2006 and 2007 in Myanmar, 54 individuals were convicted of predicate offences while only one was found guilty of money laundering under the Control of

is, laundering the proceeds of one's own criminal conduct, may not be prosecuted in certain states.[111]

An even broader definition of the scope of predicate offences is to be found in the Council of Europe Convention on Laundering, Search, Seizure and Confiscation of the Proceeds from Crime,[112] which establishes a general prohibition of money laundering, regardless of the nature of the predicate offence and of the requirement of double criminality.[113] The Convention further contemplates the possibility of extending the scope of the crime of money laundering to situations where the offender 'ought to have assumed that the property was proceeds', 'acted for the purpose of making profit', or 'acted for the purpose of promoting the carrying on of further criminal activity'.[114] This provision, however, is not mandatory. The reach of the Convention is also significantly limited by the fact that states parties may unilaterally restrict the scope of the crime to certain categories of predicate offences.[115] In the EU, a series of directives have been adopted by the Council and the European Parliament with a view to harmonizing the domestic money-laundering laws of the member states, progressively broadening the scope of predicate offences to be covered by the crime. Nonetheless, the directives set up a minimum threshold of seriousness for predicate offences, based on the length of the corresponding sentences in the domestic law of member states.[116] The AU Convention on Corruption and the Arab Convention against Corruption, for their part, contain provisions requiring the states parties to adopt legislative measures to criminalize laundering of the proceeds of corruption and related offences.[117] In the OECD Convention on Bribery, the obligation to include bribery of foreign public officials as a predicate offence of money laundering only applies to states parties that already have criminalized the laundering of the proceeds of bribery of their own public officials.[118] The Arab Convention against Transnational Organized Crime requires states parties to criminalize the laundering of proceeds derived from any of the offences defined in the Convention,[119] which includes not only the offences defined in UNCTOC and its Protocols, but also offences not specifically envisaged in these instruments, such as bank fraud, currency counterfeiting, trafficking in hazardous

Money Laundering Law 2002: see Asia/Pacific Group on Money Laundering, *Mutual Evaluation Report on Myanmar*, 10 July 2008, at 45–46.

[111] See e.g., in Germany: Strafgesetzbuch, § 261(9) *in fine*.

[112] Convention on Laundering, Search, Seizure and Confiscation of the Proceeds from Crime, 8 November 1990, entered into force on 1 September 1993, ETS no 141.

[113] Ibid, Art 6(2)(a). [114] Ibid, Art 6(3). [115] Ibid, Art 6(4).

[116] See Council Directive 91/308/EEC on prevention of the use of the financial system for the purpose of money laundering, 10 June 1991, OJ L166 (28 June 1991) 77; Directive 2001/97/EC of the European Parliament and of the Council amending Council Directive 91/308/EEC on prevention of the use of the financial system for the purpose of money laundering, 4 December 2001, OJ L344 (28 December 2001) 76; Directive 2005/60/EC of the European Parliament and of the Council on the prevention of the use of the financial system for the purpose of money laundering and terrorist financing, 26 October 2005, OJ L309 (25 November 2005) 15; Directive 2015/849 on the prevention of the use of the financial system for the purposes of money laundering or terrorist financing, 20 May 2015, OJ L141 (5 June 2015) 73.

[117] AU Convention on Corruption, Art 6; Arab Convention against Corruption, Art 4(8).

[118] OECD Convention on Bribery, Art 7.

[119] Arab Convention against Transnational Organized Crime, Art 6.

wastes, trafficking in cultural property, trafficking in endangered species, drug trafficking, and cybercrime.

7. Participation in an organized criminal group

Organized crime is, by definition, a collective enterprise. It usually involves a diversity of actors at various stages of the criminal conduct, all of whom do not necessarily take direct part in the actual perpetration of an offence. To target better those individuals whose contribution to criminal acts would otherwise be difficult to establish, certain states have created 'inchoate' or 'associative' offences under their domestic law, making it punishable to participate in a criminal enterprise. The Committee on Civil Liberties and Internal Affairs of the European Parliament comments in this regard:

> Making participation in a criminal organization a criminal offence [...] serves primarily the purpose of exposing to criminal penalties those persons who contribute substantively to the operation of a criminal organization without themselves directly committing any criminal offence. They include primarily the members at 'leadership and advisory level' within the criminal organization and also those individuals who act as protectors, advisers and promoters in the police force, the legal system, or in the political and economic world to set up what can amount to a 'buffer zone' around the criminal organization.[120]

This model has been endorsed by UNCTOC. Pursuant to Article 5, states parties must criminalize either or both of the following:

(i) Agreeing with one or more other persons to commit a serious crime for a purpose relating directly or indirectly to the obtaining of a financial or other material benefit and, where required by domestic law, involving an act undertaken by one of the participants in furtherance of the agreement or involving an organized criminal group;
(ii) Conduct by a person who, with knowledge of either the aim and general criminal activity of an organized criminal group or its intention to commit the crimes in question, takes an active part in:
   a. Criminal activities of the organized criminal group;
   b. Other activities of the organized criminal group in the knowledge that his or her participation will contribute to the achievement of the above-described criminal aim.

Sub-paragraph (i) is modelled on conspiracy offences known to common-law jurisdictions, and sub-paragraph (ii) draws on 'associative offences' found for the most part in civil-law countries. The criminalization of the 'participation in, association or conspiracy to commit' drug-related offences was also provided for by the UN Drug Convention. However, this obligation was made 'subject to the constitutional principles and basic concepts' of the legal system of each state party,[121] because no

[120] European Parliament, Committee on Civil Liberties and Internal Affairs, *Report on the draft Joint Action adopted by the Council on the basis of Article K.3 of the Treaty on European Union on making it a criminal offence to participate in a criminal organization in the Member States of the European Union*, 5 November 1997, Doc A4-0349/97, at 12.

[121] UN Drug Convention, Art 3(1)(c)(iv).

agreement as to the definition of conspiracy could be reached during the negotiations due to irreconcilable differences in domestic legal systems.[122] This problem is still apparent in sub-paragraph (i) of the UNCTOC definition, which requires a material act to be taken in furtherance of the agreement where required by domestic law. In French law, for instance, preparatory acts undertaken in furtherance of the agreement are one of the constitutive elements of the offence of *association de malfaiteurs*.[123] By contrast, in most common-law jurisdictions the agreement of the co-conspirators is sufficient to constitute the offence.[124]

The core element of the offence of participation in an organized criminal group under sub-paragraph (ii) is the concept of 'organized criminal group', defined as

> a structured group of three or more persons, existing for a period of time and acting in concert with the aim of committing one or more serious crimes or offences established in accordance with this Convention, in order to obtain, directly or indirectly, a financial or other material benefit.[125]

This definition is intended 'to include both groups with hierarchical or other elaborate structure and non-hierarchical groups'.[126] The group 'does not need to have formally defined roles for its members, continuity of its membership or a developed structure'.[127] It must 'not [be] randomly formed for the immediate commission of an offence', but acting with a view to committing a single offence is deemed sufficient, provided that the group has some degree of continued existence.[128] Commentators take the view that all members of the group need not coordinate with each other or participate jointly in the activities of the group.[129] This definition is flexible enough to encompass very different types of criminal groups, most of which are not fixed and permanent entities.[130]

The definition in the Palermo Convention further requires that the crimes considered be committed for the specific purpose of 'obtain[ing] a financial or other material benefit'. This latter requirement is a constitutive element of the

[122] David P Stewart, 'Internationalizing the War on Drugs: The UN Convention against Illicit Traffic in Narcotic Drugs and Psychotropic Substances' (1990) 18 *Denver Journal of International Law & Policy* 387, at 393.

[123] The offence is defined under Code pénal, Art 450-1. See also Cass crim, 15 December 1993, App no 93-81.240 (unreported).

[124] See, in Canada: Criminal Code (RSC, 1985, c. C-46), s 465(1) and the decision of the Supreme Court in *Papalia v R*, [1979] 2 SCR 256, at 276; in England and Wales: Criminal Law Act 1977, s 1(1); in the United States: *United States v Nash*, 229 US 373 (1913), at 378, and, regarding drug cases in particular, *United States v Shabani*, 513 US 10 (1994) (in some states, however, an overt act is necessary: see e.g. Alabama Code, § 13A-4-3(a)).

[125] UNCTOC, Art 2(a).

[126] Interpretative Notes for UNCTOC (n 22), para 4.

[127] UNCTOC, Art 2(c).

[128] McClean (n 23), at 41. See also Boister (n 104), at 132.

[129] McClean (n 23), at 41. See also Almir Maljević , *'Participation in a Criminal Organization' and 'Conspiracy': Different Legal Models against Criminal Collectives* (Duncker & Humblot, 2011), at 150.

[130] Joseph Albini observes that '[r]ather than being a criminal secret society, a criminal syndicate consists of loosely structured relationships functioning primarily because each participant is interested in furthering his own welfare': see Joseph L Albini, *The American Mafia: Genesis of a Legend* (Appleton-Century-Crofts, 1971), at 288. For example, in West Africa 'it is particularly misleading to think of organized crime groups as being solid structures resembling major corporations of crime' with a rigid hierarchy. West African criminal networks 'are generally characterized by their great fluidity

crime in both sub-paragraphs (i) and (ii). In the case of a conspiracy offence, the agreement between the conspirators must be made for the purpose of obtaining a financial or other material benefit.[131] In the case of the offence of participation in an organized criminal group, the aim and object of the group must be to obtain a financial or other material benefit. It is commonly accepted that the words 'financial or other material benefit' are 'not limited to financial, monetary or equivalent benefits'.[132] An interpretative note indicates that they should be interpreted broadly, to include, for example, sexual gratification (in the case of human trafficking).[133] It is also irrelevant that the proceeds are later used in pursuit of political ends.[134]

The crime of participation in an organized criminal group as defined by UNCTOC is not predicated on specific offences but on the notion of 'serious crime', defined as 'conduct constituting an offence punishable by a maximum deprivation of liberty of at least four years or a more serious penalty' in the domestic law of a state party.[135] A comparative study of the sentencing provisions in domestic criminal laws shows that the offences corresponding to that standard in 1999 comprised: murder, rape, assault, abduction, theft, robbery, burglary, handling stolen property, extortion, trafficking in drugs, embezzlement, bribery, fraud, counterfeiting of currency, money laundering, trafficking in human beings, smuggling of firearms, and forming or leading a criminal organization.[136] Recommendations were made by various UN bodies to urge member states to establish as a 'serious crime' in their domestic laws, in accordance with the UNCTOC definition, offences such as the production and distribution of falsified and fraudulent products, trafficking in cultural property, trafficking in endangered species, misuse and falsification of identity, kidnapping, and trafficking in fraudulent medicines.[137]

and flexibility': UNODC, *Transnational Organized Crime in the West African Region* (United Nations, 2005), at 2, 15–18.

[131] Boister (n 104), at 139.

[132] UNODC, *Legislative Guide for the Implementation of the United Nations Convention against Transnational Organized Crime and the Protocols Thereto* (United Nations, 2004), para 26.

[133] Interpretative Notes for UNCTOC (n 22), para 3.

[134] Commentators point out that even a terrorist or insurgent group may be considered as an 'organized criminal group' provided that it commits crimes 'in order to raise financial and material benefits': see Legislative Guide for the Implementation of UNCTOC (n 132), para 26. During the negotiations of UNCTOC, Uruguay 'proposed that the reference to material and financial means could end with the words "also when those benefits are sought for political or other purposes"': see Ad Hoc Committee on the Elaboration of a Convention against Transnational Organized Crime, 3rd sess (Vienna, 28 April – 3 May 1999), *Revised draft United Nations Convention against Transnational Organized Crime*, UN Doc A/AC.254/4/Rev.2, at 4–5, n 18.

[135] UNCTOC, Art 2(b).

[136] Ad Hoc Committee on the Elaboration of a Convention against Transnational Organized Crime, *Analytical Study of Serious Crime*, 30 November 1999, UN Doc A/AC.254/22.

[137] See Conference of the Parties to the United Nations Convention against Transnational Organized Crime, 6th sess (Vienna, 15–19 October 2012), *The Notion of Serious Crime in the United Nations Convention against Transnational Organized Crime—Note by the Secretariat*, 20 September 2012, UN Doc CTOC/COP/2012/CRP.4, paras 27–33.

It is worth recalling that the obligation on states parties to criminalize the offences defined under UNCTOC, including participation in an organized criminal group, applies even if the offence is not transnational in nature.[138]

In the EU, the offence of participation in an organized criminal group is defined in the Framework Decision on the fight against organized crime.[139] The definition provided by the Framework Decision, however, differs on several points from the UNCTOC definition. In particular, the offence of participation in an organized criminal group requires an active participation on the part of the offender in the criminal activities of the group, and not just in any of the group's activities.[140] Moreover, the involvement of a criminal organization is not included as a constitutive element of the offence of conspiracy but constitutes an aggravating factor.[141] The Framework Decision also establishes minimum sentencing standards [142] and provides for the liability of legal persons.[143]

Note that the Arab Convention against Transnational Organized Crime also requires states parties to criminalize the offence of participation in an organized criminal group. The offence as defined in the Convention covers both conspiracy to commit a 'serious crime' (a notion that is not defined in the Convention), and participation in the activities of an organized criminal group in connection to any of the predicate offences defined in the Convention.[144]

8. Other relevant offences

A number of treaties also require states parties to criminalize several other crimes commonly linked to organized crime, such as: trafficking in endangered species;[145] trafficking in hazardous wastes;[146] trafficking in cultural property;[147] currency counterfeiting;[148] and cybercrime, including trafficking in child

[138] UNCTOC, Art 34(2); Interpretative Notes for UNCTOC (n 22), para 59.

[139] Council Framework Decision 2008/841/JHA on the fight against organized crime, 24 October 2008, OJ L300 (11 November 2008) 42.

[140] Ibid, Art 2(a). [141] Ibid, Arts 2(b) and 3(2). [142] Ibid, Art 3(1).

[143] Ibid, Art 5. [144] Arab Convention against Transnational Organized Crime, Art 23.

[145] Convention on International Trade in Endangered Species of Wild Fauna and Flora, 3 March 1973, entered into force on 1 July 1975, 993 UNTS 244, Art VIII(1)(a); Arab Convention against Transnational Organized Crime, Art 17.

[146] Convention on the Control of Transboundary Movements of Hazardous Wastes and their Disposal, Art 9; Convention on the Ban of the Import into Africa and the Control of Transboundary Movement and Management of Hazardous Wastes within Africa, 30 January 1991, entered into force on 22 April 1998, 2101 UNTS 177, Art 9; Arab Convention against Transnational Organized Crime, Art 16(2).

[147] Convention on the Means of Prohibiting and Preventing the Illicit Import, Export and Transfer of Ownership of Cultural Property, 14 November 1970, entered into force on 24 April 1972, 823 UNTS 232, Art 8 (also offering states parties the possibility to impose administrative sanctions instead of criminal penalties); Arab Convention against Transnational Organized Crime, Art 15. See also Council of Europe Convention on Offences Relating to Cultural Property, 19 May 2017, ETS no 221 (not yet in force), replacing the European Convention on Offences Relating to Cultural Property, 23 June 1985, ETS no 119.

[148] International Convention for the Suppression of Counterfeiting Currency, 20 April 1929, entered into force on 22 February 1931, 112 LNTS 371, Art 3; Directive 2014/62/EU on the protection of the euro and other currencies against counterfeiting by criminal law, 15 May 2014, OJ L 151 (21 May 2014) 1, Art 3; Arab Convention against Transnational Organized Crime, Art 10.

pornography.[149] As pointed out above, recommendations were made by various UN bodies to urge member states to establish as a 'serious crime' in their domestic laws, in accordance with the definition of 'serious crime' under UNCTOC, offences such as the production and distribution of falsified and fraudulent products, trafficking in cultural property, trafficking in endangered species, misuse and falsification of identity, kidnapping, and trafficking in fraudulent medicines.[150]

B. Establishment of Criminal Jurisdiction

States parties to relevant crime-suppression conventions must enact legislation to ensure that their courts will be able to exercise jurisdiction over the crimes. This does not mean that there is an obligation to exercise jurisdiction in a particular case,[151] but simply that a legal basis must exist under domestic law to enable prosecution of offenders under certain conditions. In other words, the obligations deriving from these instruments with respect to criminal jurisdiction cover only prescriptive jurisdiction. In general, under international law states enjoy broad discretion in determining which principles govern the exercise of the criminal jurisdiction of their courts, provided that they do not violate a prohibitive rule of international law.[152] When, however, a treaty mandates the establishment of a given basis of jurisdiction, states parties are obliged to adopt appropriate measures in their domestic law. This section reviews the scope of states' obligation to establish criminal jurisdiction over organized crime, corruption, and related conduct under the relevant crime-suppression conventions.

1. Bases of jurisdiction

International instruments pertaining to organized crime and corruption require or simply permit states parties to establish their jurisdiction on several bases.

[149] Convention on Cybercrime, 23 November 2001, entered into force on 1 July 2004, ETS no 185, Arts 2–10; Arab Convention on Combating Information Technology Offences, 21 December 2010, entered into force on 7 February 2014, Arts 5–18, and in particular Art 16 regarding 'offences related to organized crime committed by means of information technology'; African Union Convention on Cyber Security and Personal Data Protection, 27 June 2014 (not yet in force), Arts 25 and 29–30; Optional Protocol to the Convention on the Rights of the Child on the Sale of Children, Child Prostitution and Child Pornography, Art 3(1)(c); Directive 2011/93/EU on combating the sexual abuse and sexual exploitation of children and child pornography, 13 December 2011, OJ L 335 (17 December 2011) 1, Art 5.

[150] See Note by the Secretariat (n 137), paras 27–33.

[151] McClean (n 23), at 167; Gilmore and McClean (n 1), para 4.6. However, states parties may be required to exercise their jurisdiction pursuant to the obligation *aut dedere aut judicare*: see Section C.1(d) of this chapter. Note also Art 4(1) of the Lusaka Agreement on Co-operative Enforcement Operations Directed at Illegal Trade in Wild Fauna and Flora, 8 September 1994, entered into force on 10 December 1996, 1950 UNTS 35, requiring states parties to 'take appropriate measures [...] to investigate and prosecute cases of illegal trade'.

[152] *The Case of the S.S. 'Lotus' (France v Turkey)*, PCIJ Series A no 10 (1927), at 19.

(a) Territorial jurisdiction

States parties may first be required to establish their jurisdiction over conduct taking place, in whole or in part, in their territory. Territory includes the territorial sea and the airspace.[153] By extension, a state's territorial jurisdiction also often extends to acts committed on board vessels flying its flag and aircrafts registered under its law. The obligation to establish territorial jurisdiction is found in virtually every crime-suppression convention pertaining to organized crime and corruption.[154] EU legislation also provides for an obligation to establish jurisdiction on that basis with respect to drug offences,[155] human trafficking,[156] and participation in an organized criminal group.[157]

Some instruments—essentially but not exclusively those dealing with corruption—indicate that jurisdiction on the basis of territoriality can be exercised when the offence was committed 'in whole or in part' in the forum state's territory.[158] The words 'in part' indicate that jurisdiction may be exercised even where some constitutive elements of the offence were committed abroad, as long as at least one element of the crime was committed in the forum state's territory. This applies in particular in cases of money laundering. When the territory of a state was used for a financial transaction involving proceeds of crimes entirely committed abroad, this state may assert jurisdiction over the acts of money laundering. Some states also often claim jurisdiction in respect of the predicate offences.[159] The words 'in part' notably encompass the so-called 'objective territorial

[153] See e.g. United Nations Convention on the Law of the Sea, 10 December 1982, entered into force on 16 November 1994, 1833 UNTS 3, Art 2.

[154] See UN Drug Convention, Art 4(1)(a); UNCTOC, Art 15(1); UNCAC, Art 42(1); OECD Convention on Bribery, Art 4(1); Council of Europe Convention on Action against Trafficking in Human Beings, Art 31(1)(a), (b), and (c); Criminal Law Convention on Corruption, Art 17(1)(a); Convention on the fight against corruption involving officials of the European Communities or officials of Member States of the European Union, Art 7(1)(a); AU Convention on Corruption, Art 13(1)(a); Arab Convention against Corruption, Art 9(1)(a); Inter-American Convention against Corruption, Art V(1); Inter-American Convention against Arms Trafficking, Art V(1); Arab Convention against Illicit Traffic in Narcotic Drugs and Psychotropic Substances, Art 4(1)(a); Arab Convention against Transnational Organized Crime, Art 39(1)(a); Optional Protocol to the Convention on the Rights of the Child on the Sale of Children, Child Prostitution and Child Pornography, Art 4(1); Convention on Cybercrime, Art 22(1)(a). It should be noted that the obligation to establish criminal jurisdiction pursuant to Art 15 of UNCTOC also logically applies to the offences defined under the UNCTOC Protocols: see n 22; Legislative Guide for the Implementation of UNCTOC (n 132), para 229. But see McClean (n 23), at 141.

[155] Framework Decision on the constituent elements of criminal acts and penalties in the field of illicit drug trafficking, Art 8(1)(a).

[156] Framework Decision on combating trafficking in human beings, Art 6(1)(a).

[157] Framework Decision on the fight against organized crime, Art 7(1)(a).

[158] OECD Convention on Bribery, Art 4(1); Criminal Law Convention on Corruption, Art 17(1)(a); Convention on the fight against corruption involving officials of the European Communities or officials of Member States of the European Union, Art 7(1)(a); AU Convention on Corruption, Art 13(1)(a); Arab Convention against Transnational Organized Crime, Art 39(1)(a). For UNCAC, see Interpretative Notes for UNCAC (n 59), para 41. Within the EU, see Framework Decision on the constituent elements of criminal acts and penalties in the field of illicit drug trafficking, Art 8(1)(a); Framework Decision on combating trafficking in human beings, Art 6(1)(a); Framework Decision on the fight against organized crime, Art 7(1)(a).

[159] This is the case in France, where former Gabonese President Omar Bongo (now deceased), incumbent President of Equatorial Guinea Teodoro Obiang Nguema Mbasogo, and incumbent

principle' (also known as 'principle of ubiquity'), whereby the offence is regarded as having been committed in the territory of a state when one of its constitutive elements—often a specific outcome or effect—takes place in the territory of that state.[160] The objective territorial principle is particularly relevant in cases of conspiracies formed abroad.[161] Where proof of an overt act is required by domestic law, jurisdiction can be asserted if one of the conspirators acts in furtherance of the conspiracy in the territory of the forum state.[162] When the existence of such an act cannot be proven, or where it is not an element of the crime under the relevant domestic law, domestic courts have applied the objective territorial principle broadly. For instance, English courts can exercise jurisdiction if some of the conspirators continue to act in concert in England in pursuance of an initial agreement formed abroad.[163] In the United States, the objective territorial principle applies to '[a]cts done outside a jurisdiction, but intended to produce and producing detrimental effects within it'.[164] As a US court of appeals noted, '[u]nderlying this principle is the theory that the "detrimental effects" constitute an element of the offense and since they occur within the country, jurisdiction is properly invoked under the territorial principle'.[165] French courts similarly consider that, in the absence of an overt act in French territory, jurisdiction can be asserted over a conspiracy formed abroad if the crimes contemplated by the conspirators are committed in French territory.[166]

Congolese President Denis Sassou Nguesso, as well as members of their families, are under investigation on suspicion of having embezzled public funds in their respective countries and of having laundered the criminal proceeds in French territory (case known as *l'affaire des biens mal acquis*). Teodoro Nguema Obiang Mangue, Vice-President of Equatorial Guinea and son of President Obiang, was found guilty as charged: see T corr Paris, 32ème ch, 27 October 2017. For an overview of the developments in the case, see Transparency International France, 'Biens mal acquis : les dates clefs', https://transparency-france.org/aider-victimes-de-corruption/biens-mal-acquis/dates-clefs/. See also Gabriel Roujou de Boubée, 'Compétence française pour des détournements de fonds publics commis au préjudice d'États africains', *Recueil Dalloz* (2009) no 22, p 1520.

160 The existence of the objective territorial principle was noted by the ICJ in *Lotus* (n 152), at 23. On the objective territorial principle of jurisdiction generally, see Harvard Law School Research in International Law, 'Codification of International Law, Part II: Jurisdiction with Respect to Crime' (1935) 29 *American Journal of International Law Supplement* 435, at 487 ff.

161 On the jurisdictional challenges posed by conspiracies, see generally Joshua D A Blackmore, 'The Jurisdictional Problem of the Extraterritorial Conspiracy' (2006) 17 *Criminal Law Forum* 71.

162 See e.g., in France: Cass crim, 3 November 1970, App no 70-90.953, *Bull crim* (1970), no 285, p 689.

163 This is known in England and Wales as the 'continuing act doctrine': see *Director of Public Prosecutions v Doot and Others*, [1973] 1 All ER 940.

164 *Strassheim v Daily*, 221 US 280 (1911), at 285. Where, however, the detrimental effect is not an element of the crime, jurisdiction can be asserted on the basis of the effects doctrine.

165 *United States v Pizzarusso*, 388 F2d 8 (2nd Cir 1968), at 10.

166 See Cass crim, 20 February 1990, App nos 89-86.610 and 89-86.611, *Bull crim* (1990), no 84, p 216. French courts apply the so-called *théorie du résultat* to assert jurisdiction over acts committed abroad when the result of one of the constitutive elements of the offence manifests itself in French territory.

(b) Active personality

According to the active personality principle, jurisdiction may be exercised over crimes committed abroad when the offender is a national of the forum state. Among the crime-suppression conventions pertaining to organized crime and corruption, only a few impose an obligation for states parties to establish their jurisdiction over acts committed by their nationals. That is the case of the Arab Convention against Transnational Organized Crime.[167] Despite their ambiguous language, it seems that the AU Convention on Corruption and the Arab Convention against Corruption also require states parties to establish jurisdiction on that basis.[168] The OECD Convention on Bribery also mandates states parties to establish their jurisdiction on the basis of the nationality of the offender, but merely with respect to states parties that already use the active personality principle as a basis for exercising jurisdiction in their legal system.[169] The UN Drug Convention, UNCTOC, and UNCAC, for their part, expressly permit states parties to establish jurisdiction on the basis of the offender's nationality.[170]

The way in which the active personality principle is addressed in relevant European instruments differs slightly. With regards to organized crime offences, EU member states must establish their jurisdiction over acts committed by their nationals, but this obligation is qualified as states remain free to opt out or to apply this jurisdictional rule only in specific cases or circumstances.[171] However, member states that, under their domestic law, do not extradite their own nationals remain obliged to establish jurisdiction on the basis of the active personality principle for acts committed abroad.[172] States parties to the Convention on the fight against corruption involving officials of the European Communities or officials of Member States of the European Union must establish jurisdiction on the basis of active personality, but may give a notification with a view to restricting its application.[173] The same approach has been adopted by the Council of Europe in the Convention on

[167] Arab Convention against Transnational Organized Crime, Art 39(1)(c).

[168] AU Convention on Corruption, Art 13(1)(b) (Art 13(1) provides that '[e]ach State Party has jurisdiction' in the cases defined under each sub-paragraph. This could be interpreted as a mere recognition of potential bases of jurisdiction under the laws of states parties, and not as an obligation to establish jurisdiction. This provision, however, must be interpreted in good faith and in light of the object and purpose of the Convention (VCLT, Art 31(1)). It would make little sense for the Convention not to create any obligation for states parties to establish their jurisdiction over the conduct it aims at suppressing); Arab Convention against Corruption, Art 9(1)(d) (non-official translations are available in English, with slightly different wordings).

[169] OECD Convention on Bribery, Art 4(2).

[170] UN Drug Convention, Art 4(b)(i); UNCTOC, Art 15(2)(b); UNCAC, Art 42(2)(b).

[171] Framework Decision on the constituent elements of criminal acts and penalties in the field of illicit drug trafficking, Art 8(1)(b) and (c), and (2); Framework Decision on combating trafficking in human beings, Art 6(1)(b) and (c), and (2); Framework Decision on the fight against organized crime, Art 7(1)(b) and (c).

[172] Framework Decision on the constituent elements of criminal acts and penalties in the field of illicit drug trafficking, Art 8(3); Framework Decision on combating trafficking in human beings, Art 6(3); Framework Decision on the fight against organized crime, Art 7(3).

[173] Convention on the fight against corruption involving officials of the European Communities or officials of Member States of the European Union, Art 7.

Action against Trafficking in Human Beings,[174] the Criminal Law Convention on Corruption,[175] and the Convention on Cybercrime.[176]

Finally, applicable treaties often require states parties to establish their jurisdiction over acts committed by their nationals when the offender is present in their territory and they do not extradite him.[177] This is particularly relevant in the EU because civil-law countries generally do not extradite their own nationals.[178] Other states, by contrast, generally prefer to extradite their nationals rather than establish extraterritorial jurisdiction on the basis of active personality in order to prosecute them.[179]

(c) Passive personality

In accordance with the passive personality principle, criminal jurisdiction may be exercised over crimes committed abroad when the victim is a national of the forum state.[180] In general, crime-suppression conventions pertaining to organized crime and corruption do not oblige states parties to enact legislation allowing prosecution on the basis of the passive personality principle. In the case of certain crimes such as corruption, arms trafficking, or money laundering, this is understandable, as these crimes are not offences against the person. Yet in respect of other crimes where the exercise of jurisdiction on the basis of passive personality would be possible, such as

[174] Council of Europe Convention on Action against Trafficking in Human Beings, Art 31(1)(d) and (2).

[175] Criminal Law Convention on Corruption, Art 17(1)(b) and (c), and (2).

[176] Convention on Cybercrime, Art 22(1)(d) and (2).

[177] UN Drug Convention, Art 4(2)(a)(ii); UNCTOC, Art 15(3); UNCAC, Art 42(3); Council of Europe Convention on Action against Trafficking in Human Beings, Art 31(3); Arab Convention against Illicit Traffic in Narcotic Drugs and Psychotropic Substances, Art 4(2)(a)(ii); Criminal Law Convention on Corruption, Art 17(3); Inter-American Convention against Corruption, Art V(3); Arab Convention against Corruption, Art 9(1)(f); Inter-American Convention against Arms Trafficking, Art V(3); Optional Protocol to the Convention on the Rights of the Child on the Sale of Children, Child Prostitution and Child Pornography, Art 4(3); Convention on Cybercrime, Art 22(3). This prescription is closely linked to the principle *aut dedere aut judicare*, which creates an obligation for a requested state to submit the case to its competent authorities for the purpose of prosecution (i.e. to exercise jurisdiction), when the alleged offender is present in its territory and that state chooses not to extradite him (see Section C.1(d) of this chapter). These are two separate, yet interconnected, obligations. To be able to prosecute their own nationals in these circumstances, states parties must logically have an adequate basis of jurisdiction in their domestic law.

[178] See e.g., in France: Code de procédure pénale, Art 696-4, 1°; in Germany: Grundgesetz, Art 16(2); in Spain: Ley 4/1985 de Extradición Pasiva, Art 3(1). See generally Jean-Marc Thouvenin, 'Le principe de non extradition des nationaux' in SFDI, *Droit international et nationalité – Colloque de Poitiers* (Pedone, 2012) 127.

[179] For instance, the United States 'believe[s] it preferable to eliminate situations in which [it] cannot extradite [its] nationals rather than create jurisdiction to prosecute them because [it] cannot extradite them'. See US Senate, 101st Congress, 1st sess, *United Nations Convention against Illicit Traffic in Narcotic Drugs and Psychotropic Substances*, Exec. Rept. 101-15 (US Government Printing Office, 1989), at 55.

[180] See e.g., in France: Code pénal, Art 113-7; in Germany: Strafgesetzbuch, § 7(1). The French doctrine, for a time, considered that jurisdiction over acts committed against French nationals was an expression of the protective principle (*competence réelle*): see Henri Donnedieu de Vabres, *Les principes modernes du droit pénal international*, first published 1928 (reprinted edn, Panthéon-Assas, 2004), at 92, 105–107.

human trafficking and sexual exploitation of children, relevant instruments rarely contemplate the adoption of legislation to establish jurisdiction on the basis of the victim's nationality. The only treaties to impose an obligation on states parties to establish their jurisdiction over a crime committed against one of their nationals are the Arab Convention against Transnational Organized Crime and the Arab Convention against Corruption.[181] In other treaties, jurisdiction on the basis of passive personality is left at the discretion of states parties.[182] This is maybe partly due to states' general distrust in the potentially far-reaching exercise of extraterritorial jurisdiction.[183] In general, common-law countries are more favourable to facilitating extradition in order to have the offender prosecuted in the state where the offence was committed.[184]

(d) The effects doctrine

Jurisdiction can be grounded in the 'effects doctrine' to encompass criminal acts that have a substantial impact in, or a clear nexus with, the territory of the forum state.[185] This doctrine should be distinguished from the 'objective territorial principle'.[186] Despite its controversial nature,[187] the effects doctrine is recognized as a potential basis for exercising jurisdiction in the major international instruments dealing with organized crime and related conduct. The establishment of jurisdiction on this particular basis, however, is generally not mandatory. Under the UN Drug Convention

[181] Arab Convention against Transnational Organized Crime, Art 39(1)(c); Arab Convention against Corruption, Art 9(1)(c).

[182] See e.g. Optional Protocol to the Convention on the Rights of the Child on the Sale of Children, Child Prostitution and Child Pornography, Art 4(2)(b); Council of Europe Convention on Action against Trafficking in Human Beings, Art 31(1)(e) (providing for the establishment of jurisdiction over an offence committed against a national of a state party), and paragraph (2) (allowing states parties to reserve their 'right not to apply or to apply only in specific cases or conditions the jurisdiction rules laid down in [sub paragraph 1(e)]').

[183] For instance, during the negotiations of UNCAC, Mexico and other delegations expressed the concern that criminalizing bribery of foreign public officials could be interpreted as allowing the exercise of extraterritorial jurisdiction: see Ad Hoc Committee for the Negotiation of a Convention against Corruption, 2nd sess (Vienna, 17–28 June 2002), *Revised Draft United Nations Convention against Corruption*, 26 March 2002, UN Doc A/AC.261/3/Rev.1, n 151.

[184] Neil Boister, *Penal Aspects of the UN Drug Conventions* (Kluwer Law International, 2001), at 247 ff. For example, Australia has jurisdiction over drug offences committed abroad by foreigners when the offender is present in Australian territory, provided that 'no steps have been taken by the foreign country [...] for the surrender of the person', or '[extradition] proceedings taken by that country [...] have not resulted in the person being surrendered' (Crimes (Traffic in Narcotic Drugs and Psychotropic Substances) Act 1990, s 12(2)).

[185] An interpretative note to UNCTOC indicates that 'the term "substantial effects" is intended to cover situations where an offence has had a substantial consequential adverse effect on another State Party, for example where the currency of one State Party is counterfeited in another State Party and the organized criminal group has put the counterfeit currency into global circulation'; see Interpretative Notes for UNCTOC (n 22), para 8. Although this note is concerned with the definition of the transnational character of an offence, it clearly draws on the effects doctrine of jurisdiction.

[186] Roger O'Keefe, 'Universal Jurisdiction: Clarifying the Basic Concept' (2004) 2 *Journal of International Criminal Justice* 735, at 739, n 16. This distinction is often misunderstood.

[187] See e.g. Boister (n 184), at 280 (deploring 'extravagant interpretations' of the effects doctrine in drug trafficking cases).

and the Arab Convention against Illicit Traffic in Narcotic Drugs and Psychotropic Substances, jurisdiction may be exercised over acts committed abroad 'with a view to the commission' of an offence within the territory of the forum state.[188] Such formulation is chiefly intended to cover conspiracy-type offences. This approach is also that of UNCTOC and UNCAC, although in these conventions the application of the effects doctrine is only prescribed with respect to the offences of participation in an organized criminal group and money laundering.[189] An obligation to establish jurisdiction on the basis of the effects doctrine can only be found in the Arab Convention against Transnational Organized Crime, which requires states parties to establish their jurisdiction over crimes having an effect on their territory,[190] as well as in the Arab Convention against Corruption, which requires states parties to establish their jurisdiction over a crime 'committed outside the state party's territory with the aim of committing the offence within its territory'.[191] The AU Convention on Corruption, for its part, provides that states parties 'ha[ve] jurisdiction' over acts having 'deleterious or harmful consequences or effects' in their territory.[192] Whether this formulation entails an obligation for states parties to establish their jurisdiction on the basis of the effects doctrine is unclear.

The effects doctrine is particularly relevant in cases of inchoate conspiracies formed abroad. The courts of the US Fifth Circuit, for instance, assert jurisdiction when there is 'evidence that the defendants intended their conspiracy to be consummated within the nation's borders'.[193] In other words, the detrimental effect need not be realized as long as intended effect may be proven. The Privy Council of the United Kingdom, in a case concerning Hong-Kong, has also recognized that jurisdiction can be established on this basis.[194]

[188] UN Drug Convention, Art 4(1)(b)(iii); Arab Convention against Illicit Traffic in Narcotic Drugs and Psychotropic Substances, Art 4(1)(b)(iii).

[189] UNCTOC, Art 15(2)(c); UNCAC, Art 42(2)(c).

[190] Arab Convention against Transnational Organized Crime, Art 39(1)(a).

[191] Arab Convention against Corruption, Art 9(1)(e).

[192] AU Convention on Corruption, Art 13(1)(d).

[193] *United States v Mann*, 615 F2d 668 (5th Cir 1980), at 671. See also *United States v Ricardo*, 619 F2d 1124 (5th Cir 1980). Both cases dealt with charges of conspiracy to import drugs. The courts, however, asserted jurisdiction on the basis of the objective territorial principle. US courts tend to conflate the objective territorial principle and the effects doctrine, blurring the fundamental distinction between them. When the conspirators did not act in furtherance of the conspiracy and the crimes contemplated by the conspirators were not committed in the territory of the forum state, jurisdiction cannot be asserted on the basis of territoriality because nothing happened in the territory of the forum state. As Mann noted, for the objective territorial principle to apply, '[t]he effect occurring within the country must be the fact which completes the offence; neither more nor less remote facts which could loosely be described as "effects" are sufficient' (Frederick Alexander Mann, 'The Doctrine of Jurisdiction in International Law' (1964) 111 *Recueil des cours de l'Académie de droit international* 1, at 86). Therefore, those cases should properly be read as applications of the effects doctrine.

[194] See the decision of the Privy Council in *Samchai Liangsiriprasert v United States*, [1991] 1 AC 225, at 251 ('a conspiracy entered into in Thailand with the intention of committing the criminal offence of trafficking in drugs in Hong Kong is justiciable in Hong Kong even if no overt act pursuant to the conspiracy has yet occurred in Hong Kong').

(e) The protective principle

The 'protective principle' allows the exercise of jurisdiction over conduct threatening vital interests of the forum state, such as its national security. While this principle may be used to assert jurisdiction over certain acts committed abroad by nationals of the forum state where that state does not otherwise apply the active personality principle, it may also be relied on against aliens.[195] The protective principle is almost never mentioned in treaties on organized crime and corruption, most probably because of controversies surrounding abuses of the protective doctrine.[196] Three notable exceptions are UNCAC, the AU Convention on Corruption, and the Arab Convention against Corruption. UNCAC adopts an ambiguous formulation prescribing the establishment of jurisdiction when the offence is committed 'against' the forum state.[197] The language of the AU Convention on Corruption is more precise, providing for jurisdiction to be exercised over acts affecting the 'vital interests' of the forum state.[198] Similarly, the Arab Convention against Corruption requires states parties to establish their jurisdiction over crimes committed 'against the interests of the state party'.[199] Whether a particular situation warrants the application of the protective principle depends on the domestic law of the forum state. For instance, in the United States the protective principle is applied broadly to assert jurisdiction over offences which 'have a "potentially adverse effect" upon security or governmental functions'.[200] These include customs laws,[201] thereby allowing the exercise of jurisdiction over a conspiracy to smuggle drugs into US territory.

(f) Universal jurisdiction

The UN Drug Convention, UNCTOC, and UNCAC permit states parties to establish their jurisdiction over organized crime, corruption, and related offences when the alleged offender is present in their territory and they do not extradite him.[202] The AU Convention on Corruption and the Arab Convention against

[195] See Harvard Research in International Law (n 160), at 543 ff.

[196] See e.g., in the context of the United States: M Lawrence Noyer, 'High Seas Narcotics Smuggling and Section 955a of Title 21: Overextension of the Protective Principle of International Jurisdiction' (1982) 50 *Fordham Law Review* 688.

[197] UNCAC, Art 42(2)(d). The *travaux préparatoires* indicate that this formulation was preferred to a proposal suggesting to prescribe the establishment of jurisdiction when the offence was committed 'against the affected State': see Ad Hoc Committee for the Negotiation of a Convention against Corruption, 3rd sess (Vienna, 30 September – 11 October 2002), *Revised draft United Nations Convention against Corruption*, 5 July 2002, UN Doc A/AC.261/3/Rev.1/Add.1, Art 50(1)(c *bis*). It seems that the drafters intended to refer to the protective principle: see UNODC, *Technical Guide to the United Nations Convention against Corruption* (United Nations, 2009) at 135–36.

[198] AU Convention on Corruption, Art 13(1)(d).

[199] Arab Convention against Corruption, Art 9(1)(c).

[200] *United States v Pizzarusso* (n 165), at 10–11. See also *United States v James-Robinson*, 515 F Supp 1340 (SD Fla 1981), at 1344–45.

[201] American Law Institute, *Restatement of the Law Third: The Foreign Relations Law of the United States*, vol 1 (American Law Institute Publishers, 1987), at 240, comment *f*.

[202] UN Drug Convention, Art 4(2)(b); UNCTOC, Art 15(4); UNCAC, Art 42(4).

Corruption go a step further by requiring states parties to do so.[203] Such provisions create a broad expansion of jurisdiction. Where the alleged offender is not a national of the state party, they amount to providing for a subsidiary form of universal jurisdiction.[204] Subsidiary universal jurisdiction is explicitly provided for in the International Convention for the Suppression of Counterfeiting Currency, which requires states parties to exercise jurisdiction over foreigners for an offence committed abroad, provided that a prior request for extradition cannot be granted.[205]

(g) *Possible residual bases of jurisdiction*

Many instruments permit the exercise of extraterritorial jurisdiction in accordance with domestic law.[206] This covers bases of jurisdiction not addressed by the treaties, for example jurisdiction over acts committed by habitual residents of the forum state, as known in some legal systems,[207] and potentially universal jurisdiction.[208] In UNCAC and UNCTOC, however, the addition of the terms 'without prejudice to norms of general international law' arguably poses some limits to extraterritorial jurisdictional claims. The meaning of this provision remains contentious, and the extent to which it allows extraterritorial jurisdiction beyond the basis explicitly provided for in the treaties is not clear.[209]

2. Concurrent jurisdiction

Conflicts may arise between different states asserting jurisdiction for the same offence. This is particularly likely to occur in cases of organized crime, which often involves a transnational element. Concurrent jurisdiction can arise when the constitutive elements of a crime are committed in several countries, or when third states claim extraterritorial jurisdiction, for example on the basis of the personality principle.[210] To avoid conflicts, some crime-suppression conventions require states

[203] AU Convention on Corruption, Art 13(1)(c); Arab Convention against Corruption, Art 9(2).

[204] See Neil Boister, 'The Trend to Universal Extradition over Subsidiary Universal Jurisdiction in the Suppression of Transnational Crime' (2003) *Acta Juridica* 287, at 304–10. Universal jurisdiction is 'subsidiary' because it must be established as an alternative to extradition.

[205] International Convention for the Suppression of Counterfeiting Currency, Art 9.

[206] See e.g. UN Drug Convention, Art 4(3); UNCTOC, Art 15(6); UNCAC, Art 42(6).

[207] This is, for example, the case in Thailand in relation to drug offences: see Act on Measures for the Suppression of Offenders in an Offence Relating to Narcotics 1991, s 5(1).

[208] See e.g., in Germany, Strafgesetzbuch, § 6(4) (establishing universal jurisdiction over human trafficking as a 'crime against internationally protected interests'); in Spain: Ley Orgánica 6/1985 del Poder Judicial, Art 23(4)(e) (establishing universal jurisdiction over drug trafficking). It is worth noting that these states have also established their jurisdiction over any crime committed abroad by aliens when the crime in question is among those that these states have undertaken by treaty to prosecute (Strafgesetzbuch, § 6(9); Ley Orgánica del Poder Judicial, Art 23(4)(h)).

[209] Gilmore and McClean (n 1), para 4.40; McClean (n 23), at 172.

[210] Problems may also theoretically arise in case of acts committed on board aircrafts, since joint registration of aircrafts has been allowed by the International Civil Aviation Organization despite the prohibition of dual registration under the Chicago Convention: see Action of the Council, 62nd sess (19 September–15 December 1967), ICAO Doc 8743-C/978, at 26, and Convention on International Civil Aviation, 7 December 1944, entered into force on 4 April 1947, 15 UNTS 295, Art 18.

parties asserting jurisdiction to consult one another and coordinate legal action with a view to determining the most appropriate forum for prosecution.[211] The EU Framework Decision on the fight against organized crime also provides guidelines on how to solve concurrent jurisdictional claims.[212]

C. International Cooperation in Criminal Matters

Mutual legal assistance and other international cooperation mechanisms in criminal matters form the cornerstone of the international legal regime to combat organized crime and corruption. These mechanisms are crucial to effective criminal-law enforcement. This section primarily focuses on the obligations of states parties with respect to extradition proceedings, and also offers an overview of the range of other mutual legal assistance mechanisms provided for in the universal crime-suppression conventions pertaining to organized crime and corruption.

1. Extradition

Without compulsory mechanisms to regulate the surrender of alleged offenders by one state party to another for the purpose of prosecution, prospects to hold perpetrators accountable for organized crime or corruption would be slight. While extradition procedures between states are governed chiefly by bilateral and sometimes regional agreements,[213] universal treaties such as the UN Drug Convention, UNCTOC, and UNCAC have established a bare-bones framework to facilitate extradition proceedings. The following developments survey the scope of the obligations of states parties regarding extradition.

[211] See e.g. UNCTOC, Art 15(5); UNCAC, Art 42(5); Convention on Cybercrime, Art 22(5). Some domestic courts adopt an approach based on the doctrine of *forum non conveniens*, taking into consideration a number of questions, such as: 'where was the impact of the offence felt or likely to have been felt'; 'which jurisdiction has the greater interest in prosecuting the offence'; 'which police force played the major role in the development of the case'; 'which jurisdiction has laid charges'; 'which jurisdiction has the most comprehensive case'; 'which jurisdiction is ready to proceed to trial'; 'where is the evidence located'; 'whether the evidence is mobile'; 'the number of accused involved and whether they can be gathered together in one place for trial'; 'in what jurisdiction were most of the acts in furtherance of the crime committed'; 'the nationality and residence of the accused'; and 'the severity of the sentence the accused is likely to receive in each jurisdiction'. See *United States of America v Swystun* (1987), 50 Man R (2d) 129, at 133–34, endorsed by the Canadian Supreme Court in *United States of America v Cotroni; United States of America v El Zein*, [1989] 1 SCR 1469, at 1498–99.

[212] Framework Decision on the fight against organized crime, Art 7(2).

[213] In the EU, however, extradition procedures are now regulated by EU legislation: see Council Framework Decision 2002/584/JHA on the European arrest warrant and the surrender procedures between Member States, 13 June 2002, OJ L190 (18 July 2002) 1 (Framework Decision on the European arrest warrant), which supplanted pre-existing treaties, such as the Convention on Simplified Extradition Procedure between the Member States of the European Union, 10 March 1995, OJ C78 (30 March 1995) 2, the Convention drawn up on the basis of Article K.3 of the Treaty on European Union, relating to extradition between the Member States of the European Union, 27 September 1996, OJ C313 (23 October 1996) 12, and, within the broader context of the Council of Europe, the European Convention on Extradition, 13 December 1957, entered into force on 18 April 1960, ETS no 24 (and its Additional Protocols).

(a) Legal basis for extradition

The relevant crime-suppression conventions contain provisions aiming at ensuring that organized crime, corruption, and related conduct will be extraditable offences. First, such offences are deemed to be automatically included as extraditable offences in existing extradition treaties between the states parties[214] as well as in their domestic law.[215] Secondly, states parties are under an obligation to include such offences in future extradition treaties to be concluded between them.[216] Thirdly, states parties that do not make extradition conditional on the existence of a treaty must recognize such offences as extraditable offences.[217]

Finally, nearly all relevant treaties provide that the treaty itself must be able to be relied on as a legal basis for extradition between states parties not otherwise bound by an extradition treaty.[218] In the absence of any applicable extradition treaty, states parties to the AU Convention on Corruption are required to use the Convention as a basis for extradition.[219]

(b) Requirement of double criminality

Under UNCTOC and UNCAC, obligations in relation to extradition apply only insofar as the offence for which extradition is sought is punishable under the domestic law of both the requesting state and the requested state.[220] While the requirement of

[214] UN Drug Convention, Art 6(2); UNCTOC, Art 16(3); UNCAC, Art 44(4); Arab Convention against Illicit Traffic in Narcotic Drugs and Psychotropic Substances, Art 6(3); Criminal Law Convention on Corruption, Art 27(1); OECD Convention on Bribery, Art 10(1); AU Convention on Corruption, Art 15(2); Inter-American Convention against Corruption, Art XIII(2); Arab Convention against Corruption, Art 23(1); Inter-American Convention against Arms Trafficking, Art XIX(2); Optional Protocol to the Convention on the Rights of the Child on the Sale of Children, Child Prostitution and Child Pornography, Art 5(1); International Convention for the Suppression of Counterfeiting Currency, Art 10; Convention on Cybercrime, Art 24(2).

[215] OECD Convention on Bribery, Art 10(1); AU Convention on Corruption, Art 15(2).

[216] UN Drug Convention, Art 6(2); UNCTOC, Art 16(3); UNCAC, Art 44(4); Arab Convention against Illicit Traffic in Narcotic Drugs and Psychotropic Substances, Art 6(3); Criminal Law Convention on Corruption, Art 27(1); Inter-American Convention against Corruption, Art XIII(2); Arab Convention against Corruption, Art 23(1); Inter-American Convention against Arms Trafficking, Art XIX(2); Optional Protocol to the Convention on the Rights of the Child on the Sale of Children, Child Prostitution and Child Pornography, Art 5(1); International Convention for the Suppression of Counterfeiting Currency, Art 10. Under the Arab Convention against Corruption, this is merely optional (Art 23(7)).

[217] UN Drug Convention, Art 6(4); UNCTOC, Art 16(6); UNCAC, Art 44(7); Criminal Law Convention on Corruption, Art 27(4); AU Convention on Corruption, Art 15(4); Inter-American Convention against Corruption, Art XIII(4); Inter-American Convention against Arms Trafficking, Art XIX(4); Optional Protocol to the Convention on the Rights of the Child on the Sale of Children, Child Prostitution and Child Pornography, Art 5(3); International Convention for the Suppression of Counterfeiting Currency, Art 10; Convention on Cybercrime, Art 24(4).

[218] UN Drug Convention, Art 6(3); UNCTOC, Art 16(4); UNCAC, Art 44(5); Criminal Law Convention on Corruption, Art 27(2); OECD Convention on Bribery, Art 10(2); Arab Convention against Corruption, Art 23(5); Inter-American Convention against Corruption, Art XIII(3); Inter-American Convention against Arms Trafficking, Art XIX(3); Optional Protocol to the Convention on the Rights of the Child on the Sale of Children, Child Prostitution and Child Pornography, Art 5(2); Convention on Cybercrime, Art 24(3).

[219] AU Convention on Corruption, Art 15(3).

[220] UNCTOC, Art 16(1); UNCAC, Art 44(1).

double criminality has been abandoned in the EU with respect to organized crime, corruption, and related offences,[221] it remains in use in many states, including common-law jurisdictions,[222] which explains why the requirement of double criminality was included in the provisions of UNCTOC and UNCAC. UNCAC, however, encourages states parties to grant extradition irrespective of double criminality.[223] There is no mention of double criminality in the UN Drug Convention.[224]

For the purposes of double criminality, which is a question of domestic law, it is commonly accepted by domestic courts that an exact identity in the denomination of the offence and in each of its constitutive elements is not required.[225] It is usually sufficient that the essential elements of the offence are substantially the same.[226] But double criminality may require that the act for which extradition is requested must have been punishable under the law of the requested state at the time it was committed.[227] In addition, it may be necessary that the requested state had established its jurisdiction over the crime at the relevant period. When, for example, the requested state lacked jurisdiction because the crime was committed outside its territory by a foreign national, double criminality may preclude extradition to the requesting state.[228]

[221] See the list of offences in Framework Decision on the European arrest warrant, Art 2(2). In practice, however, member states have been reluctant to abandon completely the requirement of double criminality and have sometimes reintroduced it through the back door: see Gérard Cahin, 'La double incrimination dans le droit de l'extradition' (2013) 117 *Revue générale de droit international public* 579, at 603–608; Elies van Sliedregt, 'The Dual Criminality Requirement' in Elies van Sliedregt and Nico Keijzer (eds), *The European Arrest Warrant in Practice* (TMC Asser, 2010) 40, at 61–64.

[222] See, in Australia: Extradition Act 1988, s 19(2)(c); in the Bahamas: Extradition Act 1994, s 5(1)(a)(ii) and (b)(ii); in Canada: Extradition Act (SC, 1999, c. 18), s 3(1)(b); in New Zealand: Extradition Act 1999, s 4(2); in the United Kingdom: Extradition Act 2003, ss 64–65 and 137–38; in the United States: 18 USC § 3181(b)(1). See also London Scheme for Extradition within the Commonwealth, Art 2(2) (note that the Scheme is not a treaty). Double criminality is also required in other legal systems: see e.g., in China: Extradition Law of the People's Republic of China (Order of the President no 42), Art 7(1); in Israel: Extradition Law 5714-1954, s 2(a); and in Russia: Constitution of the Russian Federation, Art 63(2).

[223] UNCAC, Art 44(2).

[224] Stessens points out that the silence of the UN Drug Convention 'is logical in view of the fact that all parties are obliged under the convention to incriminate [...] drug trafficking' (Stessens (n 105), at 226).

[225] UNCAC, Art 43(2). See also *Model Treaty on Extradition*, Art 2(2), annexed to UN General Assembly Resolution 45/116, 14 December 1990, UN Doc A/RES/45/116, as amended by Resolution 52/88, 12 December 1997, UN Doc A/RES/52/88.

[226] During the negotiations of UNCTOC, Australia proposed to include a paragraph recalling this principle in the provisions pertaining to extradition, but this was eventually not deemed necessary. See Ad Hoc Committee on the Elaboration of a Convention against Transnational Organized Crime, 4th sess (Vienna, 28 June – 9 July 1999), *Proposals and contributions received from Governments on the draft United Nations Convention against Transnational Organized Crime–Australia: amendment to the revised draft United Nations Convention against Transnational Organized Crime*, 1 July 1999, UN Doc A/AC.254/L.48.

[227] See *R v Bow Street Metropolitan Stipendiary Magistrate and Others, ex parte Pinochet Ugarte (No 3)*, [2000] 1 AC 147, at 195 (Lord Browne-Wilkinson). This was the first time in English law that double criminality was made referable to the date of alleged commission.

[228] See e.g., in France: CA Paris, 11 January 1977, reproduced in (1976) 22 *Annuaire français de droit international* 937 (refusing the extradition to Israel of Raji Yousef Ben Hanna, involved in the hostage-taking at the 1972 Munich Olympic Games).

(c) Grounds for refusal

Crime-suppression conventions on organized crime, corruption, and related conduct generally do not spell out the circumstances in which extradition may be refused.[229] Instead, extradition is made 'subject to the conditions provided for by the law of the requested state or by applicable extradition treaties, including the grounds on which the requested state may refuse extradition'.[230] As a result, the grounds for refusal under the applicable domestic law apply unless otherwise provided. Of particular interest for our analysis of state organized crime are three exceptions found in many jurisdictions, namely the so-called 'political offence' exception, the discrimination clause, and the exception concerning fiscal offences.[231] Note that under UNCTOC and UNCAC, the requested state must, where appropriate, consult with the requesting state before refusing extradition.[232]

(i) Political offence exception

It is a well-established principle in many states that extradition may or must be refused if requested in relation to offences of a political character.[233] This ground of refusal is explicitly provided for in the Arab Convention against Transnational Organized Crime.[234] There is no customary definition of a 'political offence' in international law.[235] In practice, the characterization of political offences is left to

[229] With the exception of the Arab Convention against Transnational Organized Crime, which in Art 31 lists specific grounds of refusal that states parties may invoke to deny extradition. This provision seems without prejudice to the right of states parties to rely on other grounds for refusal provided for in their domestic law.

[230] UN Drug Convention, Art 6(5); UNCTOC, Art 16(7); UNCAC, Art 44(8); Criminal Law Convention on Corruption, Art 27(4); OECD Convention on Bribery, Art 10(4); AU Convention on Corruption, Art 15(5); Inter-American Convention against Corruption, Art XIII(5); Inter-American Convention against Arms Trafficking, Art XIX(5); Convention on Cybercrime, Art 24(5).

[231] Jurisdictional immunities are also often invoked by the requested state if the person sought is one of its officials. This issue is dealt with in detail in Chapter 4, Section B.4(a).

[232] UNCTOC, Art 16(16); UNCAC, Art 44(17).

[233] See e.g., in the Bahamas: Extradition Act 1994, s 7(1)(a); in Brazil: Constitution of the Federative Republic of Brazil, Art 5(52); in Canada: Extradition Act, s 46(1)(c); in China: Extradition Law of the People's Republic of China, Art 8(3); in France: Code de procédure pénale, Art 696-4, 2°; in Germany: Gesetz über die internationale Rechtshilfe in Strafsachen, § 6(1); in India: Extradition Act, 1962, s 31(a); in Israel: Extradition Law, s 2B(a)(1); in South Africa: Extradition Act 62 of 1967, s 15; in Spain: Ley de Extradición Pasiva, Art 4(1); in Switzerland: Loi fédérale sur l'entraide internationale en matière pénale, Art 3(1); in the United States: 18 USC § 3181(b)(2). See also Implementation Review Group of the United Nations Convention against Corruption, 7th sess (Vienna, 20–24 June 2016), *Implementation of Chapter IV (International Cooperation) of the United Nations Convention against Corruption (review of Articles 43–50): Thematic report prepared by the Secretariat*, 27 April 2016, UN Doc CAC/COSP/IRG/2016/8, para 16.

[234] Arab Convention against Transnational Organized Crime, Art 31(5).

[235] José Puente Egido, 'L'extradition en droit international : problèmes choisis' (1991) 231 *Recueil des cours de l'Académie de droit international* 9, at 238. See also Christine van den Wijngaert, *The Political Offence Exception to Extradition: The Delicate Problem of Balancing the Rights of the Individual and the International Public Order* (Kluwer, 1980), at 103–104. During the negotiations of the UN Drug Convention, the delegate of Norway, speaking on behalf of Nordic countries, stated that they 'did not accept any restriction on their absolute freedom to assess which offences were political or politically motivated, and had consequently never accepted any language attempting to define such offences in any treaty of international instrument': see United Nations Conference for the Adoption of a Convention against Illicit Traffic in Narcotic Drugs and Psychotropic Substances (Vienna, 25 November – 20 December 1988), *Official Records*, Summary Records of Meetings of Committee I, 27th meeting

the appreciation of the executive or, in some legal systems, of domestic courts.[236] This exercise rests on a combination of objective and subjective criteria. While the nature of the offence and the circumstances surrounding its commission are usually conclusive in determining its political character, the motives of the offender, as well as considerations of proportionality, may also be relevant.[237]

The UN Drug Convention provides that drug offences shall not be considered political offences for the purposes of refusing extradition, although this exclusion remains subject to the domestic law of each state party.[238] Similarly, UNCAC requires states parties whose laws so permit not to consider corruption offences as political offences, but only in cases where they use the Convention as a basis for extradition.[239] Note that other crime-suppression conventions are more stringent, prohibiting states parties from refusing extradition 'on the sole ground that it concerns a political offence or an offence connected with a political offence or an offence inspired by political motives'.[240]

An Explanatory Report to the Council of Europe Convention on Laundering, Search, Seizure and Confiscation of the Proceeds from Crime indicates that drug offences and money laundering as defined under the UN Drug Convention are not to be considered political offences for the purposes of the Convention.[241] Within the EU, the political offence exception has disappeared entirely for the offences subject to the European arrest warrant procedure.[242]

(12 December 1988), at 169, para 35. Neither is there a general definition of political offences in domestic law. In the context of the United Kingdom, Lord Salmon wrote: 'No exhaustive definition of an offence of a political character is possible and none has been attempted': see *Tzu-Tsai Cheng v Governor of Pentonville Prison*, [1973] AC 931, at 961. In Germany, a definition was provided under the 1929 Extradition Law, but it was abandoned in subsequent legislation. The definition used to read as follows: 'Political offences are punishable acts which are directed immediately against the existence or the security of the State, the Head of State or a member of government as such, the institutions and organs of the State established by the constitution, the voting rights of the citizens, or the maintenance of peaceful foreign relations' (Deutsches Auslieferungsgesetz, § 3(2), author's translation).

[236] Puente Egido (n 235), at 173–74.

[237] Ibid, at 169. For a comparative analysis of the definition of the political offences in domestic case law, see ibid, at 173–238; Torsten Stein, *Die Auslieferungsausnahme bei politischen Delikten: Normative Grenzen, Anwendung in der Praxis und Versuch einer Neuformulierung* (Springer, 1983), at 180–337; van den Wijngaert (n 235), at 111–32.

[238] UN Drug Convention, Art 3(10).

[239] UNCAC, Art 44(4).

[240] See e.g. International Convention for the Suppression of Terrorist Bombings, 15 December 1997, entered into force on 23 May 2001, 2149 UNTS 256, Art 11; International Convention for the Suppression of Acts of Nuclear Terrorism, 13 April 2005, entered into force on 7 July 2007, 2445 UNTS 89, Art 15; International Convention for the Suppression of the Financing of Terrorism, 9 December 1999, entered into force on 10 April 2002, 2178 UNTS 197, Art 14.

[241] Council of Europe, *Explanatory Report to the Convention on Laundering, Search, Seizure and Confiscation of the Proceeds from Crime*, 8 November 1990, para 63. Consider also Art 12(1)(b)(i) of the non-binding London Scheme for Extradition within the Commonwealth, which specifies that 'offences of a political character' do not include 'offences established under any multilateral international convention to which the requesting and the requested countries are parties, the purpose of which is to prevent or repress a specific category of offences and which imposes on the parties an obligation either to extradite or to prosecute the person sought'.

[242] The list of permitted grounds for refusal does not include the political offence exception: see Framework Decision on the European arrest warrant, Arts 3 and 4. Before the adoption of the European arrest warrant, certain offences had already been excluded from the scope of the political offence exception: see Convention relating to extradition between the Member States of the European Union, Art 5.

(ii) Discrimination clause

At the same time, extradition may be refused under the relevant universal conventions when the request, as opposed to the offence, is politically motivated.[243] Under the UN Drug Convention, UNCTOC, and UNCAC, the requested state may refuse extradition if

> [it] has substantial grounds for believing that the request has been made for the purpose of prosecuting or punishing a person on account of that person's sex, race, religion, nationality, ethnic origin or political opinions or that compliance with the request would cause prejudice to that person's position for any one of these reasons.[244]

This provision is known as the discrimination clause. It is also present in EU legislation regulating the surrender of alleged offenders between member states.[245]

(iii) Fiscal offence exception

Under UNCTOC and UNCAC, states parties may not refuse extradition 'on the sole ground that the offence is also considered to involve fiscal matters'.[246] This provision is particularly relevant for money laundering cases.

(d) Obligation to extradite or prosecute

The obligation *aut dedere aut judicare*, according to which states parties must take steps to initiate criminal proceedings against a suspected offender found in their territory when they do not extradite him,[247] is a standard provision in crime-suppression conventions. In the treaties pertaining to organized crime and corruption, it comes in a variety of shades. In UNCTOC and UNCAC, it is formulated as follows:

> A State Party in whose territory an alleged offender is found, if it does not extradite such person in respect of an offence to which this article applies solely on the ground that he or she is one of its nationals, shall, at the request of the State Party seeking extradition, be obliged to submit the case without undue delay to its competent authorities for the purpose of prosecution.[248]

243 Former members of the Canadian delegation to the Conference for the adoption of the UN Drug Convention point out that 'few [delegations] were prepared to concede that states should be required to cooperate when a request made pursuant to a Convention offence was only a cover to apprehend and persecute an individual for political reasons': D W Sproule and Paul St-Denis, 'The UN Drug Trafficking Convention: An Ambitious Step' (1989) 27 *Canadian Yearbook of International Law* 263, at 273–74.

244 UNCTOC, Art 16(14); UNCAC, Art 44(15). The wording of Art 6(6) of the UN Drug Convention differs slightly.

245 See Decision on the European arrest warrant, preamble, 12th recital.

246 UNCTOC, Art 16(15); UNCAC, Art 44(16).

247 The formulation of the obligation *aut dedere aut judicare* varies from one treaty to another, and its customary status remains uncertain: see *Fourth report on the obligation to extradite or prosecute (aut dedere aut judicare), by Zdzislaw Galicki, Special Rapporteur*, 31 May 2011, UN Doc A/CN.4/648, at 17–24; M Cherif Bassiouni and Edward M Wise, *Aut Dedere Aut Judicare: The Duty to Extradite or Prosecute in International Law* (Martinus Nijhoff, 1995), at 20–25, 43–69.

248 UNCTOC, Art 16(10); UNCAC, Art 44(11). See also, with slightly different wordings: OECD Convention on Bribery, Art 10(3); Criminal Law Convention on Corruption, Art 27(5); Arab Convention against Corruption, Art 23(11); Inter-American Convention against Arms Trafficking, Art

In this case, the obligation on a requested state party to submit the case to its competent prosecutorial authorities applies solely when extradition is refused on the ground that the person concerned is one of its nationals.[249] In the UN Drug Convention, the obligation applies not only when the requested state party refuses extradition on the ground that the offence was committed by one of its nationals, but also when it does so on the ground that the offence was committed within its territory.[250] In other treaties, the obligation applies more generally when the requested state refuses extradition on the ground that it has jurisdiction over the crime.[251] Under the Optional Protocol to the Convention on the Rights of the Child on the Sale of Children, Child Prostitution and Child Pornography, states parties refusing extradition on the basis of the nationality of the offender are not required to 'submit the case without undue delay', but merely to 'take suitable measures to submit the case' for prosecution.[252] Those important variations notwithstanding, it is striking that in treaties pertaining to organized crime and corruption the obligation *aut dedere aut judicare* is framed differently than in many other crime-suppression conventions, where the obligation is typically formulated as follows:

> The State Party in the territory of which the alleged offender is present shall, if it does not extradite that person, be obliged, without exception whatsoever and whether or not the offence was committed in its territory, to submit the case without undue delay to its competent authorities for the purpose of prosecution.[253]

XIX(6); Optional Protocol to the Convention on the Rights of the Child on the Sale of Children, Child Prostitution and Child Pornography, Art 5(5).

[249] A note to UNCTOC suggests that 'States Parties should also take into consideration the need to eliminate safe havens for offenders who commit heinous crimes in circumstances not covered by [the provisions on the obligation *aut dedere aut judicare*]' (Interpretative Notes for UNCTOC (n 22), para 31).

[250] UN Drug Convention, Art 6(9) in conjunction with Art 4(2)(a). Under Arts 6(9)(b) and 4(2)(b) of the Convention, if a state party chooses to establish its jurisdiction over acts committed by a suspected offender found in its territory when it does not extradite him (that is, irrespective of the ground for refusal), then the obligation *aut dedere aut judicare* is also triggered irrespective of the ground for refusal. The early drug conventions did not limit the application of the obligation *aut dedere aut judicare* to specific grounds for refusal: see Single Convention on Narcotic Drugs, Art 36(2)(a)(iv); Convention on Psychotropic Substances, Art 22(2)(a)(iv).

[251] AU Convention on Corruption, Art 15(6); Criminal Law Convention on Corruption, Art 27(5); Inter-American Convention against Corruption, Art XIII(6); Convention on Cybercrime, Art 24(6). See also, with a different wording, Arab Convention against Transnational Organized Crime, Art 30(3).

[252] Optional Protocol to the Convention on the Rights of the Child on the Sale of Children, Child Prostitution and Child Pornography, Art 5(5).

[253] See e.g. Convention for the Suppression of Unlawful Acts against the Safety of Maritime Navigation, 10 March 1988, entered into force on 1 March 1992, 1678 UNTS 222, Art 10(1); Convention for the Suppression of Unlawful Seizure of Aircraft, 16 December 1970, entered into force on 14 October 1971, 860 UNTS 105, Art 7; Convention on the Prevention and Punishment of Crimes against Internationally Protected Persons, including Diplomatic Agents, 14 December 1973, entered into force on 20 February 1977, 1035 UNTS 167, Art 7; International Convention against the Taking of Hostages, 17 December 1979, entered into force on 3 June 1983, 1316 UNTS 205, Art 7; International Convention for the Suppression of the Financing of Terrorism, Art 10; International Convention for the Suppression of Acts of Nuclear Terrorism, Art 11(1); International Convention for the Suppression of Terrorist Bombings, Art 8. See also Convention against Torture and Other Cruel, Inhuman or Degrading Treatment or Punishment, 10 December 1984, entered into force on 26 June 1987, 1465 UNTS 85, Art 7(1) (in which the words 'without exception whatsoever and whether or not the offence was committed in its territory' do not appear).

In this latter case, the obligation on a state party to submit the case to its competent prosecutorial authorities applies irrespective of the reason why that state chooses not to extradite the person sought. In particular, there is no mention of the necessity of an extradition request, and the obligation *aut dedere aut judicare* applies 'irrespective of the existence of a prior request for the extradition of the suspect', as held by the ICJ in relation to the UN Convention against Torture and Other Cruel, Inhuman or Degrading Treatment or Punishment (Convention against Torture).[254] By contrast, the obligation *aut dedere aut judicare* as defined in the crime-suppression conventions pertaining to organized crime and corruption is triggered only after a state party has been presented with an extradition request.

The so-called 'obligation to prosecute' does not mean that states parties must necessarily put the alleged offender on trial. States parties are obliged merely to submit the case to their competent authorities for the purpose of prosecution. An investigation must be initiated without delay and conducted with diligence[255] but, if the evidence is insufficient, prosecution need not ensue.[256] Nor is there a free-standing obligation to extradite. As the ICJ concluded, '[e]xtradition is an option offered to the State by the Convention, whereas prosecution is an international obligation under the Convention, the violation of which is a wrongful act engaging the responsibility of the State'.[257]

2. Mutual legal assistance and other international cooperation mechanisms

International cooperation in criminal matters is not limited to extradition. Law enforcement authorities are also encouraged to cooperate at all stages of criminal proceedings. While mutual legal assistance between states is generally regulated in detail by regional treaties[258] or bilateral agreements, international instruments pertaining to organized crime and corruption also contain basic provisions on mutual legal assistance. In particular, the provisions of the UN Drug Convention, UNCTOC, and UNCAC aim at setting minimum standards for states parties that are not bound by mutual legal assistance treaties.[259] These provisions apply without prejudice to other

[254] *Questions relating to the Obligation to Prosecute or Extradite (Belgium v Senegal)*, Judgment, ICJ Rep 2012, p 422, at 456, para 94.

[255] Ibid, at 460, paras 112–15. See also UNCTOC, Art 16(10); UNCAC, Art 44(11); Convention on Cybercrime, Art 24(6) (providing that the prosecutorial authorities of the requested state party 'shall take their decision and conduct their proceedings in the same manner as in the case of any other offence of a grave nature under the domestic law of that State Party').

[256] *Questions relating to the Obligation to Prosecute or Extradite* (n 254), at 455, paras 90 and 94.

[257] Ibid, at 456, para 95.

[258] See e.g., for the EU: Convention on Mutual Assistance in Criminal Matters between the Member States of the European Union, 29 May 2000, OJ C197 (12 July 2000) 3; for the ECOWAS: Convention on Mutual Assistance in Criminal Matters, 29 July 1992, entered into force on 28 October 1998, 2329 UNTS 301; for the Americas: Inter-American Convention on Mutual Assistance in Criminal Matters, 23 May 1992, entered into force on 14 April 1996, OASTS no 75; for the Caribbean: Caribbean Treaty on Mutual Legal Assistance in Serious Criminal Matters, 6 July 2005; for the ASEAN: Treaty on Mutual Legal Assistance in Criminal Matters, 29 November 2004, entered into force on 1 June 2005, 2336 UNTS 271.

[259] See UN Drug Convention, Art 7(7); UNCTOC, Art 18(7); UNCAC, Art 46(7).

treaties on mutual legal assistance.[260] Nonetheless, where the provisions of the UN Drug Convention and UNCTOC require a higher level of assistance, commentators disagree as to whether priority should be given to these instruments.[261] It seems that, in accordance with the general principles of the law of treaties, precedence should be given to the *lex posterior*.[262] This section briefly reviews the scope of the regime established by the UN Drug Convention, UNCTOC, and UNCAC.

(a) Scope

States parties are under an obligation to 'afford one another the widest measure of mutual legal assistance in investigations, prosecution and judicial proceedings' with respect to organized crime, corruption, and related offences.[263] Mutual legal assistance may be requested for any of the following purposes:

(a) Taking evidence or statements from persons;
(b) Effecting service of judicial documents;
(c) Executing searches and seizures, and freezing;
(d) Examining objects and sites;
(e) Providing information, evidentiary items and expert evaluations;
(f) Providing originals or certified copies of relevant documents and records, including government, bank, financial, corporate or business records;
(g) Identifying or tracing proceeds of crime, property, instrumentalities or other things for evidentiary purposes;
(h) Facilitating the voluntary appearance of persons in the requesting State [...];
(i) Any other type of assistance that is not contrary to the domestic law of the requested State [...];
(j) Identifying, freezing and tracing proceeds of crime [...];
(k) The recovery of assets [...].[264]

Requests for mutual legal assistance are usually received, processed, and executed by central authorities or other specialized agencies designated by each state party.[265]

[260] UN Drug Convention, Art 7(6); UNCTOC, Art 18(6); UNCAC, Art 46(6).

[261] See Gilmore and McClean (n 1), para 7.20; McClean (n 23), at 214. See *contra* Boister (n 184) at 305. The problem is the same in respect of UNCAC.

[262] See VCLT, Art 30(3) (providing: 'When all the parties to the earlier treaty are parties also to the later treaty but the earlier treaty is not terminated or suspended in operation [...], the earlier treaty applies only to the extent that its provisions are compatible with those of the later treaty').

[263] UN Drug Convention, Art 7(1); UNCTOC, Art 18(1); UNCAC, Art 46(1). See also Criminal Law Convention on Corruption, Art 26(1); OECD Convention on Bribery, Art 9(1); AU Convention on Corruption, Art 18(1); Inter-American Convention against Corruption, Art XIV(1); Inter-American Convention against Arms Trafficking, Art XVII(1).

[264] UNCAC, Art 46(3). This list has progressively expanded: see and compare UNCTOC, Art 18(3), and UN Drug Convention, Art 7(2).

[265] UN Drug Convention, Art 7(8); UNCTOC, Art 18(13); UNCAC, Art 46(13).

In addition to allowing mutual legal assistance on an ad hoc basis, states parties are required generally to improve the exchange of information and facilitate coordination between their respective law enforcement agencies.[266] International cooperation is also required or encouraged in relation to joint investigations,[267] special investigative techniques such as controlled delivery,[268] the confiscation of proceeds of crime and the recovery of assets,[269] training programmes,[270] and research and trend analysis,[271] and for the purposes of providing technical assistance to, and enhancing capacity building in, developing countries.[272]

(b) *Formal requirements*

Formal requirements for mutual legal assistance requests tend to vary from one state to another. Technicalities in the law of the requested state can be challenging for the law enforcement and judicial authorities of the requesting state when swift action is necessary. To make things easier, the UN Drug Convention, UNCTOC, and UNCAC establish minimum formal requirements for submitting a request.[273] Moreover, standards have been set out to address the question of the language of the request,[274] which in practice proves problematic, particularly in states where language is a politically sensitive issue.[275]

(c) *Grounds for refusal*

Relevant crime-suppression conventions prohibit states parties from refusing to grant a request for mutual legal assistance on certain grounds. Because bank secrecy laws can dramatically hinder law enforcement in money-laundering cases, the UN Drug Convention, UNCTOC, and UNCAC, among other instruments, forbid refusal of a request for mutual legal assistance on the ground of bank secrecy.[276] Importantly, this provision is not part of the subsidiary package applicable in the absence of other mutual legal assistance treaties.[277] Rather, it applies to all requests for mutual legal assistance in criminal matters between states parties, regardless of other applicable instruments. UNCTOC and UNCAC also provide that mutual

[266] UN Drug Convention, Art 9(1)(a) and (b); UNCTOC, Art 27; UNCAC, Art 48.
[267] UN Drug Convention, Art 9(1)(c); UNCTOC, Art 19; UNCAC, Art 49.
[268] UN Drug Convention, Art 11; UNCTOC, Art 20; UNCAC, Art 50.
[269] UN Drug Convention, Art 5(4); UNCTOC, Arts 13 and 14; UNCAC, Arts 51–59.
[270] UN Drug Convention, Art 9(2); UNCTOC, Art 29(2) and (4); UNCAC, Art 60(2) and (3).
[271] UN Drug Convention, Art 9(3); UNCTOC, Art 28(2); UNCAC, Art 60(4).
[272] UN Drug Convention, Art 10; UNCTOC, Art 30; UNCAC, Art 62.
[273] UN Drug Convention, Art 7(10); UNCTOC, Art 18(15); UNCAC, Art 46(15).
[274] UN Drug Convention, Art 7(9); UNCTOC, Art 18(14); UNCAC, Art 46(14).
[275] Some states will deny a request not translated into their official language: see Implementation Review Group of UNCAC (n 233), para 40.
[276] UN Drug Convention, Art 7(5); UNCTOC, Art 18(8); UNCAC, Art 46(8). See also Convention on Laundering, Search, Seizure and Confiscation of the Proceeds from Crime, Art 18(7); Criminal Law Convention on Corruption, Art 26(3); OECD Convention on Bribery, Art 9(3); Inter-American Convention against Corruption, Art XVI(1).
[277] Recall the introduction to Section C.2 of this chapter.

legal assistance may not be refused on the ground that the offence is considered to involve fiscal matters.[278]

At the same time, the UN Drug Convention, UNCTOC, and UNCAC contain several grounds on which states parties may refuse to grant a request for mutual legal assistance. First, under UNCTOC and UNCAC states parties may decline mutual legal assistance on the ground of absence of double criminality.[279] In UNCAC, where the basic principles of their legal system so permit, states parties are nevertheless required to render assistance that does not involve coercive action irrespective of double criminality.[280] Secondly and more importantly, grounds for refusal include where 'the requested State Party considers that execution of the request is likely to prejudice its sovereignty, security, *ordre public* or other essential interests'.[281] An interpretative note indicates that the expression 'essential interests' is meant to cover both the discrimination clause and the political offence exception.[282] Finally, states parties may also postpone the execution of a request for mutual legal assistance 'on the ground that it interferes with an ongoing investigation, prosecution or judicial proceeding'.[283]

While states parties are free to rely on any of these grounds to refuse to render mutual legal assistance, they are required to provide an explanation for their refusal in order 'to substantiate [their] good faith in refusing the request'.[284]

D. Seizure and Confiscation of Proceeds of Crime and Other Property

The purpose of targeting illicitly obtained assets is to deprive offenders of the means to further their agenda, and to deter future crimes by increasing the perceived cost of engaging in criminal conduct. Confiscated assets also generate substantial resources to improve law enforcement responses, and can fund compensation for victims. A number of international instruments on organized crime and corruption contain provisions for the confiscation and seizure of proceeds of crime. The measures provided for under the UN Drug Convention, UNCTOC, and UNCAC must be adopted 'to the greatest extent possible within the domestic legal system' of each state party.[285] This section discusses the extent of states parties' obligations concerning the confiscation and seizure of property by reviewing, first, the types of measures required and, second, the categories of assets liable to confiscation. It then discusses the possibility offered by the relevant conventions to reverse the burden of proof in confiscation proceedings.

278 UNCTOC, Art 18(22); UNCAC, Art 46(22).

279 UNCTOC, Art 18(9); UNCAC, Art 46(9)(b).

280 UNCAC, Art 46(9)(b).

281 UN Drug Convention, Art 7(15)(b); UNCTOC, Art 18(21)(b); UNCAC, Art 46(21)(b).

282 Interpretative Notes for UNCTOC (n 22), para 42.

283 UN Drug Convention, Art 7(17); UNCTOC, Art 18(25); UNCAC, Art 46(25).

284 *Certain Questions of Mutual Assistance in Criminal Matters (Djibouti v France)*, Judgment, ICJ Rep 2008, p 177, at 231, para 152. See also at 229, para 145.

285 UN Drug Convention, Art 5(9); UNCTOC, Art 12(1) and (9); UNCAC, Art 31(1) and (10).

1. Types of measures required

The measures targeting illicit assets required by the relevant crime-suppression conventions fall into two categories, namely confiscation, on the one hand, and freezing and seizure, on the other.

(a) Confiscation

States parties to the conventions in question must adopt measures necessary to enable the confiscation of proceeds of crime and other property.[286] Confiscation means 'the permanent deprivation of property by order of a court or other competent authority'.[287] The term 'forfeiture' is often used as a synonym, especially in the United States. Confiscation is to be distinguished from those measures, namely seizure and freezing, not entailing deprivation of property rights.[288]

Confiscation proceedings may be criminal or civil. In France, the confiscation of criminal proceeds is a penalty decided by a judge in criminal proceedings.[289] In England and Wales, confiscation may similarly, at least on the one hand, be ordered by a criminal court upon conviction. It is not necessary to establish that the targeted assets were directly derived from a specific offence; rather, confiscation may be ordered if the court is satisfied that the accused leads a 'criminal lifestyle', that is to say, if he is found to have benefited from his general criminal conduct.[290] On the other hand, the confiscation of illicitly obtained assets in England and Wales may also be undertaken through civil proceedings,[291] in which event the standard of proof is that of the balance of probabilities.[292] In the United States, too, the proceeds of crime may be subject to both criminal[293] and civil forfeiture.[294] In the latter case, the US government may bring *in rem* proceedings against property suspected of being, or having been obtained through, proceeds of crime.[295] Such civil confiscation measures do not

[286] UN Drug Convention, Art 5(1); UNCTOC, Art 12(1); UNCAC, Art 31(1); Criminal Law Convention on Corruption, Art 19(3); Convention on Laundering, Search, Seizure and Confiscation of the Proceeds from Crime, Art 2(1); Council of Europe Convention on Action against Trafficking in Human Beings, Art 23(3); OECD Convention on Bribery, Art 3(3); AU Convention on Corruption, Art 16(1)(b).

[287] UN Drug Convention, Art 1(f); UNCTOC, Art 1(g); UNCAC, Art 1(g).

[288] See Financial Action Task Force, *International Standards on Combating Money Laundering and the Financing of Terrorism and Proliferation: The FATF Recommendations* (June 2017), at 111 ('Confiscation or forfeiture takes place through a judicial or administrative procedure that transfers the ownership of specified funds or other assets to be transferred to the State. In this case, the person(s) or entity(ies) that held an interest in the specified funds or other assets at the time of the confiscation or forfeiture loses all rights, in principle, to the confiscated or forfeited funds or other assets. Confiscation or forfeiture orders are usually linked to a criminal conviction or a court decision whereby the confiscated or forfeited property is determined to have been derived from or intended for use in a violation of the law').

[289] Code pénal, Art 131-21. On the confiscation of assets in France (with a comparative outlook), see Thomas Ballot, 'Réflexions sur les sanctions patrimoniales à la lumière du recouvrement des avoirs issus de la corruption transnationale' (2013) 77 *Revue de science criminelle et de droit pénal comparé* 321.

[290] Proceeds of Crime Act 2002, s 6(4). The notion of 'criminal lifestyle' is further defined under s 10.

[291] Ibid, ss 240 ff. [292] Ibid, s 241(3). [293] 18 USC § 982.

[294] 18 USC § 981. See also 21 USC § 881(a)(6) for the forfeiture of the proceeds of drug offences.

[295] On *in rem* forfeiture in the United States, see generally Stephan D Cassella, *Asset Forfeiture Law in the United States* (2nd edn, Juris, 2013), at 31–37, 213–472, and *passim*.

require that the owner of the assets be convicted or even prosecuted for any crime,[296] and the standard of proof is probable cause.[297]

(b) *Freezing and seizure*

States parties are further required by the relevant conventions to adopt measures necessary to enable the freezing or seizure of proceeds of crime and other property.[298] Freezing and seizure are defined as measures 'temporarily prohibiting the transfer, conversion, disposition or movement of property or temporarily assuming custody or control of property on the basis of an order issued by a court or other competent authority'.[299] Unlike confiscation, freezing and seizure do not entail deprivation of property rights. Although international instruments do not distinguish between freezing and seizure and often use these terms interchangeably, there is a technical difference between the two, namely that in the case of seizure the competent authority often takes control over the property for the purposes of administration or management.[300]

An asset freeze is usually ordered as a provisional measure aimed at preventing the transfer of funds in anticipation of confiscation.[301] Once the illicitly obtained assets have been traced and identified, a freeze can be ordered and implemented with a view to eventual confiscation. States parties are required to empower their courts or other competent authorities to order that bank, financial, or commercial records be made available or seized. Bank secrecy laws may not justify non-compliance with a court order.[302]

2. Property liable to confiscation

Confiscation measures can target a variety of assets. The definition of 'property' is itself very broad, covering 'assets of every kind, whether corporeal or incorporeal, movable or immovable, tangible or intangible, and legal documents or instruments evidencing title to, or interest in, such assets'.[303] At the same time, confiscation

[296] See *United States v $734,578.82 in U.S. Currency*, 286 F3d 641 (3rd Cir 2002), at 657; *United States v Sandini*, 816 F2d 869 (3rd Cir 1987), at 872.

[297] 18 USC § 981(b)(2)(B).

[298] UN Drug Convention, Art 5(2); UNCTOC, Art 12(2); UNCAC, Art 31(2); Council of Europe Convention on Laundering, Search, Seizure and Confiscation of the Proceeds from Crime, Art 11(1); Criminal Law Convention on Corruption, Art 23(1); OECD Convention on Bribery, Art 3(3); AU Convention on Corruption, Art 16(1)(a).

[299] See e.g. UN Drug Convention, Art 1(l); UNCTOC, Art 1(f); UNCAC, Art 1(f).

[300] See FATF Recommendations (n 288), at 117 and 120–21.

[301] See e.g., in England and Wales: Proceeds of Crime Act 2002, ss 40 and 41; in France: Code de procédure pénale, Art 706-103, paragraph 1.

[302] UN Drug Convention, Art 5(3); UNCTOC, Art 12(6); UNCAC, Art 31(7); Criminal Law Convention on Corruption, Art 23(2) and (3); Council of Europe Convention on Laundering, Search, Seizure and Confiscation of the Proceeds from Crime, Art 4(1); AU Convention on Corruption, Art 17(1) and (3).

[303] See e.g. UN Drug Convention, Art 1(q); UNCTOC, Art 1(d); UNCAC, Art 2(d); Council of Europe Convention on Laundering, Search, Seizure and Confiscation of the Proceeds from Crime, Art 1(b).

measures face limitations with respect to state property. An interpretative note to UNCTOC recalls that the rules of international law governing state immunity, in particular immunity from pre- and post-judgment measures of constraint, continue to apply. As a result, 'property belonging to a foreign State and used for non-commercial purposes may not be confiscated except with the consent of the foreign State'.[304] This is in line with customary international law.[305]

(a) *Proceeds of crime and related property*

First, states parties must take appropriate measures to enable the confiscation of proceeds of crime or other property of identical value.[306] Proceeds of crime are defined as 'any property derived from or obtained, directly or indirectly, through the commission of an offence'.[307] Confiscation must be enabled in relation to the crimes defined under the relevant instruments.[308]

Under the UN Drug Convention, UNCTOC, and UNCAC, confiscation must also be made possible with respect to property into which proceeds of crime have been transformed or converted, in part or in full.[309] This applies even if the assets are no longer in the hands of the offender.[310] In addition, when proceeds of crime have been intermingled with property acquired from legitimate sources, states parties must enable the confiscation of such property up to the assessed value of the intermingled proceeds.[311] Furthermore, income or other benefits derived from proceeds of crime, from property into which proceeds of crime have been transformed or converted, or from property with which proceeds of crime have been intermingled, must also be liable to confiscation.[312] An even broader basis for the confiscation of proceeds of crime is provided for in the Council of Europe Convention on Laundering, Search, Seizure and Confiscation of the Proceeds from Crime, which, instead of listing different types of property subject to confiscation, defines proceeds of crime as 'any economic advantage from criminal offences'.[313]

304 Interpretative Notes for UNCTOC (n 22), para 21.

305 See *Jurisdictional Immunities of the State (Germany v Italy; Greece intervening)*, Judgment, ICJ Rep 2012, p 99, at 148, para 118; Convention on Jurisdictional Immunities of States and Their Property, 2 December 2004, UN Doc A/59/49 (not yet in force), Art 19. For an analysis of the challenges posed by sovereign immunity in confiscation proceedings, see Chapter 4, Section B.5.

306 UN Drug Convention, Art 5(1)(a); UNCTOC, Art 12(1)(a); UNCAC, Art 31(1)(a); Convention on Laundering, Search, Seizure and Confiscation of the Proceeds from Crime, Art 2(1); Criminal Law Convention on Corruption, Art 19(3); Council of Europe Convention on Action against Trafficking in Human Beings, Art 23(3); OECD Convention on Bribery, Art 3(3); AU Convention on Corruption, Art 16(1).

307 UN Drug Convention, Art 1(p); UNCTOC, Art 1(e); UNCAC, Art 2(e).

308 A notable exception is the Council of Europe Convention on Laundering, Search, Seizure and Confiscation of the Proceeds from Crime, which applies by default to all criminal offences.

309 UN Drug Convention, Art 5(6)(a); UNCTOC, Art 12(3); UNCAC, Art 31(4).

310 Gilmore and McClean (n 1), para 5.43; McClean (n 23), at 145.

311 UN Drug Convention, Art 5(6)(b); UNCTOC, Art 12(4); UNCAC, Art 31(5).

312 UN Drug Convention, Art 5(6)(c); UNCTOC, Art 12(5); UNCAC, Art 31(6).

313 Convention on Laundering, Search, Seizure and Confiscation of the Proceeds from Crime, Art 1(a). Under Art 2(2), however, states parties may restrict the scope of application of the Convention to specific crimes.

In the case of money laundering, the proceeds of the crime are also those of the predicate offences. As a result, when the proceeds of crimes committed in one state party are laundered in another, the latter is entitled to take action against assets which might otherwise have remained outside its jurisdiction.[314]

(b) *Instrumentalities*

States parties are also required to enable the confiscation of property, materials, equipment, or other instrumentalities used in or destined for use in organized crime and corruption offences.[315] The expression 'destined for use' indicates that property may be confiscated even if no offence was actually committed. According to an interpretative note to UNCTOC, this requires 'an intention of such a nature that it may be viewed as tantamount to an attempt to commit a crime'.[316] An interpretative note to UNCAC also indicates that 'the term "instrumentalities" should not be interpreted in an overly broad manner'.[317]

The confiscation of instrumentalities in the context of drug offences is used in respect of not only the drugs themselves but also precursor chemicals, laboratory facilities, and other items involved in the drug-manufacturing process. In the context of corruption offences, it allows for the confiscation of bribes. As regards arms trafficking, the Inter-American Convention against Arms Trafficking requires states parties to confiscate 'firearms, ammunition, explosives, and other related materials that have been illicitly manufactured or trafficked'.[318]

3. Reversal of the burden of proof

To facilitate confiscation proceedings, whether criminal or civil, some international instruments encourage states parties to consider reversing the onus of proof to make it incumbent on the offender to demonstrate the licit origin of his property[319]—in other words, to establish a presumption that assets held by a person convicted of an offence are proceeds of crime.[320] Although this evidentiary technique can be effective,

[314] Stessens (n 105), at 217. For a recent illustration, see *affaire des biens mal acquis* (n 159).

[315] UN Drug Convention, Art 5(1)(b); UNCTOC, Art 12(1)(b); UNCAC, Art 31(1)(b); Convention on Laundering, Search, Seizure and Confiscation of the Proceeds from Crime, Art 2(1); Criminal Law Convention on Corruption, Art 19(3); Council of Europe Convention on Action against Trafficking in Human Beings, Art 23(3); OECD Convention on Bribery, Art 3(3); AU Convention on Corruption, Art 16(1)(a).

[316] Interpretative Notes for UNCTOC (n 22), para 22.

[317] Interpretative Notes for UNCAC (n 59), para 63.

[318] Inter-American Convention against Arms Trafficking, Art VII(1).

[319] See UN Drug Convention, Art 5(7); UNCTOC, Art 12(7); UNCAC, Art 31(8).

[320] Such a presumption applies in England and Wales, where the concept of 'criminal lifestyle' plays a central role in confiscation proceedings (see n 290). It also applies in French law, where the offender has been convicted of an offence punishable by at least five years of imprisonment and which has generated direct or indirect profit (Code pénal, Art 131-21, para 5).

it raises concerns over the presumption of innocence[321] and the protection against double jeopardy[322] guaranteed by international human rights law.[323]

E. Conclusion

The survey of the treaty obligations of states parties to crime-suppression conventions pertaining to organized crime and corruption conducted in this chapter lays the foundation for an analysis of the limits of these instruments in cases of state organized crime. The argument to follow will highlight the shortcomings, for the specific purpose of combating state organized crime, of the legal framework presented in this chapter, and discuss potential avenues of action to develop international legal responses to state organized crime.

[321] The European Court of Human Rights, however, has repeatedly upheld the conformity of confiscation measures, whether criminal or civil, with the European Convention on Human Rights. See in particular *Phillips v United Kingdom*, App no 41087/98, ECHR 2001-VII, paras 34–36 (ruling that confiscation measures do not amount to a 'criminal charge' within the meaning of Art 6(2) of the Convention since their purpose is not the conviction or acquittal of the accused).

[322] As regards civil confiscation, the International Association of Penal Law takes the view that 'non-criminal prosecutions and decisions with an equivalent punitive function as well should bar a new prosecution': Resolutions of the XVIIth International Congress of Penal Law (Beijing, 12–19 September 2004), Section IV: Concurrent National and International Criminal Jurisdiction and the Principle '*Ne bis in idem*' in José Luis de la Cuesta (ed), *Resolutions of the Congresses of the International Association of Penal Law (1926–2004)* (Érès, 2009) 203, at 204. See also R Thomas Naylor, 'Follow-the-Money Methods in Crime Control Policy' in Margaret E Beare (ed), *Critical Reflexions on Transnational Organized Crime, Money Laundering, and Corruption* (University of Toronto Press, 2003) 256, at 281–82.

[323] See ICCPR, Art 14(2) and (7); Convention for the Protection of Human Rights and Fundamental Freedoms, Art 6(2); Protocol No 7 to the Convention for the Protection of Human Rights and Fundamental Freedoms, 22 November 1984, entered into force on 1 November 1988, 1525 UNTS 195, Art 4(1).

4

The Limits of Applicable Crime-suppression Conventions

This chapter highlights the limits of relevant international criminal law instruments in cases of state organized crime, with a view to demonstrating the need for dedicated legal responses against this phenomenon at the international level. First, it stresses that the fragmentation of the applicable law undermines the establishment of coherent standards across national jurisdictions. Secondly, it discusses the procedural shortcomings of the enforcement model provided by these instruments when applied to cases of state organized crime. The chapter finally draws attention to the failure of the existing law to perform a crucial expressive function with respect to state organized crime, arguing that, because international law does not adequately take account of the involvement of state officials and resources in organized crime, it fails to address the unique harm and wrongfulness inherent in state organized crime.

A. Fragmentation of the Law

The suppression of state organized crime would require a unified and coherent legal regime, yet the applicable law is fragmented. Such lack of coherence results from a combination of three factors. First, the multiplication of international instruments pertaining to organized crime and corruption has created a patchwork of overlapping and sometimes uneven legal regimes. Secondly, the wording of certain provisions allows for significant variations in the implementation of the relevant treaties. Thirdly, in these instruments the permissive use of reservations has created discrepancies among states parties.

1. Normative dispersal

The fragmentation of the applicable law is attributable, first, to 'the piecemeal approach of international criminal law'[1] and the dispersal of norms across different instruments. Different aspects of both substantive and procedural law relevant to the suppression of organized crime and corruption are regulated by at least

[1] M Cherif Bassiouni, 'Introduction' in Dawn L Rothe and Christopher W Mullins (eds), *State Crime: Current Perspectives* (Rutgers University Press, 2011), at 15.

eleven universal treaties, and fourteen regional instruments.[2] While many provisions overlap to a significant extent, the legal regime established by these instruments, when considered as a whole, is far from uniform and coherent. On the macro level, discrepancies are evident when comparing the provisions of universal crime-suppression conventions with those of regional instruments. The difference is striking as between, on the one hand, the UN Drug Convention, UNCTOC, and UNCAC, which contain elaborate provisions on extradition and mutual legal assistance in criminal matters, and, on the other, their regional counterparts, which lay down only basic requirements in this regard. Yet, regional instruments are occasionally more advanced. For instance, the Inter-American, AU, and Arab conventions against corruption require states parties to criminalize abuse of functions and, subject to the fundamental principles of their domestic law, illicit enrichment, whereas the provisions of UNCAC regarding abuse of functions and illicit enrichment are not mandatory for states parties.[3] On the micro level, slight variations of language, from one treaty to another, in clauses dealing with a same subject, translate into different legal obligations and may result in inconsistent practices. For example, there are at least four different legal standards for the obligation *aut dedere aut judicare* in different treaties.[4]

2. Provisions with broad or permissive language

Fragmentation also results from the discretion left to states parties by overly flexible provisions phrased in a broad or permissive language, most likely as a result of drafting compromises necessary to secure sufficient participation in the treaties. Where the required standards are defined in broad or unspecific terms by the treaty, implementation will not be consistent across states parties, undermining domestic

[2] Namely, for universal treaties: the UN Drug Convention, UNCTOC, the UNCTOC Human Trafficking Protocol, the UNCTOC Migrants Smuggling Protocol, the UNCTOC Firearms Protocol, UNCAC, the Convention on International Trade in Endangered Species of Wild Fauna and Flora, the Convention on the Control of Transboundary Movements of Hazardous Wastes and their Disposal, the Convention on the Means of Prohibiting and Preventing the Illicit Import, Export and Transfer of Ownership of Cultural Property, the International Convention for the Suppression of Counterfeiting Currency, and the Optional Protocol to the Convention on the Rights of the Child on the Sale of Children, Child Prostitution and Child Pornography; for regional treaties: the Arab Convention against Illicit Traffic in Narcotic Drugs and Psychotropic Substances, the Arab Convention against Transnational Organized Crime, the Arab Convention against Corruption, the AU Convention on Corruption, the OECD Convention on Bribery, the Convention on the fight against corruption involving officials of the European Communities or officials of Member States of the European Union, the Criminal Law Convention on Corruption, the Inter-American Convention against Corruption, the Inter-American Convention against Arms Trafficking, the Inter-American Convention on International Traffic in Minors, the Convention on Laundering, Search, Seizure and Confiscation of the Proceeds from Crime, the Convention on Cybercrime, the Arab Convention on Combating Information Technology Offences, and the Convention on the Ban of the Import into Africa and the Control of Transboundary Movement and Management of Hazardous Wastes within Africa—to which should be added relevant pieces of EU legislation.

[3] See and compare, on the one hand, UNCAC, Arts 15–20, and, on the other, Inter-American Convention against Corruption, Arts VI–IX, AU Convention on Corruption, Arts 4, 5(1), and 8, and Arab Convention against Corruption, Art 4(6) and (7).

[4] Recall Chapter 3, Section C.1(d).

law enforcement against the type of crime contemplated by the treaty as well as international cooperation. This problem is particularly acute in the implementation of the offence of participation in an organized criminal group defined under UNCTOC. The very broad definition of 'organized criminal group' provided by UNCTOC has been implemented with significant discrepancies in the domestic law of states parties. Some states parties that already had within their domestic law offences for the fight against organized crime did not adapt their legislation to match the UNCTOC definition, while legislation adopted in other states parties for the purpose of implementing the provisions of UNCTOC has taken many forms depending on domestic practices and conceptions of what constitutes a criminal organization.[5] Similarly, Boister argues that the concept of 'serious crime' is so unspecific that UNCTOC 'cannot be used to prescribe to states parties what to criminalize and when to use its provisions, because the discretion remains with those parties'.[6] A similar issue arises with some regional instruments requiring states parties to criminalize acts that are defined nowhere in the treaty.[7]

Moreover, discrepancies in domestic laws persist where states parties are left free not to adopt certain measures, for example in the case of Article 20 of UNCAC, which merely requires states parties to 'consider' establishing illicit enrichment as a criminal offence. In 2016, the Implementation Review Group of UNCAC[8] noted that in half of the states parties under review, illicit enrichment had not been established as a criminal offence.[9]

3. Reservations

The last element of fragmentation is the possibility for states parties to make reservations to key provisions of the relevant treaties. While the availability of reservations is necessary to encourage maximum participation in the treaties,[10] allowing

[5] See the analysis in Neil Boister, 'The UN Convention against Transnational Organized Crime 2000' in Pierre Hauck and Sven Peterke (eds), *International Law and Transnational Organized Crime* (Oxford University Press, 2016) 126, at 140–41.

[6] Ibid, at 149.

[7] See Arab Convention against Corruption, Art 4; Arab Convention on Combating Information Technology Offences, Art 16.

[8] The Implementation Review Group is an organ of the Conference of States Parties to UNCAC tasked with overviewing the review process within the framework of the Mechanism established pursuant to Art 63(7) of UNCAC to review the implementation of the Convention in the domestic law of states parties. See Conference of the States Parties to the United Nations Convention against Corruption, 3rd sess (Doha, 9–13 November 2009), Resolution 3/1.

[9] Implementation Review Group of UNCAC, 7th sess (Vienna, 20–24 June 2016), *Implementation of Chapter III (Criminalization and Law Enforcement) of the United Nations Convention against Corruption (review of Articles 15–29): Thematic report prepared by the Secretariat*, 15 April 2016, UN Doc CAC/COSP/IRG/2016/6, para 14. Those findings are based on the first review cycle, including data from 123 states parties.

[10] See Alain Pellet, 'Article 19 – Convention of 1969' in Olivier Corten and Pierre Klein (eds), *The Vienna Conventions on the Law of Treaties: A Commentary* (Oxford University Press, 2011) 405, at 418–19 ('The prerequisite of universality coerces to open as broadly as possible the rights of States to formulate reservations which, evidently, facilitate universal participation in treaties').

reservations to certain provisions strongly undermines the foundations of the law relevant to the suppression of state organized crime.

For example, the concept of 'serious crime', upon which the applicability of UNCTOC is premised, is understood by Ukraine to apply to offences punished by a sentence of at least five years of imprisonment, and not four as required under Article 2(b) of UNCTOC.[11] Panama, for its part, does not adhere to the provisions of the UN Drug Convention requiring states parties to enable confiscation in value.[12] Moreover, Ethiopia and Yemen have declared themselves not bound by the provisions of Article 44 of UNCAC, which governs extradition proceedings with respect to the offences defined under the Convention.[13] Vietnam has done the same with respect to Article 6 of the UN Drug Convention pertaining to extradition.[14]

Given that a key objective of the UN Drug Convention, UNCTOC, and UNCAC is to foster international cooperation against organized crime and corruption,[15] reservations excluding the applicability of the provisions governing extradition seem to be incompatible with the object and purpose of the treaties,[16] and could therefore be considered impermissible[17] and devoid of legal effect.[18]

Reservations are also problematic in the particular case of the Convention on International Trade in Endangered Species of Wild Fauna and Flora. When the list of endangered species is amended to include a new species, states parties have the possibility to formulate a reservation in order not to be bound by the provisions of

[11] Reservation of Ukraine, 21 May 2004, 2261 UNTS 286.

[12] Reservation of Panama, 13 January 1994, 1762 UNTS 259. However, Panama did not make reservations to similar provisions of UNCTOC and UNCAC.

[13] Reservation of Yemen, 7 November 2005, 2349 UNTS 367; Reservation of Ethiopia, 26 November 2007, 2482 UNTS 310.

[14] Reservation of Vietnam, 4 November 1997, 1996 UNTS 436.

[15] UN Drug Convention, preamble, 14th recital; UN General Assembly Resolution 55/25, 15 November 2000, UN Doc A/RES/55/25, preamble, 7th and 9th recitals; UNCAC, preamble, 4th recital.

[16] According to the ILC, '[a] reservation is incompatible with the object and purpose of the treaty if it affects an essential element of the treaty that is necessary to its general tenor, in such a way that the reservation impairs the *raison d'être* of the treaty' (Guide to Practice on Reservations to Treaties, in *Report of the International Law Commission* (63rd sess), UN Doc A/66/10/Add.1 in *Yearbook of the International Law Commission* (2011), vol 2(II), at 351, Principle 3.1.5). See also Pellet (n 10), at 450–51 (speaking of the 'efficiency', '*rasion d'être*', and 'fundamental core' of the treaty).

[17] VCLT, Art 19(c); Guide to Practice on Reservations to Treaties (n 16), at 403, Principle 3.3.1.

[18] Guide to Practice on Reservations to Treaties (n 16), at 509, Principle 4.5.1; Pellet (n 10), at 478, 481. State practice indicates that the validity of reservations does not depend on the objection or the acceptance by other contracting states: see Guide to Practice on Reservations to Treaties (n 16), at 520, Principle 4.5.2, and commentaries thereunder. The jurisprudence of the ICJ is not conclusive on this point: see *Reservations to the Convention on the Prevention and Punishment of the Crime of Genocide*, Advisory Opinion, ICJ Rep 1951, p 15, at 24, 26 (ruling that each contracting state has to appraise the permissibility of reservations independently and that the legal effects of a reservation deemed incompatible with the object and purpose of the treaty will depend on the objection or the acceptance by other contracting states); but see *Armed Activities on the Territory of the Congo (New Application: 2002) (Democratic Republic of the Congo v Rwanda)*, Order of 10 July 2002, ICJ Rep 2002, p 219, at 246, para 72, and Jurisdiction and Admissibility, Judgment, ICJ Rep 2006, p 6, at 32, para 67 (undertaking an independent assessment of the permissibility of a reservation with regard to the object and purpose of a treaty). On the doctrinal controversies concerning the objective or subjective admissibility of reservations, see Jean Kyongun Koh, 'Reservations to Multilateral Treaties: How International Legal Doctrine Reflects World Vision' (1982) 23 *Harvard International Law Journal* 71, at 73–76 and *passim*.

the Convention with respect to the trade in specimens of the species in question.[19] As a result, although all states parties are required to criminalize illicit trafficking in endangered species, trade in a particular species may constitute a criminal offence in some states parties but not in others.[20]

B. Procedural Limits Hindering Law Enforcement

Treaties pertaining to organized crime and corruption are subject to significant procedural limits in cases of state organized crime. A number of such limits result from the provisions of the treaties themselves. The existing instruments rest on an imperfect compromise between two models of enforcement, accommodating both the interests of certain states favouring the use of extraterritorial jurisdiction and extradition, and the concerns of other states over the respect of their sovereignty.[21] In politicized cases involving senior state officials, this mixed model often proves deficient. It is suggested, first, that the provisions governing jurisdiction are ineffective in cases of state organized crime. The same can be said, secondly, of the provisions regulating extradition and mutual legal assistance in criminal matters. Thirdly and consequently, it is argued that the obligation *aut dedere aut judicare* is framed too narrowly in the relevant instruments.

In addition, the existing crime-suppression conventions remain subject to procedural bars under general international law. Criminal proceedings involving state officials may be hindered by jurisdictional immunities and similar legal principles precluding domestic courts from exercising jurisdiction over the conduct of foreign state officials. The law of immunities can also hinder the confiscation of property.

1. The limits of territorial jurisdiction

The crime-suppression model adopted in treaties pertaining to organized crime and corruption is centred on territorial jurisdiction. The jurisdictional provisions in the relevant crime-suppression conventions often do not explicitly encompass the objective territorial principle. Some instruments, notably crime-suppressions conventions against corruption, allow states to make use of the objective territorial principle, but generally do not require them to do so.[22] It is difficult to discern

[19] Convention on International Trade in Endangered Species of Wild Fauna and Flora, Art XV(3).

[20] See generally Gwyneth G Stewart, 'Enforcement Problems in the Endangered Species Convention: Reservations Regarding the Reservation Clauses' (1981) 14 *Cornell International Law Journal* 429.

[21] Neil Boister, 'The Trend to Universal Extradition over Subsidiary Universal Jurisdiction in the Suppression of Transnational Crime' (2003) *Acta Juridica* 287, at 312–13.

[22] See OECD Convention on Bribery, Art 4(1); Criminal Law Convention on Corruption, Art 17(1)(a); Convention on the fight against corruption involving officials of the European Communities or officials of Member States of the European Union, Art 7(1)(a); AU Convention on Corruption, Art 13(1)(a); Arab Convention against Transnational Organized Crime, Art 39(1)(a). For UNCAC, see Ad Hoc Committee for the Negotiation of a Convention against Corruption, *Interpretative Notes for the Official Records (travaux préparatoires) of the Negotiation of the United Nations Convention against Corruption*, 7 October 2003, UN Doc A/58/422/Add.1, para 41. Within the EU, see Framework

the rationale for not recognizing objective territoriality in respect of other crimes, especially offences related to transnational trafficking in drugs or human beings. Moreover, applicable instruments make very little use of the effects and protective doctrines of jurisdiction.[23]

This marked preference for territoriality makes sense when the state of the *locus delicti* is willing and able to prosecute the offender. When, however, senior officials of that state are involved in the commission of a serious offence, it is often unlikely that proceedings will be initiated in the latter state as long as the perpetrators hold an influential position, especially if their crimes were committed pursuant to state policy. Even in states with a strong tradition of judicial independence, domestic prosecutorial authorities and courts are not immune to corruption or coercion. As a result, prospects for holding perpetrators responsible may be contingent on the prosecutorial policy of third states in a position to claim concurrent jurisdiction. The effectiveness of the extradition-based model of enforcement, depending as it does 'as much on the political willingness of requested states to assume the international obligation to fight crime as upon their legal capacity to do so', is compromised in 'the most highly politicized cases where extradition proves impossible'.[24] The exercise of jurisdiction against senior public officials of a state by the authorities of another state indeed tends to generate a high level of tension.[25] This problem could partially be solved if, in contrast to the present situation,[26] the obligation *aut dedere aut judicare* were framed in the relevant treaties so as to require a requested state party, should it not extradite an alleged offender, to initiate proceedings itself.

2. Obstacles to international cooperation in criminal matters

The provisions governing extradition and mutual legal assistance in criminal matters in the relevant treaties can in some circumstances prove inadequate in proceedings concerning senior public officials involved in state organized crime.

(a) Inapplicability of UNCTOC and its Protocols to purely domestic criminality

Although states parties are required to criminalize conduct defined under UNCTOC and its Protocols irrespective of the existence of a transnational element,[27] the

Decision on the constituent elements of criminal acts and penalties in the field of illicit drug trafficking, Art 8(1)(a); Framework Decision on combating trafficking in human beings, Art 6(1)(a); Framework Decision on the fight against organized crime, Art 7(1)(a). EU legislation is more permissive.

[23] Recall Chapter 3, Sections B.1(d) and (e).

[24] Boister (n 21), at 313.

[25] See e.g. the position of the AU Assembly condemning the use by non-African states of universal jurisdiction against African leaders: Decision 199 (XI), 'Decision on the Report of the Commission on the Abuse of the Principle of Universal Jurisdiction', 1 July 2008 ('The abuse of the Principle of Universal Jurisdiction is a development that could endanger International law, order and security' and '[t]he political nature and abuse of the principle of universal jurisdiction [...] is a clear violation of the sovereignty and territorial integrity of [African] States').

[26] See Section B.3 of this chapter.

[27] UNCTOC, Art 34(2); Ad Hoc Committee on the Elaboration of a Convention against Transnational Organized Crime, *Interpretative Notes for the Official Records (travaux préparatoires) of the*

application of UNCTOC 'to the prevention, investigation and prosecution' of such offences is limited to situations 'where the offence is transnational in nature'.[28] An offence is 'transnational in nature' if

(*a*) It is committed in more than one State;
(*b*) It is committed in one State but a substantial part of its preparation, planning, direction or control takes place in another State;
(*c*) It is committed in one State but involves an organized criminal group that engages in criminal activities in more than one State; or
(*d*) It is committed in one State but has substantial effects in another State.[29]

The mechanisms of international cooperation in criminal matters established in UNCTOC remain inapplicable to organized crime committed in a purely domestic context. This may cause difficulty if, for example, the surrender of a suspect or the testimony of key witnesses can be obtained only with the assistance of a state with which the forum state does not share any extradition or other mutual legal assistance treaty.

(b) *The 'essential interests' clause*

It is problematic that under the UN Drug Convention, UNCTOC, and UNCAC, mutual legal assistance may be refused by the requested state if the request is deemed 'to prejudice its sovereignty, security, *ordre public* or other essential interests'.[30] The ICJ has observed that such clauses grant states parties 'a very considerable discretion'.[31] A commentator suggests that '[t]he provision is so broadly worded that it provides a blanket opt-out provision undermining mutual legal assistance'.[32] Although the 'essential interest' clause remains subject to the requirement of good faith,[33] it can provide a basis for dismissing requests for assistance formulated in connection to an investigation concerning politically sensitive allegations. Interestingly, the United States has interpreted this provision as allowing it to 'deny a request for assistance when the designated authority [. . .] has specific information that a senior government official who will have access to information to be provided under [the UN Drug Convention] is engaged in or facilitates the production or distribution of illegal drugs'.[34]

Negotiation of the United Nations Convention against Transnational Organized Crime and the Protocols Thereto, 3 November 2000, UN Doc A/55/383/Add.1, para 59.

[28] UNCTOC, Art 3(1). [29] Ibid, Art 3(2).

[30] UN Drug Convention, Art 7(15)(b); UNCTOC, Art 18(21)(b); UNCAC, Art 46(21)(b).

[31] *Certain Questions of Mutual Assistance in Criminal Matters (Djibouti v France)*, Judgment, ICJ Rep 2008, p 177, at 229, para 145.

[32] Neil Boister, *Penal Aspects of the UN Drug Conventions* (Kluwer Law International, 2001), at 321.

[33] *Certain Questions of Mutual Assistance in Criminal Matters* (n 31), at 229, para 145; VCLT, Art 26.

[34] Declaration of the United States of America, 20 December 1988, 1582 UNTS 406, at 406–407.

(c) *Denial of assistance in cases of concurrent investigations*

Under the UN Drug Convention, UNCTOC, and UNCAC, states parties may postpone the execution of a request for mutual legal assistance on the ground that the request 'interferes with an ongoing investigation, prosecution or judicial proceeding'.[35] Although, as a matter of international law, states remain obliged to perform their treaty obligations in good faith and in particular to refrain from acts that would defeat the object and purpose of the treaty,[36] in effect this may allow states parties to use sham proceedings as a pretext to defer assistance indefinitely.

(d) *The requirement of double criminality*

The requirement of double criminality, which remains 'a standard condition for extradition' in many states,[37] can also undermine international cooperation in criminal matters. Under UNCTOC and UNCAC, states parties may still deny mutual legal assistance or extradition on the ground that the offence for which assistance or extradition is requested is not criminalized under their domestic law.[38] The recognition of the requirement of double criminality in UNCTOC and UNCAC poses several problems.

At first sight, the persistence of the requirement of double criminality may appear of little relevance, given that all states parties are obliged to criminalize the same criminal conduct.[39] In UNCTOC, however, the provisions defining the offence of participation in an organized criminal group offer states parties a choice between two alternatives with distinct constitutive elements.[40] Moreover, in UNCTOC the notion of 'serious crime'[41] covers very different forms of criminal conduct and, as a

[35] UN Drug Convention, Art 7(17); UNCTOC, Art 18(25); UNCAC, Art 46(25).

[36] Recall Chapter 2, Section C.2.

[37] Implementation Review Group of the United Nations Convention against Corruption, 7th sess (Vienna, 20–24 June 2016), *Implementation of Chapter IV (International Cooperation) of the United Nations Convention against Corruption (review of Articles 43–50): Thematic report prepared by the Secretariat*, 27 April 2016, UN Doc CAC/COSP/IRG/2016/8, para 13.

[38] UNCTOC, Arts 16(1) and 18(9); UNCAC, Arts 44(1) and 46(9). However, in the majority of states parties to UNCAC under review during the first review cycle, double criminality is not a requirement for granting mutual legal assistance: see Implementation Review Group of UNCAC (n 37), para 35.

[39] See Gérard Cahin, 'La double incrimination dans le droit de l'extradition' (2013) 117 *Revue générale de droit international public* 579, at 593–94. During the negotiations of UNCAC, some delegations expressed the view that double criminality might not be required 'if it was sufficiently clear which offences would be covered': see Ad Hoc Committee for the Negotiation of a Convention against Corruption, 3rd sess (Vienna, 30 September – 11 October 2002), *Revised draft United Nations Convention against Corruption*, 5 July 2002, UN Doc A/AC.261/3/Rev.1/Add.1, n 72.

[40] Recall Chapter 3, Section A.7. Issues of double criminality arise for example in relation to complex offences under US law such as 'continuing criminal enterprise' (21 USC § 848(b)) and offences defined under the Racketeer Influenced and Corrupt Organizations Act (18 USC §§ 1961–1968): see Jonathan O Hafen, 'International Extradition: Issues Arising under the Dual Criminality Requirement' (1992) *Brigham Young University Law Review* 191, at 208–14; Steven A Bernholz, Martin J Bernholz, and G Nicolas Herman, 'International Extradition in Drug Cases' (1985) 10 *North Carolina Journal of International Law and Commercial Regulation* 353, at 358 ff.

[41] UNCTOC, Arts 2(a), 3(1)(b), and 5.

result, for any offence falling under this label 'no obligation to extradite arises unless th[e] dual criminality requirement is fulfilled'.[42]

Furthermore, the requirement of double criminality may be particularly problematic when the definition of the offence for which extradition is sought refers to predicate offences, as is the case with money laundering[43] or participation in an organized criminal group. When the relevant predicate offence is not criminalized in the law of the requested state party, extradition may be refused.

In addition, the requirement of double criminality may not be satisfied when the law of the requested state party does not itself employ the jurisdictional basis on which the requesting state party asserts jurisdiction. Observers note that 'insistence upon correspondence of jurisdiction for the particular offence in question may prove to be a major obstacle to extradition'.[44] For example, extradition requests emanating from the United States in respect of drug offences have repeatedly been denied by states that do not assert the extensive extraterritorial jurisdiction provided for by US law.[45]

Lastly, the requirement of double criminality may have the perverse effect of allowing states parties to refuse extradition so long as they do not take appropriate steps to comply with their obligation to establish particular offences in their domestic law. Although it is a central principle of the law of treaties that '[a] party may not invoke the provisions of its internal law as justification for its failure to perform a treaty',[46] in practice it would not be wholly unthinkable for a state party to deny extradition on that basis with the intention of shielding an alleged offender from foreign criminal proceedings.

(e) The evidentiary threshold

Extradition in respect of corruption and organized crime can also be undermined because the existing treaties do not resolve discrepancies between states parties with regard to the evidence required to be provided in support of a request. In 2012, the Implementation Review Group of UNCAC recorded a '[l]ack of uniformity [...] in terms of evidentiary threshold prescribed by domestic laws in order to grant extradition'.[47] Common-law countries usually require that the requesting state provide

[42] UNODC, *Legislative Guide for the Implementation of the United Nations Convention against Transnational Organized Crime and the Protocols Thereto* (United Nations, 2004), para 417.

[43] Some states adhere to the requirement of double criminality concerning the predicate offences of money laundering: see Guy Stessens, *Money Laundering: A New International Law Enforcement Model* (Cambridge University Press, 2000), at 228–29, and the examples cited therein. During the negotiations of UNCTOC, Poland suggested specifying that '[t]he establishment of double criminality with respect to money-laundering is not conditional upon the predicate offence': see Ad Hoc Committee on the Elaboration of a Convention against Transnational Organized Crime, 4th sess (Vienna, 28 June – 9 July 1999), *Proposals and contributions received from Governments—Poland*, 18 May 1999, UN Doc A/AC.254/5/Add.7. This provision, however, did not appear in the final draft of the Convention.

[44] Boister (n 21), at 298. [45] See Hafen (n 40), at 214–24. [46] See VCLT, Art 27.

[47] Implementation Review Group of UNCAC, 3rd sess (Vienna, 18–22 June 2012), *Implementation of Chapter IV (International Cooperation) of the United Nations Convention against Corruption: Thematic report prepared by the Secretariat*, 12 June 2012, UN Doc CAC/COSP/IRG/2012/CRP.2, para 23. See also the latest findings of the Implementation Review Group of UNCAC (n 37), para 25.

evidence in support of the request.[48] Australia and the United Kingdom generally demand that the requesting state make out a prima facie case,[49] although the United Kingdom exempts a number of states from this condition.[50] By contrast, civil-law countries generally do not mandate an evidentiary threshold for extradition,[51] although evidentiary issues may nonetheless arise. For example, Peru's request to Chile to have former Peruvian President Alberto Fujimori extradited on charges of crimes against humanity and corruption was rejected in first instance, on the ground that the charges were insufficiently supported by evidence.[52]

(f) The political offence exception

The political offence exception is a well-established ground for refusal in many states.[53] Offences defined in the UN Drug Convention and UNCAC are in principle not to be considered political offences, with the qualification that domestic law may still provide otherwise.[54] No such limitation applies in respect of the offences defined in UNCTOC and its Protocols. Moreover, in contrast to the terrorism conventions,[55] nothing in crime-suppression conventions pertaining to organized crime and corruption precludes states parties from refusing extradition on the ground that the crime is connected to a political offence.[56] In the Arab Convention against Transnational Organized Crime, the political offence exception is even enshrined as a valid ground for refusing extradition.[57]

The political offence exception was successfully raised by notorious arms trafficker Viktor Bout before the Criminal Court of Bangkok to oppose his extradition to the United States on charges of conspiracy linked to illicit arms trade with the Revolutionary Armed Forces of Colombia. The Court refused to grant the

48 See e.g., in Canada: Extradition Act (SC 1999, c. 18), s 33(3)(a).

49 See, in Australia: Extradition Act 1988, ss 11(4) and (5) and 19(2); in the United Kingdom: Extradition Act 2003, s 84(1). The authorities of the requesting state must submit evidence which would be sufficient to open an inquiry in relation to the offence.

50 See Extradition Act 2003, s 84(7); Extradition Act 2003 (Designation of Part 2 Territories) Order 2003, SI 2003/3334, and the countries listed therein (which include France, Germany, the Netherlands, Russia, and the United States).

51 See e.g. the requirements in France: Code de procédure pénale, Art 696-8.

52 Decision of Judge Orlando Álvarez, 11 July 2007. On appeal, the Supreme Court found that there was sufficient evidence to support some of the charges, allowing Alberto Fujimori to be extradited to Peru (Corte Suprema, 21 September 2007, Case no 2242-06, reproduced in English in ILDC 1443 (CL 2007)). See Rodrigo Lledó Vásquez, 'Comentarios sobre la Sentencia de Extradición de Alberto Fujimori Fujimori' (2008) 4 *Anuario de Derechos Humanos* 107.

53 See n 37.

54 UN Drug Convention, Art 3(10); UNCAC, Art 44(4).

55 See e.g. International Convention for the Suppression of Terrorist Bombings, Art 11; International Convention for the Suppression of Acts of Nuclear Terrorism, Art 15; International Convention for the Suppression of the Financing of Terrorism, Art 14.

56 For an illustration of the argument that financial crimes may be connected to a political offence, see e.g. *Jiménez v Aristeguieta*, 311 F2d 547 (5th Cir 1962), at 558–60 (concerning extradition proceedings initiated in the United States by Venezuela with a view to obtaining the surrender of former Venezuelan President Marcos Pérez Jiménez, notably on charges of embezzlement. Jiménez argued that the financial crimes for which he was sought by Venezuela were connected to murders committed for political purposes. The argument was rejected by the Court).

57 Arab Convention against Transnational Organized Crime, Art 31(5).

extradition request on the ground that the offence for which Bout was charged was a political offence, his activities constituting 'political support' to the insurgents.[58] Extradition could be challenged on this ground in cases of criminal activities carried out against the interests of a foreign state, for instance in the case of covert operations designed to destabilize a foreign government. Boister points out that 'rebel groups in the developing world that use drug trafficking as a source of funding may counter that they have a legitimate claim to the [political offence] exception and especially so if they believe that supporting the supply of drugs to the developed world is simply one way of prosecuting a political struggle'.[59] Although this claim would probably be inoperative in a state party to the UN Drug Convention,[60] a similar argument could be made in respect of many crimes not expressly excluded from the scope of political offences, especially where such crimes are committed by public officials in furtherance of state policy.

(g) The discrimination clause

The decision to prosecute serving or former heads of state has often proven to be motivated by purely political considerations.[61] As a safeguard against abuses of the criminal justice system for political ends by a requesting state party, international instruments pertaining to organized crime and corruption permit a requested state party to refuse extradition where there are 'substantial grounds for believing that the request has been made for the purpose of prosecuting or punishing a person on account of that person's [...] political opinions'.[62] The flip side of the discrimination clause is that it allows any politically exposed person sought for extradition to claim to be a victim of political machinations on the part of the requesting state.[63]

[58] *Prosecutor v Viktor Bout*, 11 August 2009, Black Case no 3/2551, certified English translation, at 49. The ruling was overturned in appeal: see *Prosecutor v Viktor Bout*, 24 May 2010, Red Case no 5581-5582/2553, certified English translation, at 26.

[59] Boister (n 32), at 255.

[60] Art 3(10) of the UN Drug Convention indicates that drug offences are not to be regarded as 'politically motivated'—with the important qualification that this obligation remains subject to 'the constitutional limitations and fundamental domestic law of the Parties'. The United States interprets this provision to mean that 'if a Party recognizes a limitation to its obligation to co-operate for offences committed for political reasons, such as drug trafficking to raise money for a political group, that limitation shall not apply'. See US Senate, 101st Congress, 1st sess, *United Nations Convention against Illicit Traffic in Narcotic Drugs and Psychotropic Substances*, Exec Rept 101-15 (US Government Printing Office), at 34.

[61] See e.g. Naomi Roht-Arriaza, 'Prosecutions of Heads of State in Latin America' in Ellen L Lutz and Caitlin Reiger (eds), *Prosecuting Heads of State* (Cambridge University Press, 2009) 46, at 68–69.

[62] UN Drug Convention, Art 6(6); UNCTOC, Art 16(14); UNCAC, Art 44(15).

[63] Note that, in some jurisdictions, the argument will be examined under the political offence exception: see José Puente Egido, 'L'extradition en droit international : problèmes choisis' (1991) 231 *Recueil des cours de l'Académie de droit international* 9, at 169. For example, in France the political offence exception is interpreted broadly, placing emphasis not uniquely on the character of the offence, but also on the motives allegedly underlying the extradition request: see Code de procédure pénale, Art 696-4, 2°; CE (ass), *Moussa Koné*, 3 July 1996, Case no 169219. This might not be familiar to American jurists. In the United States, courts have steadily held that '[t]he status of the offence committed, whether a political offence or not, is to be determined by the circumstances attending the alleged crime at the time of its commission and not by the motives of those who subsequently handle the prosecution' (see e.g. *García-Guillern v United States*, 450 F2d 1189 (5th Cir 1971), at 1192, where the extradition of the

The political-discrimination argument is frequently raised in high-profile organized crime and corruption cases. The person sought will not hesitate to claim to be the victim of abusive proceedings driven by political considerations, for example because political rivals, or foreign powers, have a vested interest in putting him on trial. Several emblematic cases can be cited. A French appellate court opposed Georgia's request for the extradition of former Georgian Defence Minister Davit Kezerashvili in relation to charges of corruption and organized crime, on the ground that the charges were politically motivated.[64] Another example is the judicial saga concerning the extradition of Jorge Luis Ochoa Vásquez, co-founder of the Medellín cartel. When the United States and Colombia respectively requested Spain to surrender Ochoa, the Spanish Audiencia Nacional ordered extradition to Colombia, rejecting the United States' request on the ground that the indictment was 'immersed in a political context'.[65]

Furthermore, because the political-discrimination argument often gives rise to issues of conflict of jurisdiction between the judiciary and the executive, proceedings may be significantly delayed. In the *Ochoa* case, after the Audiencia Nacional had authorized extradition to Colombia, the Spanish government moved to claim jurisdiction to decide on the concurrent extradition requests and summoned the Court to refrain from intervening in the execution of the order.[66] In the United States, where the final decision is taken by the Secretary of State after determination by the judiciary that the person is extraditable,[67] courts of appeals are generally reluctant to examine the argument and leave it to the Department of State to decide in last instance whether to surrender the defendant in light of the specific circumstances of the case.[68] However, the position of the case law is not clear. In *Nicosia v Wall*, Panama requested the surrender of Hildebrando Nicosia Pérez, former Minister of the Presidency of the Panamanian government, on charges of abuse of functions. The judges of the Fifth Circuit, recognizing the 'obvious [...] distinct political overtones' of the case, held that it belonged to the court of first instance to decide whether the defendant's argument was well-founded.[69]

defendant, a former Director General of the Ministry of Education of Peru, was requested in relation to charges of embezzlement).

[64] CA Aix-en-Provence, ch inst, 27 February 2014, decision no 58/EXT/2014. A similar case arose in 2011 when Egypt requested Spain to extradite Hussein Salem Fawzi, a close relation of former Egyptian President Hosni Mubarak, on charges of trading in influence. To oppose his surrender, Salem claimed that Egypt's request formed part of a process of political persecution against politicians and business people associated with the former regime. The tribunal, however, did not need to examine the argument, as extradition was refused on the ground that the applicant had acquired Spanish citizenship. See Tribunal Constitucional, Decision no 232/2012, 10 December 2012, BOE no 10 (2013), p 25.

[65] Audiencia Nacional, Sala de lo Penal, Decisions of 20 March 1986 and 7 May 1986, Extradition Files nos 35/1984, 8/1985, and 31/1985.

[66] See *Conflicto de jurisdicción planteado por el Delegado del Gobierno en la Comunidad Autónoma de Madrid a la Sala de lo Penal de la Audiencia Nacional*, no 12/1986, 9 July 1986, BOE no 205 (1986), p 30060.

[67] See 18 USC § 3184; American Law Institute, *Restatement of the Law Third: The Foreign Relations Law of the United States*, vol 1 (American Law Institute Publishers, 1987), at 582 ff (§ 478 and comments thereunder).

[68] See e.g. *García-Guillern v United States* (n 63), at 1192.

[69] *Nicosia v Wall*, 442 F2d 1005 (5th Cir 1971), at 1006–1007.

3. The limited scope of the obligation *aut dedere aut judicare*

The abundance of possible bars to extradition in treaties pertaining to organized crime and corruption is not counterbalanced by an adequate obligation to initiate an investigation for the purpose of prosecution if extradition is refused. Under many of the relevant instruments, the obligation on a requested state party to submit the case to its competent authorities for the purpose of prosecution is triggered only if extradition is refused 'on the ground that [the person concerned] is one of its nationals'.[70] This formulation is narrower than that found in many other crime-suppression conventions, in two respects. First, under these other conventions the obligation to initiate an investigation is not dependent on the prior refusal of an extradition request.[71] States parties are required to submit the case to their competent authorities as soon as the alleged offender is present in their territory, unless they choose to extradite him to another state.[72] Secondly, many instruments explicitly indicate that states parties are obliged to submit the case to their competent authorities for the purpose of prosecution 'without exception whatsoever',[73] which implies that, in a case where a prior request for extradition is denied, an investigation must be initiated regardless of the ground for refusal.

Even in cases where the requested state party is obliged to submit the case to its competent authorities for the purpose of prosecution, the manner in which the competent authorities are to proceed remains largely unregulated by international law. UNCTOC, UNCAC, and the Council of Europe Convention on Cybercrime simply indicate that '[t]hose authorities shall take their decision and conduct their proceedings in the same manner as in the case of any other offence of a grave nature under the domestic law of that State Party'.[74] The ICJ did not provide much guidance as to the exact scope of the obligation to prosecute, and the threshold required for a state to discharge its obligation seems to be a low one.[75] This is not an issue in states where prosecutorial independence is guaranteed, but may become problematic where prosecutors are subject to the influence of the executive. Domestic authorities may decide to terminate investigations without bringing charges, even if the evidence is sufficient to go to trial. Alternatively, a lenient plea bargain or a

[70] See UNCTOC, Art 16(10); UNCAC, Art 44(11). See also, with slightly different wordings: OECD Convention on Bribery, Art 10(3); Criminal Law Convention on Corruption, Art 27(5); Arab Convention against Corruption, Art 23(11); Inter-American Convention against Arms Trafficking, Art XIX(6); Optional Protocol to the Convention on the Rights of the Child on the Sale of Children, Child Prostitution and Child Pornography, Art 5(5).

[71] See e.g. Convention for the Suppression of Unlawful Acts against the Safety of Maritime Navigation, Art 10(1); Convention for the Suppression of Unlawful Seizure of Aircraft, Art 7; Convention on the Prevention and Punishment of Crimes against Internationally Protected Persons, including Diplomatic Agents, Art 7; International Convention against the Taking of Hostages, Art 7; International Convention for the Suppression of the Financing of Terrorism, Art 10; International Convention for the Suppression of Acts of Nuclear Terrorism, Art 11(1); International Convention for the Suppression of Terrorist Bombings, Art 8. See also Convention against Torture, Art 7(1).

[72] See *Questions relating to the Obligation to Prosecute or Extradite (Belgium v Senegal)*, Judgment, ICJ Rep 2002, p 422, at 456, paras 94–95.

[73] See the instruments cited in n 71 (to the exception of the Convention against Torture).

[74] UNCTOC, Art 16(10); UNCAC, Art 44(11); Convention on Cybercrime, Art 24(6).

[75] Recall Chapter 3, Section C.1(d).

pardon may be offered to the offender. The obligation *aut dedere aut judicare*, as formulated in the relevant crime-suppression conventions, does not provide much safeguard against the possible abuse by states parties of their criminal justice system to shield the offender from punishment. Such conduct on the part of a state may constitute a breach of the obligation under the law of treaties to perform treaty obligations in good faith and in particular to refrain from acts that would defeat the object and purpose of the treaty.[76] Nonetheless, a state's lack of good faith may be difficult to establish in matters where domestic prosecutorial authorities enjoy significant discretion.

What is more, a state party that fails to fulfil its obligation to submit the case to its competent authorities for the purpose of prosecution is under no obligation to extradite the alleged offender. As the ICJ noted, extradition is merely 'an option offered to the State'.[77] As a result, state responsibility cannot be incurred for failure to extradite.[78]

In view of the above, it is doubtful whether the obligation *aut dedere aut judicare*, as formulated in international instruments pertaining to organized crime and corruption, is apt to fulfil the purpose of 'preventing suspects from escaping the consequences of their criminal responsibility'[79] in cases of state organized crime.

4. Obstacles to the exercise of jurisdiction over foreign state officials and their conduct

There is only so much crime-suppression conventions can do to lift barriers to prosecution and extradition. Certain fundamental principles in both international and domestic law have the potential to hinder the exercise of jurisdiction by domestic courts in relation to state organized crime. This section focuses on the effect on domestic criminal proceedings, first, of the jurisdictional immunities that, as a matter of international law, one state must accord the officials of another state and, secondly, of the Anglo-American act of state doctrine. The former renders internationally unlawful in certain circumstances the exercise of criminal jurisdiction over foreign state officials, while the latter operates as a ground of non-justiciability which compels a domestic court to decline to exercise its jurisdiction in relation to certain matters involving a foreign state.

[76] Recall Chapter 2, Section C.2.

[77] *Questions relating to the Obligation to Prosecute or Extradite* (n 72), at 456, para 95.

[78] In *Questions relating to the Obligation to Prosecute or Extradite*, Belgium tried to argue that, as a result of Senegal's breach of its primary obligation to submit the case to its competent authorities for the purpose of prosecution, Senegal was under a secondary obligation to cease the internationally wrongful act by extraditing Hissène Habré to Belgium. The Court did not follow this argument: see ibid, at 461, paras 118–21.

[79] Ibid, at 455, para 91. See also at 461, para 120.

(a) *Jurisdictional immunities of foreign state officials*

It is a well-established principle of international law that state officials must, in certain circumstances, be accorded immunity from the criminal jurisdiction of other states. The immunities that, as a matter of international law, states are required to accord to foreign state officials apply at all stages of the criminal justice process. State officials are not only immune from prosecution before the courts of another state, but also may not be subjected to any measure of judicial constraint,[80] such as an arrest warrant[81] or a subpoena to give testimony as a suspect in an ongoing investigation.[82] The immunity of state officials has the potential to frustrate investigations and extradition proceedings significantly.

The material and temporal scope of the immunities enjoyed by state officials vary depending on the position occupied by the official when proceedings are brought and on the nature of the acts under consideration. The challenges posed by jurisdictional immunities in different scenarios of state organized crime are best illustrated in light of the traditional distinction between immunities *ratione materiae* and *ratione personae*.

(i) Immunity *ratione materiae*

Immunity *ratione materiae* from foreign criminal jurisdiction is a manifestation of sovereign immunity.[83] It shields officials and ex-officials of a state from the criminal jurisdiction of foreign courts in respect of all acts carried out in their capacity as officials of the state. Under customary international law, all serving and former officials of a state, irrespective of their position in the hierarchy of the state, must be accorded immunity *ratione materiae* from foreign criminal jurisdiction, so long as the charges concern acts carried out in their official capacity.[84]

The difficulty consists in determining which acts performed by a public official may be considered to have been committed in an official capacity for the purpose

[80] *Certain Questions of Mutual Assistance in Criminal Matters* (n 31), at 237, para 170.

[81] *Arrest Warrant of 11 April 2000 (Democratic Republic of the Congo v Belgium)*, Judgment, ICJ Rep 2002, p 3, at 22, para 54, and at 29, para 70.

[82] See *Certain Questions of Mutual Assistance in Criminal Matters* (n 31), at 243, para 191: 'it has not been "concretely verified" before [the Court] that the acts which were the subject of the summonses as *témoins assistés* issued by France were indeed acts within the scope of their duties as organs of State'. The Court seems to imply that summonsing a state official to give testimony concerning acts carried out in his official capacity would contravene jurisdictional immunity. However, a mere invitation to give testimony as a witness does not (ibid, at 237, para 171, and at 240, para 179). Neither does the commencement of a preliminary investigation: see *Second report on immunity of State officials from foreign criminal jurisdiction, by Roman Anatolevich Kolodkin, Special Rapporteur*, 10 June 2010, UN Doc A/CN.4/631, para 42, and the authorities cited therein.

[83] Immunity *ratione materiae* is a corollary of the sovereign equality of states: see *Jurisdictional Immunities of the State (Germany v Italy; Greece intervening)*, Judgment, ICJ Rep 2012, p 99, at 123, para 57 (as illustrated by the maxim *par in parem non habet imperium*, attributed to Bartolus de Saxoferrato, *Tractatus represaliarum* (1354), Questio I/3, para 10).

[84] For a detailed review of the authorities supporting this view, see *Immunity of State officials from foreign criminal jurisdiction, memorandum by the Secretariat*, 31 March 2008, UN Doc A/CN.4/596, paras 166–73.

of defining the scope of immunity *ratione materiae* in criminal proceedings.[85] The concept of 'act performed in an official capacity' is also central to the rules governing attribution of conduct to the state for the purposes of state responsibility.[86] The extent to which the criteria for attribution should be considered relevant for the purpose of determining the scope of jurisdictional immunities is disputed.[87] Successive special rapporteurs appointed by the ILC to work on the topic of the immunity of state officials from foreign criminal jurisdiction have adopted different views.[88] If one considers that the regime of jurisdictional immunities should be aligned with the principles of the law of state responsibility governing attribution of conduct to the state, then one also has to accept that the 'classification of the conduct of an official as official conduct does not depend on the motives of the person or the substance of the conduct. The determining factor is that the official is acting in a capacity as such'.[89] As a result, acts *ultra vires*—including acts considered criminal under the law of the official's own state—as well as acts performed by a public official for private motives but under the guise of state authority, may be covered by immunity *ratione materiae* under international law.[90] Taken to its final conclusion, this proposition would completely shield the officials of a state from criminal responsibility before the courts of another state for criminal conduct performed under the guise of official authority.

State practice, however, does not follow this approach. In judicial decisions rendered by domestic courts, *ultra vires* acts or acts committed for private motives, which may be attributed to the state under the law of state responsibility, are generally not considered 'official acts' for the purposes of the law of jurisdictional immunities.[91]

[85] Note that the distinction between *acta jure imperii* and *acta jure gestionis* made for the purpose of delineating the scope of state immunity in civil matters is irrelevant when it comes to immunity *ratione materiae* in criminal proceedings: see *Fourth Report on the immunity of State officials from foreign criminal jurisdiction, by Concepción Escobar Hernández Special Rapporteur*, 29 May 2015, UN Doc A/CN.4/686, paras 30, 65, 120.

[86] Recall Chapter 2, Section B.1.

[87] See Chimène I Keitner, 'Categorizing Acts by State Officials: Attribution and Responsibility in the Law of Foreign Official Immunity' (2016) *Duke Journal of Comparative & International Law* 451 (concluding that '[a]ttribution cannot be the sole basis for determining whether or not a state official should be held personally responsible by a foreign court'); Luigi Condorelli and Claus Kress, 'The Rules of Attribution: General Considerations' in James Crawford, Alain Pellet, and Simon Olleson (eds), *The Law of International Responsibility* (Oxford University Press, 2010) 221, at 228 (noting that the attribution to a state of the conduct of an organ of that state for the purposes of state responsibility does not *ipso facto* imply that the person acting as an organ of the state may benefit from jurisdictional immunity *ratione materiae* under international law).

[88] See Second report on immunity of state officials (n 82), paras 24–27; Secretariat memorandum on the immunity of state officials (n 84), at 156 (identifying 'strong reasons for aligning the immunity regime with the rules on attribution of conduct for purposes of State responsibility'); see *contra* Fourth report on immunity of state officials (n 85), paras 111–17 (questioning the usefulness of the rules on attribution for the purposes of immunity).

[89] Second report on immunity of state officials (n 82), para 27. See also ARSIWA Commentary in *Report of the International Law Commission* (53rd sess), UN Doc A/56/10 in *Yearbook of the International Law Commission* (2001), vol II(2), at 42, para 13 (noting that '[i]t is irrelevant for this purpose that the person concerned may have had ulterior or improper motives or may be abusing public power. Where such a person acts in an apparently official capacity, or under colour of authority, the actions in question will be attributable to the State').

[90] Second report on immunity of state officials (n 82), paras 29–31.

[91] See the analysis in Fourth report on immunity of state officials (n 85), paras 49–60.

In her report on the material scope of immunity *ratione materiae*, the ILC Special Rapporteur concluded that immunity only applies with respect to acts attributable to the state that also involve the exercise of governmental authority, such as 'activities occurring during the implementation of State policies and decisions that involve the exercise of sovereignty'.[92] The ILC provisionally adopted draft Article 2(f) defining an 'act performed in an official capacity' as 'any act performed by a State official in the exercise of State authority'.[93] This presupposes 'a direct connection between the act and the exercise of State functions and powers',[94] for example when the act in question is performed 'in the interests of the State'.[95] The Commission, while noting that the rules governing attribution to the state for the purposes of state responsibility should be considered as a point of departure for ascertaining whether the conduct of a public official may be considered to be 'performed in an official capacity', pointed out that the principles concerning the attribution of acts *ultra vires* 'd[id] not seem generally applicable'. In the view of the Commission, 'acts performed by an official purely for their own benefit and in their own interest cannot be considered as acts performed in an official capacity, even though they may appear to have been performed officially'.[96] Whether conduct may be considered to have been 'performed in the exercise of state authority' must be assessed in view of the facts and circumstances of each particular case.[97]

The difficulty in determining whether a particular criminal act can be considered to fall within that category appears at its most acute in cases of state organized crime. As noted by the Special Rapporteur with respect to cases of corruption and misappropriation of state property:

> practice shows that, in a number of the cases, it was not easy to determine clearly whether the act concerned was official or private, in particular since the act in question was only capable of being performed because of the official status of its perpetrator and the latter's ability to take advantage of the State structure, sometimes by means of acts that were ostensibly official.[98]

The analysis of the phenomenon of state organized crime in Chapter 1 has suggested that specific modes of governance prevalent in kleptocratic regimes blur the distinction between the private and public spheres. In this context, criminal acts perhaps more commonly considered to further private interests could be regarded as acts of government.[99] Whether such acts may be considered to have been performed in the exercise of state authority, with the consequence that immunity *ratione materiae* would preclude foreign criminal proceedings, remains open to question. State practice in point is scarce and not uniform. In general, domestic courts tend to reject immunity pleas in cases of drug trafficking, corruption, embezzlement of public funds,

[92] Ibid, paras 95, 119.
[93] See *Report of the International Law Commission* (68th sess), UN Doc A/71/10 in *Yearbook of the International Law Commission* (2016), vol II(2), para 250.
[94] Ibid, Commentary, para 3. [95] Ibid, para 6. [96] Ibid, para 5.
[97] Ibid, para 10.
[98] *Fifth Report on the immunity of State officials from foreign criminal jurisdiction, by Concepción Escobar Hernández Special Rapporteur*, 14 June 2016, UN Doc A/CN.4/701, para 231.
[99] Recall Chapter 1, Section B.2 and Chapter 2, Section B.1(b).

and money laundering.[100] The line of reasoning followed by domestic courts is either that such acts cannot, by definition, be considered to fall within the official duties of a public official,[101] or that they were committed for the perpetrator's personal benefit. For instance, in the case concerning Teodoro Nguema Obiang Mangue, Vice-President in charge of Defence and State Security and former Minister for Agriculture and Forestry of Equatorial Guinea, charged with money laundering and embezzlement of public funds, the French Court of Cassation rejected the defendant's plea of immunity on the ground that the acts for which he was charged had been committed for private ends.[102] Similarly, in a case involving charges of money laundering brought against former Panamanian ruler Manuel Noriega, a French court of first instance rejected Noriega's plea of immunity *ratione materiae*, on the ground that the offence had been committed for private ends independently of the defendant's functions as head of state.[103] However, in that same case the Court drew a distinction between money laundering and the predicate offence of drug trafficking, apparently suggesting *a contrario* that the drug trafficking could be considered to have been committed in an official capacity and therefore to entail immunity.[104] Other judicial decisions suggest that immunity *ratione materiae* may be applicable in certain cases of state organized crime. The Swiss Federal Tribunal notably considered that it could not transmit the bank records of former Filipino President Ferdinand Marcos pursuant to a US request for mutual legal assistance relating to charges of embezzlement and abuse of functions, in the absence of a waiver of immunity on the part of the Philippines.[105] In another case concerning the applicability of the act of state doctrine, a US court of appeals overruled an injunction ordering the freezing of Marcos's assets, considering that the misappropriation of assets in a dictatorship may constitute an exercise of sovereign authority.[106] It is therefore impossible to infer from state practice a general rule or principle to the effect

[100] See ILC Report (68th sess) (n 93), para 13, and the cases cited therein. See also Fourth report on immunity of state officials (n 85), para 58.

[101] Note the contradiction in cases of corruption, which according to the UNCAC definition necessarily occurs 'in the exercise of the official duties' of a public official and therefore does not apply to acts *ultra vires*: recall Chapter 3, Section A.4.

[102] Cass crim, 15 December 2015, App no 15-83.156, *Bull crim* (2015), no 292, p 578.

[103] T corr Paris, 11ème ch, *Administration des Douanes et Droits Indirects c/ Noriega*, 7 July 2010, Case no 8935669013.

[104] Ibid (stating without further explanation that 'because the means employed do not concern the offence of drug trafficking, but that of laundering, [...] such means could have been used by any offender irrespective of the functions exercised by a head of state' (author's translation)).

[105] TF, Ière Cour de droit public, *Ferdinand et Imelda Marcos c. Office fédéral de la police*, 2 November 1989, BGE 115 Ib 496, reproduced in English in 102 ILR 198, para 5(d). The tribunal noted that the Philippines had validly waived Marcos' immunity, and granted the request for mutual legal assistance. The government of the Philippines paradoxically took the view that 'the acquisition of any personal wealth by President and Mrs Marcos cannot constitute public, governmental or official action by the Philippine Government, even if such enrichment was achieved by the use or the purported use of governmental authority'.

[106] *Republic of the Philippines v Marcos*, 818 F2d 1473 (9th Cir 1987) (*Marcos II*). The 'act of state' doctrine is a domestic doctrine of non-justiciability applied in common-law jurisdictions, distinct from immunity *ratione materiae* under international law. This case is discussed in greater detail in Section B.4(b) of this chapter.

of excluding immunity *ratione materiae* in cases of drug trafficking, corruption, or misappropriation of public property.[107] Interestingly, the possibility that acts of corruption and embezzlement of public funds may be covered by immunity under domestic law is contemplated by Article 30(2) of UNCAC, which provides that states parties shall take measures

> to establish or maintain, in accordance with its legal system and constitutional principles, an appropriate balance between any immunities or jurisdictional privileges accorded to its public officials for the performance of their functions and the possibility, when necessary, of effectively investigating, prosecuting and adjudicating offences established in accordance with this Convention.

In cases of state organized crime, where senior public officials take advantage of their official position and use the resources of the state to commit crimes, such crimes can arguably be considered to have been performed in the exercise of state authority.

This conclusion applies in particular in cases of covert operations carried out by the secret services of a state in the territory of another state under the instructions of senior state officials and in pursuance of state policy. In the words of Lord Lloyd in *Pinochet (No 1)*,

> [w]here a person is accused of organising the commission of crimes as the head of the government, [...] and carrying out those crimes through the agency of [...] the secret service, the inevitable conclusion must be that he was acting in [an official] capacity and not in a personal or private capacity.[108]

It has been suggested that immunity *ratione materiae* need not be granted to covert agents operating in the territory of the forum state without its knowledge and consent,[109] but the existence of a customary exception to immunity in these circumstances remains open to question.

[107] The ILC, at its 69th session, did not include corruption and drug offences within the list of 'crimes under international law in respect of which immunity *ratione materiae* shall not apply' (see draft Art 7, 10 July 2017, UN Doc A/CN.4/L.893). The Special Rapporteur and other academics had proposed to recognize the existence of a general limitation excluding the applicability of immunity *ratione materiae* in all cases of corruption: see Fifth report on the immunity of state officials (n 98), para 234; Institut de droit international, 'Resolution on Immunities from Jurisdiction and Execution of Heads of State and of Government in International Law' (2001) 69 *Annuaire de l'Institut de droit international* 743, Art 13(2). See also Christian Dominicé, 'Quelques observations sur l'immunité de juridiction pénale de l'ancien chef d'État' (1999) 103 *Revue générale de droit international public* 297, at 304 (regarding acts of embezzlement and drug trafficking). State practice supporting this latter view is scarce: see e.g., in Switzerland: TF, Ière Cour de droit public, *Evgeny O. Adamov gegen Bundesamt für Justiz*, 22 December 2005, Case no 1A.288/2005, para 3.4.2 (holding that 'the purpose of immunity from criminal jurisdiction is not to grant impunity to former members of government for corruption (or any other common crimes committed in a private capacity)' (author's translation)).

[108] *R v Bow Street Metropolitan Stipendiary Magistrate and Others, ex parte Pinochet Ugarte (No 1)*, [2000] 1 AC 61, at 95. Although this judgment was held void because of an appearance of bias of one of the Law Lords (see *R v Bow Street Metropolitan Stipendiary Magistrate and Others, ex parte Pinochet Ugarte (No 2)*, [2000] 1 AC 119), Lord Lloyd's reasoning retains its cogency.

[109] See Second report on immunity of state officials (n 82), para 85, and the authorities cited therein. See also the decision of a British court in *Khurts Bat v Investigating Judge of the Federal Court of Germany*, [2013] QB 349 (refusing to uphold the immunity of the Head of the National Security Office of Mongolia for his involvement in the kidnapping of a Mongolian national in France).

Finally, one should mention the existence of a number of domestic judicial decisions excluding immunity *ratione materiae* in cases of torture, crimes against humanity, and war crimes.[110] Whether these should be considered as evidence of a potential rule of customary international law establishing limitations or exceptions to immunity *ratione materiae* in respect of international crimes is disputed,[111] and, in any event, the existence of such a rule of customary international law is not supported by *opinio juris*.[112]

In view of the above considerations, it is evident that the principles of international law governing the immunity *ratione materiae* of state officials from foreign criminal jurisdiction can constitute a serious impediment to the prosecution of public officials involved in state organized crime.

(ii) Immunity *ratione personae*

As recalled by the ICJ in the *Arrest Warrant* case, 'in international law it is firmly established that, as also diplomatic and consular agents, certain holders of high-ranking office in a State, such as the Head of State, Head of Government and Minister for Foreign Affairs, enjoy immunities from jurisdiction in other States, both civil and criminal'.[113] This type of immunity specifically granted to diplomats and certain

[110] Concerning the crime of torture, see, in England, *R v Bow Street Metropolitan Stipendiary Magistrate and Others, ex parte Pinochet Ugarte (No 3)*, [2000] 1 AC 147, at 266–67 (Lord Saville), 277–78 (Lord Millett); concerning war crimes and crimes against humanity, see, in the Netherlands, Hof Amsterdam, 20 November 2000, *LJN* AA8395 (*Bouterse* case), reproduced in English in (2000) 3 *Yearbook of International Humanitarian Law* 677, para 4.2; in Italy, C Cass, Sez I penale, 24 July 2008, Decision no 31171/2008 (*Lozano* case), reproduced in English in ILDC 1085 (IT 2008); in Switzerland, TPF, *A c. Ministère public de la Confédération, B et C*, 25 July 2012, Case no BB.2011.140 (*Nezzar* case), para 5.4.3.

[111] For views in favour of an exception to immunity *ratione materiae* in cases of international crimes, see Fifth report on the immunity of state officials (n 98), paras 179–80; Institut de droit international, 'Resolution on the Immunity from Jurisdiction of the State and of Persons Who Act on Behalf of the State in Case of International Crimes' (2009) 73 *Annuaire de l'Institut de droit international* 227, Art III(1), and Resolution on Immunities from Jurisdiction and Execution of Heads of State and of Government in International Law (n 107), Art 13(2); Dapo Akande and Sangeeta Shah, 'Immunities of State Officials, International Crimes, and Foreign Domestic Courts' (2011) 21 *European Journal of International Law* 815; Paola Gaeta, 'Immunity of States and State Officials: A Major Stumbling-Block to Judicial Scrutiny?' in Antonio Cassese (ed), *Realizing Utopia: The Future of International Law* (Oxford University Press, 2012) 227. See also *Prosecutor v Tihomir Blaškić*, Case no IT-95-14, Judgment on the Request of the Republic of Croatia for Review of the Decision of Trial Chamber II of 18 July 1997, 29 October 1997, para 41 (*obiter dictum*). For views rejecting the existence of any exception, see Second report on immunity of state officials (n 82), para 90; Joanne Foakes, *The Position of Heads of State and Senior Officials in International Law* (Oxford University Press, 2014), at 149–60; Roger O'Keefe, 'An "International Crime" Exception to Immunity of State Officials from Foreign Criminal Jurisdiction: Not Currently, Not Likely' (2015) 109 *AJIL Unbound* 167. The latter view is strongly supported by statements made by the ICJ: see *Arrest Warrant* (n 81), at 25, para 61 (stating that 'a court of one State may try a former Minister for Foreign Affairs of another State [...] in respect of acts committed during [his] period of office in a private capacity', therefore implying *a contrario* that immunity *ratione materiae* remains valid with respect to crimes committed in an official capacity), and at 25, para 59 (stressing that 'although various international conventions on the prevention and punishment of certain serious crimes impose on States obligations of prosecution or extradition, thereby requiring them to extend their criminal jurisdiction, such extension of jurisdiction in no way affects immunities under customary international law'—implicitly addressing the ratio of *Pinochet (No 3)*).

[112] O'Keefe (n 111), at 168.

[113] *Arrest Warrant* (n 81), at 20–21, para 51. See also *Certain Questions of Mutual Assistance in Criminal Matters* (n 31), at 236–37, para 170.

high-ranking state officials is distinct from the immunity *ratione materiae* enjoyed by all serving and former state officials in respect of acts carried out in their official capacity. Immunity *ratione personae* from foreign criminal jurisdiction is absolute. During his time in office, it serves to shield its beneficiary completely from criminal proceedings in foreign courts, even in relation to charges concerning purely private acts and acts performed prior to his time in office.[114] It is worth stressing that international law does not recognize the existence of any exception to immunity *ratione personae* in relation to particular types of crimes.[115]

The challenge is to identify those state officials who benefit from immunity *ratione personae*. The issue is uncontroversial in the case of diplomatic agents,[116] state representatives in a special mission,[117] and members of permanent delegations to the UN and other international organizations,[118] who enjoy treaty-based immunity from the criminal jurisdiction of the host and transit states. Under customary international law, heads of state, heads of government, and ministers of foreign affairs also enjoy absolute immunity from foreign criminal jurisdiction during their time in office.[119] It remains unclear, however, whether other 'holders of high-ranking

[114] *Arrest Warrant* (n 81), at 22, paras 54–55; *Certain Questions of Mutual Assistance in Criminal Matters* (n 31), at 237, para 170. See also Secretariat memorandum on the immunity of state officials (n 84), paras 137–40, and the authorities cited therein.

[115] See Fifth report on the immunity of state officials (n 98), paras 110, 121, 237; *Arrest Warrant* (n 81), at 24, para 58. Consider also *Jurisdictional Immunities of the State* (n 83), at 141, para 95 (recalling the ICJ's previous ruling in *Arrest Warrant*, and stating that 'the fact that a Minister for Foreign Affairs was accused of criminal violations of rules which undoubtedly possess the character of *jus cogens* did not deprive the Democratic Republic of the Congo of the entitlement which it possessed as a matter of customary international law to demand immunity on his behalf'). For isolated instances of state practice to the contrary, see, in Belgium: Loi relative à la répression des infractions graves aux Conventions internationales de Genève du 12 août 1949 et aux Protocoles I et II du 8 juin 1977, 16 juin 1993, as amended by Loi relative à la répression des violations graves de droit international humanitaire, 10 February 1999, Art 5(3) (excluding jurisdictional immunity of all state officials for war crimes); and in France: Cass crim, 13 March 2001, App no 00-87.215, *Bull crim* (2001), no 64, p 218 (*Gaddafi* case) (noting the existence of exceptions to immunity for certain crimes, but refusing to include the crime of terrorism within the scope of such exceptions).

[116] Vienna Convention on Diplomatic Relations, 18 April 1961, entered into force on 24 April 1964, 500 UNTS 95, Art 31(1); *United States Diplomatic and Consular Staff in Tehran (United States of America v Iran)*, Judgment, ICJ Rep 1980, p 3, at 37, para 79.

[117] Convention on Special Missions, 8 December 1969, entered into force on 21 June 1985, 1400 UNTS 231, Art 31(1). For an illustration involving charges of drug trafficking in Germany, see BGH, 27 February 1984, Decision no 3 StR 396/83, BGHSt 32, 275 (*Tabatabai* case), reproduced in English in 80 ILR 411 (according immunity to an Iranian special envoy on the basis of an agreement between Iran and Germany defining the terms of the special mission and concluded after his arrest).

[118] Convention on the Privileges and Immunities of the United Nations, 13 February 1946, entered into force on 17 September 1946, 1 UNTS 15, Art IV, s 11(g); Vienna Convention on the Representation of States in their Relations with International Organizations of a Universal Character, 14 March 1975, UN Doc A/CONF.67/16 (not yet in force), Art 30(1) and (3).

[119] *Arrest Warrant* (n 81), at 22, para 54; *Certain Questions of Mutual Assistance in Criminal Matters* (n 31), at 236–37, para 170. See also Convention on Special Missions, Art 21; Convention on Jurisdictional Immunities of States and Their Property, Art 3(2). For a discussion of the scope of jurisdictional immunities predating the judgments of the ICJ, see Arthur Watts, 'The Legal Position in International Law of Heads of States, Heads of Governments and Foreign Ministers' (1994) 247 *Recueil des cours de l'Académie de droit international* 9, in particular at 54, 106–108.

office' are entitled to immunity *ratione personae*.[120] Given the paucity of cases the question remains unanswered. Notable developments include the refusal by magistrates' courts in England, on grounds of immunity, to issue arrest warrants against a minister of defence[121] and a minister of commerce and international trade.[122] Although in the draft articles provisionally adopted to date by the ILC immunity *ratione personae* appears limited to the 'troika',[123] the issue is not settled yet. In cases of state organized crime involving a range of high-ranking officials, the scope of immunities *ratione personae* is likely to be disputed, as illustrated by Equatorial Guinea's application to the ICJ requesting the Court to declare that France violated its obligations under international law by initiating criminal proceedings against the Vice-President of Equatorial Guinea in charge of Defence and State Security.[124]

(b) The act of state doctrine and other grounds of non-justiciability

The 'act of state' doctrine—or, more accurately, the 'foreign act of state' doctrine—is 'a judicial self-restraint doctrine'[125] whereby 'the courts of one country will not sit in judgment on the acts of the government of another done within its own territory'.[126] It is a doctrine not of international law[127] but of domestic law in certain common-law jurisdictions.[128]

In England and Wales, a similar principle of non-justiciability known as the *Buttes* doctrine precludes domestic courts from adjudicating upon acts of a foreign state carried out outside its territory 'by virtue of sovereign authority'.[129] For example, the English courts have declined in one case to examine the international legality of acts carried out by CIA officials 'implementing US policy' abroad.[130] The *Buttes* non-justiciability rule is, however, subject to limitations. The courts will

[120] For a discussion of the beneficiaries of immunity *ratione personae*, see *Preliminary report on immunity of State officials from foreign criminal jurisdiction, by Roman Anatolevich Kolodkin, Special Rapporteur*, 29 May 2008, UN Doc A/CN.4/601, paras 117–21.

[121] *Re Mofaz*, 12 February 2004, 128 ILR 709; *Re Barak*, 29 September 2009, City of Westminster Magistrates' Court (unreported).

[122] *Re Bo Xilai*, 8 November 2005, 128 ILR 713.

[123] See *Report of the International Law Commission* (65th sess), UN Doc A/68/10, draft Art 3 and commentary, at 58–65, in particular para 12.

[124] *Immunities and Criminal Proceedings (Equatorial Guinea v France)*, Application Instituting Proceedings, 13 June 2016.

[125] Brigitte Stern, 'Immunities for Heads of State: Where Do We Stand?' in Mark Lattimer and Philippe Sands (eds), *Justice for Crimes against Humanity* (Hart Publishing, 2003) 73, at 77.

[126] See, in the United States: *Underhill v Hernandez*, 168 US 250 (1897), at 252; in England: *A.M. Luther and Co v James Sagor and Co*, [1921] KB 532, at 548.

[127] See the views of domestic courts, e.g., in the United States: *Banco Nacional de Cuba v Sabbatino*, 376 US 398 (1964), at 421; in Germany: BGH, 3 November 1992, Decision no 5 StR 370/92, BGHSt 39, 1 (*Mauerschützen Fall*), reproduced in English in 100 ILR 364, at 372 (rejecting the appellants' argument on the ground that the act of state doctrine is unknown in Germany).

[128] For an analysis of the development of the act of state doctrine in England and the United States, see Michael Singer, 'The Act of State Doctrine of the United Kingdom: An Analysis, with Comparisons to United States Practice' (1981) 75 *American Journal of International Law* 283.

[129] *Buttes Gas and Oil Co v Hammer (No 3)*, [1982] AC 888, at 932.

[130] See *R (on the application of Khan) v Secretary of State for Foreign and Commonwealth Affairs*, [2014] EWCA Civ 24 (concerning drone strikes in Pakistan).

not refrain from assessing the legality, whether under domestic or international law, of a foreign state's act 'where it is plain beyond dispute that a clearly established norm of international law has been violated'.[131] The English act of state and *Buttes* doctrines, being purely judge-made, cannot apply where the court is directed by statute to adjudicate a particular issue.[132] As a result, there is no scope for a plea of non-justiciability on such bases in criminal proceedings.[133] That being said, both doctrines remain applicable in civil confiscation proceedings.

In US law, such limitations do not apply. No exception is made where the conduct under consideration is alleged to be unlawful under customary international law,[134] and the act of state doctrine is applicable in criminal proceedings. On several occasions, a plea of act of state has been invoked before US courts by foreign heads of state accused of drug trafficking and corruption. For instance, the issue arose in a case concerning a petition of *habeas corpus* filed by former Venezuelan president Marcos Pérez Jiménez to oppose his extradition to Venezuela on corruption charges.[135] Jiménez argued that as the former dictator of Venezuela, he was himself the 'sovereign' and that the financial crimes for which his extradition was sought were acts of the sovereign. The Court of Appeals for the Fifth Circuit rejected the argument, ruling that Jiménez was merely an executive of the sovereign state of Venezuela, and that as a matter of law, acts of embezzlement are not acts of sovereignty but common crimes committed for his personal benefit 'in violation of his position and not in pursuance of it'.[136] An analogous conclusion was reached by the District Court for the Southern District of Florida in the trial of Manuel Noriega. The line of reasoning adopted by the Court to reject Noriega's contention is as follows:

> The Court fails to see how Noriega's alleged drug trafficking and protection of money launderers could conceivably constitute public action taken on behalf of the Panamanian state. Certainly no evidence has been presented to this effect, despite Defendant's burden of proof on the issue. [. . .] The indictment in this case charges a series of private acts committed by the defendant for his own personal financial enrichment. It does not allege, and cannot reasonably be construed to charge, that Noriega participated in a racketeering enterprise and conspired to import cocaine into the United States in furtherance of Panama's state policy or to serve some overriding national interest. The fact that Noriega is alleged to have utilized his official position to engage in criminal activity does not, as Defendant suggests, cast his actions in a public light; as we well know, government officials are as capable of exploiting their positions of power for private, selfish ends as they are for public purpose. The inquiry is not whether Noriega used his official position to engage in the challenged acts, but whether those acts were taken on behalf of Noriega instead of Panama.[137]

[131] See *Kuwait Airways Corp v Iraqi Airways Co (Nos 4 and 5)*, [2002] AC 883, at 1109, para 140 (Lord Hope). This would be the case, for example, 'where there is a grave infringement of human rights': see *Khan* (n 130), para 28 (yet the Court in this case still refused to examine the claimant's contention that the CIA had committed crimes against humanity and war crimes (paras 51–52)).

[132] See *Pinochet (No 1)* (n 108), at 107 (Lord Nicholls).

[133] But see Lord Lloyd's opinion in *Pinochet (No 1)*, taking the view that the Court should decline jurisdiction on the basis of the *Buttes* doctrine (at 102–104).

[134] See *Banco Nacional de Cuba v Sabbatino* (n 127), at 428–37.

[135] *Jiménez v Aristeguieta* (n 56).

[136] Ibid, at 557–58.

[137] *United States v Noriega*, 746 F Supp 1506 (SD Fla 1990), at 1522.

The fact that Noriega used the resources of the state for criminal purposes was not considered by the Court to be a relevant consideration.

A similar issue was litigated in asset forfeiture proceedings initiated by the Philippines against its former president, Ferdinand Marcos. The Philippines alleged that Marcos had acquired his wealth through unlawful expropriation decrees and other illicit methods. Two contradictory decisions were rendered by two courts of appeals in this case. In the first, the Court of Appeals for the Second Circuit, drawing a 'distinction between acts of Marcos as head of state, which may be protected from judicial scrutiny even if illegal under Philippines law, and his purely private acts', concluded that Marcos had not met his burden to prove that his wealth had been acquired though official acts, and rejected his claim on the facts.[138] The Court stressed the difficulty of distinguishing between public and private acts in this case,[139] which illustrates the legal challenges posed by kleptocratic modes of governance. But in the second decision, the Court of Appeals for the Ninth Circuit, reversing the burden of proof, could not conclude that Marcos' property had not been acquired in the performance of his official capacity and overruled the injunction ordering the freezing of assets.[140] As the Court pointed out: '[t]hat one of the motives behind a particular governmental act may have been selfish, or that it was intended to serve otherwise improper ends, does not make that act any less the pronouncement of the sovereign'.[141] The Court concluded on a cynical note: 'Offensive as such absolute government may be to our sense of justice, no legal restraints can prevail against dictatorial power. A dictator can do whatever he can get away with. A court of law in this country simply cannot second-guess how that power is exercised'.[142]

As these cases show, the act of state doctrine is relied on by kleptocrats to escape the jurisdiction of foreign courts, sometimes successfully. As pointed out in relation to immunity *ratione materiae*, in kleptocratic regimes the distinction between official and private acts may be difficult to draw, giving ground for a defendant to argue that his acts could be considered as acts of government.[143] The cases cited above illustrate the challenges of adjudicating cases where the apparatus of the state is so deeply involved in criminal conduct that it becomes almost impossible to untangle the interconnection of the private and official spheres. In jurisdictions where the act of state doctrine and similar grounds of non-justiciability are recognized, the conduct of foreign state officials involved in state organized crime could, in certain circumstances, escape judicial scrutiny.

[138] *Republic of the Philippines v Marcos*, 806 F2d 344 (2nd Cir 1986), at 359–60.

[139] Ibid, at 359. [140] *Marcos II* (n 106). [141] Ibid, at 1485.

[142] Ibid, at 1489. For a critique of this decision, see Tracie A Sundack, '*Republic of the Philippines v Marcos*: The Ninth Circuit Allows a Former Ruler to Invoke the Act of State Doctrine against a Resisting Sovereign' (1988) 38 *American University Law Review* 225.

[143] Recall Section B.4(a)(i) of this chapter.

5. Immunity from enforcement measures of state property and property belonging to a head of state

The rules of international law governing the immunity of certain property from pre- and post-judgment measures of constraint pose certain challenges to the confiscation of proceeds of crime in cases of state organized crime. First, in many cases sovereign immunity shields state property from enforcement measures. Secondly, property owned by a head of state is sometimes considered to be immune from measures of constraint.

(a) Immunity of state property

In cases of state organized crime, there may be doubts as to whether certain assets are privately or state-owned, notably where illicitly obtained assets are intermingled with state property. Asset confiscation regimes established pursuant to existing treaties, whether criminal or civil, risk being ineffective in this situation because of the immunity granted to state property. Pursuant to Article 18 of the UN Convention on Jurisdictional Immunities of States and Their Property, state property cannot be subject to pre-judgment measures of constraint, such as attachment or arrest, in connection with a proceeding before a court of another state, unless the state has consented to the taking of such measures. Article 19 further provides that state property cannot, without the state's consent, be subject to post-judgment foreign measures of constraint, 'unless and to the extent that [...] it has been established that the property is specifically in use or intended for use by the State for other than government non-commercial purposes and is in the territory of the State of the forum'. These provisions are commonly considered to codify customary international law.[144]

Although criminal proceedings are not explicitly excluded from the scope of the Convention, the general understanding is that the latter applies only to civil proceedings.[145] Nonetheless, 'the rules of customary international law continue to govern matters not regulated by the provisions of the [...] Convention'.[146] As far as criminal confiscation proceedings are concerned, it is probable that, as a matter of customary international law, foreign state property remains immune from any

[144] See Chester Brown and Roger O'Keefe, 'Article 18' and 'Article 19' in Roger O'Keefe and Christian J Tams (eds), *The United Nations Convention on Jurisdictional Immunities of States and Their Property: A Commentary* (Oxford University Press, 2013), respectively at 306 and 327. The ICJ ruled that 'there is at least one condition that has to be satisfied before any measure of constraint may be taken against property belonging to a foreign State: that the property in question must be in use for an activity not pursuing government non-commercial purposes [...]' (*Jurisdictional Immunities of the State* (n 83), at 148, para 118). Although the reference to 'any measure of constraint' may be taken to suggest that the 'commercial use' exception also applies to pre-judgment measures of constraint, the Court's *dictum* seems to be limited to post-judgment measures of constraint within the meaning of Art 19 of the Convention: see Brown and O'Keefe, 'Article 18', at 307.

[145] See UN General Assembly Resolution 59/38, 2 December 2004, UN Doc A/RES/59/38, para 2; Roger O'Keefe, 'The "General Understandings"' in O'Keefe and Tams (n 144), at 19–21.

[146] Convention on Jurisdictional Immunities of States and Their Property, preamble, 5th recital.

pre- or post-judgment measure of constraint, such as asset freezes and confiscation.[147] Whether the 'commercial use' exception used in civil proceedings would apply in this context remains open to question.

The test for determining whether property falls under the 'commercial use' exception does not depend on the nature or origin of the assets, but rather on the purpose for which they are used or intended to be used by the state.[148] In certain jurisdictions, state property is presumed to serve public purposes and domestic courts will defer to the qualification made by the foreign state.[149]

Article 21 of the UN Convention on Jurisdictional Immunities of States and Their Property further lists specific categories of property that do not to fall under the 'commercial use' exception and therefore remain immune from any measure of constraint, subject to a waiver by the state:

(*a*) property, including any bank account, which is used or intended for use in the performance of the functions of the diplomatic mission of the State or its consular posts, special missions, missions to international organizations or delegations to organs of international organizations or to international conferences;
(*b*) property of a military character or used or intended for use in the performance of military functions;
(*c*) property of the central bank or other monetary authority of the State;
(*d*) property forming part of the cultural heritage of the State or part of its archives and not placed or intended to be placed on sale;
(*e*) property forming part of an exhibition of objects of scientific, cultural or historical interest and not placed or intended to be placed on sale.

[147] Since the evolution from an absolute to a restrictive doctrine of state immunity in civil proceedings did not affect the immunity of states in connection with criminal proceedings (Hazel Fox and Philippa Webb, *The Law of State Immunity* (3rd edn, Oxford University Press, 2013), at 89), there is no reason to believe that the absolute doctrine of state immunity, which renders state property immune from any foreign measure of constraint (ibid, at 482), does not apply to criminal confiscation proceedings. See also Xiaodong Yang, *State Immunity in International Law* (Cambridge University Press, 2012), at 427 (taking the view that 'under current international law, States qua States still enjoy absolute immunity from criminal proceedings').

[148] See Brown and O'Keefe, 'Article 19' (n 144), at 323; Xiaodong (n 147), at 362–73. In some jurisdictions, other considerations are taken into account, such as the legality of the activities from which property was derived. For example, in the United States assets obtained in violation of international law may be subject to enforcement measures: see 28 USC § 1610(a)(3). This principle was endorsed by the International Law Association: see *Draft Articles for a Convention on State Immunity*, 1982, (1983) 22 ILM 287, Art VIII(A)(3).

[149] See August Reinisch, 'European Court Practice Concerning State Immunity from Enforcement Measures' (2006) 14 *European Journal of International Law* 803, at 829–33, and the cases cited therein. See in particular the *Philippine Embassy Bank Account* case decided by the German Federal Constitutional Court, 2 BvM 1/76, 13 December 1977, BVerfGE 46, 342, reproduced in English in 65 ILR 146, at 189, holding: 'For the executing authorities of the receiving State to require the sending State, without its consent, to provide details concerning the existence or the past, present or future purposes of funds in such an account would constitute interference, contrary to international law, in matters within the exclusive competence of the sending State. On the other hand, general international law does not prohibit asking the sending State to substantiate the fact that a given account is one that is used for the continued performance of the functions of its diplomatic mission. As regards the substance and form of such substantiation, the State of the forum must of course, in accordance with international law, be satisfied with due assurances from a competent authority of the sending State'.

Commentators suggest that this provision partly reflects customary international law.[150]

Difficulties arise where there are doubts as to whether property is privately or state-owned and notably where illicitly obtained assets are intermingled with state property, as may be the case in certain situations of state organized crime. A study of obstacles to asset recovery conducted by the World Bank and UNODC found that 'immunity acts as a barrier where, for example, bank accounts are set up in the name of a jurisdiction but are used to finance personal expenses of dishonest officials who attempt to claim immunity on the basis that the activities related to state sovereignty'.[151] This problem is illustrated by the dispute between Equatorial Guinea and France regarding an alleged breach of Equatorial Guinea's sovereign immunity as a result of the decision of French investigating magistrates to seize a building suspected of having been purchased by Teodoro Nguema Obiang Mangue with embezzled public funds. Equatorial Guinea claims that the building in question is state property used by its diplomatic mission. The ICJ has granted Equatorial Guinea's request for provisional measures, ordering France to take all appropriate measures to ensure the inviolability of the premises.[152] A similar problem arose in confiscation proceedings carried out in Switzerland pursuant to a request by the United States for mutual legal assistance concerning assets suspected of having been illicitly obtained by Kazakh President Nursultan Nazarbayev. Kazakhstan argued that the targeted assets were state property and that they were destined to be used for public purposes. A Swiss court acknowledged that it could not exclude the possibility that the assets were in fact intended to be used for sovereign purposes, and quashed the decision of the investigating magistrate to seize documents concerning the suspicious bank accounts.[153]

(b) Immunity of property belonging to a head of state

Property privately owned by a head of state is sometimes considered to be immune from measures of constraint.[154] This aspect of the immunity and inviolability of

[150] Chester Brown and Roger O'Keefe, 'Article 21' in O'Keefe and Tams (n 144), at 346.

[151] Stolen Asset Recovery Initiative (World Bank and UNODC), *Barriers to Asset Recovery: An Analysis of the Key Barriers and Recommendations for Action* (International Bank for Reconstruction and Development, 2011), at 71.

[152] *Immunities and Criminal Proceedings (Equatorial Guinea v France)*, Request for the Indication of Provisional Measures, Order of 7 December 2016, para 48.

[153] Chambre d'accusation du canton de Genève, Decision of 29 June 2000. The federal court, however, ruled that immunity did not apply because 'the intrinsic nature of the operation intended to be carried out by the state' did not meet the definition of 'public purpose' (author's translation): see TF, Ière Cour de droit public, Decision of 8 December 2000, Case no 1P.581/2000, and Decision of 25 June 2001, Case no 1A.94/2001.

[154] See Watts (n 119), at 69–70; Foakes (n 111), at 99–100. Precedents are scarce: see in particular the decision of a Belgian court in *Consorts Mobutu c. SA Cotoni*, 29 December 1988, (1989) *Revue de jurisprudence de Liège, Mons et Bruxelles* 169, reproduced in English in 91 ILR 259 (vacating the conservatory attachment of immovable property belonging to former Zairian ruler Mobutu Sese Seko on grounds of immunity).

heads of state remains a grey area in international law.[155] The International Law Institute noted that '[p]roperty belonging personally to a Head of State and located in the territory of a foreign State may not be subject to any measure of execution except to give effect to a final judgement, rendered against such Head of State'.[156] However, the Institute took the view that provisional measures such as asset freezes may be taken '[w]hen serious doubt arises as to the legality of the appropriation of fund or any other asset held by, or on behalf of, the Head of State'.[157] The contours of the immunity of property belonging to a head of state remain fuzzy. If recognized and enforced by domestic courts, such immunities have the potential to hinder asset confiscation proceedings in cases of state organized crime.

C. Failure to Take into Account the Involvement of State Organs and Resources in Organized Crime

Under the law as it currently stands, a public official involved in state organized crime can be convicted under domestic law for his participation in the commission of offences such as drug trafficking, abuse of functions, participation in an organized criminal group, or money laundering. Yet a conviction on such charges would not represent the full extent of the offender's blameworthiness and of the criminogenic forces at play in state organized crime. Beyond the practical issues analysed above, a fundamental shortcoming of the existing international legal framework arguably lies in its failure to take into account the involvement of state officials and the use of state resources in organized crime. Our examination of the substantive provisions of crime-suppression conventions requiring states parties to criminalize organized crime, corruption, and related conduct shows that the former are almost completely silent on the crucial issue of the involvement of state officials and of the diversion of state resources for criminal purposes. Even though a handful of instruments do provide for aggravating circumstances when the offender is a public official acting in an official capacity,[158] in the vast majority of cases this dimension is completely ignored. Most crime-suppression conventions do not contemplate the involvement of

[155] On the occasion of its work on the jurisdictional immunities of states and their property, the ILC considered a proposal by Special Rapporteur Sucharitkul to include a provision addressing the issue. Draft Art 25(2) used to read as follows: 'No measures of attachment or execution may be taken in respect of property of a personal sovereign or head of State if they cannot be taken without infringing the inviolability of his person or of his residence'. See *Eighth report on jurisdictional immunities of States and their property, by Mr. Sompong Sucharitkul, Special Rapporteur*, 3 March 1986, UN Doc A/CN.4/396 in *Yearbook of the International Law Commission* (1986), vol II(1), at 31. The proposal was rejected, but for reasons that do not challenge the validity of this principle: see Records of the 1944th meeting, 13 May 1986 in *Yearbook of the International Law Commission* (1986), vol I, at 17.

[156] Resolution on Immunities from Jurisdiction and Execution of Heads of State and of Government in International Law (n 107), Art 4(1).

[157] Ibid, Art 4(2).

[158] See UN Drug Convention, Art 3(5)(e); EU Directive on preventing and combating trafficking in human beings and protecting its victims, Art 4(3); Council of Europe Convention on Action against Trafficking in Human Beings, Art 24(c).

senior public officials in organized criminal activities.[159] Nor do they contemplate the use of the material and human resources of the state for criminal purposes. It is true that a few existing offences adequately capture certain aspects of state organized crime. For instance, the prohibition of abuse of functions in UNCAC covers criminal acts carried out in the discharge of official duties for the purpose of obtaining an undue advantage.[160] Similarly, the offence of improper use of state property, as defined in the Inter-American Convention against Corruption, requires that the offender act 'because of, or in the performance of, his functions' and for the purpose of obtaining a benefit.[161] But neither of these are offences which states parties to the relevant conventions are obliged to criminalize.

The silence of international law regarding these particular issues is problematic. Ignoring the involvement of state organs in organized criminal activities is ignoring the wrong inherent in state organized crime and the harm it causes. Providing for aggravated punishment is not sufficient to reflect the qualitative difference between regular cases of organized crime and cases involving state officials abusing their authority to participate in organized crime. This difference matters because it reflects normative considerations about the nature of the wrong inherent in, and of the harm caused by, state organized crime.[162]

Similar considerations underpin the criminalization of genocide. As Judge Shahabuddeen wrote in his opinion in the *Jelisić* genocide case adjudicated by the ICTY Appeals Chamber, discussions about the legal definition of genocide as opposed to other crimes are not merely academic; they are concerned with 'recording the true extent of [a defendant's] criminal conduct on allegations of gravity'.[163] The seriousness of certain international crimes such as genocide or terrorism derives from the specific intent with which these crimes are committed, which in itself justifies that conduct which could be punishable as murder or as other 'regular' offences against the person be criminalized as a separate offence with distinctive constitutive elements. Constitutive elements reflecting the purpose for which certain crimes are committed, or the means through which they are committed, or the context in which they are committed, set these crimes apart from other offences. The difference, therefore, is not merely quantitative—as reflected in the aggravated

[159] Note that the involvement of public officials in organized crime is criminalized as such in certain domestic legislation. See e.g., in India: Maharashtra Control of Organized Crime Act, 1999, s 24 (which provides: 'Whoever being a public servant renders any help or support in any manner in the commission of organized crime [...], whether before or after the commission of any offence by a member of an organized crime syndicate or abstains from taking lawful measures under this Act or intentionally avoids to carry out the directions of any Court or of the superior police officers in this respect, shall be punished with imprisonment of either description for a term which may extend to three years and also with fine').

[160] UNCAC, Art 19.

[161] Inter-American Convention against Corruption, Art XI(1)(b).

[162] A similar argument was made by Kofele-Kale, who argued that existing corruption offences 'do not adequately convey the full force' of the concept of 'patrimonicide': see Ndiva Kofele-Kale, 'Patrimonicide: The International Economic Crime of Indigenous Spoliation' (1995) 28 *Vanderbilt Journal of Transnational Law* 45, at 56–58.

[163] *Prosecutor v Goran Jelisić*, Case no IT-95-10, Appeals Judgment, 5 July 2001, Partial Dissenting Opinion of Judge Shahabuddeen, para 25.

punishment incurred—but truly qualitative—as reflected in the separate denomination of the crime.

As already noted in Chapter 2, it is from the perspective of expressivism that international law's omission to consider and attach legal consequences to the involvement of state organs in organized crime is the most consequential.[164] This normative void undermines the expressive potential of international law with respect to organized crime and corruption in general. Legal norms can only communicate the wrongfulness of conduct and influence behaviour if they label and describe the wrongdoing accurately. As far as state organized crime is concerned, existing international criminal law instruments are inadequate to fulfil this function.

Raphael Lemkin, with his study of genocide and his proposal to adopt a convention specifically dedicated to preventing and punishing genocide as an international crime, demonstrated how new ways to conceive of criminal phenomena may require new normative approaches.[165] It is important that the law be tailored to the dynamics of crime. The particular and distinctive quality of the wrong inherent in state organized crime should be formally reflected in the law. A qualitative distinction should accordingly be drawn between ordinary cases of organized crime or corruption, and cases involving the diversion of state resources for criminal purposes by the highest authorities of the state acting in the pursuit of profit. It is this latter dimension that distinguishes state organized crime from ordinary economic crime and that would arguably justify establishing state organized crime as a distinct international crime.

D. Conclusion

Existing crime-suppression conventions are, *de lege lata*, inadequate to combat state organized crime. First, the applicable law is fragmented into different legal regimes implemented unevenly across national jurisdictions. Secondly, the current international crime-suppression model rests on a territorial approach to jurisdiction that is likely to be ineffective in politically sensitive cases. Thirdly, certain mechanisms applicable to extradition proceedings, such as the political offence exception, the discrimination clause, and the 'essential interests' clause, can be relied on by suspected offenders or requested states parties to undermine international cooperation in criminal matters. Fourthly, the narrow formulation of the obligation *aut dedere aut judicare* in the relevant conventions can in certain circumstances allow offenders to escape punishment. Fifthly, the legal regime established by the relevant instruments remains subject to the international law of jurisdictional immunities, which in certain cases shields state officials from foreign criminal proceedings as well as

164 Recall Chapter 2, Section E. For a discussion of expressivist theories of law and of their relevance to my argument, see Chapter 5, Section A.2.

165 Raphael Lemkin, *Axis Rule in Occupied Europe: Laws of Occupation, Analysis of Government, Proposals for Redress*, first published 1944 (The Lawbook Exchange, 2005), at 79. See also generally John Cooper, *Raphael Lemkin and the Struggle for the Genocide Convention* (Palgrave Macmillan, 2008).

state property from measures of foreign judicial constraint in confiscation proceedings. Sixthly, and most importantly, the existing law does not adequately take into consideration the involvement of state organs in organized crime and the diversion of state resources for criminal purposes, and therefore fails to fulfil a crucial expressive function.

Many of the issues identified in this chapter are archetypal manifestations of state sovereignty in international law. The prerogatives of state sovereignty exist and are preserved under international law for legitimate reasons, but they can also present an enduring obstacle to the effective suppression of international crimes where the interests of a state or those of its most powerful representatives are at risk of being compromised. Nonetheless, the above analysis suggests that some of the shortcomings of the existing law are not irremediable, and that there is a need for dedicated legal responses to state organized crime. In keeping with the assumption that as a matter of legal policy, endeavours to suppress state organized crime should be targeted primarily at individuals, the final part of the book will elaborate a normative justification for establishing state organized crime as an international crime, and put forward proposals to develop international legal mechanisms specifically designed to hold perpetrators accountable.

PART III

INTERNATIONAL LEGAL MECHANISMS FOR THE SUPPRESSION OF STATE ORGANIZED CRIME

5

A Normative Justification for Establishing State Organized Crime as an International Crime

Few would deny that state organized crime is intuitively 'wrong' and that something ought to be done about it. Yet before a remedial course of action can be prescribed, it is necessary to understand what makes the phenomenon of state organized crime reprehensible in general and in particular from the perspective of international law. This is the concern of the present chapter, which presents a normative justification for establishing state organized crime as an international crime. State organized crime is not *de lege lata* a crime under international law, either pursuant to treaty or custom. There are, however, sound normative reasons to establish state organized crime as an international crime. The argument is advanced in three steps. First, this chapter reflects on the social function of criminalization generally to identify guiding principles and set up a theoretical framework. Then, it discusses the concept of 'international crime' and undertakes an empirical analysis of the dynamics of criminalization at the international level to identify elements underlying the establishment of international crimes. In light of this normative framework, it finally suggests reasons to establish state organized crime as an international crime.

A. Theoretical Aspects of Criminalization

Criminalization is the norm-making process through which states prohibit and make punishable certain acts or omissions as criminal offences. Prior to examining how criminalization is conceptualized and how it operates in the international sphere, it is useful to consider some general theoretical aspects to understand what sort of conduct is typically considered eligible for criminalization, and why. This section outlines some fundamental principles of criminalization theory.

1. General principles of criminalization

Criminalization theory does not provide a legal basis for enacting or striking down legislation. It seeks to put forward a normative justification for establishing certain types of conduct as criminal offences[1] and accordingly to delineate a perimeter

[1] See Robert Cryer, 'The Doctrinal Foundations of International Criminalization' in M Cherif Bassiouni (ed), *International Criminal Law*, vol I: *Sources, Subject, and Contents* (3rd edn, Martinus

for the proper reach of the criminal law. While it is doubtful that a single theory can satisfyingly explain the rationales underlying criminalization,[2] criminalization theory offers useful indicators of the values that the law should protect or enforce. Criminalization theory is a form of ethical-normative theory, providing a framework for normative evaluation.[3] This section presents different approaches to criminalization theory developed by common-law and continental legal scholarship.

(a) *The deontological approach: legal moralism*

Legal moralists believe that 'all and only moral wrongs should be prohibited by the criminal law'.[4] According to this approach, wrongfulness is evaluated by reference to the principles and standards of a particular moral code. While legal moralism provides an intuitive model for criminalization, it does not satisfyingly overcome obstacles posed by moral and cultural relativism.[5] What may be considered morally objectionable in one particular social and cultural context may be acceptable in another, and may evolve over time. The challenge of relativism is particularly acute in the international context, characterized as it is by a plurality of cultural, social, and moral repertoires.[6]

The difficulty of relying on a moralist discourse in criminal-law theory has given rise to a 'moral arguphobia',[7] leading many criminal-law theorists to avoid references to ethical principles and to seek alternatives to legal moralism. Some argue that 'wrongfulness by itself does not even establish a *pro tanto* claim for criminalization' and that 'conduct is eligible for criminalization only when it involves further effects'.[8] To impose objective limits on the use of coercive power by the state, it appears necessary to take into consideration the consequences of the conduct being considered for criminalization.

Nijhoff, 2008) 107, at 127 (arguing that the models proposed by criminalization theory are 'understandable abstractions from the facts of criminalization' that can 'give structure' to the progressive development of the law).

[2] To account realistically for the rationales underlying criminalization, such a theory would indeed have to take into consideration all social, political, and human factors involved in law-making.

[3] The field of normative ethics 'is concerned with the articulation and the justification of the fundamental principles that govern [moral evaluation]'. See Julia Driver, 'Normative Ethics' in Frank Jackson and Michael Smith (eds), *The Oxford Handbook of Contemporary Philosophy* (Oxford University Press, 2007) 31, at 31.

[4] Michael S Moore, *Placing Blame: A Theory of the Criminal Law* (Oxford University Press, 2010), at 754. See also at 645, 662.

[5] This problem is acknowledged by Moore: see ibid, at 652, 662–63.

[6] On cultural relativism in international law, see generally René-Jean Dupuy (ed), *The Future of International Law in a Multicultural World* (Martinus Nijhoff, 1984); Götz Schulze (ed), *Kulturelle Relativität des internationalen Rechts* (Nomos, 2014).

[7] Douglas N Husak, *Philosophy of Criminal Law* (Rowman & Littlefield, 1987), at 231.

[8] Andrew Simester and Andreas von Hirsch, *Crimes, Harms, and Wrongs: On the Principles of Criminalization* (Hart Publishing, 2011), at 141.

(b) Consequentialist approaches

In most legal systems, the criminal law is perceived as a means to protect certain interests of the community. Anglo-American criminalization theory revolves around the well-known 'harm principle'. According to John Stuart Mill, 'the only purpose for which power can be rightfully exercised over any member of a civilized community, against his will, is to prevent harm to others'.[9] The harm principle justifies criminalizing conduct that results in 'the thwarting, setting back, or defeating of an interest'.[10] The concept of a legally protectable interest is narrowly conceived. It consists of individual welfare interests, that is to say, 'interest[s] in achieving and maintaining that minimum level of physical and mental health, material resources, economic assets, and political liberty that is necessary [to achieve] well-being',[11] as well as of 'public interests' shared by all individuals.[12]

In civil-law countries, the proper reach of the criminal law is conceptualized through similar models, such as the *Rechtsgut* doctrine in Germany[13] and the *principio di offensività* in Italy.[14] While in Germany this principle does not appear to be justiciable,[15] in Italy it has been endorsed on some occasions by the Constitutional Court.[16] Both theories provide that criminalization is justified only in so far as conduct infringes or threatens[17] legally protected goods. These goods (*Rechtsgüter*, or

[9] John Stuart Mill, *On Liberty* (London, 1859), chap. I, para 9.

[10] Joel Feinberg, *The Moral Limits of the Criminal Law*, vol 1: *Harm to Others* (Oxford University Press, 1987), at 33, 36.

[11] Ibid, at 37–63.

[12] Ibid, at 63–64, 221–25. Similarly, the International Association of Penal Law refers to the concept of 'social harm': Resolutions of the XVIth International Congress of Penal Law: 'The Criminal Justice System Facing the Challenge of Organized Crime' (Budapest, 5–11 September 1999) in José Luis de la Cuesta (ed), *Resolutions of the Congresses of the International Association of Penal Law (1926–2004)* (Érès, 2009) 175, at 179.

[13] See generally Roland Hefendehl, Andreas von Hirsch, and Wolfgang Wohlers (eds), *Die Rechtsgutstheorie: Legitimationsbasis des Strafrechts oder dogmatisches Glasperlenspiel?* (Nomos, 2003). This theory was first expounded by Johannes Birnbaum as follows: 'among those actions that tend to be punished as crimes in all states some are of the type by which first of all certain persons are violated in one of the goods to be guaranteed to all by state power and others of the type in which the action directly deprives, diminishes or endangers one of these goods in relation to the community. Thus it is possible to determine the classification of crimes as a whole according to the [...] nature of the good primarily threatened or diminished by the action'. See Johann Michael Franz Birnbaum, 'Über das Erforderniß einer Rechtsverletzung zum Begriffe des Verbrechens, mit besonderer Rücksicht auf den Begriff der Ehrenkränkung' (1834) 15 *Archiv des Criminalrechts (Neue Folge)* 149, at 178; translation in Markus D Dubber (ed), *Foundational Texts in Modern Criminal Law* (Oxford University Press, 2014) 389, at 399. The *Rechtsgutslehre* is a doctrine that aims at setting substantive limits to the repressive power of the state (*systemkritische Funktion der Rechstgutslehre*).

[14] See generally Vittorio Manes, *Il principio di offensività nel diritto penale. Canone di politica criminale, criterio ermeneutico, parametro di ragionevolezza* (Giappichelli, 2005).

[15] The German Constitutional Court does not endorse the *Rechtsgutslehre* when assessing whether a given criminal prohibition conforms to the constitution. The Court applies a proportionality test, verifying that the proposed offence is suitable, necessary, and adequate to achieve a legitimate purpose pursued by the legislator. See Decision no 2 BvR 392/07, 26 February 2008, BVerfGE 120, 224, para 39 (regarding the legality of the prohibition of incest).

[16] See e.g. C Cost, Decision no 189/1987, 21 May 1987; Decision no 519/1995, 28 December 1995.

[17] For the argument that acts presenting a mere threat to a protected interest may legitimately be prohibited, see e.g. Günther Jakobs, 'Kriminalisierung im Vorfeld einer Rechtsgutsverletzung' (1985) 97

beni giuridici) are '[a]ll facts or established goals that are necessary for the free development of the individual's personality, the realization of his or her civil rights and the functioning of a political system which is based on these objectives',[18] as well as collective and universal goods.[19] They are akin to the 'interests' protected by the harm principle.[20]

All of the consequentialist theories come to similar conclusions regarding moral wrongs. They posit that morally reprehensible conduct should not be criminalized unless it endangers a protected interest.[21] They also face a common difficulty, namely, that of defining and delineating legally protected 'interests' or 'goods'. Because the definition of interests that may legitimately be protected through the criminal law is sometimes vague and abstract,[22] it has been argued that the *Rechtsgutslehre* and the harm principle fail to provide sufficiently reliable criteria to evaluate the legitimacy of criminal-law norms.[23] It has also been pointed out that because the identification and delineation of interests worthy of protection depend on broader normative considerations, these theories are not a genuine alternative to legal moralism.[24] Consequentialist theories do, however, provide a clearer and more rigorous framework for delineating the scope and reach of the criminal law.

2. The expressive function of criminal law

Expressivist accounts of law theorize how meaning is communicated by legal norms and how it is received and internalized by the norms' addressees.[25] Drawing on

Zeitschrift für die gesamte Strafrechtswissenschaft 751 (discussing the concept of *Vorfeldkriminalisierung* in German criminal-law theory).

[18] Claus Roxin, *Strafrecht: allgemeiner Teil*, vol I: *Grundlagen. Der Aufbau der Verbrechenslehre* (4th edn, C.H. Beck, 2006), at 16 (translation in Carl Constantin Lauterwein, *The Limits of Criminal Law: A Comparative Analysis of Approaches to Legal Theorizing* (Ashgate, 2010), at 10).

[19] Roxin (n 18), at 17, 38–40; Roland Hefendehl, *Kollektive Rechtsgüter im Strafrecht* (Heymanns, 2002). Public interests are sometimes understood to include those which constitute a fundamental normative framework necessary for the state to protect and enforce individual rights: see Roland Hefendehl, 'Die Materialisierung von Rechtsgut und Deliktsstruktur' (2002) 149 *Goltdammer's Archiv für Strafrecht* 21, at 25.

[20] See Andreas von Hirsch, 'Der Rechtsgutsbegriff und das „Harm Principle"' in Hefendehl, von Hirsch, and Wohlers (n 13), at 17–18. See also nn 11 and 12.

[21] Roxin (n 18), at 19–20.

[22] See e.g. Hans-Heinrich Jescheck and Thomas Weigend, *Lehrbuch des Strafrechts: Allgemeiner Teil* (5th edn, Duncker & Humblot, 1996), at 257 (defining *Rechtsgüter* as 'abstract values of the social order protected by law' (author's translation)). See *contra* Roxin (n 18), at 28 (arguing that concepts of too high a degree of abstraction, such as 'public peace', are not *Rechtsgüter*).

[23] Kurt Seelmann, 'Rechtsgutskonzept, „Harm Principle" und Anerkennungsmodell als Strafwürdigkeitskriterien' in Hefendehl, von Hirsch, and Wohlers (n 13), at 262.

[24] See Husak (n 7), at 231–37. See also Moore (n 4), at 753 (arguing that the underlying reason for defining harm to others as a precondition to criminalization is precisely that harming others is in most cases morally wrong).

[25] The label 'expressivist theories of law' refers to a diversified doctrinal field. For an overview, see Cass R Sunstein, 'On the Expressive Function of Law' (1996) 144 *University of Pennsylvania Law Review* 2021; Elizabeth S Anderson and Richard H Pildes, 'Expressive Theories of Law: A General Restatement' (2000) 148 *University of Pennsylvania Law Review* 1503; Matthew D Adler, 'Expressive Theories of Law: A Skeptical Overview' (2000) 148 *University of Pennsylvania Law Review* 1363; Alan Strudler, 'The Power of Expressive Theories of Law' (2001) 60 *Maryland Law Review* 492.

expressivist literature concerned with the communicative function of the law, by which it is meant law's ability to operate as normative statements affirming and conveying values to legal subjects, this section discusses the role of law in affirming normative standards and condemning transgressive conduct.

(a) *Consequentialist expressivist theories*

Law-making may be conceptualized as an act of communication. Consequentialist expressivist theories of law are concerned with the effect of normative statements on the addressees of a norm. Such expressivist accounts draw on 'rational choice' theory, positing that the actions of individuals reflect rational choices made in order to maximize benefits and to limit costs.[26] On this view, normative statements can be made 'to affect social norms and in that way ultimately to affect both judgments and behavior'.[27] Expressivist considerations are particularly relevant in the criminal law, where criminalization is conceived of as a moral appeal to legal subjects to refrain from engaging in criminal conduct.[28] Over time, criminalization fulfils a norm-nurturing function, which contributes to anchoring values and norms into society.[29]

In the international sphere, too, law has 'potential for changing the social meaning of particular behavior by altering the social cost of undertaking that behavior'.[30] Some authors argue that the actions of governments are driven in part by a need for recognition and esteem within the international community.[31] International law exercises in this way a distinct 'normative pressure' on its subjects.[32]

(b) *Deontological expressivist theories*

The persuasiveness of expressivist theories of law does not depend only on how successful a norm can be in shaping normative standards and affecting the conduct of legal subjects. Normative statements have value regardless of their intended or actual effects. They can be issued solely for the purpose of affirming principles and values.[33]

[26] See Robert Cooter, 'Expressive Law and Economics' (1998) 27 *Journal of Legal Studies* 585.

[27] Sunstein (n 25), at 2025. Accordingly, 'any support for "statements" should be rooted [...] in plausible judgments about its effects on social norms and hence in "on balance" judgements about its consequences' (at 2045). As Hart observed, '[a] legislature cannot introduce a new rule and give it the status of a moral rule just by its *fiat*' (Herbert L A Hart, *The Concept of Law* (2nd edn, Clarendon Press, 1994), at 230).

[28] Simester and von Hirsch (n 8), at 14.

[29] Paul H Robinson, 'Why Does the Criminal Law Care What the Layperson Thinks Is Just? Coercive Versus Normative Crime Control' (2000) 86 *Virginia Law Review* 1839, at 1868.

[30] Alex Geisinger and Michael Ashley Stein, 'A Theory of Expressive International Law' (2007) 60 *Vanderbilt Law Review* 75, at 83–84.

[31] Contrary to pure rational-choice theorists, these authors argue that the 'desire to be members of international society [...] exists separately from other preferences—it is a preference for esteem and not a preference for material or economic benefit—and can serve as a powerful influence on the willingness of States to conform to law' (ibid, at 111).

[32] Ibid, at 94 and *passim*.

[33] Cass R Sunstein, 'Incommensurability and Valuation in Law' (1994) 92 *Michigan Law Review* 779, at 823.

In this way, law fulfils a constitutive function by embodying the ethical code of the community. This is particularly true of the criminal law. Punishment in the criminal law is a vector for moral censure.[34] As Feinberg points out,

> punishment is a conventional device for the expression of attitudes of resentment and indignation, and of judgments of disapproval and reprobation, either on the part of the punishing authority himself or of those "in whose name" the punishment is inflicted. Punishment, in short, has a *symbolic significance*.[35]

The same symbolic significance is attached to criminalization. Criminalization operates as both an *ex ante* critical-moral communication of the wrongfulness of an act, and a commitment to impose justified punishment. In short, prohibitions in the criminal law speak with 'a moral voice'.[36]

(c) *The function of labelling*

The definition and labelling of offences, as well as the prescribed punishment, establish a scale of gravity in the criminal law.[37] Because murder and criminally negligent homicide are not regarded alike by society, they are treated and labelled differently under the criminal law. Criminalization must therefore seek to reflect, through the labelling of the offence and the definition of its constitutive elements, the specific wrongfulness and harm inherent in the prohibited conduct.

3. Conclusion

The fact that certain acts or omissions are perceived as a threat to individual or collective interests indispensable to the social order is considered a legitimate reason for establishing such conduct as a criminal offence. Criminalization in turn constitutes a statement of condemnation of the conduct in question. For such condemnation to be meaningful normatively, it must reflect the nature and seriousness of the harm, which requires that the prohibited conduct be appropriately defined and labelled by law. These considerations may not be determinative for law-makers, but they are nevertheless relevant when considering whether to criminalize conduct. The next section discusses their validity and relevance in the international sphere, to

[34] See Robin Antony Duff, *Trials and Punishments* (Cambridge University Press, 1986), at 233–45; Dan M Kahan, 'The Secret Ambition of Deterrence' (1999) 113 *Harvard Law Review* 413, at 419–25; Deidre Golash, 'The Justification of Punishment in the International Context' in Larry May and Zachary Hoskins (eds), *International Criminal Law and Philosophy* (Cambridge University Press, 2010) 201, at 217 ff.

[35] Joel Feinberg, *Doing and Deserving: Essays in the Theory of Responsibility* (Princeton University Press, 1970), at 98 (emphasis in the original). Expressivist accounts of punishment are clearly retributivist.

[36] Simester and von Hirsch (n 8), at 10–14. See also Immi Tallgren, 'The Sensibility and Sense of International Criminal Law' (2002) 13 *European Journal of International Law* 561, at 592 (conceiving international criminal law as 'the loudspeaker echoing the values of the international community', 'sending *ex ante* messages', and 'disseminating information on common values').

[37] See Dan M Kahan, 'What Do Alternative Sanctions Mean?' (1996) 63 *University of Chicago Law Review* 591, at 598 (noting that '[t]he expressive theory [...] explains the relative seriousness of different forms of wrongdoing').

determine whether they can influence the progressive development of international criminal law.

B. International Criminalization

Compared to the models developed in domestic criminal-law scholarship, criminalization theory in international law remains underdeveloped. This is due in part to the qualitative differences between domestic legal orders and the international legal order. While at the domestic level criminalization commonly occurs through the enactment of statutes by the legislature, in international law the positing of certain acts or omissions as a crime may originate from a variety of sources. International criminalization commonly occurs through the adoption by states of multilateral treaties or through their participation in the formation of customary law, but it may also arguably involve a decision of the UN Security Council requiring states to establish certain conduct as a criminal offence in their domestic law.[38] Criminalization theory at the international level is also crippled by the theoretical limbo surrounding the definition of the concept of 'international crime'. This section aims at defining a framework within which to make a theoretical argument for the international criminalization of state organized crime. It begins by addressing definitional issues surrounding the concept of 'international crime' and with an empirical analysis of the criminalization process at the international level. Identifying attributes common to several existing international crimes, it then shows that international criminalization seeks to safeguard specific interests.

1. The concept of international crime

International law scholarship has yet to reach an agreement about the meaning of the term 'international crime'. The view commonly considered to be prevailing, at least until recently, is that an international crime is a crime giving rise to individual criminal responsibility directly under international law, irrespective of domestic criminalization.[39] The tenants of this view accordingly draw a distinction between 'international' and 'transnational' crimes, the latter being crimes that states parties

[38] The Security Council acting under Chapter VII of the UN Charter can require UN member states to criminalize certain conduct, as it did in several resolutions. For an analysis of the 'legislative' power of the Security Council, see Chapter 7, Section B.1. The UN and international organizations in general play an important role in the genesis of criminal-law norms at the international level: see Frank Meyer, *Strafrechtsgenese in Internationalen Organizationen: Eine Untersuchung der Strukturen und Legitimationsvoraussetzungen strafrechtlicher Normbildungsprozesse in Mehrebenensystemen* (Nomos, 2012), in particular at 202–49.

[39] Se e.g. Kai Ambos, *Treatise on International Criminal Law*, vol I: *Foundations and General Part* (Oxford University Press, 2013), at 54; Otto Triffterer, *Dogmatische Untersuchungen zur Entwicklung des materiellen Völkerstrafrechts seit Nürnberg* (E. Albert, 1966), at 34; Hervé Ascensio, Emmanuel Decaux, and Alain Pellet, 'Présentation de la 1ère partie : Essai de classification et principe de légalité' in Hervé Ascensio, Emmanuel Decaux, and Alain Pellet (eds), *Droit international pénal* (2nd edn, Pedone, 2012) 93, at 93–95; Robert Cryer, *Prosecuting International Crimes: Selectivity and the International Criminal Law Regime* (Cambridge University Press, 2005), at 1–2. See also the ILC's definition of crimes against the peace and security of mankind: Draft Code of Crimes against the Peace and Security of Mankind in

to crime-suppression conventions are required to establish as criminal offences in their domestic law.[40] They often also consider that an international crime is a crime over which an international criminal tribunal may exercise jurisdiction.[41] Some authors deduce the existence of international crimes not only from formal criteria but also from a priori normative principles grounded in natural law, arguing that in order to qualify as an international crime, conduct needs to reach a certain threshold of gravity or to violate the fundamental values of the international community.[42] On this view, international crimes are typically associated with peremptory norms of international law (*jus cogens*).[43] And, finally, for some positivist scholars the concept of international crime includes any conduct defined as a crime by international law, whether treaty or custom, irrespective of whether such crimes can be considered to give rise to individual criminal responsibility directly under international law, and regardless of any particular substantive criterion.[44]

For the reasons convincingly put forward by O'Keefe to dispel common misconceptions about the concept of international crime,[45] this study adheres to the latter view. For the purposes of the following analysis, an 'international crime' is therefore understood to mean any conduct defined as a crime by international law, whether pursuant to treaty or custom. This formal definition does not differentiate between so-called 'core' international crimes and 'transnational' crimes. While the latter are often excluded from the definition of international crimes, one can actually argue with Heller that many of the crimes defined in crime-suppression conventions 'have

Report of the International Law Commission (48th sess), UN Doc A/51/10 in *Yearbook of the International Law Commission* (1996), vol II(2), Art 1(2).

[40] See e.g. Robert Cryer et al (eds), *An Introduction to International Criminal Law and Procedure* (3rd edn, Cambridge University Press, 2014), at 4; Neil Boister, *An Introduction to Transnational Criminal Law* (Oxford University Press, 2012), at 18–19; Ascensio, Decaux, and Pellet (n 39), at 94–95.

[41] See e.g. Cryer et al (n 40), at 4–5; Ascensio, Decaux, and Pellet (n 39), at 94.

[42] See e.g. M Cherif Bassiouni, 'International Crimes: The *Ratione Materiae* of International Criminal Law' in Bassiouni (n 1), at 133; Paola Gaeta, 'International Criminalization of Prohibited Conduct' in Antonio Cassese (ed), *The Oxford Companion to International Criminal Justice* (Oxford University Press, 2009) 63, at 66; David Luban, 'A Theory of Crimes against Humanity' (2004) 29 *Yale Journal of International Law* 85, at 98–103; Athos G Tsoutsos, 'Facteurs déterminant la notion du crime international' (1954) 7 *Revue hellénique de droit international* 164, at 168–69. See also the ILC's commentary to the 1996 Draft Code of Crimes against the Peace and Security of Mankind, in ILC Report (48th sess) (n 39), at 27, para 1 ('these heinous crimes shock the conscience of mankind, violate some of the most fundamental rules of international law and threaten international peace and security').

[43] See e.g. M Cherif Bassiouni, 'International Crimes: *Jus Cogens* and *Obligatio Erga Omnes*' (1996) 59 *Law and Contemporary Problems* 63; Stefan Kadelbach, '*Jus Cogens*, Obligations *Erga Omnes* and Other Rules – The Identification of Fundamental Norms' in Christian Tomuschat and Jean-Marc Thouvenin (eds), *The Fundamental Rules of the International Legal Order: Jus Cogens and Obligations Erga Omnes* (Martinus Nijhoff, 2006) 21, at 39; Larry May, *Crimes against Humanity: A Normative Account* (Cambridge University Press, 2005), at 24–39.

[44] See Roger O'Keefe, *International Criminal Law* (Oxford University Press, 2015), at 56, 60, 84; M Cherif Bassiouni, 'The Penal Characteristics of Conventional International Criminal Law' (1983) 15 *Case Western Reserve Journal of International Law* 27, at 28–29; Cryer (n 1), at 107; Yoram Dinstein, 'International Criminal Law' (1985) 20 *Israel Law Review* 206, at 221.

[45] O'Keefe (n 44), at 50–61.

an even stronger positivist claim to international status than some of the core international crimes'.[46] The positivist stance is grounded in a rigorous empirical analysis of existing norms of international criminal law and state practice pertaining to the definition and suppression of crime.

The analysis of the historical process of international criminalization shows that states have criminalized diverse conduct for a variety of reasons on an ad hoc basis, without following a distinguishable doctrinal line.[47] The decision to criminalize conduct at the international level is generally driven more by pragmatic concerns (that is, the strengthening of international cooperation and the elimination of loopholes to ensure the efficiency of law enforcement across national jurisdictions) than by the desire to protect and enforce the interests of an 'international community', as distinct from those of states. Moreover, individual criminal responsibility for international crimes derives in most if not all cases from domestic law and not directly from international law.[48] Whether the establishment of an international legal framework for the suppression of a particular crime amounts to 'criminalization' in any meaningful sense can be called into question. Nonetheless, the fact that states choose to address certain crimes by means of international law, but not other crimes, indicates that broader considerations are at play. The choice to have recourse to international law as a normative vehicle is dictated in part by the will to declare conduct reprehensible as a matter of international law, because such conduct has implications which go beyond sole domestic interests. An analysis of the object and purpose of existing international criminal law instruments, as expressed in their respective preambles,[49] suggests that states are guided by certain criteria and, more specifically, by the intention to protect specific interests deemed worthy of protection through international law. To that extent, it makes sense to speak of 'international criminalization'.

[46] Kevin Jon Heller, 'What Is an International Crime? (A Revisionist History)' (2017) 58 *Harvard International Law Journal* 353, at 356.

[47] Cryer (n 1), at 127; Bassiouni (n 44), at 28; Éric David, 'Les valeurs, politiques et objectifs du droit pénal international à l'heure de la mondialisation' in Association internationale de droit pénal, *International Criminal Law: Quo Vadis?*—Proceedings of the International Conference held in Siracusa, Italy, 28 November – 3 December 2002, Nouvelles études pénales no 19 (Érès, 2004) 157, at 157.

[48] See Heller (n 46), at 390–91 (arguing that international crimes are not crimes under international law but crimes that states are required by international law to establish as criminal offences within their domestic law).

[49] For the purpose of interpreting a treaty, preambles are relevant in determining the will of the contracting parties and in particular the object and purpose of the treaty: see VCLT, Art 31(2); *Reservations to the Convention on the Prevention and Punishment of the Crime of Genocide*, Advisory Opinion, ICJ Rep 1951, p 15, at 23; *Colombian-Peruvian Asylum Case (Colombia v Peru)*, Judgment, ICJ Rep 1950, p 266, at 282; Richard Gardiner, *Treaty Interpretation* (Oxford University Press, 2008), at 186, 196–97; Mark E Villiger, *Commentary on the 1969 Vienna Convention on the Law of Treaties* (Martinus Nijhoff, 2009), at 44, 428. Preambles are also indicative of the motives underlying the adoption of a resolution by the UN Security Council: see Michael C Wood, 'The Interpretation of Security Council Resolutions' (1998) 2 *Max Planck Yearbook of United Nations Law* 73, at 86, 90.

2. Interests protected by international criminalization

When it comes to the interests or 'legal goods' that states—the 'legislators', as it were, of international law—consider worthy of protection by enacting substantive international criminal law norms, there is no common denominator.[50] There are, however, various recurring themes. International instruments contain indications as to what kind of conduct is considered by states to be eligible for criminalization as a matter of international law. Analysing these indicators cannot provide 'self-evident predictive criteria' for identifying international crimes,[51] but it can help to establish a normative basis for the progressive development of international criminal law[52] in relation to state organized crime.

It is often said that international crimes are acts that adversely affect internationally protected interests.[53] Based on an analysis of existing international crimes established by treaty, this section identifies interests that states have considered worthy of protection by means of international criminal law. These interests are not the only ones that may have guided the establishment of international crimes, but they are relevant for the purposes of my argument concerning the criminalization of state organized crime. The interests in question are: the protection against the abuse of state authority, the maintenance of international peace and security, the more effective protection of human rights, the promotion of the rule of law, and the maintenance of normal international relations necessary for interstate cooperation.

(a) Protection against the abuse of state authority

States show a propensity for criminalizing as a matter of international law reprehensible acts committed by individuals in the exercise of state power. The underlying normative rationale for criminalizing conduct involving an abuse of state authority is that such conduct amounts to a betrayal of trust on the part of individuals entrusted with the responsibility and authority to uphold the law and protect the people under their jurisdiction.[54] This conception of public office as 'a position of

[50] The difficulty in finding a 'general or conceptual definition of crimes' was stressed by some members of the ILC while working on a Draft Code of Crimes against the Peace and Security of Mankind: see ILC Report (48th sess) (n 39), at 77, para 113. The members of the Commission, however, agreed that it was useful to identify some distinctive features of crimes against the peace and security of mankind: see *Report of the International Law Commission* (47th sess), UN Doc A/50/10 in *Yearbook of the International Law Commission* (1995), vol II(2), at 18, para 47, and at 19, paras 56–57.

[51] Cryer (n 1), at 126. See also Dinstein (n 44), at 221.

[52] Cryer (n 1), at 127–28.

[53] See e.g. Bassiouni (n 42), at 133; Ambos (n 39), at 65–67; Neil Boister, ''Transnational Criminal Law'?' (2003) 14 *European Journal of International Law* 953, at 965–68 and *passim*; Tallgren (n 36), at 585–86; Gerhard Werle, *Principles of International Criminal Law* (2nd edn, TMC Asser, 2009), at 31–32. See also *Attorney-General of the Government of Israel v Adolf Eichmann*, 29 May 1962, 36 ILR 277, at 291; *Third Report on the Draft Code of Offences against the Peace and Security of Mankind, by Mr. Doudou Thiam, Special Rapporteur*, 8 April 1985, UN Doc A/CN.4/387 in *Yearbook of the International Law Commission* (1985), vol II(1), at 70–71, paras 61–63.

[54] See M Cherif Bassiouni, 'Introduction' in Dawn L Rothe and Christopher W Mullins (eds), *State Crime: Current Perspectives* (Rutgers University Press, 2011), at 4; Stanley Cohen, 'Human Rights and Crimes of the State: The Culture of Denial' (1993) 26 *Australian & New Zealand Journal of Criminology* 97, at 101. The idea that states have a duty to protect the safety of their citizens was central to Hobbes' understanding of natural law: see Thomas Hobbes, *Leviathan, or The Matter, Forme and Power of a*

trust, implying a duty to act in the public interest' is enshrined in the International Code of Conduct for Public Officials adopted by the UN General Assembly.[55]

(i) Public sector corruption

Abuse of state authority is the hallmark of corruption offences. As noted in Chapter 3, corruption as defined by UNCAC and UNCTOC presupposes an act or omission by a public official 'in the exercise of his official duties'.[56] Similarly, embezzlement of public funds consists in the misappropriation by a public official of property entrusted to him 'by virtue of his position'.[57]

(ii) Aggression

Since the emergence of the concept of crimes against peace after the Second World War, what is now called the crime of aggression has been considered an international crime, even if its definition has remained uncertain. Since 2010, the crime of aggression is defined in Article 8*bis*(1) of the Rome Statute of the International Criminal Court[58] (ICC Statute or Rome Statute) as:

> the planning, preparation, initiation or execution, by a person in a position effectively to exercise control over or to direct the political or military action of a State, of an act of aggression which, by its character, gravity and scale, constitutes a manifest violation of the Charter of the United Nations.[59]

An 'act of aggression', as defined in Article 8*bis*(2), requires 'the use of armed force by a State'.[60] The idea of abuse of state authority is inherently embedded in the constitutive elements of the crime of aggression.

(iii) Crimes against humanity

Under the Rome Statute, the first and to date only treaty to provide a definition of crimes against humanity, crimes against humanity must be committed 'pursuant to or in furtherance of a State or organizational policy'.[61] While crimes against humanity may be committed by non-state actors and the requisite policy need not be

Common-whealth Ecclesiasticall and Civill (London, 1651), chapter XXX, para 1 ('The office of the Soveraign, (be it a Monarch, or an Assembly), consisteth in the end, for which he was trusted with the Soveraign Power, namely the procuration of *the safety of the people*; to which he is obliged by the Law of Nature [...]. But by Safety here, is not meant a bare Preservation, but also all other Contentments of life').

[55] *International Code of Conduct for Public Officials*, Principle 1, annexed to General Assembly Resolution 51/59, 28 January 1997, UN Doc A/RES/51/59.

[56] UNCAC, Art 15; UNCTOC, Art 8(1).

[57] UNCAC, Art 17.

[58] Rome Statute of the International Criminal Court, 17 July 1998, entered into force on 1 July 2002, 2187 UNTS 3.

[59] Whether this definition comports with customary international law is an open question, although the requirement of state involvement is uncontested.

[60] See also *Definition of Aggression*, annexed to UN General Assembly Resolution 3314 (XXIX), 14 December 1974, UN Doc A/RES/3314 (XXIX), Art 1.

[61] ICC Statute, Art 7(2)(a).

that of a state or state-like organization,[62] the definition in the Rome Statute indicates that the execution of state policy can nonetheless be constitutive of a crime against humanity.[63] This again suggests that as a matter of international law, states consider the execution of certain abusive state policies eligible for criminalization.

(iv) Torture

Article 1 of the Convention against Torture defines torture as

> any act by which severe pain or suffering, whether physical or mental, is intentionally inflicted on a person for such purposes as obtaining from him or a third person information or a confession, punishing him for an act he or a third person has committed or is suspected of having committed, or intimidating or coercing him or a third person, or for any reason based on discrimination of any kind, when such pain or suffering is inflicted by or at the instigation of or with the consent or acquiescence of a public official or other person acting in an official capacity.[64]

The involvement of a person clothed in state authority is a constitutive element of the crime.[65] This requirement was already apparent in the UN General Assembly's Declaration on the Protection of All Persons from Being Subjected to Torture and Other Cruel, Inhuman or Degrading Treatment or Punishment,[66] which was held

[62] See *Situation in the Republic of Kenya*, Situation no ICC-01/09, Decision Pursuant to Article 15 of the Rome Statute on the Authorization of an Investigation into the Situation in the Republic of Kenya, 31 March 2010, para 92. Under the Statutes of the International Criminal Tribunal for the former Yugoslavia (ICTY) and of the International Criminal Tribunal for Rwanda (ICTR), the involvement of a state is not an element of the crime. Nor is the existence of a policy or plan: see *Prosecutor v Dragoljub Kunarac and others*, Case no IT-96-23 and 23/1, Appeals Judgment, 12 June 2002, para 98; *Prosecutor v Ferdinand Nahimana and others*, Case no ICTR-99-52, Appeals Judgment, 28 November 2007, para 922.

[63] The wording of the Rome Statute is also used in the Statute of the Supreme Iraqi Criminal Tribunal: see Law of the Iraqi Higher Criminal Court, Law no (10) 2005, *Official gazette of the Republic of Iraq*, no 4006 (18 October 2005), Art 12(2)(A). Furthermore, state practice has confirmed that state policy is considered a determinant element of crimes against humanity. See, for the United States: *United States v Josef Altstötter and others* (*Justice* case) in *Trials of War Criminals before the Nuremberg Military Tribunals under Control Council Law No 10* (US Government Printing Office, 1949–1953), vol III, at 973, 984; *United States v Otto Ohlendorf and others* (*Einsatzgruppen* case) in *Trials of War Criminals before the Nuremberg Military Tribunals under Control Council Law No 10* (US Government Printing Office, 1949–1953), vol IV, at 498; in France: Cass crim, 3 June 1988, App no 87-84.240, *Bull crim* (1988), no 246, p 637 (*Barbie* case); Cass crim, 27 November 1992, App no 92-82.409, *Bull crim* (1992), no 394, p 1082 (*Touvier* case); in Canada: *R v Finta*, [1994] 1 SCR 701, at 823.

[64] Art 1 continues: 'It does not include pain or suffering arising only from, inherent in or incidental to lawful sanctions'.

[65] The ICTY, however, has adopted a different definition of torture as a crime against humanity or a war crime (see *Kunarac and others* (n 62), paras 145–48). On the difference between torture as a treaty crime and torture as an underlying offence of crimes against humanity or war crimes, and the requirement of the involvement of a state official under international criminal law, see Paola Gaeta, 'When Is the Involvement of State Officials a Requirement for the Crime of Torture?' (2008) 6 *Journal of International Criminal Justice* 183.

[66] *Declaration on the Protection of All Persons from Being Subjected to Torture and Other Cruel, Inhuman or Degrading Treatment or Punishment*, annexed to UN General Assembly Resolution 3452 (XXX), 9 December 1975, UN Doc A/RES/3452 (XXX), Art 1.

by the Supreme Court Chamber of the Extraordinary Chambers in the Courts of Cambodia (ECCC) to reflect customary international law as early as 1975–1979.[67]

(v) Enforced disappearance

Like torture within the meaning of the Convention against Torture, enforced disappearance as defined in the International Convention for the Protection of All Persons from Enforced Disappearance[68] can be committed only 'by agents of the State or groups of persons acting with the authorization, support or acquiescence of the State'.[69] This element of the crime featured in the earlier declaration on enforced disappearance by the UN General Assembly.[70]

(b) Maintenance of international peace and security

States have also established as international crimes conduct they consider a threat to international peace and security. References to the maintenance of international peace and security as a rationale for international criminalization can be found in particular in multilateral treaties for the suppression of crimes associated with terrorism,[71] and also in the Rome Statute in relation to the crime of aggression, genocide, crimes against humanity, and war crimes.[72]

(c) Protection of human rights

Fundamental rights are guaranteed by and protected at the international level primarily through treaties imposing an obligation on states parties to respect and protect human rights within their jurisdiction. In addition, international law requires states to criminalize particular conduct amounting to human rights abuses, so that such abuses entail individual criminal responsibility. The desire to strengthen the

[67] *Kaing Guek Eav alias Duch*, Case no 001/18-07-2007/ECCC, Appeal Judgment, 3 February 2012, para 205. See also *Prosecutor v Anto Furundžija*, Case no IT-95-17/1, Appeals Judgment, 21 July 2000, para 111.

[68] International Convention for the Protection of All Persons from Enforced Disappearance, 20 December 2006, entered into force on 23 December 2010, 2716 UNTS 3.

[69] Ibid, Art 2.

[70] UN General Assembly Resolution 47/133, *Declaration on the Protection of All Persons from Enforced Disappearance*, 18 December 1992, UN Doc A/RES/47/133, preamble, 3rd recital.

[71] See Convention on the Prevention and Punishment of Crimes against Internationally Protected Persons, including Diplomatic Agents, preamble, 1st recital; International Convention against the Taking of Hostages, preamble, 1st recital; Convention for the Suppression of Unlawful Acts against the Safety of Maritime Navigation, preamble, 1st recital; International Convention for the Suppression of Terrorist Bombings, preamble, 1st recital; International Convention for the Suppression of the Financing of Terrorism, preamble, 1st recital; International Convention for the Suppression of Acts of Nuclear Terrorism, preamble, 1st recital. The maintenance of international peace and security similarly motivated the UN Security Council's decision to require UN member states to criminalize terrorist acts: see Resolution 1373 (2001), preamble, 3rd recital.

[72] ICC Statute, preamble, 3rd recital.

protection of human rights has motivated the creation of several international crimes, as made explicit in treaties criminalizing torture,[73] enforced disappearance,[74] and slavery.[75] It has also underpinned the prohibition of genocide and crimes against humanity.[76]

(d) Promotion of the rule of law

When criminalizing certain conduct at the international level, states have also occasionally referred to the rule of law as an interest worthy of protection, notably concerning corruption offences.[77] The rule of law as understood at the international level

> refers to a principle of governance in which all persons, institutions and entities, public and private, including the State itself, are accountable to laws that are publicly promulgated, equally enforced and independently adjudicated, and which are consistent with international human rights norms and standards. It requires, as well, measures to ensure adherence to the principles of supremacy of law, equality before the law, accountability to the law, fairness in the application of the law, separation of powers, participation in decision-making, legal certainty, avoidance of arbitrariness and procedural and legal transparency.[78]

Beyond its formal and substantive dimensions,[79] the rule of law as a structural concept refers to 'fundamental principles which are characteristic of a legally ordered community and which provide a long-term quasi-constitutional framework within which particular rules of law operate'.[80] It constitutes a fundamental normative framework necessary for the state to protect and enforce individual rights.[81]

[73] Convention against Torture, preamble, 3rd and 4th recitals.

[74] International Convention for the Protection of All Persons from Enforced Disappearance, preamble, 1st, 2nd, and 3rd recitals.

[75] Supplementary Convention on the Abolition of Slavery, the Slave Trade, and Institutions and Practices Similar to Slavery, preamble, 3rd recital.

[76] Although the Rome Statute does not make explicit reference to human rights in its preamble, the latter refers to the 'Purposes and Principles of the Charter of the United Nations' (7th recital), which include 'promoting and encouraging respect for human rights and for fundamental freedoms' (UN Charter, Art 1(3)). The ambition of protecting individuals against certain gross human rights violations is explicit in the case of the prohibition of apartheid as a crime against humanity: see International Convention on the Suppression and Punishment of the Crime of Apartheid, 30 November 1973, entered into force on 18 July 1976, 1015 UNTS 243, preamble, 1st and 2nd recitals.

[77] UNCAC, preamble, 1st recital; Criminal Law Convention on Corruption, preamble, 4th recital; AU Convention on Corruption, preamble, 3rd recital.

[78] Report of the UN Secretary-General, *The rule of law and transitional justice in conflict and post-conflict societies*, 23 August 2004, UN Doc S/2004/616, para 6. See also Report of the UN Secretary-General, *The rule of law at the national and international levels: comments and information received from Governments*, 11 July 2007, UN Doc A/62/121.

[79] See Paul Craig, 'Formal and Substantive Conceptions of the Rule of Law: An Analytical Framework' (1997) *Public Law* 467.

[80] Arthur Watts, 'The International Rule of Law' (1993) 36 *German Yearbook of International Law* 15, at 22.

[81] UN General Assembly Resolution 61/39, 4 December 2006, UN Doc A/RES/61/39 (stating that 'the advancement of the rule of law at the national and international levels is essential for [...] the protection of all human rights and fundamental freedoms').

The theme of the rule of law has gained increasing traction internationally.[82] Notwithstanding occasional suspicion on the part of some states,[83] the rule of law has been formally endorsed as a 'core value' which states have 'committ[ed] [them]-selves to actively protecting and promoting'.[84] Although this commitment may be considered as an unequivocal expression of *opinio juris*, it remains unclear whether there is an obligation under international law to respect and promote the rule of law, and what the contours of such an obligation would be. Some argue that the rule of law is nothing more than a general aspirational principle affirming political ideals with reference to already existing legal rules.[85] Be that as it may, the rule of law is an emerging principle of international law deemed relevant by states when it comes to criminalizing conduct at the international level.

(e) *Maintenance of normal international relations necessary for interstate cooperation*

Finally, in the Convention on the Prevention and Punishment of Crimes against Internationally Protected Persons, including Diplomatic Agents, states have criminalized conduct 'creat[ing] a serious threat to the maintenance of normal international relations which are necessary for co-operation among States'.[86] This points

[82] The increasing significance of the rule of law is evidenced by numerous international instruments: see in particular, for the UN: Resolution 61/39, preamble, 7th recital (expressing the conviction 'that the promotion of and respect for the rule of law at the national and international levels, as well as justice and good governance, should guide the activities of the United Nations and its Member States'); for the Council of Europe: Statute of the Council of Europe, 5 May 1949, entered into force on 3 August 1949, 87 UNTS 103, Art 3; for the AU: Constitutive Act of the African Union, 11 July 2000, entered into force on 26 May 2001, 2158 UNTS 3, Art 4(m); for the OAS: *Declaration of Santiago on Democracy and Public Trust: A New Commitment to Good Governance for the Americas*, 10 June 2003, Doc no AG/DEC.31 (XXXIII-O/03). On the emergence of international standards concerning domestic governance, see generally Jacques-Yvan Morin, 'L'État de droit : émergence d'un principe du droit international' (1995) 254 *Recueil des cours de l'Académie de droit international* 9; Helmut Philip Aust and Georg Nolte, 'International Law and the Rule of Law at the National Level' in Michael Zürn, André Nollkaemper, and Randall Peerenboom (eds), *Rule of Law Dynamics in an Era of International and Transnational Governance* (Cambridge University Press, 2012) 48.

[83] See e.g. UN General Assembly Sixth Committee, 62nd sess, Summary record of the 14th meeting, 15 November 2007, UN Doc A/C.6/62/SR.14, para 49 (statement of the representative of Sudan: 'The principle of the rule of law should not be used as a tool for applying political pressure, and developing States should be allowed to pursue their aspirations for development without interference in their internal affairs'); UN General Assembly Sixth Committee, 62nd sess, Summary record of the 16th meeting, 19 November 2007, UN Doc A/C.6/62/SR.16, paras 29 (statement of the representative of Tunisia), 96 (statement of the representative of Syria). Concerns have been expressed that the rule of law may be used as a vector of hegemony in international relations: see Jacques Chevallier, 'État de droit et relations internationales' (2006) 7 *Annuaire français de droit international* 4, at 5.

[84] UN General Assembly Resolution 60/1, *2005 World Summit Outcome*, 16 September 2005, UN Doc A/RES/60/1, para 119. See also UN General Assembly Resolution 55/2, *United Nations Millennium Declaration*, 8 September 2000, UN Doc A/RES/55/2, para 9.

[85] Olivier Corten, 'L'État de droit en droit international : quelle valeur juridique ajoutée ?' in Société française de droit international, *L'État de droit en droit international – Colloque de Bruxelles* (Pedone, 2009) 11.

[86] Convention on the Prevention and Punishment of Crimes against Internationally Protected Persons, including Diplomatic Agents, preamble, 2nd recital.

to the existence of a distinct interest deemed worthy of protection by means of international criminal law.

3. The potential expressive function of international criminalization

Expressivist considerations have rarely to date been a driving force of international criminalization.[87] The case of genocide, however, shows that expressivism can be a rationale for international criminalization in its own right. Although acts of genocide had already been punishable as crimes against humanity since the Nuremberg trial, genocide has been recognized by states as a discrete international crime.[88] It has come to involve a particular stigma not conveyed by other terms, and summons up specific normative assumptions.[89] In the words of Judge Shahabuddeen, charges of genocide reflect 'the need to describe the true extent of [a defendant's] criminal conduct'.[90]

A significant number of international instruments express states' moral condemnation of conduct defined as international crimes,[91] even if this was not the ultimate rationale for establishing the international crime in question. This suggests that expressivist concerns play a role when criminalizing particular conduct at the international level.[92] As Amman points out, the absence of effective enforcement of international criminal law norms does not render them any less meaningful, as 'words of long-dormant instruments' may 'beg[i]n to assume a palpable quality'.[93]

[87] Barbara M Yarnold, 'Doctrinal Basis for the International Criminalization Process' (1994) 8 *Temple International and Comparative Law Journal* 85, at 114 (acknowledging that 'conduct is criminalized more often on the basis of policy as opposed to principle'). Recall also Section B.1 of this chapter.

[88] See UN General Assembly Resolution 96 (I), 11 December 1946, UN Doc A/RES/96 (I); Genocide Convention, Art I.

[89] For an analysis of the signification and evocative power of the crime of genocide, see Diane-Marie Amman, 'Group Mentality, Expressivism, and Genocide' (2002) 2 *International Criminal Law Review* 93, at 124–31; Payam Akhavan, *Reducing Genocide to Law: Definition, Meaning, and the Ultimate Crime* (Cambridge University Press, 2012).

[90] *Prosecutor v Goran Jelisić*, Case no IT-95-10, Appeals Judgment, 5 July 2001, Partial Dissenting Opinion of Judge Shahabuddeen, para 26.

[91] See in particular Genocide Convention, preamble, 3rd recital (calling genocide 'an odious scourge'); UN General Assembly Resolution 96 (I) (stating that genocide 'is contrary to moral law'); Declaration on the Protection of All Persons from Enforced Disappearance (n 70), preamble, 4th recital ('[c]onsidering that enforced disappearance undermines the deepest values of any society'); UN General Assembly Resolution 2627 (XXV), Declaration on the Occasion of the Twenty-fifth Anniversary of the United Nations, 24 October 1970, UN Doc A/RES/2627 (XXV), para 7 (calling apartheid 'a crime against the conscience and dignity of mankind'); ICC Statute, preamble, 2nd recital (speaking of 'unimaginable atrocities that deeply shock the conscience of humanity').

[92] See Boister (n 53), at 967 (arguing that the international criminalization process may be driven by 'a sufficiently influential cosmopolitan belief that [...] conduct should be outlawed in all states because of its moral repugnance'); Antonio Cassese, *International Criminal Law* (2nd edn, Oxford University Press, 2008), at 11 (arguing that rules criminalizing conduct internationally 'are intended to protect *values* considered important by the whole international community'—emphasis in the original); Ethan A Nadelmann, 'Global Prohibition Regimes: The Evolution of Norms in International Society' (1990) 44 *International Organization* 479, in particular at 480–81 (arguing that '[i]nternational prohibition regimes [...] give force and symbolic representation to the moral values, beliefs, and prejudices of those who make the laws').

[93] Amman (n 89), at 122.

The value of expressivist theories of law is all too often discounted in international legal scholarship. Legal realists argue that ethical-legal considerations are simply rhetoric used by states for strategic purposes.[94] Critical legal scholars such as Koskenniemi suggest that 'the turn to ethics, too, is a politics',[95] and that the invocation of universal normative principles is the manifestation of a hegemonic technique.[96] Others do not share such radical scepticism.[97] They remind us that international law is grounded in ethics and that it provides a space for the articulation, confrontation, and endorsement of ethical-normative claims.[98] International criminal law in particular is a domain in which such claims can be given meaning through the establishment by states of a legal framework for the suppression of reprehensible conduct.

C. Reasons to Establish State Organized Crime as an International Crime

In light of the above, it is argued that there are persuasive reasons to establish state organized crime as an international crime. The criminalization of state organized crime can be justified normatively under principles of criminalization theory, as this phenomenon entails a specific harm distinct from other international crimes which infringes or threatens interests that states deem worthy of protection by way of international criminalization. The distinctive wrong of state organized crime can be broken down in five propositions: (1) state organized crime involves a reprehensible exercise of state authority or the execution of a reprehensible state policy; (2) it threatens international peace and security; (3) it can involve human rights abuses; (4) it undermines the rule of law and good governance; and (5) it subverts the proper functioning of interstate cooperation.

1. State organized crime as an abuse of state authority

State organized crime is a form of organizational deviance. Chapter 1 described how senior state officials involved in state organized crime abuse the prerogatives conferred by their official position for criminal purposes. They highjack the states' resources to plan, organize, and carry out criminal activities, sometimes systematically

[94] See e.g. Jack L Goldsmith and Eric A Posner, 'Moral and Legal Rhetoric in International Relations: A Rational Choice Perspective' (2002) 31 *Journal of Legal Studies* 115.

[95] Martti Koskenniemi, '"The Lady Doth Protest Too Much": Kosovo, and the Turn to Ethics in International Law' (2002) 65 *Modern Law Review* 159, at 173.

[96] Martti Koskenniemi, 'International Law and Hegemony: A Reconfiguration' (2004) 17 *Cambridge Review of International Affairs* 197.

[97] See e.g. Pierre-Marie Dupuy, 'Some Reflections on Contemporary International Law and the Appeal to Universal Values: A Response to Martti Koskenniemi' (2005) 16 *European Journal of International Law* 131 (suggesting the danger of '[a] passionate demand for self-scrutiny lead[ing] to paralysis' (at 136)).

[98] See generally Donald Earl Childress III (ed), *The Role of Ethics in International Law* (Cambridge University Press, 2012).

and on a large scale. In many instances, state organized crime is committed not for the purpose of private gain, but in pursuance of state policy. State organized crime is rendered possible by the perpetrators' privileged access to the state's material, financial, human, and political resources, its means of coercion, and its intelligence and diplomatic networks. Perpetrators have the power to shape domestic and international policies, enjoy a high level of authority over civil servants, the police, and the army, and can influence or interfere with the legislative process. In some cases, orders coming from the highest authorities of the state follow a top-down chain of command to be implemented by the rank-and-file perpetrators.

State organized crime as a form of system criminality has much in common with certain international crimes such as aggression, crimes against humanity, torture, or enforced disappearance, which are commonly planned, directed, and committed by individuals who abuse their official authority and harness the state's resources for criminal ends. It is the combination of '[s]tructural and organizational conditions with [...] individual predilections and positions' which makes such crimes possible.[99] Crimes involving state officials acting in their official capacity may be conceptualized as a combination of 'crimes of authority' and 'crimes of obedience'.[100] They are usually committed within the framework of a hierarchical system where policies designed by decision-makers are implemented at various levels of the system and instructions are transmitted through a chain of command to be eventually put into effect by the physical perpetrators of the crimes. In addition, state officials who have the power to prevent or punish criminal activities choose to turn a blind eye to crimes committed by individuals under their authority or control.

Conceptualizing state organized crime as an abuse of state authority is central to delineating the distinct harm and wrongfulness that justify the positing of state organized crime as an international crime distinct from regular organized crime offences. This is reflected in the definition of state organized crime, which requires 'the use of the resources of the state by a public official in a position to shape or influence the actions of the state'. By prioritizing their personal interest over the public interest, or by committing or facilitating crimes in the name of the public interest, the perpetrators of state organized crime violate the trust placed by the public in the state and its representatives.

2. State organized crime as a threat to international peace and security

Reasons to consider state organized crime as a threat to international peace and security are both formal and substantive. As regards the former, the practice of the UN Security Council shows that the phenomenon of organized crime in general and situations amounting to state organized crime in particular have been characterized as threats to the peace—this point will be addressed in detail at a later stage.[101] It is,

[99] Dawn L Rothe, *State Criminality: The Crime of All Crimes* (Lexington Books, 2009), at 4.

[100] Herbert C Kelman, 'The Policy Context of International Crimes' in André Nollkaemper and Harmen van der Wilt (eds), *System Criminality in International Law* (Cambridge University Press, 2009) 26, at 26–29.

[101] See Chapter 7, Sections A.2(b) and C.1(b).

however, necessary to go beyond this purely formal argument and to understand in substance the nature of the threat presented by state organized crime.[102]

Organized criminal activities, and state organized crime in particular, often go hand in hand with armed violence. The analysis in Chapter 1 showed that state organized crime often fuels armed conflicts, in relation to which crimes such as aggression, genocide, crimes against humanity, and war crimes may be committed for the satisfaction of economic and financial interests.[103] The case of the Taliban regime also shows that state organized crime can be closely linked to international terrorism,[104] which constitutes a threat to the peace.[105] In addition, state organized crime is sometimes paired with covert operations in the territory of foreign states, which constitutes a breach of the principle of non-intervention[106] and, in certain circumstances, of the prohibition against the use of force.[107]

Beyond its concrete manifestations in a particular case, organized crime as a general phenomenon may be characterized as a threat to the peace.[108] Organized criminal activities have 'negative economic and social implications'[109] undermining the foundations of the state and destroying social and human capital.[110] Organized crime, and state organized crime in particular, operate as long-term destabilizing

[102] Several authors have suggested reasons to consider certain organized criminal activities as threats to the peace: see e.g. Daniel Pickard, 'When Does Crime Become a Threat to International Peace and Security?' (1998) 12 *Florida Journal of International Law* 1 (regarding drug trafficking); Ndiva Kofele-Kale, 'Patrimonicide: The International Economic Crime of Indigenous Spoliation' (1995) 28 *Vanderbilt Journal of Transnational Law* 45, at 62–68 (regarding large-scale misappropriation of a country's resources by corrupt officials).

[103] Recall Chapter 1, Section B.3.

[104] Recall Chapter 1, Section C.3. The UN Security Council noted that 'means of financing [terrorism] include but are not limited to the use of proceeds derived from crime, including the illicit cultivation, production and trafficking of narcotic drugs and their precursors originating and transiting through Afghanistan' (Resolution 1988 (2011), 17 June 2011, UN Doc S/RES/1988 (2011), para 5; Resolution 2082 (2012), 17 December 2012, UN Doc S/RES/2082 (2012), para 4), and noted more generally a 'close connection between international terrorism and transnational organized crime, illicit drugs, money-laundering, illegal arms trafficking, and illegal movement of nuclear, chemical, biological and other potentially deadly materials' (Resolution 1373 (2001), para 4). See also Tamara Makarenko, 'The Crime-Terror Continuum: Tracing the Interplay between Transnational Organized Crime and Terrorism' (2004) 6 *Global Crime* 129.

[105] See e.g. Resolution 1373 (2001), preamble, 3rd recital; Resolution 2133 (2014), 27 January 2014, UN Doc S/RES/2133 (2014).

[106] Recall Chapter 2, Section C.4.

[107] *Military and Paramilitary Activities in and against Nicaragua (Nicaragua v United States of America)*, Merits, Judgment, ICJ Rep 1986, p 14, at 108, para 205 ('The element of coercion, which defines, and indeed forms the very essence of, prohibited intervention, is particularly obvious in the case of an intervention which uses force, either in the direct form of military action, or in the indirect form of support for subversive or terrorist armed activities within another State. [. . .] These forms of action are therefore wrongful in the light of both the principle of non-use of force, and that of non-intervention').

[108] For an analysis of relevant Security Council practice, see Chapter 7, Section A.2(b).

[109] UN General Assembly Resolution 55/25, preamble, 7th recital.

[110] UNODC, *Crime and Development in Africa* (United Nations, June 2005), at 67. See also Sonja Licht, 'The Threat of Organized Crime to State and Human Security' in *State and Human Security in the "Age of Terrorism": The Role of Security Sector Reform*—Compilation of presentations made at the second joint seminar of the United Nations Office at Geneva (UNOG) and the Geneva Centre for the Democratic Control of Armed Forces (DCAF) held on 26 January 2004 (United Nations Office at Geneva, 2004.

factors, both domestically and internationally. The deleterious effects of this phenomenon pose a clear threat to international peace and security.

3. State organized crime as a cause of human rights abuses

State organized crime adversely impacts internationally guaranteed human rights, either directly by violating certain rights, or indirectly by being conducive to human rights abuses. To begin with, certain criminal activities carried out by state officials or state-controlled entities for profit purposes directly infringe fundamental rights. For example, when military officials are involved in the trafficking of women for the purpose of sexual exploitation,[111] the prohibition of slavery may be violated.[112] It may also be argued that the systematic pillage of natural resources by state officials violates the right of a people freely to dispose of its natural wealth and resources[113] recognized by international human rights instruments.[114] While the debate regarding the legal contours of this concept is not entirely settled,[115] the collective right of indigenous peoples to dispose of their natural resources is enforceable before certain international human rights courts and treaty bodies,[116] whether as an autonomous right[117] or as a component of the right to property.[118] In the case of

[111] Recall the case of Bento dos Santos Kangamba, a general of the Angolan armed forces, charged in Brazil with trafficking women for the purpose of sexual exploitation. For extracts of the indictment, see TRF 3a região, HC 0031957-43.2013.4.03.0000/SP, Relator Desembargador Federal Paulo Fontes, Decision of 12 December 2013, e-DJF3 (18 December 2013), 334.

[112] Recall Chapter 2, Section C.7.

[113] See Ndiva Kofele-Kale, *The International Law of Responsibility for Economic Crimes: Holding State Officials Individually Liable for Acts of Fraudulent Enrichment* (2nd edn, Routledge, 2016), at 79–111; W Michael Reisman, 'Editorial Comments: Harnessing International Law to Restrain and Recapture Indigenous Spoliations' (1989) 83 *American Journal of International Law* 56, at 57.

[114] ICCPR, Art 1(2); International Covenant on Economic, Social and Cultural Rights, 16 December 1966, entered into force on 3 January 1976, 993 UNTS 3, Art 1(2); African Charter on Human and Peoples' Rights, Art 21(1).

[115] The right of peoples freely to dispose of their natural resources is closely related to the principle of permanent sovereignty over natural resources, which applies in international relations between states (recall Chapter 2, Section C.5). With the development of the rights of indigenous peoples (see UN General Assembly, *United Nations Declaration on the Rights of Indigenous Peoples*, annexed to Resolution 61/295, 13 September 2007, UN Doc A/RES/61/295), a corollary emerged in the form of a fundamental right held by peoples vis-à-vis the state as duty bearer. The question of how these concepts relate to each other, and the uncertainty surrounding the identification of right holders, is part of the broader discussion on the nature, scope, and status of collective rights. See generally Philip Alston (ed), *People's Rights (Collected Courses of the Academy of European Law)* (Oxford University Press, 2001); James Crawford (ed), *The Rights of Peoples* (Clarendon Press, 1988); Peter Jones, 'Human Rights, Group Rights and Peoples' Rights' (1999) 21 *Human Rights Quarterly* 80.

[116] Note that the Human Rights Committee traditionally dismisses claims based on collective rights as inadmissible: see e.g. *Chief Bernard Ominayak and Lubicon Lake Band v Canada*, 26 March 1990, Com no 167/1984, UN Doc CCPR/C/38/D/167/1984, para 13.3; *R. L. and others v Canada*, 1 April 1989, Com no 358/1989, UN Doc CCPR/C/43/D/358/1989, para 6.2.

[117] See cases before the African Commission on Human and Peoples' Rights: *Social and Economic Rights Action Center and Center for Economic and Social Rights v Nigeria*, 27 October 2001, Com no 155/96, paras 55–58; *Centre for Minority Rights Development (Kenya) and Minority Rights Group International on behalf of Endorois Welfare Council v Kenya*, 25 November 2009, Com no 276/03, paras 255–68.

[118] See cases before the Inter-American Court of Human Rights: *Case of the Yakye Axa Indigenous Community v Paraguay*, Judgment, 17 June 2005, Series C no 125, para 137; *Case of the Kichwa Indigenous People of Sarayaku v Ecuador*, Judgment, 27 June 2012, Series C no 245, para 146.

the *Armed Activities on the Territory of the Congo*, where Uganda was found responsible for acts of looting, plundering, and exploitation of Congolese natural resources committed by members of its armed forces, the ICJ referred to the right of a dispossessed people to receive reparations in case of spoliation, but it did not indicate whether Uganda was under an obligation to provide reparations on that basis.[119]

Another way in which state organized crime may be linked to human rights violations is where the criminal activities involved generate a particular risk for certain groups of people to be subjected to a treatment prohibited under international human rights law. For example, labourers working in narcotics laboratories or illegal mining sites may be subjected to forced labour. In certain instances, workers even suffered arbitrary detentions, sexual abuse, torture, and extrajudicial killings on the part of the police and the military.[120] In a similar vein, it has been alleged that widespread and systematic land-grabbing committed by the ruling elite in Cambodia for self-enrichment has engendered other crimes such as forcible transfer, murder, illegal imprisonment, other inhumane acts, and persecution, amounting to crimes against humanity.[121] State organized crime may also be directly linked to human rights violations where proceeds of organized criminal activities are used by the state to fund covert operations involving assassinations, torture, or enforced disappearance.[122]

Finally, the culture of secrecy surrounding state organized crime inevitably leads governments to endeavour to suppress attempts to expose their involvement in criminal activities. Freedom of expression, in particular the freedom of the press, may be threatened.

4. State organized crime as a subversion of the rule of law and good governance

State organized crime also fundamentally disregards the rule of law and internationally promoted standards of good governance. According to the World Bank:

> Good governance is epitomized by predictable, open, and enlightened policymaking (that is, transparent processes); a bureaucracy imbued with a professional ethos; an executive arm of government accountable for its actions, and a strong civil society participating in public affairs; and all behaving under the rule of law.[123]

[119] *Armed Activities on the Territory of the Congo (Democratic Republic of the Congo v Uganda)*, Judgment, ICJ Rep 2005, p 168, at 252, para 245.

[120] See Human Rights Watch, *Diamonds in the Rough: Human Rights Abuses in the Marange Diamond Fields of Zimbabwe* (June 2009), at 24–46; US diplomatic cable, Embassy Harare, 'Regime Elites Looting Deadly Diamond Field' (12 November 2008) 08HARARE1016 (reporting the death of 100 labourers shot by police forces in Zimbabwean mines exploited by corrupt government officials).

[121] Global Diligence, 'Communication under Article 15 of the Rome Statute of the International Criminal Court: The Commission of Crimes against Humanity in Cambodia', 7 October 2014.

[122] This was, for instance, the scenario of the Susurluk scandal in Turkey: recall Chapter 1, Section C.2(a).

[123] International Bank for Reconstruction and Development, *Governance: The World Bank's Experience* (IBRD, 1994), at vii.

The UN Security Council has repeatedly stressed that organized crime has a negative impact on governance and the rule of law.[124] The harm caused by state organized crime goes beyond the corrupting influence commonly associated with organized crime. Where senior public officials, vested with the responsibility and authority to uphold the law on behalf and in the interest of the people, abuse their authority for criminal purposes, usually in violation of domestic law and with complete impunity, there can be no rule of law. Where organized crime becomes a tool of political, economic, and social control in the hands of a government, governance cannot be transparent, and the state imperils the rights of its citizens.

5. State organized crime as an abuse of sovereignty undermining interstate cooperation

Finally, state organized crime undermines the foundations of the international legal order based on interstate cooperation. International law rests on the principle of sovereign equality of states.[125] Institutions such as consensualism and sovereign immunity are direct expressions of this principle. In this context, cooperation between states is essential for international law to fulfil its purposes.[126] This is particularly true of the international legal framework for combating organized crime and corruption. Crime-suppression conventions are designed after a classic model of interstate cooperation, whereby states parties bear the responsibility to take appropriate measures in their domestic law and to cooperate to bring perpetrators to justice.[127]

Sovereign equality, beyond its purely formal dimension, also presupposes a certain conception of sovereignty and participation in international relations. While '[e]ach State has the right freely to choose and develop its political, social, economic and cultural systems',[128] state sovereignty also entails 'the duty to comply fully and in good faith with its international obligations'.[129] Sovereignty is not synonymous

[124] See e.g. Resolution 2048 (2012), 18 May 2012, UN Doc S/RES/2048 (2012), preamble, 13th recital ('expressing concern that [...] the impact of illicit drug trafficking and organized crime in Guinea-Bissau ha[s] significantly hampered efforts to establish rule of law and good governance and tackle impunity and corruption'); Resolution 2120 (2013), 10 October 2013, UN Doc S/RES/2120 (2013), preamble, 18th recital (expressing concern 'at the serious harm that opium cultivation, production and trafficking and consumption continue to cause to the security, development and governance of Afghanistan as well as to the region and beyond').

[125] See UN General Assembly Resolution 2625 (XXV); *Jurisdictional Immunities of the State (Germany v Italy; Greece intervening)*, Judgment, ICJ Rep 2012, p 99, at 123, para 57 (describing sovereign equality of states as 'one of the fundamental principles of the international legal order'). See also UN Charter, Art 2(1) (providing: 'The Organization is based on the principle of the sovereign equality of all its Members'); Final Act of the Conference on Security and Co-operation in Europe, Principle I.

[126] See Christoph Schreuer, 'State Sovereignty and the Duty of States to Cooperate – Two Incompatible Notions?' in Jost Delbrück (ed), *International Law of Cooperation and State Sovereignty—*Proceedings of the International Symposium of the Kiel Walther-Schücking-Institute of International Law, May 23–26, 2001 (Duncker & Humblot, 2002) 163, at 164 (describing cooperation as 'a factual precondition for international relations and international law' and 'a metalegal factual basis for international law').

[127] Recall Chapter 3.

[128] UN General Assembly Resolution 2625 (XXV).

[129] Ibid.

with absolute liberty. It is relative in that it remains subject to the limits posed by international law.[130]

This conception of sovereignty and international relations cannot possibly fit in with situations where senior public officials, acting in their capacity as officials of the state, freely abuse the prerogatives of sovereignty to commit crimes in blatant disregard for some of the most fundamental principles of international law, and at the same time claim the benefit of sovereign immunity and of other mechanisms designed to protect the sovereign interests of the state.[131] One of the most noxious effects of state organized crime is to subvert the normative foundations of the international legal architecture of crime-suppression based on inter-state cooperation.

D. Conclusion

This chapter has put forward theoretical reasons to criminalize state organized crime through international law. It is suggested that the positing of state organized crime as an international crime would be consistent with principles of criminalization at the international level. State organized crime threatens interests that states deem worthy of protection by way of international criminalization, constituting as it does an abuse of state authority, a threat to international peace and security, a violation of internationally guaranteed human rights, and a subversion of the rule of law and of the proper functioning of interstate cooperation. In addition, criminalizing state organized crime would fulfil an important expressive function. Accordingly, it is suggested that states should consider criminalizing state organized crime through international law, either by adopting a universal multilateral treaty or by using the power of the UN Security Council acting under Chapter VII of the UN Charter.

[130] See Hans Kelsen, 'The Principle of Sovereign Equality of States as a Basis for International Organization' (1944) 53 *Yale Law Journal* 207, at 208; Paul Guggenheim, 'Les principes de droit international public' (1952) 80 *Recueil des cours de l'Académie de droit international* 1, at 84–85. For an overview of doctrines of relative sovereignty, see generally Djura Ninčić, *The Problem of Sovereignty in the Charter and in the Practice of the United Nations* (Martinus Nijhoff, 1970), at 9–15. For further analysis of the 'legal' and 'pure fact' approaches to sovereignty and their implications, see Martti Koskenniemi, *From Apology to Utopia: The Structure of International Legal Argument* (2nd edn, Cambridge University Press, 2005), at 224–302.

[131] The same idea underpins a number of Security Council resolutions expressing 'concern that [the Democratic Republic of North Korea] is abusing the privileges and immunities accorded under the Vienna Conventions on Diplomatic and Consular Relations': see Resolution 2270 (2016), 2 March 2016, UN Doc S/RES/2270 (2016), preamble, 10th recital; Resolution 2321 (2016), 30 November 2016, UN Doc S/RES/2321 (2016), preamble, 7th recital.

6

A Convention for the Suppression of State Organized Crime

This chapter proposes the adoption and discusses the contents of a universal multilateral treaty requiring states parties to establish state organized crime as a criminal offence in their domestic law, to adopt adequate provisions to allow for the effective suppression of the specified crime, and to refrain from participating in or supporting organized criminal activities. While such a treaty cannot realistically be expected to solve all the problems identified in Part II of this volume, it can nevertheless remedy certain of the limits of international law in cases of state organized crime, namely the absence of a coherent regime and of a criminal offence designed specifically to deal with the involvement of senior public officials in organized crime, the inadequacy of a territorial approach to jurisdiction in such cases, the narrow formulation of the obligation *aut dedere aut judicare*, and, last but not least, the absence of a primary rule of international law prohibiting state participation in organized crime.

Multilateral treaties are the 'workhorses' of the international legal order, and 'serve as the vehicle *par excellence* of community interest'.[1] When states believe that 'existing multilateral provisions do not adequately address' a particular issue, they may conclude a new treaty to fill the gaps[2] and 'ensure that the specific contemporary problems of fighting crime are effectively addressed'.[3] Organized crime and corruption are matters that states have chosen to address at the international level by way of crime-suppression conventions and of other international mechanisms providing for the establishment of minimum standards across domestic criminal laws.[4] It is

[1] Bruno Simma, 'From Bilateralism to Community Interest in International Law' (1994) 250 *Recueil des cours de l'Académie de droit international* 217, at 322–23.

[2] See the grounds cited in the preambles to the International Convention for the Suppression of Terrorist Bombings, 8th recital; and in the International Convention for the Suppression of the Financing of Terrorism, 11th recital.

[3] UN General Assembly Resolution 53/112, 9 December 1998, UN Doc A/RES/53/112, preamble, 2nd recital.

[4] This trend is most vividly illustrated in the realm of the EU, where Member States have consented to limiting their sovereign rights by granting the EU competence to set minimum standards concerning the definition of offences 'in the areas of particularly serious crime with a cross-border dimension', such as corruption or organized crime: see Treaty on the Functioning of the European Union (consolidated version), OJ C83 (30 March 2010) 47, Art 83. In addition to the textual legal bases in the treaties, the EU also has competence to take measures relating to the criminal law of Members States where such measures appear necessary to ensure the effectiveness of EU law: see *Commission of the European Communities v Council of the European Union*, Case no C-176/03, [2005] ECR I-7907, paras 48, 52.

argued that this effort could be taken to the next level by adopting a multilateral treaty criminalizing the involvement of senior state officials in organized crime. As suggested in Chapters 4 and 5, criminalizing state organized crime through international law is called for on both practical and theoretical grounds. The proposed treaty goes a step further than classic crime-suppression conventions by also prohibiting states parties from participating in or supporting organized criminal activities, thereby opening the door for the international responsibility of states parties for their involvement in organized crime.

This chapter begins by defining the constitutive elements of the proposed offence of 'state organized crime'. It then discusses provisions regulating jurisdictional issues, the obligation *aut dedere aut judicare*, and grounds for refusal in mutual legal assistance. It also proposes a provision prohibiting states parties from engaging in state organized crime. Finally, it briefly addresses the issue of reservations.

A. The Elements of the Crime

State organized crime has so far been defined for the purposes of our analysis as 'the use, by a public official in a position to shape or influence the actions of a state and acting in concert with a structured group, of the resources of the state to commit or facilitate the commission of acts criminalized in international law, in order to obtain a financial or other material benefit'. While this definition captures the characteristics of state organized crime as a criminological object, it does not meet the formal standards required for the definition of a criminal offence. A provision requiring states parties to criminalize state organized crime could be drafted as follows:

Criminalization

1. Each State Party shall adopt such legislative and other measures as may be necessary to establish as criminal offences the following, when committed by a public official in a position effectively to shape or influence the actions of a state, and acting in concert with a structured group for the purpose of obtaining, directly or indirectly, a financial or other material benefit:
   (a) using the material, financial, or human resources of that state to commit or facilitate the commission of any of the crimes listed in paragraph 2, knowing or having reason to know that such resources are used to commit or facilitate the commission of such crimes;
   (b) agreeing to use the material, financial, or human resources of that state to commit or facilitate the commission of any of the crimes listed in paragraph 2 and, where required by domestic law, involving an act undertaken by one of the participants in furtherance of the agreement.
2. For the purposes of paragraph 1, 'crimes' shall mean:
   (a) drug manufacturing and trafficking, as defined in Article 3, sub-paragraph 1(a), of the United Nations Convention against Illicit Traffic in Narcotic Drugs and Psychotropic Substances;
   (b) trafficking in human beings, as defined in Article 5, paragraph 1, and Article 3 of the Protocol to Prevent, Suppress and Punish Trafficking in Persons, Especially Women

and Children, supplementing the United Nations Convention against Transnational Organized Crime;

(c) sale of children and trafficking in child pornography, as defined in Article 3, paragraph 1, of the Optional Protocol to the Convention on the Rights of the Child on the Sale of Children, Child Prostitution and Child Pornography;

(d) smuggling of migrants, as defined in Article 6, paragraph 1, and Article 3 of the Protocol against the Smuggling of Migrants by Land, Sea and Air, supplementing the United Nations Convention against Transnational Organized Crime;

(e) trafficking in firearms, as defined in Article 5, paragraph 1, and Article 3 of the Protocol against the Illicit Manufacturing of and Trafficking in Firearms, Their Parts and Components and Ammunition, supplementing the United Nations Convention against Transnational Organized Crime;

(f) illicit exploitation of natural resources, as defined in Article 28L*bis* of the Statute of the African Court of Justice and Human Rights, as amended by the Protocol on Amendments to the Protocol on the Statute of the African Court of Justice and Human Rights;

(g) trafficking in endangered species, as defined in Article VIII, sub-paragraph 1(a), of the Convention on International Trade in Endangered Species of Wild Fauna and Flora;

(h) illegal traffic in hazardous wastes, as defined in Article 9, paragraph 1, of the Convention on the Control of Transboundary Movements of Hazardous Wastes and their Disposal;

(i) illicit export and import of cultural property, as defined in Article 6, paragraph b, and Article 7, sub-paragraph b(i), of the Convention on the Means of Prohibiting and Preventing the Illicit Import, Export and Transfer of Ownership of Cultural Property;

(j) currency counterfeiting, as defined in Article 3 of the International Convention for the Suppression of Counterfeiting Currency;

(k) cybercrime, as defined in Articles 2 to 10 of the Council of Europe Convention on Cybercrime;

(l) corruption, as defined in Article 15 and Article 16 of the United Nations Convention against Corruption;

(m) trading in influence, as defined in Article 18 of the United Nations Convention against Corruption;

(n) embezzlement of public funds, as defined in Article 17 of the United Nations Convention against Corruption;

(o) laundering of the proceeds of crime, as defined in Article 6, paragraph 1, of the United Nations Convention against Transnational Organized Crime;

(p) genocide, as defined in Article II of the Convention on the Prevention and Punishment of the Crime of Genocide;

(q) crimes against humanity, as defined in Article 7 of the Rome Statute of the International Criminal Court;

(r) war crimes, as defined in Article 8 of the Rome Statute of the International Criminal Court;

(s) the crime of aggression, as defined in Article 8*bis* of the Rome Statute of the International Criminal Court.

3. The knowledge, purpose, or agreement referred to in paragraph 1 may be inferred from objective factual circumstances.

An additional provision could define relevant terms as follows:

Use of terms

For the purposes of this Convention,

(a) 'public official' shall mean (i) any person holding a legislative, executive, administrative or judicial office of a State Party, whether appointed or elected, whether permanent or temporary, whether paid or unpaid, irrespective of that person's seniority; (ii) any other person who performs a public function, including for a public agency or public enterprise, or provides a public service, as defined in the domestic law of the State Party and as applied in the pertinent area of law of that State Party; (iii) any other person defined as a 'public official' in the domestic law of a State Party;

(b) 'structured group' shall mean a group of three or more persons existing for a period of time that is not randomly formed for the immediate commission of an offence and that does not need to have formally defined roles for its members, continuity of its membership, or a developed structure;

(c) 'other material benefit' shall mean any material advantage, to the exclusion of the satisfaction of purely political motives;

(d) 'proceeds of crime' shall mean any property derived from or obtained, directly or indirectly, through the commission of any of the offences listed in sub-paragraphs 2(a) to (n) and (p) to (s) of [the provision defining state organized crime].

These two provisions define the constitutive elements of the criminal offence of 'state organized crime'. The definition of the offence is clear and precise, as required by the principle of legality.[5] The denomination 'state organized crime' is sufficiently explicit to conform to the principle of fair labelling.[6]

The following commentary elaborates on the *actus reus and the mens rea* of the proposed crime, explaining the facts intended to be covered by each element of the crime.

1. Actus reus

The actus reus of the proposed crime contains six elements, namely (i) a senior public official (ii) acting in concert with a structured group (iii) using or agreeing to use (iv) the resources of the state (v) to commit or facilitate the commission of (vi) one or more predicate offences. The definition does not require that the crime involve a transnational element.

[5] On the requirement of certainty, see the decisions of the European Court of Human Rights in *Kokkinakis v Greece*, 25 May 1993, Series A no 260-A, para 52, and *Cantoni v France*, 15 November 1996, *Reports of Judgments and Decisions* 1996-V, paras 29–32. On the principle of legality generally in international criminal law, see Kenneth S Gallant, *The Principle of Legality in International and Comparative Criminal Law* (Cambridge University Press, 2009).

[6] According to the principle of fair labelling, 'the label applied to an offence ought fairly to represent the offender's wrongdoing': see Andrew Ashworth, 'The Elasticity of *Mens Rea*' in Colin F H Tapper (ed), *Crime, Proof and Punishment: Essays in Memory of Sir Rupert Cross* (Butterworths, 1981) 45, at 53; Glanville Williams, 'Convictions and Fair Labelling' (1983) 42 *Cambridge Law Journal* 85; James Chalmers and Fiona Leverick, 'Fair Labelling in Criminal Law' (2008) 71 *Modern Law Review* 217.

(a) *'A public official in a position effectively to shape or influence the actions of a state'*

State organized crime is by definition committed by or at the instigation of individuals entrusted with public power, that is, public officials. A public official is defined as

> (i) any person holding a legislative, executive, administrative or judicial office of a State Party, whether appointed or elected, whether permanent or temporary, whether paid or unpaid, irrespective of that person's seniority; (ii) any other person who performs a public function, including for a public agency or public enterprise, or provides a public service, as defined in the domestic law of the State Party and as applied in the pertinent area of law of that State Party; (iii) any other person defined as a 'public official' in the domestic law of a State Party.

The definition, which is also that of UNCAC,[7] complements a functional approach with a formal approach based on a reference to the domestic law of each state party.

Because the wrongfulness of state organized crime resides in an abuse of state authority by individuals entrusted with prominent public functions,[8] the circle of potential offenders should be restricted to individuals who enjoy a certain degree of power and influence in the apparatus of the state. Rather than using formal criteria to delineate the required threshold of authority, such as the official position of the offender as determined under domestic law, it would be preferable to adopt a functional test placing emphasis on the authority effectively enjoyed by the individuals involved. Accordingly, the offender must be 'in a position effectively to shape or influence the actions of a state'.

To that extent, state organized crime is similar to the crime of aggression. In determining which political leaders should be held responsible for the crime of aggression, the Special Working Group on the Crime of Aggression decided to limit the scope of criminal responsibility to persons 'in a position effectively to exercise control over or to direct the political or military action of a state'.[9] However, for the purposes of the suppression of state organized crime it seems more adequate to adopt the lower threshold suggested by some delegations of the Special Working Group, namely that the offender be in a position to 'shape or influence the actions of a State',[10] a standard originally articulated in the German *High Command* case.[11]

[7] UNCAC, Art 2(a).

[8] Recall Chapter 5, Section C.1.

[9] ICC Statute, Art 8*bis*(1).

[10] *Report of the Special Working Group on the Crime of Aggression*, annexed to *Official Records of the Assembly of States Parties to the Rome Statute of the International Criminal Court*, 5th sess (New York, 29 January – 1 February 2007), Doc no ICC-ASP/5/35, at 10, para 13. On the difference between these different standards, see generally Kevin Jon Heller, 'Retreat from Nuremberg: The Leadership Requirement in the Crime of Aggression' (2007) 18 *European Journal of International Law* 477.

[11] *United States v Wilhelm von Leeb and others* (*High Command* case) in *Trials of War Criminals before the Nuremberg Military Tribunals under Control Council Law No 10* (US Government Printing Office, 1949–1953), vol XI, at 489 ('It is not a person's rank or status, but his power to shape or influence the policy of his state, which is the relevant issue for determining his criminality under the charge of crimes against peace').

The 'shape-or-influence' test remains sufficiently high to exclude rank-and-file participants, while being flexible enough to include middle- to high-level perpetrators, depending on the circumstances of the case.

The words 'shape or influence' require that the offender be in a position to participate or otherwise play a role in the decision-making processes of a state. Accordingly, public officials involved in the mere implementation or execution of state policies are not covered by the proposed definition of the offence of state organized crime. The words 'actions of a state' further indicate that the offender must be able to shape or influence 'the deeds of the [...] establishments of the State aimed at achieving particular objectives', and therefore 'to dictate quite specific outcomes'.[12]

The phrase 'in a position effectively to' establishes a functional test, requiring the offender's material ability to shape or influence the actions of a state. In assessing whether the offender possesses such ability, inspiration can be drawn from the jurisprudence of international criminal courts and tribunals concerning superior responsibility. Under customary international law, the responsibility of military commanders requires 'effective command and control',[13] that is, the material ability to exercise authority.[14] While formal indicators such as the offender's *de jure* powers may be relevant, they are not in themselves sufficient, as effective control is a question of fact.[15]

Because the definition 'focuses on *de facto* [authority] rather than formal status, [it] is not *per se* limited to political leaders and/or members of government'.[16] In practice, it would be likely to include heads of state (in systems of government where the head of state is an executive position), heads of government (president or prime minister, depending on the system of government of the state concerned), members of government (e.g. ministers of home and foreign affairs, defence, investment and trade, and so on), members of parliament, military commanders (especially in situations of armed conflict), and senior diplomatic agents, as well as any other individual enjoying sufficient discretion and authority to act with limited constraint and oversight, such as senior intelligence officials. The definition could also include judges from the highest judicial bodies of a state, to the extent that they have the authority indirectly to influence or even dictate policy through their rulings, typically

[12] Carrie McDougall, *The Crime of Aggression under the Rome Statute of the International Criminal Court* (Cambridge University Press, 2013), at 180 (commenting on the definition of the leadership requirement of the crime of aggression).

[13] ICC Statute, Art 28(a).

[14] See *Prosecutor v Zejnil Delalić and others* (*Čelebići* case), Case no IT-96-21, Appeals Judgment, 20 February 2001, paras 196–98.

[15] Ibid, para 197; *Prosecutor v Enver Hadžihasanović and Amir Kubura*, Case no IT-01-47, Appeals Judgment, 22 April 2008, para 21. In particular, the ability to issue orders may be an indicator of effective control, but it is not a determining criterion: see *Prosecutor v Tihomir Blaškić*, Case no IT-95-14, Appeals Judgment, 29 July 2004, paras 69, 485; *Prosecutor v Dario Kordić and Mario Čerkez*, Case no IT-95-14/2, Appeals Judgment, 17 December 2004, para 847.

[16] Kai Ambos, 'The Crime of Aggression after Kampala' (2010) 53 *German Yearbook of International Law* (2010) 463, at 490 (commenting on the definition of the leadership requirement in the crime of aggression).

but not exclusively in public-law matters. In federal states, this definition would also include senior officials of the federated entities, provided that they enjoy sufficient power and autonomy from the federal government in the particular matter under consideration. Last but not least, it could also potentially include influential political or diplomatic advisers proven to enjoy significant *de facto* authority.

The definition, however, would probably exclude public officials entrusted with local functions (e.g. district councillors or mayors), judges from lower courts, or law enforcement officials (e.g. police or customs officers), as well as rank-and-file civil servants tasked with purely administrative functions. But again, there may be exceptions since the ability to shape or influence the actions of a state is a question of fact, which depends on the circumstances of each case.

(b) 'Acting in concert with a structured group'

The definition of state organized crime proposed here employs terms defined in UNCTOC. A structured group is defined as 'a group of three or more persons existing for a period of time',[17] 'that is not randomly formed for the immediate commission of an offence and that does not need to have formally defined roles for its members, continuity of its membership or a developed structure'.[18] Commentators suggest that a group acting with a view to committing a single offence would qualify, provided that the group has some degree of continued existence.[19]

The words 'acting in concert with' indicate that some degree of communication, agreement, and coordination between the perpetrator and the group is necessary. It is not required, however, that the perpetrator and each member of the group know about their respective activities. Nor is it required that all members of the group coordinate with each other[20] or with the perpetrator.

The definition is flexible enough to encompass different scenarios of state organized crime. It would apply, first, to situations where state officials act in concert with non-state actors to engage in illicit activities. State officials act 'in concert with' a criminal group when they act jointly with the group in the pursuance of a particular objective, for example by providing logistical support to the group for their activities, or more generally when they make arrangements with the group. It is not necessary that the perpetrator be in direct contact with the members of the group, as long as a sufficient connection can be established through state officials or agents acting under his control or instructions. Secondly, where the officials involved do not cooperate with private criminals but instead engage in criminal activities directly, they can constitute an organized criminal group in their own right. For instance, the definition would cover corruption schemes involving a plurality of state officials acting in concert to share profits.

[17] UNCTOC, Art 2(a). [18] Ibid, Art 2(c).

[19] David McClean, *Transnational Organized Crime: A Commentary on the UN Convention and its Protocols* (Oxford University Press, 2007), at 41.

[20] Ibid.

(c) 'Using' or 'agreeing to use'

The proposed offence of state organized crime covers both the use of state resources, that is, the decision to employ, deploy, or otherwise have recourse to the resources of the state for criminal purposes, and the agreement to do so. As with many crimes involving senior state officials, the connection between the perpetrator and the commission of the predicate offence may be difficult to establish. To avoid setting too high an evidentiary threshold, the proposed offence of state organized crime extends to the mere agreement to engage in criminal activities. Where required by domestic law, additional proof of an overt act in furtherance of the conspiracy is necessary.[21] In the case of a conspiracy, the official may be held responsible for the offence of state organized crime even though the predicate offence was actually not committed.

(d) 'The material, financial, or human resources of the state'

A public official's mere condonation of criminal activities does not constitute state organized crime. This crime requires the active contribution of a public official abusing his authority and using the resources of the state to further a criminal agenda. As seen in Chapter 1, a range of public facilities and equipment can be used for criminal purposes, such as buildings, offices, vehicles, vessels, weapons, airports, military bases, and diplomatic pouches. Public funds are diverted to sponsor criminal activities, or are directly embezzled by state officials for their personal benefit. The human resources of the state, including rank-and-file civil servants, military and police staff, employees of state-owned corporations, and secret services agents are also harnessed for criminal purposes. A general distinction can be drawn between cases where state resources are used as instrumentalities by state officials to commit a crime, cases where state resources are used to facilitate the commission of a crime by non-state actors, and cases where state property is itself the object of the crime.[22]

(e) 'To commit or facilitate the commission of'

The proposed definition of the offence of state organized crime encompasses both the commission and the active facilitation of a predicate offence. The use of state resources must either be instrumental in or otherwise aid the commission of criminal acts by any individual, not necessarily a member of the criminal group. In the case of a mere agreement to use state resources, such intended use must be calculated to commit or facilitate the commission of a predicate offence.

To determine whether state resources were used or intended to be used 'to commit or facilitate the commission of' crimes, each state party can apply the relevant principles of its domestic law, for example the test applicable in the confiscation of instrumentalities.[23] In certain jurisdictions, the test is whether property is used or

[21] Recall Chapter 3, Section A.7.

[22] Recall Chapter 1, Section E.

[23] Recall Chapter 3, Section D.2(b).

intended to be used 'in connection with' the commission of a crime.[24] A stricter approach would be to determine whether the use of such property has had or would have had a substantial effect on the commission of the crime.[25]

(f) Predicate offences

The principle of legality requires that the predicate offences linked to the proposed offence of state organized crime be clearly identifiable to potential offenders. To avoid the lack of specificity of the concept of 'serious crime' under UNCTOC, and the excessive discretion it leaves to states parties, paragraph 2 of the proposed definition does not follow the approach adopted in UNCTOC with respect to predicate offences. Instead, it identifies specific offences, corresponding to conduct that states parties to crime-suppression conventions pertaining to organized crime and corruption are required to establish as criminal offences or otherwise to make punishable in their domestic law. Some of the offences included in this list, such as trafficking in endangered species and trafficking in cultural property, are offences that UN member states were urged to establish as a 'serious crime' within the ambit of UNCTOC.[26] Note that sub-paragraph 2(f) also includes within the list of predicate offences the crime of illicit exploitation of natural resources, as defined under the amended Statute of the ACJHR.[27] Sub-paragraph 2(o) includes as a predicate offence the laundering of the proceeds of crime, by which is meant property derived from or obtained, directly or indirectly, through the commission of any of the other predicate offences of state organized crime. Finally, the list of predicate offences also includes in sub-paragraphs 2(p) to (s) genocide, crimes against humanity, war crimes, and the crime of aggression, which in some circumstances may be committed for the purpose of obtaining a financial or other material benefit.

Defining the predicate offences of state organized crime by referring to crimes defined in separate treaties, including regional instruments, comes with difficulties, as some states that are not party to these instruments would have to consent to be bound by the definition of the offences provided in these instruments before considering becoming a party to the proposed convention. However, that difficulty is not insurmountable, as most of the treaties to which the proposed provision refers have already been widely ratified.[28] Moreover, states may find reassurance in the legal

[24] See e.g. the Australian Proceeds of Crime Act 2002 (Cth), s 329(2).

[25] In England and Wales, the test is whether the use of the property to be confiscated was 'an integral part of the offence'; in other words, whether the offence could have been committed without such property: see *R v Lidster*, [1976] RTR 240, at 242; *R v Boothe*, (1987) 9 Cr App R (S) 8, at 10.

[26] See Conference of the Parties to the United Nations Convention against Transnational Organized Crime, 6th sess (Vienna, 15–19 October 2012), *The Notion of Serious Crime in the United Nations Convention against Transnational Organized Crime—Note by the Secretariat*, 20 September 2012, UN Doc CTOC/COP/2012/CRP.4, paras 27–33.

[27] See Chapter 8, Section B.3(a).

[28] Note that the Council of Europe Convention on Cybercrime was ratified or acceded to by a number of non-member states from almost all regions of the world, such as Australia, Japan, Panama, and the United States.

certainty offered by a precise and exhaustive definition of state organized crime. Yet the fact remains that the inclusion of some crimes on this list, such as the crime of aggression, is likely to be met with robust opposition on the part of states.

2. Mens rea

The mental element of state organized crime is twofold. The chapeau to paragraph 1 of the proposed provision requires, first, specific intent. That is, the perpetrator must act 'for the purpose of obtaining, directly or indirectly, a financial or other material benefit'. In addition, the species of the offence outlined in sub-paragraphs 1(a) and (b) each have their own specific mens rea requirements. In the situation described in sub-paragraph 1(a), it is necessary, first, that the perpetrator uses the resources of the state intentionally and, secondly, that he knows or has reasons to know that in doing so he is contributing to the commission of a crime. In the situation described in sub-paragraph 1(b), it is understood that any agreement must necessarily be intentional.

(a) *'For the purpose of obtaining, directly or indirectly, a financial or other material benefit'*

As with standard organized crime, state organized crime is driven by financial or other material motives, although political considerations are commonly also at play. Accordingly, one of the conditions of culpability for the proposed offence of state organized crime is that the perpetrator act with the specific intent to obtain 'directly or indirectly, a financial or other material benefit'. In keeping with the general understanding that the term 'financial or other material benefit' in UNCTOC is 'not limited to financial, monetary or equivalent benefits',[29] the proposed treaty defines 'other material benefit' as 'any material advantage, to the exclusion of the satisfaction of purely political motives'. It is irrelevant that the expected benefits are ultimately intended to be used for political ends. Conduct motivated by political considerations will fall outside the definition of organized crime only where no other potential material advantage is expected by the perpetrators. 'Other material benefits' could include, for instance, control over territory rich with natural resources.[30] Pursuant to paragraph 3 of the definition, the purpose pursued by the perpetrator may be inferred from objective factual circumstances.

The definition of 'other material benefits', in accordance with the ordinary meaning of the term 'material', does not encompass intangible advantages, such as political or strategic advantages. In certain cases, state officials may provide support to organized criminal groups for political purposes, without expecting any financial

[29] Recall Chapter 3, Section A.7. The bottom line is that the perpetrator must not act solely out of political motivations.

[30] Cf, in the context of the definition of a 'criminal organization' under Canadian criminal law, *R v Leclerc*, [2001] RJQ 747, para 316 (ruling that a 'material benefit' includes an increased presence on a particular territory to deal in narcotics). See also *R v Pereira*, 2008 BCSC 184, para 180.

or economic profit in return. For instance, although US officials in charge of CIA covert operations in South-East Asia during the Cold War did provide logistical support to local armed groups involved in drug trafficking, there is no evidence that they received a share of the profit generated by the traffic, or any remuneration in exchange for their support.[31] Similarly, in the case of the 'Susurluk scandal' in Turkey, it is unclear whether proceeds from organized criminal activities were shared with or used by Turkish officials.[32] Whether such borderline cases should be characterized as state organized crime or as simple complicity in organized crime depends on the interpretation of the term 'other material benefit' and, ultimately, on the facts of the case.

It may be questioned whether the intent to obtain a financial or other material benefit is compatible with genocidal intent or the discriminatory intent of persecution as a crime against humanity. The case law seems to answer this question in the affirmative. For the purposes of establishing the subjective element of the crime of genocide, the personal motives of the perpetrator are irrelevant, as long as it is established that he acted with the required specific intent.[33] Similarly, motive is irrelevant for establishing crimes against humanity.[34] Criminal responsibility for state organized crime involving genocide or persecution as a predicate offence may therefore be incurred if the perpetrator's genocidal or discriminatory intent was driven by material considerations—a 'motive behind the motive', as it were.[35]

Finally, it should be noted that the perpetrator need not be the final beneficiary of the financial or other material benefits. Neither does the perpetrator need to expect that the benefits would be derived from criminal activities. What matters is that he uses or agrees to use the resources of the state for the purpose of obtaining a financial or other material benefit. Sub-paragraph 1(a) provides that criminal responsibility is incurred even when the perpetrator does not know with certainty that the resources of the state would be used for criminal purposes.

(b) 'Knowing or having reason to know'

The proposed definition of state organized crime does not require direct proof of intent to use the resources of the state for criminal purposes. It suffices that the perpetrator knew or had reason to know that his actions would lead to the commission of crimes, in accordance with sub-paragraph 1(a), or agreed to act for criminal purposes, in accordance with sub-paragraph 1(b). For the purpose of sub-paragraph 1(a), the term 'having reason to know' indicates that, when knowledge cannot be established directly, it may be imputed on the basis of relevant circumstances. Senior

[31] Recall Chapter 1, Section C.2(b). [32] Recall Chapter 1, Section C.2(a).

[33] *Prosecutor v Goran Jelisić*, Case no IT-95-10, Appeals Judgment, 5 July 2001, paras 49 and 71; *Prosecutor v Clément Kayishema and Obed Ruzindana*, Case no ICTR-95-1, Appeals Judgment, 1 June 2001, para 161; *Prosecutor v Eliézer Niyitegeka*, Case no ICTR-96-14, Appeals Judgment, 9 July 2004, para 53.

[34] *Prosecutor v Duško Tadić*, Case no IT-94-1, Appeals Judgment, 15 July 1999, paras 255–70.

[35] See Paul Behrens, 'Genocide and the Question of Motives' (2012) 10 *Journal of International Criminal Justice* 501, at 522.

state officials in possession of information pointing to the fact that state resources have been or risk being used for criminal purposes may not turn a blind eye to the activities of their subordinates.

The wording of sub-paragraph 1(a) is modelled after the law of superior responsibility in the statutes of the ad hoc international criminal tribunals.[36] The test for determining whether the perpetrator had 'reason to know' is a subjective one. Courts must consider 'the specific situation of the superior concerned at the time in question'.[37] A superior may be held responsible 'only if information was available to him which would have put him on notice of offences committed [or about to be committed] by subordinates'.[38] The perpetrator must have received 'sufficiently alarming information to justify further inquiry'[39]—that is, 'some general information' pointing to 'possible unlawful acts'.[40] It is not necessary to prove that the perpetrator consciously disregarded information at his disposal, as would be required to establish the responsibility of civilian superiors under the Rome Statute.[41] Neither is it required that the accused acquainted himself with the information—the fact that such information was available to him is a sufficient condition of responsibility.[42] When the superior is in possession of sufficient information, he cannot claim not to have known of the crimes of his subordinates. Responsibility is incurred *a fortiori* in case of wilful blindness.[43] However, in contrast to the broader, negligence-based standard established by the Rome Statute for military commanders,[44] the accused is not expected to seek out information in the first place.[45]

[36] See Statute of the International Criminal Tribunal for the former Yugoslavia, annexed to *Report of the Secretary-General pursuant to paragraph 2 of resolution 808 (1993)*, 3 May 1993, UN Doc S/25704 and Add.l, Art 7(3); Statute of the International Criminal Tribunal for Rwanda, annexed to UN Security Council Resolution 955 (1994), 8 November 1994, UN Doc S/RES/955 (1994), Art 6(3); Statute of the Special Court for Sierra Leone, annexed to Agreement between the United Nations and the Government of Sierra Leone on the establishment of the Special Court for Sierra Leone, 16 January 2002, entered into force on 12 April 2002, 2178 UNTS 138, Art 6(3).

[37] *Čelebići* Appeals Judgment (n 14), para 239. See also ICC Statute, Art 28(a)(i).

[38] *Čelebići* Appeals Judgment (n 14), para 241; *Blaškić* Appeals Judgment (n 15), para 62.

[39] *Hadžihasanović and Kubura* Appeals Judgment (n 15), para 28; *Prosecutor v Milorad Krnojelac*, Case no IT-97-25, Appeals Judgment, 17 September 2003, para 155.

[40] *Čelebići* Appeals Judgment (n 14), para 238; *Prosecutor v Ignace Bagilishema*, Case no ICTR-95-1A, Appeals Judgment, 3 July 2002, para 42.

[41] Art 28(b)(i). The standard of the Rome Statute for civilian superiors is indeed stricter than the formula 'having reason to know': see Greg R Vetter, 'Command Responsibility of Non-Military Superiors in the International Criminal Court (ICC)' (2000) 25 *Yale Journal of International Law* 89, at 123–24.

[42] *Čelebići* Appeals Judgment (n 14), para 239.

[43] See *Prosecutor v Zejnil Delalić and others* (*Čelebići* case), Case no IT-96-21, Trial Judgment, 16 November 1998, para 387 (superior responsibility 'takes as its point of departure the principle that a superior is not permitted to remain wilfully blind to the acts of his subordinates').

[44] Under Art 28(a)(i) of the Rome Statute, it is sufficient that a military commander 'should have known' of the crimes. The test, however, is not purely objective, as the assessment must be undertaken in light of 'the circumstances at the time'. See *Prosecutor v Jean-Pierre Bemba Gombo*, Case no ICC-01/05-01/08, Decision Pursuant to Article 61(7)(a) and (b) of the Rome Statute on the Charges of the Prosecutor Against Jean-Pierre Bemba Gombo, 15 June 2009, paras 432–34. For an analysis of the ambiguity generated by this standard, see Kai Ambos, 'Superior Responsibility' in Antonio Cassese, Paola Gaeta, and John R W D Jones (eds), *The Rome Statute of the International Criminal Court: A Commentary*, vol I (Oxford University Press, 2002) 823, at 864–69.

[45] *Čelebići* Appeals Judgment (n 14), para 226; *Blaškić* Appeals Judgment (n 15), para 62.

B. Obligations Concerning the Establishment and Exercise of Jurisdiction

Provisions governing the establishment and exercise of jurisdiction over state organized crime have to take into account the peculiarities of this crime. The impact of state organized crime often goes beyond the borders of the state involved to affect other states. In some cases, it is even designed to affect another state, for example by destabilizing its government. The objective territorial principle, the protective principle, and the effects doctrine are likely to play a crucial role in prosecuting suspects. Considering the political sensitivity of allegations of state organized crime, extraterritorial jurisdictional claims and requests for extradition in respect of the offence can be expected to generate strong diplomatic tensions. The proposal here is to harness this potential for tension to exert leverage on the state that is in the better position to prosecute the offender, by triggering the obligation *aut dedere aut judicare*. Enabling the exercise of jurisdiction on multiple bases would create a broad potential for extradition proceedings, and may thereby contribute to pressuring the requested state to initiate proceedings.

1. Obligation to establish jurisdiction

A treaty for the suppression of state organized crime might usefully include a provision to the following effect:

Jurisdiction

1. Each State Party shall adopt such measures as may be necessary to establish its jurisdiction over the offence established in accordance with this Convention when:
   (a) the offence is committed, in whole or in part, in its territory;
   (b) the offence is committed, in whole or in part, on board a vessel that is flying its flag or an aircraft that is registered under its laws at the time that the offence is committed; or
   (c) the offence is committed by one of its nationals.
2. For the purposes of sub-paragraph 1(a), the offence shall be regarded as having been committed in the territory of a State Party when one of the constitutive elements of the offence takes place in the territory of that State Party.
3. Subject to the fundamental principles of its domestic law, each State Party shall also adopt such measures as may be necessary to establish its jurisdiction over the offence established in accordance with this Convention when the offence is committed outside its territory,
   (a) with a view to the commission of one of the crimes listed in [the provisions defining the predicate offences of state organized crime] within its territory; or
   (b) when the offence affects its vital interests or otherwise has deleterious or harmful consequences or effects in its territory.
4. Each State Party shall also take such measures as may be necessary to establish its jurisdiction over the offence established in accordance with this Convention when the alleged offender is present in its territory and it does not extradite him or her.

5. If a State Party exercising its jurisdiction under this article has been notified, or has otherwise learned, that any other States Parties are conducting an investigation, prosecution or judicial proceeding in respect of the same conduct, the competent authorities of those States Parties shall, as appropriate, consult one another with a view to coordinating their actions.
6. This Convention shall not exclude the exercise of any criminal jurisdiction established by a State Party in accordance with its domestic law.

Pursuant to these provisions, states parties would be required to establish their jurisdiction on several bases. This is merely an obligation to create adequate legal bases to assert jurisdiction, not an obligation to exercise jurisdiction by way of prosecution. First, sub-paragraph 1(a) provides for the establishment of jurisdiction on the basis of territoriality. Sub-paragraph 1(b) provides for the establishment of jurisdiction over acts committed on board vessels and aircrafts. The words 'in whole or in part' indicate that jurisdiction may be established even where some elements of the offences are committed abroad. Paragraph 2 further specifies that states parties are required to establish territorial jurisdiction when at least one of the constitutive elements of the offence takes place in their territory (this covers both objective and subjective territoriality). Sub-paragraph 1(a) and paragraph 2 would provide a legal basis for prosecuting state organized crime where, for example, the predicate offences are committed in the territory of the forum state, even if all the other elements of the crime are committed abroad. In certain jurisdictions, it would also apply to conspiracies formed abroad, even where proof of an overt act is not required by law or cannot be established.[46]

Secondly, sub-paragraph 1(c) requires states to establish jurisdiction on the basis of the nationality of the offender (or 'active personality'). In practice, this provision may prove largely redundant, as senior state officials, who are most commonly nationals of the state on behalf of which they exercise their functions, are most likely to commit the elements of the crime in the territory of that state. It is not inconceivable, however, that perpetrators might commit the offence in the territory of another state.

Thirdly, paragraph 3 provides for the establishment of extraterritorial jurisdiction on the basis of the protective principle and the effects doctrine, respectively in sub-paragraphs (a) and (b), subject to the fundamental principles of the domestic law of each state party. The caveat is necessary in light of the reluctance of many states to assert extraterritorial jurisdiction on these bases, at least beyond the purview of a very narrow range of offences. The protective principle would be particularly relevant in the case of covert operations or state-sponsored drug trafficking designed to destabilize the government of the forum state.

Paragraph 4 requires states parties to establish their jurisdiction when the offender is present in their territory and they do not extradite him, irrespective of the issuance of a prior extradition request—which amounts to requiring states parties to establish subsidiary universal jurisdiction.[47]

[46] Recall Chapter 3, Section B.1(a).

[47] Recall Chapter 3, Section B.1(f).

Paragraph 5 encourages interstate cooperation in cases of concurrent jurisdictional claims to allow proceedings to be conducted in the state in the best position to prosecute the offender.[48]

Paragraph 6, a standard provision in international criminal conventions, permits states parties to establish jurisdiction on such other bases as may be provided for in their domestic law. The precise import of such a provision remains uncertain, although, given the width of the preceding paragraphs, this uncertainty is likely to be of little practical significance.

2. Obligation to extradite or prosecute

The obligation *aut dedere aut judicare* is the cornerstone of the proposed legal regime. The relevant provisions of the proposed treaty might be drafted as follows:

Extradition

1. A State Party in whose territory an alleged offender is found shall, if it does not extradite such person in respect of the offence defined in [the provision defining state organized crime], be obliged, without exception whatsoever, to submit the case without undue delay to its competent authorities for the purpose of prosecution.
2. The authorities referred to in paragraph 1 shall take their decision in the same manner as in the case of any other offence of a grave nature under the domestic law of that State Party. The investigation shall be conducted independently and impartially and without unjustified delay, in a manner consistent with an intent to ascertain whether the person concerned should be prosecuted. [...][49]

Paragraph 1 requires states parties to submit the case to their competent authorities for the purpose of prosecution if they do not extradite the person concerned. The wording corresponds to the traditional formulation of the obligation *aut dedere aut judicare* found in many crime-suppression conventions,[50] but differs from the

[48] Many factors can be taken into account to determine the most appropriate forum. Some domestic courts adopt an approach based on the doctrine of *forum non conveniens*, taking into consideration a number of questions, such as: 'where was the impact of the offence felt or likely to have been felt'; 'which jurisdiction has the greater interest in prosecuting the offence'; 'which police force played the major role in the development of the case'; 'which jurisdiction has laid charges'; 'which jurisdiction has the most comprehensive case'; 'which jurisdiction is ready to proceed to trial'; 'where is the evidence located'; 'whether the evidence is mobile'; 'the number of accused involved and whether they can be gathered together in one place for trial'; 'in what jurisdiction were most of the acts in furtherance of the crime committed'; 'the nationality and residence of the accused'; and 'the severity of the sentence the accused is likely to receive in each jurisdiction'. See *United States of America v Swystun*, 50 Man R (2d) 129 (1987), at 133–34, endorsed by the Canadian Supreme Court in *United States of America v Cotroni; United States of America v El Zein*, [1989] 1 SCR 1469, at 1498–99.

[49] The proposed treaty would also include the standard provisions on extradition, including those ensuring that the offence of state organized crime is included as an extraditable offence between states parties.

[50] See e.g. Convention for the Suppression of Unlawful Acts against the Safety of Maritime Navigation, Art 10(1); Convention for the Suppression of Unlawful Seizure of Aircraft, Art 7; Convention on the Prevention and Punishment of Crimes against Internationally Protected Persons, including Diplomatic Agents, Art 7; International Convention against the Taking of Hostages, Art 7;

formulation commonly found in crime-suppression conventions pertaining to organized crime and corruption. The obligation to investigate applies even in the absence of an extradition request and is triggered as soon as the relevant authorities of a state party, having knowledge of the presence of a suspected offender in the territory of that state, choose not to extradite him.[51] In other words, when a state party has reason to suspect that a senior public official residing in its territory has been involved in the commission of the offence of state organized crime, that state has an obligation promptly to open an investigation. Moreover, the obligation applies 'without exception whatsoever', which implies that, in the event that a state party rejects a request for extradition, the obligation to submit the case to its competent authorities for the purpose of prosecution is without regard to the ground on which extradition was refused.

It is thus not necessary to regulate the grounds for refusal or other bars to extradition in the domestic law of states parties. Despite their occasional downsides, the requirement of double criminality, the political offence exception, and the discrimination clause are important safeguards against potential abuses of extradition proceedings by a requesting state party, and should therefore remain valid grounds for refusal. That being said, while a requested state party to the proposed treaty retains full discretion, within the confines of good faith, to deny extradition on any ground it deems appropriate, it cannot escape its obligation to enquire into the allegations concerning the person who is the object of the request. The requested state party is obliged to initiate an investigation to determine whether there is ground to prosecute the person concerned. The obligation to open an investigation does not require the requested state party eventually to prosecute.[52]

Paragraph 2 requires the requested state party to ensure that its competent authorities conduct their investigation and take their decision whether or not to prosecute independently and impartially. The first sentence of this provision, requiring that the prosecutorial authorities of a state party 'take their decision in the same manner as in the case of any other offence of a grave nature under the domestic law of that State Party', is a standard clause in international crime-suppression conventions. The second sentence goes further by requiring that the investigation 'be conducted independently and impartially and without unjustified delay, in a manner consistent with an intent to ascertain whether the person concerned should be prosecuted'. It is inspired by the rules of the Rome Statute governing the admissibility of cases before the ICC.[53]

International Convention for the Suppression of the Financing of Terrorism, Art 10; International Convention for the Suppression of Acts of Nuclear Terrorism, Art 11(1); International Convention for the Suppression of Terrorist Bombings, Art 8. See also Convention against Torture, Art 7(1).

[51] See *Questions relating to the Obligation to Prosecute or Extradite (Belgium v Senegal)*, Judgment, ICJ Rep 2002, p 422, at 456, paras 94–95.

[52] Recall Chapter 3, Section C.1(d).

[53] See ICC Statute, Art 17(2) (defining a state's 'unwillingness genuinely to prosecute'), and Art 20(3). For an analysis of the principle of complementarity and the rules of admissibility before the ICC, see Chapter 8, Section B.1(b).

C. Regulation of Grounds for Refusal for the Purpose of Mutual Legal Assistance

The provisions on mutual legal assistance in existing treaties pose significant obstacles to law enforcement in respect of state organized crime.[54] It would be difficult to delete the 'essential interest' clause, which allows a requested state party to reject a request for mutual legal assistance if it considers that 'execution of the request is likely to prejudice its sovereignty, security, *ordre public* or other essential interests',[55] without disproportionately undermining the protection of legitimate interests of states parties. The requirement of double criminality, however, can be excluded since states parties are obliged to criminalize state organized crime in their domestic law. The relevant provision could be drafted as follows:

Mutual legal assistance

States Parties may not decline to render assistance pursuant to this article by reference to an absence of double criminality. [...][56]

A state party should not be allowed to invoke the insufficiency of its domestic law to deny mutual legal assistance where this insufficiency results from this state's breach of its obligation to criminalize state organized crime.

D. Obligation Not to Participate in Organized Crime

In parallel to the provisions designed to ensure that senior public officials involved in state organized crime may be held criminally responsible under domestic law, it is suggested to include in the proposed convention a provision prohibiting states parties from engaging in organized crime, drafted as follows:

Participation of state organs or agents in organized crime

States Parties shall not knowingly participate in, support, or facilitate any of the activities listed in sub-paragraphs 2(a) to (o) of [the provision defining state organized crime], except to the extent permitted by the principles of their domestic law governing the use of controlled delivery and of other special investigative techniques for the purpose of collecting evidence regarding the commission of an offence.

The proposed provision does not establish any explicit connection between the prohibited conduct of the state and the conduct of public officials to be criminalized by states parties. This is intended to avoid both the conceptual difficulty of imputing to the state the criminal conduct of individuals acting as its organs, and the practical

[54] Recall Chapter 4.
[55] Recall Chapter 3, Section C.2(c).
[56] The proposed treaty would also include standard provisions on mutual legal assistance.

pitfalls that may result from conditioning state responsibility on a finding that a crime has been committed by particular individuals. Rather, the proposed provision creates a distinct obligation for states parties to refrain from knowingly participating in, supporting, or facilitating specific activities that also constitute the predicate offences of state organized crime.

The scope of prohibited state conduct is defined in much more general terms than the criminal offence of state organized crime. First, there is no mention of a particular financial or economic motive for engaging in organized criminal activities. An 'intent to obtain a financial or other material benefit' can be characterized in the mind of a natural person, but it may be conceptually difficult to attribute to a state, especially in cases where public officials involved in state organized crime act for their own personal benefit and not in furtherance of state policy. Nevertheless, this essential dimension of state organized crime is not absent from the text of the proposed provision, since the prohibited activities listed as predicate offences of state organized crime entail, by nature, a form of profit. Moreover, the provision does not mention the use of state resources, as it is implicit that a state will have to use the resources at its disposal in order to 'participate in, support, or facilitate' organized criminal activities. Finally, in keeping with the indivisibility of the person of the state under international law, no distinction is made between the most senior officials of the state and other public officials. It is assumed that only senior public officials will have the authority to use the resources of the state to participate in, support, or facilitate organized criminal activities on a scale sufficient to represent a matter of concern for the states parties.

The prohibition on state participation in organized crime in the proposed provision is subject to an exception allowing states parties to implement legitimate special investigative techniques commonly used by law enforcement authorities to obtain evidence regarding the commission of a crime and the identification of suspects. These include controlled delivery, undercover operations, and other similar techniques encouraged by the UN Drug Convention, UNCTOC, and UNCAC.[57]

The list of prohibited activities does not include genocide, crimes against humanity, war crimes, and aggression, which do not in themselves entail any form of profit, and which in any event are already prohibited under customary international law.

It should be pointed out that the provision proposed here is not entirely unprecedented. As mentioned in Chapter 2, the Arab Convention against Transnational Organized Crime requires states parties to ensure that their territory will not be used for planning, carrying out, initiating, or participating in any of the crimes listed in the Convention.[58] As in the Arab Convention, the proposed provision would be placed in the architecture of the treaty after the provisions concerning the

[57] UN Drug Convention, Art 11; UNCTOC, Art 20; UNCAC, Art 50. Controlled delivery is defined as 'the technique of allowing illicit or suspect consignments to pass out of, through or into the territory of one or more States, with the knowledge and under the supervision of their competent authorities, with a view to the investigation of an offence and the identification of persons involved in the commission of the offence'.

[58] Arab Convention against Transnational Organized Crime, Art 37(1).

suppression of individual criminal conduct, to reflect the fact that the primary object of the convention is to prevent the commission of crimes by individuals.

E. Reservations

The objective of the proposed treaty is to establish a legal framework allowing for the effective prosecution of individuals involved in state organized crime and to prevent states parties from participating in or supporting organized criminal activities. The provisions discussed above are indispensable in the architecture of the treaty to fulfil these goals. Allowing reservations to these provisions would undermine the very foundations of the treaty. On the other hand, prohibiting reservations might have a disproportionate detrimental effect by discouraging states' participation in the treaty.[59]

In any event, reservations aiming at rendering inapplicable, in whole or in substantial part, the provisions discussed above, would be incompatible with the object and purpose of the treaty[60] and therefore would have to be considered impermissible[61] and devoid of legal effect.[62]

F. Conclusion

A universal multilateral treaty requiring states parties to criminalize state organized crime and to refrain from participating in organized crime would fill a normative void in international law. It would first and foremost fulfil an important expressive function by formally acknowledging the existence of the phenomenon of state organized crime, and by expressing the resolution of states parties to combat it. It would lay a legal foundation both for prosecuting perpetrators and for holding states involved in organized crime responsible for an internationally wrongful act. The proposed treaty is also designed to enhance domestic criminal law enforcement. It creates a broad obligation for states parties to establish both territorial and extraterritorial jurisdiction over the proposed crime, and widens the scope of the

[59] See Alain Pellet, 'Article 19 – Convention of 1969' in Olivier Corten and Pierre Klein (eds), *The Vienna Conventions on the Law of Treaties: A Commentary* (Oxford University Press, 2011) 405, at 418–20 (speaking of the need for the rules governing reservations to 'realize [an] equilibrium [...] between the prerequisites of universality and the integrity of the treaty').

[60] 'A reservation is incompatible with the object and purpose of the treaty if it affects an essential element of the treaty that is necessary to its general tenor, in such a way that the reservation impairs the *raison d'être* of the treaty.' See Guide to Practice on Reservations to Treaties in *Report of the International Law Commission* (63rd sess), UN Doc A/66/10/Add.1 in *Yearbook of the International Law Commission* (2011), vol 2(II), at 351, Principle 3.1.5.

[61] VCLT, Art 19(c); Guide to Practice on Reservations to Treaties (n 60), at 403, Principle 3.3.1 and commentaries thereunder.

[62] Guide to Practice on Reservations to Treaties (n 60), at 509, Principle 4.5.1 and commentaries thereunder. See also the discussion in n 18 in Chapter 4 of this volume. Whether the reserving state then becomes a party to the treaty will depend on the intention expressed by that state (ibid, at 524, Principle 4.5.3).

obligation *aut dedere aut judicare* with a view to pressuring states parties genuinely to initiate proceedings against suspected offenders present in their territory. It also prohibits states parties from denying mutual legal assistance in the absence of double criminality.

Nonetheless, the idea of an international convention for the suppression of state organized crime faces significant difficulties. To begin with, while a multilateral treaty is, in terms of legitimacy, the most satisfying means to generate obligations for states, participation in a treaty remains entirely voluntary and it is doubtful at best whether states would be willing to negotiate and conclude a treaty that would undoubtedly be perceived by many states as an unacceptable infringement in their domestic affairs. Even if the idea of a convention for the suppression of state organized crime would gain diplomatic traction, it would probably take a great many years for the treaty to be negotiated and to enter into force.[63] Moreover, assuming that such a treaty would enter into force, prosecuting individuals involved in state organized crime before domestic courts would still remain subject to a number of political and legal constraints. The prosecutorial and judicial authorities of a state attempting to investigate and prosecute senior officials of that state would be exposed to a high risk of political interference, whereas prosecution before the courts of a foreign state would be hindered by jurisdictional immunities. The proposed treaty would therefore remain subject to some—and not the least significant—of the limits identified in Chapter 4.

In view of such limitations, it is worth exploring alternative or complementary means to suppress state organized crime at the international level. Chapter 7 will consider the potential role of the UN Security Council in requiring UN member states to criminalize state organized crime and to freeze the assets of suspected offenders. Finally, Chapter 8 will discuss the potential role of international criminal courts and tribunals in prosecuting perpetrators.

[63] Consider the endeavours relating to the drafting of a Comprehensive Terrorism Convention, stalled in part because of diverging views regarding the scope of the definition of terrorism and in particular as to whether it should include 'state terrorism': see Mahmoud Hmoud, 'Negotiating the Draft Comprehensive Convention on International Terrorism: Major Bones of Contention' (2006) 4 *Journal of International Criminal Justice* 1031, at 1039–41.

7

The Potential Role of the UN Security Council in the Suppression of State Organized Crime

This chapter discusses the potential role of the UN Security Council in requiring UN member states to criminalize state organized crime and in imposing targeted financial sanctions against suspected offenders. It begins by reviewing the general conditions under which the Security Council would be entitled to adopt binding measures for the suppression of state organized crime, outlining the legal framework of the Security Council's action under Chapter VII of the UN Charter.[1] It then considers, as an alternative or a complement to the multilateral treaty proposed in Chapter 5, the adoption by the Security Council of a binding decision requiring UN member states to establish state organized crime as a criminal offence in their domestic law and to cooperate to bring offenders to justice. Finally, it suggests the imposition by the Security Council of targeted financial sanctions[2] in the form of asset freezes against individuals and entities suspected of being involved in state organized crime.

A. Legal Basis of the Security Council's Action under Articles 39 and 41 of the UN Charter

The UN Security Council is not *legibus solutus* and must act within the confines of the competences attributed to it.[3] Like any other organ of an international organization, the Security Council must act pursuant either to a power expressly provided for in the constituent instrument of the organization or to an implied power necessary to fulfil its functions.[4] This section outlines the legal requirements for the Security Council's action under Chapter VII of the UN Charter.

[1] Charter of the United Nations, 26 June 1945, entered into force on 24 October 1945, 1 UNTS xvi.

[2] 'Targeted' sanctions are also referred to as 'smart' sanctions: see David Cortright and George A Lopez (eds), *Smart Sanctions: Targeting Economic Statecraft* (Rowman & Littlefield, 2002); Matthew Craven, 'Humanitarianism and the Quest for Smarter Sanctions' (2002) 13 *European Journal of International Law* 43; Michael Brzoska, 'From Dumb to Smart? Recent Reforms of UN Sanctions' (2003) 9 *Global Governance* 519. The assumption that some measures are inherently smarter than others being disputable, preference is given to the term 'targeted sanctions'.

[3] See *Prosecutor v Duško Tadić*, Case no IT-94-1, Decision on the Defence Motion for Interlocutory Appeal on Jurisdiction, 2 October 1995, para 28.

[4] *Reparation for Injuries Suffered in the Service of the United Nations*, Advisory Opinion, ICJ Rep 1949, p 174, at 180, 182. On the determination of the scope of competence of international organizations and the doctrine of implied powers, see generally Chittharanjan F Amerasinghe, *Principles of*

1. The discretionary power of the Security Council

Bearing 'primary responsibility for the maintenance of international peace and security',[5] the Security Council has been vested with the power to take binding measures under Chapter VII of the UN Charter. In particular, Article 41 of the Charter allows the Security Council to take any 'measures not involving the use of armed force'. The competence of the Security Council under Article 41 is conditioned by Article 39, which requires that the Council first 'determine the existence of any threat to the peace, breach of the peace, or act of aggression'.

The UN Charter does not define the term 'threat to the peace' as used in Article 39. At the San Francisco Conference where the Charter was drafted, states decided 'to leave to the Council the entire decision, and also the entire responsibility for that decision, as to what constitutes a threat to the peace'.[6] In determining whether a particular situation presents a threat to international peace and security, the Security Council enjoys ample discretion.[7] The determination of the existence of a threat to the peace is 'a judgement based on factual findings and the weighing of political considerations which could not be measured by legal criteria'.[8] That is not to say, however, that the Security Council's discretion is absolutely unfettered, as the Council remains bound by the provisions of the Charter outlining the scope of its mandate.[9] Nor does it imply that the legality of the Council's action is necessarily beyond scrutiny or discussion.[10]

the Institutional Law of International Organizations (2nd edn, Cambridge University Press, 2004), at 46–49, 100, 135, 138, and *passim*.

[5] UN Charter, Art 24(1).

[6] United Nations Conference on International Organization, *Verbatim Minutes of the First Meeting of Commission III*, 13 June 1945, Doc 943 III/5, at 6.

[7] Hans Kelsen, *The Law of the United Nations: A Critical Analysis of Its Fundamental Problems* (Stevens & Sons, 1951), at 727; Nico Krisch, 'Article 39' in Bruno Simma et al (eds), *The Charter of the United Nations: A Commentary*, vol II (3rd edn, Oxford University Press, 2012) 1272, at 1275; Pierre d'Argent et al, 'Article 39' in Jean-Pierre Cot, Alain Pellet, and Mathias Forteau (eds), *La Charte des Nations Unies : Commentaire article par article*, vol I (3rd edn, Economica, 2005) 1131, at 1141–42.

[8] Erika de Wet, *The Chapter VII Powers of the United Nations Security Council* (Hart Publishing, 2004), at 135. See also Terry D Gill, 'Legal and Some Political Limitations on the Power of the UN Security Council to Exercise its Enforcement Powers Under Chapter VII of the Charter' (1995) 26 *Netherlands Yearbook of International Law* 33, at 117 ('Law is not capable of determining what does or does not constitute a threat to the peace [. . .] because legal terms of reference are irrelevant to such determinations').

[9] As the ICJ noted, '[t]he political character of an organ cannot release it from the observance of the treaty provisions established by the Charter when they constitute limitations on its powers or criteria for its judgment'. See *Admission of a State to Membership in the United Nations (Charter, Art 4)*, Advisory Opinion, ICJ Rep 1948, p 57, at 64.

[10] See Dapo Akande, 'The International Court of Justice and the Security Council: Is There Room for Judicial Control of Decisions of the Political Organs of the United Nations?' (1997) 46 *International and Comparative Law Quarterly* 309 (arguing that the ICJ would have the power to declare invalid Security Council decisions); Gill (n 8) (concluding that '[t]he far-reaching powers [of the Security Council] inevitably opens it to charges of misuse of its authority and poses the international (legal) community with the task of determining what the limits to this power are and should be' (at 134)); Alexander Orakhelashvili, 'The Power of the UN Security Council to Determine the Existence of a 'Threat to the Peace' ' (2006) 1 *Irish Yearbook of International Law* 61, at 70 ('Even if, allegedly, fifteen members of the Council believe in the ambiguity of [the concept of threat to the peace] and the consequent open-endedness of the Council's competence on this issue, the rest of the international

Once it has determined the existence of a threat to the peace under Article 39, the Security Council enjoys wide discretionary powers in choosing the measures it deems appropriate under Chapter VII in general[11] and Article 41 in particular.[12] The decisions of the Security Council adopted under Chapter VII are binding for all UN member states.[13]

2. Situations considered to constitute a threat to the peace

An examination of the Security Council's practice shows that situations considered to constitute a threat to the peace under Article 39 of the UN Charter tend to display certain features.[14] Threats to the peace notably include organized crime.

(a) *General observations*

Legal considerations may come into play when determining whether a particular situation constitutes a threat to the peace. Although the illicit character of a given situation is not essential for triggering the application of Chapter VII,[15] it has nevertheless become a relevant factor in determining the existence of a threat to the peace, in particular for the purpose of taking measures under Article 41.[16] The Security

community is certainly entitled to ask where the limits lie and, in appropriate cases, to pass judgment on the Council's determination'). Despite the lack of formal remedies the Security Council's action can incidentally be subject to some degree of judicial scrutiny: see e.g. *Tadić* Decision on Jurisdiction (n 3), paras 9–48 (assessing the legality of the creation of the ICTY by the Security Council); *Ahmed Ali Yusuf and Al Barakaat International Foundation v Council of the European Union and Commission of the European Communities*, Case no T-306/01, [2005] ECR II-3533, paras 277 ff and *Yassin Abdullah Kadi v Council of the European Union and Commission of the European Communities*, Case no T-315/01, [2005] ECR II-3649, paras 226 ff (assessing the legality of Security Council resolutions with regard to *jus cogens*).

[11] d'Argent et al (n 7), at 1165–66; de Wet (n 8), at 184; *Tadić* Decision on Jurisdiction (n 3), para 31.

[12] Here, too, 'the power of the Security Council pursuant to Article 41 is all along a discretionary one': Évelyne Lagrange and Pierre Michel Eisemann, 'Article 41' in Cot, Pellet, and Forteau (n 7), at 1204–205 (author's translation). See also *Tadić* Decision on Jurisdiction (n 3), para 35.

[13] UN Charter, Arts 25 and 48.

[14] For an analysis of the situations considered by the Security Council to constitute a threat to the peace, see generally d'Argent et al (n 7), at 1154–65; de Wet (n 8), at 149–74; Krisch (n 7), at 1278–91; Orakhelashvili (n 10), at 76–95 and *passim* (pointing out that 'the concept of a "threat to the peace", although initially dependent on discretionary determinations of the Security Council, nevertheless is a concept whose content can be identified by reference to objective and observable criteria' (at 62)).

[15] As Hans Kelsen explains, the Security Council was originally not designed 'to maintain or restore the law, but to maintain, or restore peace, which is not necessarily identical with the law. [...] Since the Security Council is completely free in its determination of what is a threat to the peace or breach of the peace, it may determine as such any conduct of a state without regard to whether this conduct constitutes the violation of an obligation stipulated by pre-existing law'. See Kelsen (n 7), at 294, 736. See *contra* Stephan Wollbrink, *A Violation of International Law as a Necessary Element of a 'Threat to the Peace' under the UN Charter* (Nomos, 2014).

[16] d'Argent et al (n 7), at 1164; Vera Gowlland-Debbas, 'Security Council Enforcement Action and Issues of State Responsibility' (1994) 43 *International and Comparative Law Quarterly* 55, at 63–66, 77; Orakhelashvili (n 10), at 82–86.

Council increasingly engages in legal characterizations amounting to quasi-judicial findings, explicitly stating that a particular situation violates international law.[17]

The notion of threat to the peace is not limited to situations involving a plurality of states but also encompasses purely domestic situations. In some cases, the Security Council's concern is to prevent repercussions in neighbouring states, but in other instances, action has been taken in the absence of an established cross-border element.[18]

Furthermore, threats to the peace are not limited to instances of armed conflict. As heads of state and government stated at a 1992 Security Council meeting, '[t]he non-military sources of instability in the economic, social [and] humanitarian [...] fields have become threats to international peace and security'.[19] The conception of 'peace' has therefore evolved from a negatively defined concept denoting the absence of war to a positive and more substantive interpretation encompassing broader considerations of security and welfare.[20] As a result, the concept of 'threat to the peace' is no longer limited to concrete conflict situations but applies to certain phenomena that create, in the abstract, significant dangers, such as arms trafficking or the illicit exploitation of natural resources.[21] That being said, observers of the Security Council's practice point out that the characterization of a particular phenomenon as a threat to the peace justifying the use of coercive measures under Chapter VII typically presupposes a link between the phenomenon in question and an actual or potential situation of conflict or armed violence in a concrete case.[22]

(b) *Organized crime as a threat to the peace*

In recent years, organized crime and in particular trafficking in drugs, arms, human beings, and wildlife, as well as money laundering and the pillage of natural resources have been characterized by the Security Council as threats to international peace and security in a significant number of resolutions[23] and

[17] For an analysis of selected situations characterized by the Security Council as violations of international law, see Keith Harper, 'Does the United Nations Security Council Have the Competence to Act as Court and Legislature?' (1994) 27 *New York University Journal of International Law and Politics* 103, at 108–26.

[18] Krisch (n 7), at 1279; d'Argent et al (n 7), at 1156; Orakhelashvili (n 10), at 78–82.

[19] Note by the President of the Security Council, 31 January 1992, UN Doc S/23500, at 3.

[20] See Krisch (n 7), at 1277–78; d'Argent et al (n 7), at 1155.

[21] See Krisch (n 7), at 1289–90; Jacob Katz Cogan, 'Stabilization and the Expanding Scope of the Security Council's Work' (2015) 109 *American Journal of International Law* 324, at 325–29.

[22] See Jurij Daniel Aston, 'Die Bekämpfung abstrakter Gefahren für den Weltfrieden durch legislative Maßnahmen des Sicherheitsrats – Resolution 1373 (2001) im Kontext' (2002) 62 *Zeitschrift für ausländisches öffentliches Recht und Völkerrecht* 257, at 288 (requiring a causal link to a situation of armed violence); de Wet (n 8), at 174–75; Krisch (n 7), at 1291 (requiring 'a concrete, acute risk of conflict'); Alexander Orakhelashvili, *Collective Security* (Oxford University Press, 2011) at 161–62 (taking the view that the phenomenon at hand must constitute a 'root cause' of conflict); Stefan Talmon, 'The Security Council as World Legislature' (2005) 99 *American Journal of International Law* 175, at 181 (requiring 'a reasonable connection between the phenomenon in question and the use of force'). On rare occasions, however, the Security Council has acted pursuant to Chapter VII to address certain phenomena in general: see Section B.1(a) of this chapter.

[23] See e.g. Resolution 1209 (1998), 19 November 1998, UN Doc S/RES/1209 (1998) (illicit arms flows to and in Africa); Resolution 1817 (2008), 11 June 2008, UN Doc S/RES/1817 (2008) (drug

presidential statements.[24] The Security Council has 'called upon' member states to 'criminalize, investigate, prosecute and ensure accountability of those who engage in transnational organized crime', in particular in arms trafficking and trafficking in persons.[25] The Security Council's growing concern over the impact of organized crime on international peace and security[26] is also apparent in resolutions stressing the link between organized crime and terrorism,[27] as well as in decisions imposing targeted sanctions under Chapter VII of the Charter against individuals involved in organized criminal activities.[28] This goes to show that in certain circumstances, the Security Council considers itself entitled under Chapter VII to take action for the purpose of suppressing organized criminal activities.[29]

manufacturing and trafficking in Afghanistan); Resolution 2066 (2012), 17 September 2012, UN Doc S/RES/2066 (2012) (drug and arms trafficking in Liberia); Resolution 2100 (2013), 25 April 2013, UN Doc S/RES/2100 (2013) (criminal networks and transnational organized crime in the Sahel region); Resolution 2103 (2013), 22 May 2013, UN Doc S/RES/2103 (2013) (drug trafficking in Guinea-Bissau); Resolution 2117 (2013), 26 September 2013, UN Doc S/RES/2117 (2013) (illicit transfer of small arms and light weapons); Resolution 2196 (2015), 22 January 2015, UN Doc S/RES/2196 (2015) (illicit trade, exploitation and smuggling of natural resources in the Central African Republic); Resolution 2227 (2015), 29 June 2015, UN Doc S/RES/2227 (2015) (transnational organized crime in the Sahel region); Resolution 2262 (2016), 27 January 2016, UN Doc S/RES/2262 (2016) (illicit trafficking, trade, exploitation and smuggling of natural resources in the Central African Republic); Resolution 2267 (2016), 26 February 2016, UN Doc S/RES/2267 (2016) (drug trafficking and related transnational organized crime in Guinea-Bissau); Resolution 2339 (2017), 27 January 2017, UN Doc S/RES/2339 (2017) (illicit trafficking, trade, exploitation and smuggling of natural resources and illicit transfer of small arms and light weapons in the Central African Republic). In a significant number of these cases, measures were taken under Chapter VII of the UN Charter.

[24] See e.g. the presidential statements of 15 November 2008, UN Doc S/PRST/2008/37 (Situation in Guinea-Bissau); 5 November 2009, UN Doc S/PRST/2009/29 (Situation in Guinea-Bissau); 8 December 2009, UN Doc S/PRST/2009/32 (Peace and security in Africa); 24 February 2010, UN Doc S/PRST/2010/4 (Threats to international peace and security); 21 February 2012, UN Doc S/PRST/2012/2 (Impact of transnational organized crime on peace, security and stability in West Africa and the Sahel region); 25 April 2012, UN Doc S/PRST/2012/16 (Threats to international peace and security); 10 December 2012, UN Doc S/PRST/2012/26 (Peace and security in Africa); and 16 July 2013, UN Doc S/PRST/2013/10 (Peace and security in Africa).

[25] Resolution 2331 (2016), 20 December 2016, UN Doc S/RES/2331 (2016), para 2(b); Resolution 2349 (2017), 31 March 2017, UN Doc S/RES/2349 (2017), para 7.

[26] Organized crime also regularly appears on the agenda of the Security Council's meetings: see e.g. Records of the 6277th meeting, 24 February 2010, UN Doc S/PV.6277; Records of the 6565th meeting, 24 June 2011, UN Doc S/PV.6565; Records of the 6717th meeting, 21 February 2012, UN Doc S/PV.6717; Records of the 6760th meeting, 25 April 2012, UN Doc S/PV.6760.

[27] Se e.g. Resolution 2195 (2014), 19 December 2014, UN Doc S/RES/2195 (2014), preamble, 7th recital; Resolution 2253 (2015), 17 December 2015, UN Doc S/RES/2253 (2015), preamble, 23rd recital; Resolution 2295 (2016), 29 June 2016, UN Doc S/RES/2295 (2016), preamble, 21st recital; Resolution 2322 (2016), 12 December 2016, UN Doc S/RES/2322 (2016), preamble, 6th recital; Resolution 2331 (2016), preamble, 6th recital; Resolution 2347 (2017), 9th recital; Resolution 2349 (2017), preamble, 8th recital ('Expressing deep concern that terrorist groups benefiting from transnational organized crime and trafficking in all forms may contribute to undermining affected States, specifically their security, stability, governance, social and economic development, and recognizing the connection between trafficking in persons, sexual violence and terrorism and other transnational organized criminal activities, which can prolong and exacerbate conflict and instability').

[28] See Section C.1(b) of this chapter.

[29] Philippe Weckel, 'Le Conseil de sécurité et la coopération judiciaire internationale' (2013) 117 *Revue générale de droit international public* 623, at 626.

3. Conclusion

Organized criminal activities can constitute a threat to the peace within the meaning of Article 39 of the UN Charter. In keeping with the wide discretionary powers granted to the Security Council to maintain international peace and security, the adoption under Article 41 of binding measures for the suppression of state organized crime, such as a decision to require UN member states to criminalize state organized crime and the imposition of targeted financial sanctions against suspected offenders, would arguably, in certain circumstances, be consistent with the legal framework established by the UN Charter.

The following sections will show that this proposition is supported by precedents[30] in the practice of the Security Council, and discuss the respective potential merits of both proposals.

B. Criminalizing State Organized Crime by Decision of the Security Council

In recent years, the UN Security Council has played an increasing role in shaping a universal legal framework for the suppression of certain criminal activities.[31] This section considers the adoption by the Security Council acting under Chapter VII of the UN Charter of a decision requiring member states to establish state organized crime as a criminal offence in their domestic law and to cooperate in its suppression. Such a decision could constitute a valuable alternative or complement to the multilateral treaty proposed in Chapter 6. This section first examines the scope and limits of what has come to be known as the 'legislative' or 'quasi-legislative' power of the Security Council,[32] before discussing the potential role of the proposed measure in the suppression of state organized crime.

[30] While the Security Council is not legally bound to act in conformity with its previous decisions, 'prior practices are often a reliable guide to future actions' and 'international lawyers and states have an incentive to read Council enforcement actions as legal precedents'. See José E Alvarez, *International Organizations as Law-makers* (Oxford University Press, 2006), at 194. See also Matthew Happold, 'Security Council Resolution 1373 and the Constitution of the United Nations' (2003) 16 *Leiden Journal of International Law* 593, at 598 (arguing that Security Council resolutions responding to particular situations 'can have precedential value'); Cogan (n 21), at 326 (arguing that the characterization of particular phenomena as threats to the peace 'sets a precedent and expectation for Council action in the future').

[31] See Weckel (n 29).

[32] See generally Vesselin Popovski, 'The Legislative Role of the Security Council's Thematic Resolutions' in Vesselin Popovski and Trudy Fraser (eds), *The Security Council as Global Legislator* (Routledge, 2014) 1; Alvarez (n 30), at 195–217; Paul C Szasz, 'The Security Council Starts Legislating' (2002) 96 *American Journal of International Law* 901; Talmon (n 22). Whether certain decisions of the Security Council amount to 'legislation' in the formal or substantive sense is open to debate. When referring to the action of the Security Council, the word 'legislative' will be used here in quotation marks.

1. The 'legislative' power of the Security Council

The decisions of the Security Council adopted in the exercise of its powers to maintain international peace and security in a particular situation are said to 'create new law for the concrete case'.[33] In recent years, however, the Security Council has imposed on UN member states obligations of a general and permanent nature designed to apply beyond the scope of a concrete case,[34] including an obligation to establish criminal offences in their domestic law.

(a) *Security Council decisions prescribing criminalization under domestic law*

The Security Council required UN member states to adopt criminal-law measures of general and permanent applicability on three occasions. In Resolution 1373 (2001), after having affirmed 'that [the terrorist attacks which took place in New York, Washington, DC, and Pennsylvania on 11 September 2001], like any act of international terrorism, constitute a threat to international peace and security',[35] the Security Council acted under Chapter VII to require member states, inter alia, to criminalize the financing, planning, preparation or perpetration of terrorist acts and to cooperate to bring perpetrators to justice.[36] In this resolution, the Security Council imposed on member states obligations that, in substance, are similar to certain obligations found in the International Convention for the Suppression of the Financing of Terrorism, which at the time had not yet entered into force.[37]

In Resolution 1540 (2004),[38] after having 'affirm[ed] that proliferation of nuclear, chemical and biological weapons, as well as their means of delivery, constitutes a threat to international peace and security',[39] the Security Council acted under Chapter VII to require member states, inter alia, to criminalize the manufacturing, acquisition, possession, development, transport, transfer, and use of nuclear material, chemical weapons, and biological weapons by non-state actors.[40] In this resolution, the Council created entirely new obligations not provided for in a pre-existing treaty.

In Resolution 2178 (2014) the Security Council, reaffirming that international terrorism constitutes a threat to international peace and security and underlining in particular 'the acute and growing threat posed by foreign terrorist fighters',[41] acted under Chapter VII of the Charter to require UN member states, inter alia, to

[33] Kelsen (n 7), at 295.

[34] For a survey of the emerging practice of the Security Council in creating norms of a general nature, see Catherine Denis, *Le pouvoir normatif du Conseil de sécurité des Nations Unies : portée et limites* (Bruylant, 2004), at 93–163.

[35] Resolution 1373 (2001), preamble, 3rd recital.

[36] Ibid, paras 1 and 2.

[37] The Security Council also called upon states to become parties the Convention as well as to other relevant treaties (ibid, para 3(d)).

[38] Resolution 1540 (2004), 28 April 2004, UN Doc S/RES/1540 (2004).

[39] Ibid, preamble, 1st recital.

[40] Ibid, para 2.

[41] Resolution 2178 (2014), 24 September 2014, UN Doc S/RES/2178 (2014), preamble, 1st and 8th recitals.

criminalize travelling abroad for the purpose of participating in terrorist acts or receiving training for terrorism, and recruitment for terrorism.[42]

The resolutions cited here aim at establishing a general legal framework for the suppression of criminal conduct in domestic legal orders. As such, they are evidence of what may arguably be described as a mechanism of international criminalization.

It should finally be noted that the Security Council has 'called upon' member states to 'criminalize [. . .] and ensure accountability of those who engage in transnational organized crime', in particular in arms trafficking and trafficking in persons,[43] which shows that the Council is also encouraging states to establish appropriate criminal offences in their domestic law for the suppression of organized crime.

(b) Legality of Security Council decisions prescribing legislative action

While Resolutions 1373 (2001) and 2178 (2014) were adopted without difficulties[44] and generally welcomed by states,[45] during the negotiations preceding the adoption of Resolution 1540 (2004) a number of states expressed the concern that the Security Council, by prescribing legislative action on the part of member states, was overstepping its mandate.[46] The Security Council's decisions requiring member states to adopt legislative measures attracted mixed criticism in the literature, a number of authors taking the view that the Council acted *ultra vires*.[47]

It has been argued, first, that the concept of 'threat to the peace' in Article 39 of the Charter does not refer to a phenomenon in general but to its actual or potential manifestations in a concrete situation.[48] Notwithstanding the fact that the concept of 'threat to the peace' is considered open to dynamic interpretation,[49] there is merit in this argument. As pointed out above, the action of the Council under Chapter VII is usually, although not exclusively, connected to an actual or potential

[42] Ibid, para 6.

[43] Resolution 2331 (2016), para 2(b); Resolution 2349 (2017), para 7.

[44] See Records of the 4385th meeting, 28 September 2001, UN Doc S/PV.4385; Records of the 7272nd meeting, 24 September 2014, UN Doc S/PV.7272. Draft Resolution 2178 (2014) was sponsored by no fewer than 103 states.

[45] See the views expressed by states in the days following the adoption of the resolutions in the official records of the plenary meetings of the General Assembly: 56th sess, 1–5 October 2001, UN Docs A/56/PV.12–22; 69th sess, 25–30 September 2014, UN Docs A/69/PV.9–20.

[46] See Records of the 4950th meeting, 22 April 2004, UN Doc S/PV.4950, at 5 (Algeria), 23 (India), and 32 (Iran), and UN Doc S/PV.4950 (Resumption 1), at 14 (Nepal) and 15 (Nigeria); Records of the 4956th meeting, 28 April 2004, UN Doc S/PV.4956, at 3 (Pakistan).

[47] For a positive reception, see Aston (n 22), at 287 (suggesting that the Security Council take similar action in other domains); Szasz (n 32), at 905 (arguing that '[i]f used prudently, this new tool will enhance the United Nations and benefit the world community, whose ability to create international law through traditional processes has lagged behind the urgent requirements of the new millennium'); Talmon (n 22). For negative views, see Björn Elberling, 'The *Ultra Vires* Character of Legislative Action by the Security Council' (2005) 2 *International Organizations Law Review* 337; Happold (n 30), at 609 (talking of a 'usurpation' of states' power to legislate). For a more nuanced position, see Ian Johnstone, 'Legislation and Adjudication in the UN Security Council: Bringing Down the Deliberative Deficit' (2008) 102 *American Journal of International Law* 275, at 299–300 (concluding: 'That the Council has the competence to act in this way does not necessarily mean it should').

[48] Elberling (n 47), at 342–43; Happold (n 30), at 599–600.

[49] See e.g. Aston (n 22), at 278–79; de Wet (n 8), at 100–109, 167. Recall also Section A.2(a) of this chapter.

situation of conflict or armed violence in a concrete case.[50] Be that as it may, at least in Resolution 1373 (2001) the Security Council did determine the existence of a concrete threat to the peace, namely the terrorist attacks of 11 September 2001, which certainly entitled the Council to act under Chapter VII.

It has also been argued that the UN Charter does not allow the Security Council to take measures of an abstract, general, and permanent nature.[51] However, while it is true that Article 41 does not explicitly authorize the Security Council to require member states to criminalize certain conduct, the list of measures provided for under Article 41 is not exhaustive and nothing in the Charter prohibits the Council from prescribing legislative action on the part of member states. The drafters granted the Council significant discretion to maintain international peace and security,[52] and there is no reason to believe that 'legislative' measures cannot be taken on the basis of Article 41 provided that a threat to the peace is validly determined pursuant to Article 39.[53]

In any event, while 'legislative' action on the part of the Security Council was initially a topic of some controversy, both states and academics have now come to accept and even embrace the possibility for the Security Council to use its powers to require states to enact rules of an abstract, general, and permanent nature.[54] Some scholars have notably made the case for harnessing the Security Council's powers under Chapter VII to overcome the limitations of the treaty-making process and states' reluctance to address emerging threats, such as climate change.[55]

In conclusion, decisions of the Security Council prescribing legislative action on the part of UN member states, such as a decision requiring states to criminalize particular conduct, conform with the UN Charter, provided that the Council first determines the existence of a threat to the peace. As suggested by Tomuschat,

> [i]f prevention is the philosophical concept underlying Article 39, then it must also be possible that the Security Council, in a more abstract manner, without having regard to the particular nature of a régime, outlaws certain activities as being incompatible with fundamental interests of the international community. [...] [The Security Council] must also be deemed empowered to enact general regulations prohibiting or restricting certain activities which, regardless of who is the author, are susceptible of putting in jeopardy international peace through the effects they are likely to produce.[56]

[50] Recall Section A.2(a) of this chapter. For a more liberal interpretation of Article 39 in support of the Security Council's 'legislative' activity, see Szasz (n 32), at 904; Talmon (n 22), at 180–81. See *contra* de Wet (n 8), at 176–77 (warning against 'an over-extension of the Security Council that would ultimately lead to the demise of the United Nations as a whole').

[51] Elberling (n 47), at 343; Happold (n 30), at 601.

[52] Recall Section A.1 of this chapter.

[53] For a similar argument, see Aston (n 22), at 280–81, 283–84; Talmon (n 22), at 181–82; Johnstone (n 47), at 299.

[54] See Jan Wouters and Jed Odermatt, '*Quis custodiet consilium securitatis*? Reflections on the Law-Making Powers of the Security Council' and Olivia Bosch, 'A Legislative Evolution: Security Council Resolution 1540 Revisited', both in Popovski and Fraser (n 32), respectively at 73 and at 112, 116.

[55] See e.g. Alan Boyle, 'International Lawmaking? Towards a New Role for the Security Council' in Antonio Cassese (ed), *Realizing Utopia: The Future of International Law* (Oxford University Press, 2012) 172.

[56] Christian Tomuschat, 'Obligations Arising for States without or against Their Will' (1993) 241 *Recueil des cours de l'Académie de droit international* 195, at 444–45.

Accordingly, it is argued that the Security Council could and should use its power under the Charter to suppress state organized crime.

2. The potential role of a Security Council decision requiring states to criminalize state organized crime

The Security Council could require UN member states to adopt legislative measures in their domestic law to suppress state organized crime. Like the treaty discussed in Chapter 6, the decision proposed here would require states to criminalize and establish their jurisdiction over state organized crime,[57] to facilitate extradition proceedings, to either extradite or prosecute suspected offenders, and to afford one another full mutual legal assistance in the suppression of state organized crime. Such a decision could usefully complement or be adopted in lieu of a convention for the suppression of state organized crime. It would be more efficient and potentially more effective than a treaty, but it may be perceived as less legitimate.[58]

(a) An efficient means of establishing a legal framework for the suppression of state organized crime

Whereas participation in a multilateral treaty occurs on a purely voluntary basis, the decisions of the UN Security Council taken under Chapter VII of the Charter are immediately binding for all UN member states[59] (that is to say, for all states).[60] A decision by the Security Council requiring states to criminalize state organized crime and to cooperate in its suppression would therefore have a reach potentially far greater than the treaty proposed in Chapter 6. It would allow for the establishment within domestic legal orders of a coherent legal framework to prosecute individuals involved in state organized crime. It would be more time-efficient than a treaty which may take years to be negotiated and to enter into force. It would also potentially be more effective than a treaty: whereas mechanisms to ensure compliance with a multilateral treaty are limited, the Security Council would have the power to adopt coercive measures against non-compliant states to enforce its decision.

Should the proposed treaty be adopted, the Security Council could also call upon states to become parties to it, as it did in Resolution 1373 (2001) in respect of the International Convention for the Suppression of the Financing of Terrorism.[61]

[57] The Security Council should provide a precise definition of the offence.

[58] See Cogan (n 21), at 333 (noting that 'legislative' action by the Security Council entails 'advantages (speed, uniformity) and disadvantages (decreased political legitimacy, lack of state consent)').

[59] UN Charter, Arts 25 and 48.

[60] Since the admission of South Sudan in July 2011, the UN now counts 193 member states. See the list of member states and their respective status of admission online at http://www.un.org/en/member-states/index.html.

[61] Resolution 1373 (2001), para 3(d).

(b) *Expressive function*

By creating norms defining state organized crime as a criminal offence, and by formally condemning states and individuals involved in state organized crime, the Security Council would fulfil an expressive function.[62] Yet the expressive potential of the Council's decisions remains weaker than that of a multilateral treaty ratified by a great number of states. In carrying out its duties for the maintenance of international peace and security, the Security Council is considered to act 'on behalf' of UN member states,[63] but in effect Security Council decisions only reflect the views of its members.

(c) *Potential legitimacy deficit*

The downside of having the Security Council circumvent the treaty-making process is that the legitimacy of the proposed decision would be weaker than that of a multilateral treaty. Decisions of the Security Council are taken by fifteen member states only, including ten elected members and five permanent members.[64] This allows a handful of states to create obligations for all states, with only limited possibility for non-member states to participate in the decision-making process. Decisions of the Council requiring states to adopt criminal-law measures could therefore be perceived by some states as an illegitimate infringement in their sovereignty. Such perception is likely to persist as long as the project of reforming membership and decision-making in the Security Council remains stalled.[65]

While concerns over the legitimacy of the Security Council's action are not to be underestimated, it should be kept in mind that all UN member states, by acceding to the Charter, have undertaken to carry out the Security Council's decisions.[66] Therefore, a Security Council decision imposing on member states a Charter-based obligation to criminalize state organized crime would be, in formal terms, as legitimate as a similar treaty-based obligation in a convention for the suppression of state organized crime. Moreover, while Security Council decisions requiring states to adopt criminal-law measures may be viewed as an intrusion into state sovereignty, they can also be analysed as a means of empowering states by leaving them the primary responsibility to take action to combat threats to the peace.[67]

3. Conclusion

A decision by the UN Security Council, acting under Chapter VII of the Charter, to require member states to establish state organized crime as a criminal offence in

[62] On the expressive function of law, see Chapter 5, Section A.2.
[63] UN Charter, Art 24(1).
[64] Ibid, Art 23(1), as amended by General Assembly Resolution 1991 (XVIII), 17 December 1963, UN Doc A/RES/1991 (XVIII).
[65] See Nico Schrijver, 'Reforming the UN Security Council in Pursuance of Collective Security' (2007) 12 *Journal of Conflict & Security Law* 127.
[66] UN Charter, Arts 25 and 48. [67] Cogan (n 21), at 339.

their domestic law and to cooperate to bring offenders to justice would conform with the UN Charter and be in line with the practice of the Security Council, provided that the Council first determines the existence of a threat to the peace. Such a decision could usefully complement or provide a substitute for the convention for the suppression of state organized crime proposed in Chapter 6. As a means of criminalizing state organized crime, a Security Council decision would be more efficient and have a reach far greater than a treaty, allowing for the rapid establishment within domestic legal orders of a legal framework for the suppression of state organized crime. Moreover, the Security Council could take a range of coercive measures against non-compliant states to enforce its decision. The proposed measure would also fulfil an expressive function.

C. Targeted Financial Sanctions against State Officials Involved in State Organized Crime

In addition to providing for mechanisms of criminal responsibility, the Security Council could also impose targeted financial sanctions in the form of asset freezes against state officials and entities suspected of being involved in state organized crime. Asset freezes, that is to say, the decision to order member states temporarily to prohibit the transfer, conversion, disposition, or movement of an individual's property or temporarily to assume custody or control of such property,[68] have in recent years become a key tool for addressing various forms of misconduct on the part of state officials.[69] Based on an analysis of the Security Council's practice, this section begins by showing that targeted financial sanctions would be legally possible in cases

[68] Recall Chapter 3, Section D.1(b).

[69] The EU also assumes a major role in imposing international sanctions. The Union has competence to adopt measures referred to in EU legal terminology as 'restrictive measures': see Treaty on European Union (consolidated version), OJ C326 (26 October 2012) 13, Art 29; Treaty on the Functioning of the European Union, Art 215. In accordance with its stated policy, the EU imposes restrictive measures 'to uphold respect for human rights, democracy, the rule of law and good governance' (Council of the EU, *Basic Principles on the Use of Restrictive Measures (Sanctions)*, 7 June 2004, Doc no 10198/1/04 REV 1, para 3). The EU has notably taken restrictive measures against senior state officials suspected of embezzling public funds, such as former Tunisian President Zine al-Abidine Ben Ali (Council Decision 2011/72/CFSP concerning restrictive measures directed against certain persons and entities in view of the situation in Tunisia, 31 January 2011, OJ L28 (2 February 2011) 62; Council Regulation 101/2011 concerning restrictive measures directed against certain persons and entities in view of the situation in Tunisia, 4 February 2011, OJ L31 (5 February 2011) 1), former Egyptian President Hosni Mubarak (Council Decision 2011/172/CFSP concerning restrictive measures directed against certain persons, entities and bodies in view of the situation in Egypt, 21 March 2011, OJ L76 (22 March 2011) 63; Council Regulation 270/2011 concerning restrictive measures directed against certain persons, entities and bodies in view of the situation in Egypt, 21 March 2011, OJ L76 (22 March 2011) 4), and former Ukrainian President Viktor Yanukovych (Council Decision 2014/119/CFSP concerning restrictive measures directed against certain persons, entities and bodies in view of the situation in Ukraine, 5 March 2014, OJ L66, (6 March 2014) 26; Council Regulation 208/2014 concerning restrictive measures directed against certain persons, entities and bodies in view of the situation in Ukraine, 5 March 2014, OJ L66 (6 March 2014) 1).

of state organized crime. It then considers the potential function and impact of targeted financial sanctions in respect of state organized crime.

1. Asset freezes and state organized crime in the practice of the Security Council

An examination of the practice of the Security Council suggests that asset freezes can be used against individuals involved in state organized crime.

(a) *Asset freezes in the practice of the Security Council*

Asset freezes have become the Security Council's instrument of choice in a variety of situations.[70] To date, asset freezes have been ordered against the following individuals and entities (in chronological order): military officers and members of an illegal government in Haiti;[71] the Taliban regime in Afghanistan[72] and persons affiliated to al-Qaida;[73] Saddam Hussein and other former senior Iraqi officials and their relatives;[74] former Liberian President Charles Taylor, his family, and other individuals supporting the Revolutionary United Front in Sierra Leone;[75] individuals impeding the peace process and responsible for human rights violations in Côte d'Ivoire[76] and Sudan;[77] individuals suspected of involvement in the terrorist attack against former Lebanese Prime Minister Rafiq Hariri;[78] senior North Korean government officials and other individuals and entities connected to North Korea's nuclear weapons programmes;[79] individuals providing support for Iran's nuclear proliferation activities

[70] Travel bans are also routinely used in conjunction with asset freezes, or independently of other types of sanctions. For an analysis of existing and past sanctions regimes, see Jeremy Matam Farrall, *United Nations Sanctions and the Rule of Law* (Cambridge University Press, 2007), at 247–463; Michael Eriksson, *Targeting Peace: Understanding UN and EU Targeted Sanctions* (Ashgate, 2011), at 59–110 (including EU restrictive measures but excluding Security Council sanctions against individuals involved in terrorism).

[71] Resolution 917 (1994), 6 May 1994, UN Doc S/RES/917 (1994) (not mandatory, as the Security Council used the words 'strongly urges').

[72] Resolution 1267 (1999), 15 October 1999, UN Doc S/RES/1267 (1999); Resolution 1333 (2000); Resolution 1390 (2002), 28 January 2002, UN Doc S/RES/1390 (2002); Resolution 1988 (2011); Resolution 2082 (2012).

[73] Resolution 1333 (2000); Resolution 1390 (2002); Resolution 1989 (2011), 17 June 2011, UN Doc S/RES/1989 (2011); Resolution 2083 (2012), 17 December 2012, UN Doc S/RES/2083 (2012); Resolution 2161 (2014), 17 June 2014, UN Doc S/RES/2161 (2014). The Security Council initially targeted the Taliban and individuals associated with al-Qaida jointly, but Resolutions 1988 (2011) and 1989 (2011) have established separate regimes.

[74] Resolution 1483 (2003), 22 May 2003, UN Doc S/RES/1483 (2003).

[75] Resolution 1521 (2003), 22 December 2003, UN Doc S/RES/1521 (2003); Resolution 1532 (2004), 12 March 2004, UN Doc S/RES/1532 (2004).

[76] Resolution 1572 (2004), 15 November 2004, UN Doc S/RES/1572 (2004); Resolution 1975 (2011), 30 March 2011, UN Doc S/RES/1975 (2011).

[77] Resolution 1591 (2005), 29 March 2005, UN Doc S/RES/1591 (2005).

[78] Resolution 1636 (2005), 31 October 2005, UN Doc S/RES/1636 (2005).

[79] Resolution 1718 (2006), 14 October 2006, UN Doc S/RES/1718 (2006); Resolution 2270 (2016); Resolution 2321 (2016); Resolution 2356 (2017), 2 June 2017, UN Doc S/RES/2356 (2017); Resolution 2371 (2017), 5 August 2017, UN Doc S/RES/2371 (2017); Resolution 2375 (2017), 11 September 2017, UN Doc S/RES/2375 (2017).

and the development of nuclear weapon delivery systems;[80] armed groups leaders in the Democratic Republic of the Congo;[81] individuals threatening peace and security, violating arms embargoes, using children in armed conflicts, and responsible for attacks against civilians in Somalia;[82] members of the Eritrean political and military leadership providing support to armed groups destabilizing the region;[83] former Libyan head of state Muammar Gaddafi and his relatives;[84] individuals undermining the peace, stability, and security of the Central African Republic[85] and of Yemen;[86] individuals associated with ISIL and the Jabhat al-Nusrah;[87] individuals threatening the stability and undermining the political transition in Libya;[88] and individuals threatening peace, security, and stability in Mali.[89]

(b) *Analysis of relevant sanctions regimes*

In some of the situations cited above, the Security Council took into consideration the existence of organized criminal activities to impose sanctions. In the case of sanctions targeting individuals associated with al-Qaida, the Security Council stressed the 'need to take measures to prevent and suppress the financing of terrorism, including from the proceeds of organized crime, inter alia, the illicit production and trafficking of drugs and their chemical precursors'.[90] In its decision imposing sanctions on individuals associated with ISIL, the Council 'express[ed] concern that terrorists benefit from transnational organized crime in some regions, including from the trafficking of arms, persons, drugs, and artefacts, and from the illicit trade in natural resources including gold and other precious metals and stones, minerals, wildlife, charcoal and oil'.[91] In the case of the Central African Republic, the Council noted with concern the 'illicit trade, exploitation and smuggling of natural resources

[80] Resolution 1737 (2006), 27 December 2006, UN Doc S/RES/1737 (2006); Resolution 1747 (2007), 24 March 2007, UN Doc S/RES/1747 (2007); Resolution 1803 (2008), 3 March 2008, UN Doc S/RES/1803 (2008); Resolution 1929 (2010), 9 June 2010, UN Doc S/RES/1929 (2010).

[81] Resolution 1807 (2008), 31 March 2008, UN Doc S/RES/1807 (2008); Resolution 1896 (2009), 7 December 2009, UN Doc S/RES/1896 (2009).

[82] Resolution 1844 (2008), 20 November 2008, UN Doc S/RES/1844 (2008); Resolution 2002 (2011), 29 July 2011, UN Doc S/RES/2002 (2011).

[83] Resolution 1907 (2009), 23 December 2009, UN Doc S/RES/1907 (2009).

[84] Resolution 1970 (2011), 26 February 2011, UN Doc S/RES/1970 (2011).

[85] Resolution 2134 (2014), 28 January 2014, UN Doc S/RES/2134 (2014); Resolution 2196 (2015); Resolution 2262 (2016); Resolution 2339 (2017).

[86] Resolution 2140 (2014), 26 February 2014, UN Doc S/RES/2140 (2014); Resolution 2216 (2015), 14 April 2015, UN Doc S/RES/2216 (2015).

[87] Resolution 2170 (2014), 15 August 2014, UN Doc S/RES/2170 (2014); Resolution 2199 (2015), 12 February 2015, UN Doc S/RES/2199 (2015); Resolution 2253 (2015). These sanctions form part of the al-Qaida sanctions regime set up by Resolution 1989 (2011).

[88] Resolution 2174 (2014), 27 August 2014, UN Doc S/RES/2174 (2014). These sanctions form part of the sanctions regime set up by Resolution 1970 (2011).

[89] Resolution 2374 (2017), 5 September 2017, UN Doc S/RES/2374 (2017).

[90] Resolution 1989 (2011), preamble, 17th recital; Resolution 2083 (2012), preamble, 17th recital; Resolution 2161 (2014), preamble, 17th recital.

[91] Resolution 2253 (2015), preamble, 23rd recital. See also Resolution 2170 (2014), para 13; Resolution 2199 (2015), paras 1–17 (addressing the illicit exploitation of oilfields and trafficking in cultural property).

including gold, diamonds and wildlife poaching and trafficking', as well as 'the illicit transfer [...] of small arms and light weapons'.[92] Finally, in the case of Mali, the Council noted 'the intensification of criminal activities such as drug trafficking and trafficking in persons', notably 'the involvement of non-state actors, notably terrorist groups, in [...] the trafficking in cultural property', and stressed 'the serious challenges posed by transnational organized crime in the Sahel region, including arms, drug and cultural property trafficking, the smuggling of migrants, [and] trafficking in persons'.[93]

The Security Council has also taken action specifically against individuals suspected of being involved in organized crime. Regarding the situation in the Central African Republic, the Council targeted individuals '[p]roviding support for armed groups or criminal networks through the illicit exploitation or trade of natural resources, including diamonds, gold, wildlife as well as wildlife products'.[94] Similarly, regarding the situation in Libya, the Council 'express[ed] its determination to use targeted sanctions' against individuals 'providing support for armed groups or criminal networks through the illicit exploitation of crude oil or any other natural resources'.[95] In a resolution addressing the illicit trafficking in cultural property by ISIL, the Security Council '[e]ncourage[d] Member States to propose listings of ISIL, Al-Qaida and associated individuals, groups, undertakings and entities involved in the illicit trade in cultural property to be considered by the [...] ISIL (Da'esh) and Al-Qaida Sanctions Committee'.[96] In response to the situation in Mali, the Council imposed sanctions inter alia against individuals providing financial support to designated entities, 'including through the proceeds from organized crime, including the production and trafficking of narcotic drugs and their precursors originating in or transiting through Mali, the trafficking in persons and the smuggling of migrants, the smuggling and trafficking of arms as well as the trafficking in cultural property'.[97]

Sanctions have also been imposed on state officials suspected of being involved in organized crime. In the case of the Taliban in Afghanistan,[98] the Security Council noted 'that the Taliban benefits directly from the cultivation of illicit opium by imposing a tax on its production and indirectly benefits from the processing and trafficking of such opium',[99] and expressed concern over the use by the Taliban of 'proceeds derived from illicit cultivation, production and trafficking of narcotic drugs and their precursors originating in and transiting through Afghanistan'.[100] In the

[92] Resolution 2339 (2017), preamble, 17th and 21st recitals. See also Resolution 2196 (2015); Resolution 2262 (2016).

[93] Resolution 2374 (2017), preamble, 9th, 12th, and 20th recitals.

[94] Resolution 2134 (2014), para 37(d); Resolution 2339 (2017), para 17(e). See also Resolution 2127 (2013), 5 December 2013, UN Doc S/RES/2127 (2013), para 56.

[95] Resolution 2174 (2014), preamble, 9th recital, and para 4(c).

[96] Resolution 2347 (2017), para 10.

[97] Resolution 2374 (2017), para 8(c).

[98] It should be noted that the Afghan government accredited to the UN at the time was not the Taliban and that the UN did not recognize the Taliban as the legitimate government of Afghanistan.

[99] Resolution 1333 (2000), preamble, 9th recital.

[100] Resolution 1988 (2011), para 5; Resolution 2082 (2012), para 4.

case of Charles Taylor's activities in Sierra Leone, the Security Council 'recognis[ed] the linkage between the illegal exploitation of natural resources such as diamonds and timber, illicit trade in such resources, and the proliferation and trafficking of illegal arms',[101] and expressed its concern over Taylor's 'control over [...] misappropriated funds and property'.[102] In a similar vein, the Security Council's decision to impose travel bans against officials of Guinea-Bissau further to the 2012 military coup was driven by concern over 'the possible increase in illicit drug trafficking as a result of the military coup' and about 'cases of looting [...] of State assets'.[103]

Finally, the Security Council has imposed sanctions against state organs and affiliated entities suspected of being involved in state organized crime. In the case of North Korea, the Council ordered the freezing of assets held by Office 39,[104] the branch of the Workers' Party Central Committee alleged to be involved in organized criminal activities to provide funding for North Korea's nuclear weapons programme,[105] as well as against financial institutions and corporations affiliated with Office 39.[106]

These examples suggest that the suspected involvement of certain individuals and in particular of state officials in organized criminal activities is a factor taken into consideration by the Security Council when determining the existence of a threat to the peace and imposing sanctions. As observers point out '[t]he contemporary targets of UN sanctions are increasingly [...] actors who are driven by a desire for personal enrichment and power'.[107]

It should be noted, however, that a suspicion that senior public officials were involved in organized criminal activities was not the decisive rationale for determining the existence of a threat to the peace and imposing sanctions in these situations. Rather, sanctions were taken in a broader context of armed conflict, human rights violations, or terrorist or nuclear threats.[108] This suggests that the Security Council, in making use of its discretionary powers under Chapter VII of the Charter to determine the existence of a threat to the peace and to impose sanctions, targets state officials suspected of being involved in organized criminal activities only where such activities are connected, either directly or indirectly, to a form of violence.

State organized crime indeed often fuels armed conflicts and insecurity in weak states.[109] As evidenced by the situation in Sierra Leone, the recourse to armed violence is often a means for perpetrators to control resources. In turn, proceeds of criminal activities are used to purchase arms and ammunition. Similarly, in Guinea-Bissau the situation of instability and insecurity generated by the coup boosted drug

[101] Resolution 1521 (2003), preamble, 7th recital.

[102] Resolution 1532 (2004), preamble, 4th recital.

[103] Resolution 2048 (2012), preamble, 9th and 15th recitals.

[104] Resolution 2270 (2016), Annex II, no 10.

[105] Recall Chapter 1, Section E.

[106] Resolution 2321 (2016), Annex II, nos 3 and 10; Resolution 2356 (2017), Annex II, no 3; Resolution 2371 (2017), Annex II, no 2.

[107] David Cortright and George A Lopez, *Sanctions and the Search for Security: Challenges to UN Action* (Lynne Rienner, 2002), at 17.

[108] This finding is consistent with the view taken in the literature that targeted sanctions are almost always imposed in conjunction with an armed conflict or an 'ongoing crisis'. See Eriksson (n 70), at 109.

[109] Recall Chapter 1, Section B.3.

trafficking which, in turn, increased the level of violence. Moreover, the situation in Afghanistan bears testimony to the fact that state organized crime is used to finance terrorist groups.[110]

Security Council resolutions responding to particular situations 'can have precedential value'.[111] The precedents analysed here suggest that in situations where state organized crime is connected to armed violence or a terrorist threat, the Security Council could determine the existence of a threat to the peace and require UN member states to freeze the assets of public officials suspected of being involved in state organized crime.

2. The potential role of targeted financial sanctions in cases of state organized crime

Asset freezes could have an impact on state officials and entities involved in state organized crime. This section begins by underscoring the prescriptive, expressive, and preventive functions of sanctions in general, before discussing the potential practical advantages of targeted financial sanctions in cases of state organized crime.

(a) The prescriptive, expressive, and preventive functions of sanctions

In the words of the Security Council, 'sanctions are an important tool under the Charter of the United Nations in the maintenance and restoration of international peace and security'.[112] Sanctions can be conceptualized as political measures designed to achieve a particular outcome. According to the UN Secretary-General, '[t]he purpose of sanctions is to modify the behaviour of a party that is threatening international peace and security'.[113] On this view, sanctions are tools of 'carrot-and-stick diplomacy',[114] 'instruments of persuasion' used 'to isolate an abusive regime or to encourage dialogue and negotiation'.[115] Their goal is to ensure compliance with particular prescriptions or norms of international law.

In addition, sanctions serve an expressive purpose. As commentators observe, 'the background against which [the Security Council]'s action under Chapter VII unfolds is profoundly normative'.[116] Sanctions constitute a normative statement—a means to express the Security Council's 'condemnation',[117]

[110] Recall Chapter 1, Section C.3. [111] Happold (n 30). See also Cogan (n 21).

[112] See e.g. Resolution 1822 (2008), 30 June 2008, UN Doc S/RES/1822 (2008), preamble, 9th recital; Resolution 1989 (2011), preamble, 8th recital; Resolution 2083 (2012), preamble, 8th recital; Resolution 2161 (2014), preamble, 8th recital.

[113] *Supplement to An Agenda for Peace: Position paper of the Secretary-General on the occasion of the fiftieth anniversary of the United Nations*, 25 January 1995, UN Doc A/50/60, para 66, endorsed in General Assembly Resolution 51/242, 15 September 1997, UN Doc A/RES/51/242.

[114] See David Cortright and George A Lopez, *The Sanction Decade: Assessing UN Strategies in the 1990s* (Lynne Riener, 2000), at 27–32.

[115] David Cortright and George A Lopez, 'Introduction: Assessing Smart Sanctions: Lessons from the 1990s' in Cortright and Lopez (n 2), at 15–16.

[116] d'Argent et al (n 7), at 1164 (author's translation).

[117] 'The Prospective Role of the United Nations in Dealing with the International Use of Force in the Post-Cold War Period: An Analysis in the Light of the Persian Gulf Crisis', Symposium (University of

'rejection',[118] as well as its 'will [...] to end unacceptable behaviour'.[119] To this extent, sanctions fulfil an expressive function similar to that of punishment in the criminal law.[120] UN officials working on sanctions management point out that targeted sanctions are effective at generating stigma, especially when combined with media coverage.[121] Yet stigma alone is not likely to bring about compliance. 'To be effective in forcing behavioural change, sanctions must be credible and enforceable.'[122]

If properly implemented, sanctions may also have a preventive effect. As noted by the UN Secretary-General, '[s]anctions [...] have the potential to [...] diminish the capacity of the protagonists' to pursue activities which threaten international peace and security.[123] Financial sanctions can 'restrict [...] access to the hard currency necessary to fund continued fighting'[124] or other activities deemed to threaten international peace and security. In particular, asset freezes are used 'to prevent and suppress the financing of terrorism and terrorist organizations, including from the proceeds of organized crime'.[125]

In short, sanctions are imposed for a variety of purposes, which 'may include deterring future wrongdoing, [...] upholding international norms, and sending messages of disapproval in response to objectionable behaviour'.[126] Targeted sanctions arguably represent a viable avenue for action against state organized crime. Sanctions could contribute to preventing further crimes, exert pressure with a view to putting an end to criminal conduct or policies, and condemn the involvement of state officials in organized criminal activities.

Before discussing further the potential practical advantages of asset freezes in cases of state organized crime, it is worth explaining why other types of targeted sanction, such as trade embargoes on specific commodities, are less likely to be effective in such cases.

Georgia School of Law, 1–2 March 1991), (1992) 22 *Georgia Journal of International and Comparative Law* 9, at 42 (remark by Professor Nico Schrijver).

118 Records of the 4128th meeting, 17 April 2000, UN Doc S/PV.4128 (General issues relating to sanctions), at 16 (statement of the representative of Argentina).

119 Ibid, at 7 (statement of the representative of the United States).

120 See de Wet (n 8), at 353 (arguing that the freezing of assets 'would constitute a sanction belonging to the criminal sphere, in light of its punitive nature, severity, as well as the stigmatisation resulting from it'). See *contra Report of the Informal Working Group of the Security Council on General Issues of Sanctions*, annexed to UN Doc S/2006/997, 22 December 2006, para 7 (indicating that 'targeted sanctions must be clearly described and understood as measures to maintain international peace and security, not as a punitive measure').

121 Eriksson (n 70), at 124.

122 Records of the 4128th meeting (n 118), at 7 (statement of the representative of the United States).

123 Report of the UN Secretary-General, *The Causes of Conflict and the Promotion of Durable Peace and Sustainable Development in Africa*, 13 April 1998, UN Doc A/52/871, para 25.

124 Records of the 4128th meeting (n 118), at 2 (statement of the Under-Secretary-General for Political Affairs). See also at 24 (statement of the representative of Canada).

125 See resolutions cited in n 90.

126 Cortright and Lopez (n 114), at 16.

(b) *The inadequacy of economic sanctions*

Economic sanctions taken against a state would be unlikely to achieve their intended objective, and have undesirable side-effects. Economic sanctions have been criticized for being 'blunt', 'counter-productive', and disproportionately harming the population of the targeted state.[127] Even where embargoes are designed to affect the ruling elite and to minimize the impact on the population, for example by targeting specific commodities only,[128] prospects of success remain limited in situations where the targeted rulers control access to resources (usually through the black market). Economic sanctions reducing the availability of certain goods can then have the perverse effect of enriching and strengthening the regime.[129] Moreover, in weak states where the economy operates largely outside of the formal system of trade, with no documentation of transactions, no official taxation regime, and no customs control, economic sanctions such as import bans, which rely on formal monitoring and controlling mechanisms, are likely to be ineffective.[130] As a result, targeted leaders generating substantial profits from the informal economy have no incentive to comply with the prescriptions of the sanctioning body, and 'rather seek to circumvent international authority by a variety of ingenious and illegal means'.[131]

In addition, targeted embargoes still entail a high social cost, causing job losses in the affected economic sector.[132] Last but not least, import bans on certain commodities may inconvenience trading partners of the targeted country,[133] which makes these states less likely to support sanctions.[134]

[127] See Position paper of the UN Secretary-General (n 113), para 70; Report of the UN Secretary-General, *We the Peoples: The Role of the United Nations in the Twenty-first Century*, 27 March 2000, UN Doc A/54/2000, para 232; Robert A Pape, 'Why Economic Sanctions Do Not Work' (1997) 22 *International Security* 90; Boris Kondoch, 'The Limits of Economic Sanctions under International Law: The Case of Iraq' (2001) 7 *International Peacekeeping* 267. For a detailed analysis of the consequences of comprehensive economic sanctions against Iraq, see *Report of the Second Panel established pursuant to the Note by the President of the Security Council of 30 January 1999 (S/1999/100), concerning the current humanitarian situation in Iraq*, annexed to UN Doc S/1999/356, 30 March 1999, paras 17–27.

[128] See e.g. Resolution 792 (1992), 30 November 1992, UN Doc S/RES/792 (1992), paras 13–14 (recommending to cease imports of logs, minerals, and gems from Cambodia); Resolution 841 (1993), 16 June 1993, UN Doc S/RES/841 (1993), para 5 (prohibiting the sale or supply of petroleum and arms to Haiti); Resolution 1306 (2000), 5 July 2000, UN Doc S/RES/1306 (2000), para 1 (prohibiting the import of rough diamonds from Sierra Leone); Resolution 1343 (2001), 7 March 2001, UN Doc S/RES/1343 (2001), para 6 (prohibiting the import of rough diamonds from Liberia); Resolution 1718 (2006), para 8 (prohibiting the sale or supply of luxury goods to North Korea).

[129] Report of the UN Secretary-General (n 127), para 231; Cortright and Lopez (n 114), at 20; Andrew Mack and Asif Khan, 'UN Sanctions: A Glass Half-Full?' in Richard M Price and Mark W Zacher (eds), *The United Nations and Global Security* (Palgrave Macmillan, 2004) 156, at 158.

[130] Cortright and Lopez (n 107), at 12–13. [131] Ibid, at 17.

[132] See e.g. the comments of the UN Secretary-General in the case of Liberia: *Report of the Secretary-General in pursuance of paragraph 13 (a) of resolution 1343 (2001) concerning Liberia*, 5 October 2001, UN Doc S/2001/939, para 34.

[133] See Position paper of the UN Secretary-General (n 113), paras 73–75; Records of the 4128th meeting (n 118), in particular at 35–36 (statement of the representative of Bulgaria) and 44 (statement of the representative of Macedonia). See also Raul Caruso, 'The Impact of International Economic Sanctions on Trade: Empirical Evidence over the Period 1960–2000' (2005) 113 *Rivista internazionale di scienze sociali* 41; Ruth Lapidoth, 'Some Reflections on the Law and Practice Concerning the Imposition of Sanctions by the Security Council' (1992) 30 *Archiv des Völkerrechts* 114, at 122–23.

[134] In the case of Liberia, France was reluctant to support a timber embargo because it imported significant volumes of Liberian timber. See Cortright and Lopez (n 107), at 7.

In short, one should be cautious about 'the expectation that economic punishment can overwhelm a state's commitment to pursue important policy goals',[135] and about the virtues of economic sanctions designed to affect certain individuals who prove capable of taking advantage of trade embargoes. By contrast, targeted financial sanctions appear better suited to fulfil their intended objectives.

(c) *Practical advantages of targeted financial sanctions*

Targeted financial sanctions are considered preferable to broader economic sanctions because they do not have undesirable side-effects.[136] They also present certain advantages in cases of state organized crime. First, they have the potential to disrupt the financial channels of state organized crime. Secondly, decisions adopted by the UN Security Council can trump the immunity of certain assets from pre-judgment measures of constraint.

(i) Disruption of crime

Financial sanctions against public officials and entities involved in organized crime would target the phenomenon of state organized crime at its source. Asset freezes would not only deny the targets access to criminal proceeds for their personal benefit, but also deprive them of the resources necessary to commit further crimes, which would, in turn, increase the cost of wrongdoing, disrupt the operational capacity of individuals and entities involved in state organized crime, and ultimately prevent future crimes.

Targeted financial sanctions are already being used to similar ends. When the UN Security Council decided to freeze the assets of individuals associated with al-Qaida and ISIL, it was pursuing the stated objective of combating the financing of terrorism, 'including from the proceeds of organized crime, inter alia, the illicit production and trafficking of drugs and their chemical precursors'.[137]

Assets frozen pursuant to a decision of the Security Council could be confiscated in the course of domestic proceedings.[138] Ordering states to freeze the assets of particular individuals suspected of being involved in state organized crime could provide an incentive for national authorities to take further steps to investigate the origin and destination of those assets and, where appropriate, to initiate proceedings for the purpose of asset confiscation or recovery.

[135] Pape (n 127), at 93.

[136] See the reasons listed in Koenraad van Brabant, *Can Sanctions Be Smarter? The Current Debate*—Report of a conference held in London, 16–17 December 1998 (Overseas Development Institute, May 1999), at 18.

[137] See resolutions cited in nn 90 and 91.

[138] See the recent practice of the EU, which adopted restrictive measures against Ukrainian officials in anticipation of domestic asset recovery proceedings: see Council Decision 2014/119/CFSP, preamble, 2nd recital ('the Council agreed to focus restrictive measures on the freezing and recovery of assets of persons identified as responsible for the misappropriation of Ukrainian State funds'); Council Regulation 208/2014, preamble, 2nd recital (idem), and Art 8(4) (regulating the exchange of financial information 'for the purpose of assisting the recovery of misappropriated funds').

(ii) Trumping immunities from measures of constraint

The immunity shielding privately owned assets intermingled with state property from foreign pre-judgment measures of constraint[139] would be trumped by the UN Security Council's authority under the Charter.[140] In carrying out its functions for the purpose of maintaining international peace and security, the Security Council is entitled to derogate from general international law.[141] Moreover, pursuant to Article 103 of the UN Charter, obligations under the Charter prevail over 'obligations under any other international agreement', in other words over other treaty obligations binding UN member states. This provision has been widely interpreted as allowing the decisions taken by the Security Council under Chapter VII to take precedence over rules of customary international law as well.[142] As a result, states implementing Security Council decisions would be permitted to freeze foreign state property otherwise immune under international law from pre-judgment measures of constraint.

(d) Conclusion

Targeted financial sanctions could be a useful tool in the fight against state organized crime and could have an impact on suspected offenders. Such sanctions would constitute an expressive response on the part of the Security Council on behalf of the international community, condemning the individuals involved and pressuring them to respect the rule of law. In practical terms, by making illicit assets unavailable to suspected offenders and by paving the way for domestic confiscation proceedings, sanctions could also prevent the individuals and entities concerned from furthering criminal agendas.

To be effective, the envisaged sanctions would need to be carefully crafted and implemented. The person and assets to be targeted should be clearly identified.

[139] Recall Chapter 3, Section D.2 and Chapter 4, Section B.5(a).

[140] A decision of the Security Council could also trump the immunity granted to property belonging to a head of state: recall Chapter 4, Section B.5(b).

[141] This view rests on Art 1(1) of the Charter, in which the words 'in conformity with the principles of justice and international law' are meant to apply only in relation to the peaceful settlement of disputes, and not to the maintenance of international peace and security: see Kelsen (n 7), at 294–95; Leland Goodrich, Edvard Hambro, and Anne Simons, *Charter of the United Nations: Commentary and Documents* (3rd edn, Columbia University Press, 1969), at 27–28; Rüdiger Wolfrum, 'Article 1' in Simma et al (n 7), vol I, at 113–14. See also Gill (n 8), at 64–68; Akande (n 10), at 318.

[142] Stefan Talmon, 'Security Council Treaty Action' (2009) 62 *Revue héllénique de droit international* 65, at 89–90, and the authorities cited therein. See also Vera Gowlland-Debbas, 'The Functions of the United Nations Security Council in the International Legal System' in Michael Byers (ed), *The Role of Law in International Politics: Essays in International Relations and International Law* (Oxford University Press, 2000) 277, at 294 (noting that 'Security Council measures have also, on the basis of authorizations to States, resulted in the temporary suspension of (non-imperative) rules of customary international law'); and the views expressed by the Council and by the Commission of the EU in *Yusuf and Al Barakaat v Council* (n 10), para 207 and *Kadi v Council* (n 10), para 156 ('The obligations imposed on a Member of the United Nations under Chapter VII of the Charter of the United Nations prevail over every other international obligation to which the member might be subject. In that way Article 103 of the Charter makes it possible to disregard any other provision of international law, whether customary or laid down by convention, in order to apply the resolutions of the Security Council').

Sanctions committees and monitoring mechanisms should be established to conduct regular reviews of the sanctions regimes and provide assistance to UN member states to strengthen implementation capacity. De-listing procedures and appropriate remedies should also be open to designated individuals and entities.[143]

D. Conclusion

The UN Security Council could arguably play a role in the suppression of state organized crime. In situations involving armed violence or a terrorist threat, state organized crime can be characterized as a threat to the peace, which opens the door for the adoption by the Security Council of binding measures under Chapter VII of the UN Charter. The Security Council, enjoying broad discretion in the choice of measures necessary to maintain international peace and security, could require UN member states to establish state organized crime as a criminal offence in their domestic law and to cooperate to bring offenders to justice. Such a decision could usefully complement or provide a substitute for a multilateral treaty for the purpose of establishing state organized crime as an international crime. As a means of criminalizing state organized crime, it would be more efficient and have a reach far greater than a treaty, but its legitimacy and expressive capacity would be weaker. Furthermore, the Security Council could require member states to freeze the assets of senior state officials and entities suspected of being involved in state organized crime. Such sanctions would fulfil prescriptive, expressive, and preventive functions. The measures proposed in this chapter can be taken in conformity with the UN Charter and would be in line with the contemporary practice of the Security Council.

[143] On the design and implementation of targeted sanctions, see generally Swiss Confederation, UN Secretariat, and Watson Institute for International Studies, Brown University, *Targeted Financial Sanctions: A Manual for Design and Implementation—Contributions from the Interlaken Process* (Watson Institute for International Studies, Brown University, 2001); Peter Wallensteen, Carina Staibano, and Mikael Eriksson, *Making Targeted Sanctions Effective: Guidelines for the Implementation of UN Policy Options—Results from the Stockholm Process on the Implementation of Targeted Sanctions* (Department of Peace and Conflict Research, Uppsala University, 2003). For an analysis of the rule of law issues surrounding the imposition of sanctions, and policy recommendations to enhance transparency, consistency, equality, due process, and proportionality in the practice of the Security Council, see Farrall (n 70), at 183–240.

8

The Potential Role of International Criminal Tribunals in the Suppression of State Organized Crime

This chapter discusses the potential role of international criminal courts and tribunals in prosecuting individuals suspected of being involved in state organized crime. A treaty or a UN Security Council decision requiring states to criminalize state organized crime and to cooperate to bring offenders to justice would not solve all enforcement problems. The difficulties inherent in prosecuting serving or former senior government officials may still thwart law enforcement before domestic courts, whether in the state having custody of the alleged offender or in a state requesting extradition.[1] As prospects for holding offenders accountable before domestic courts are uncertain, it is worth exploring alternatives. A number of obstacles undermining law enforcement at the domestic level could be overcome by prosecuting offenders involved in state organized crime before an international criminal court or tribunal.

This idea of recourse to an international criminal court or tribunal to combat organized crime is not new. The UN General Assembly contemplated the possibility of prosecuting individuals involved in drug trafficking before an international criminal court and requested the ILC to consider the issue.[2] The Commission, in its work on a Draft Statute for an International Criminal Court, included crimes defined under the UN Drug Convention in the list of 'exceptionally serious crimes of international concern' under the jurisdiction of the proposed court.[3] The idea has been echoed in legal scholarship advocating the inclusion of drug trafficking and of other crimes such as money laundering, participation in transnational organized crime, and corruption within the jurisdiction of an international criminal court.[4]

[1] Recall Chapter 4, Section B.

[2] Resolution 44/39, 4 December 1989, UN Doc A/RES/44/39.

[3] See Draft Statute for an International Criminal Court, Art 20(e) and the crimes listed in the Annex, Item 9, in *Report of the International Law Commission* (46th sess), UN Doc A/49/10 in *Yearbook of the International Law Commission* (1994), vol II(2), at 38, 68. Offences related to drug trafficking had also been included by the ILC in the 1991 version of its Draft Code of Crimes against the Peace and Security of Mankind: see *Report of the International Law Commission* (43rd sess), UN Doc A/46/10 in *Yearbook of the International Law Commission* (1991), vol II(2), at 97 (Art 25). They were eventually deleted in the final draft.

[4] See M Cherif Bassiouni and Christopher L Blakesley, 'The Need for an International Criminal Court in the New International World Order' (1992) 25 *Vanderbilt Journal of Transnational Law* 151; William N Gianaris, 'The New World Order and the Need for an International Criminal Court' (1992)

Confronting the Shadow State: An International Law Perspective on State Organized Crime. Henri Decœur. © Henri Decœur 2018. Published 2018 by Oxford University Press.

Yet investigating cases of state organized crime and prosecuting perpetrators before an international criminal court or tribunal would come with difficulties perhaps even greater than those associated with prosecuting offenders domestically. This chapter first discusses practical and theoretical considerations in favour of prosecuting offenders before an international criminal court. It then outlines the respective pros and cons of different possible mechanisms, considering in turn the ICC, ad hoc tribunals, and the ACJHR.

A. Advantages of International Criminal Courts and Tribunals

In cases of state organized crime, proceedings before an international criminal court or tribunal could present certain advantages over those conducted by domestic criminal justice authorities. First, jurisdictional immunities are generally considered unavailable before existing international criminal courts and tribunals. Secondly, international criminal courts and tribunals may present better assurances that cases will be investigated genuinely. Thirdly, concurrent claims of jurisdiction are, at least as a matter of law, more easily resolved between an international criminal court or tribunal and domestic courts than between domestic courts *inter se*. Fourthly, international criminal courts and tribunals generally have adequate capacity to deal with cases of complex system criminality involving high-level state officials. Lastly, and perhaps most importantly, international criminal courts and tribunals fulfil a distinct expressive function.

1. Trumping jurisdictional immunities

Jurisdictional immunities, whether pursuant to domestic or international law, are generally considered inoperative before international criminal courts and tribunals. The constitutive instruments of the Nuremberg and Tokyo international military tribunals, of the ICTY and of the ICTR, and of the ICC provide that the

16 *Fordham International Law Journal* 88; Molly McConville, 'A Global War on Drugs: Why the United States Should Support the Prosecution of Drug Traffickers in the International Criminal Court' (2000) 37 *American Criminal Law Review* 75; Bryan F MacPherson, 'Building an International Criminal Court for the 21st Century' (1998) 13 *Connecticut Journal of International Law* 1; Yannick Radi, 'Du « dilemme du prisonnier » au « jeu d'intégration » : l'internationalisation de l'incrimination pénale de la corruption active transnationale' in Daniel Dormoy (ed), *La corruption et le droit international* (Bruylant, 2010) 169, at 205–11; Gerhard Kemp, 'The United Nations Convention against Transnational Organized Crime: A Milestone in International Criminal Law' (2001) 14 *African Journal of Criminal Justice* 152, at 167; Ndiva Kofele-Kale, *The International Law of Responsibility for Economic Crimes: Holding State Officials Individually Liable for Acts of Fraudulent Enrichment* (2nd edn, Routledge, 2016), at 392. One could also discern a similar motivation in the *Corpus Juris* project to establish a European Public Prosecutor vested with the authority to investigate and prosecute cases of EU budgetary fraud and corruption: see Mireille Delmas-Marty (ed), *Corpus Juris: Introducing Penal Provisions for the Purpose of the Financial Interests of the European Union* (Economica, 1997); John R Spencer, 'The *Corpus Juris* Project and the Fight against Budgetary Fraud' (1998) 1 *Cambridge Yearbook of European Legal Studies* 77.

official position of the accused shall not relieve him from criminal responsibility.[5] Jurisdictional immunities as such are further explicitly rejected as a procedural bar in the ICC Statute.[6] They were also considered inapplicable by the Appeals Chamber of the Special Court for Sierra Leone (SCSL).[7] State officials can (or 'could', for most of the ad hoc tribunals have closed) therefore be held criminally responsible before these courts regardless of their position in the hierarchy of the state and irrespective of whether they acted in their capacity as officials of the state. Some scholars accordingly defend the existence of a general principle of customary international law excluding jurisdictional immunities before any international criminal court or tribunal.[8] However, state practice and *opinio juris* does not support that view, as evidenced by the adoption, by the fifty-four member states of the Assembly of Heads of States and Government of the African Union (AU), of the amended Statute of the ACJHR, in which jurisdictional immunities *ratione personae* are recognized as a valid bar to the exercise of the Court's criminal jurisdiction.[9] Despite an established practice excluding jurisdictional immunities before international criminal courts and tribunals, as a matter of international law no general customary rule to that effect can be ascertained. Only state consent, as expressed for instance through ratification of a treaty, or a decision taken by the Security Council acting under Chapter VII of the UN Charter to derogate from customary international law, can have the effect of barring immunity for public officials before an international court.[10]

[5] Charter of the International Military Tribunal, Art 7, annexed to Agreement for the Prosecution and Punishment of the Major War Criminals of the European Axis, 8 August 1945, entered into force on 8 August 1945, 82 UNTS 279; Charter of the International Military Tribunal for the Far East, Art 6, annexed to Supreme Commander for the Allied Powers, 'Special Proclamation, Establishment of an International Military Tribunal for the Far East', 19 January 1946, TIAS 1589; ICTY Statute, Art 7(2); ICTR Statute, Art 6(2); ICC Statute, Art 27(2).

[6] ICC Statute, Art 27(2).

[7] *Prosecutor v Charles Ghankay Taylor*, Case no SCSL-03-01, Decision on Immunity from Jurisdiction, 31 May 2004.

[8] See e.g. Paola Gaeta, 'Official Capacities and Immunities' in Antonio Cassese, Paola Gaeta, and John R W D Jones (eds), *The Rome Statute of the International Criminal Court: A Commentary*, vol I (Oxford University Press, 2002) 975, at 991; Antonio Cassese, *International Criminal Law* (2nd edn, Oxford University Press, 2008), at 311–12; Arthur Watts, 'The Legal Position in International Law of Heads of States, Heads of Governments and Foreign Ministers' (1994) 247 *Recueil des cours de l'Académie de droit international* 9, at 84.

[9] See Section B.3(c) of this chapter. Commentators rightly observe that 'as a matter of customary international law, it is difficult to see how a rule of customary international law can form when the African Union, representing more than a quarter of states, rejects the said rule'. See Dire Tladi, 'Immunities (Article 46A*bis*)' in Gerhard Werle and Moritz Vormbaum (eds), *The African Criminal Court: A Commentary on the Malabo Protocol* (TMC Asser, 2016) 203, at 214.

[10] See Rosanne van Alebeek, *The Immunity of States and Their Officials in International Criminal Law and International Human Rights Law* (Oxford University Press, 2008), at 276–90; Dapo Akande, 'International Law Immunities and the International Criminal Court' (2004) 98 *American Journal of International Law* 407, at 415–19; Joanne Foakes, *The Position of Heads of State and Senior Officials in International Law* (Oxford University Press, 2014), at 204. Two authorities often cited as evidence of the existence of a general rule of customary international law excluding jurisdictional immunities before international criminal courts and tribunals, namely the Nuremberg Principles formulated by the ILC (*Principles of International Law Recognized in the Charter and Judgment of the Nürnberg Tribunal*, Principle III, affirmed in UN General Assembly Resolution 95 (I), 11 December 1946, UN Doc A/RES/95 (I)), and the ICJ's ruling in *Arrest Warrant of 11 April 2000 (Democratic Republic of the Congo v Belgium)*, Judgment, ICJ Rep 2002 3, at 25–26, para 61, do not support that view. The former were

In keeping with the practice followed by states for the establishment of most international criminal courts and tribunals, an international criminal court or tribunal established (or adapted) with a view to exercising jurisdiction over state organized crime could trump jurisdictional immunities, provided that a legal basis to that effect is included in its constitutive instrument. Similarly, the act of state doctrine, being a purely domestic legal principle, would be inapplicable.

2. Alleviating concurrence of jurisdiction

Because state organized crime usually affects more than one state, several states could claim jurisdiction over an alleged offender. When states with concurrent jurisdiction disagree as to where the alleged offender ought to be prosecuted, or, more plausibly, as to whether he should be prosecuted at all, international law provides no or little guidance to determine the appropriate forum. Prosecuting state organized crime before an international court would avoid the difficulties arising from a horizontal concurrence of jurisdiction between states by replacing it with a vertical concurrence, governed by rules that regulate the allocation of cases between domestic and international courts.[11] The diplomatic frictions generated by what Mégret calls states' 'strong sense of ownership' about crime[12] could be less pronounced if an international tribunal having 'the legitimacy and imprimatur of the international community' were to assert jurisdiction.[13] Prosecution before an international criminal court or tribunal might then appear as a legitimate compromise in politically sensitive cases such as those involving high-level state officials.[14]

3. Ensuring genuine investigation

Another reason to prosecute individuals involved in state organized crime before an international criminal court or tribunal is to allow the investigation to be conducted

not intended to reflect customary law, as 'the task of the Commission was not to express any appreciation of these principles as principles of international law but merely to formulate them' (*Report of the International Law Commission* (1st sess), UN Doc A/925 (A/4/10) in *Yearbook of the International Law Commission* (1949), at 282, para 26), and the latter does nothing more than taking note of the unavailability of immunities 'before certain international criminal courts', according to the provisions of the constitutive instruments of these courts.

[11] Neil Boister, 'The Exclusion of Treaty Crimes from the Jurisdiction of the Proposed International Criminal Court: Law, Pragmatism, Politics' (1998) 3 *Journal of Conflict & Security Law* 27, at 34. For an analysis of the principles of complementarity and primacy, see Sections B.1(b) and B.2(b) of this chapter.

[12] Frédéric Mégret, 'In Defense of Hybridity: Towards a Representational Theory of International Criminal Justice' (2005) 38 *Cornell International Law Journal* 725, at 739.

[13] Ibid, at 732. See also Boister (n 11), at 38 ('a neutral and representative ICC would not be as likely to exhibit bias, and sending an alleged offender to it would be less offensive to national pride'). That is not to say that prosecution before an international criminal court or tribunal does not generate tension: see Sections B.1(d) and B.2(d) of this chapter (recounting the difficulties faced by the ICC and ad hoc tribunals in prosecuting senior state officials).

[14] See Bassiouni and Blakesley (n 4), at 164–68, 172–73; Gianaris (n 4), at 109–10; and MacPherson (n 4), at 27.

in conditions that would be more likely to satisfy basic requirements of independence and impartiality than an investigation conducted by certain national authorities. The political dimension of cases involving serving senior officials of a state may undermine the ability or willingness of the prosecutorial and judicial organs of that state to investigate independently and impartially. Prosecutorial and judicial authorities may either refrain from taking any steps to investigate a case, or attempt to shield the individual concerned from foreign criminal proceedings by conducting a sham investigation or trial. For instance, the existence of an investigation may be used by a state as a pretext to postpone the execution of a request for mutual legal assistance on the ground that executing the request would interfere with an ongoing investigation, prosecution, or judicial proceeding.[15] In many states, pending prosecution also bars extradition to another state.[16] Once a verdict has been rendered, double jeopardy may forbid that the accused be tried again or extradited to another state.[17] In situations where the suspect is a serving senior official of the forum state, and in particular if he acted pursuant to state policy, doubts may legitimately be expressed as to the willingness of the state genuinely to conduct proceedings and to bring the offender to justice, even in states with a strong tradition of judicial independence. In states where the ruling elite exercises significant informal influence through patronage networks and has recourse to corruption, duress, or violence to maintain a position of dominance, domestic prosecutorial authorities and courts may prove powerless. Drumbl suggests that, in this context, '[i]nternational intervention can be salutary to the extent that it purges corrupt practices. [...] *In situ* legal institutions can be deeply susceptible to political interference and manipulation by State actors'.[18] By contrast, international criminal courts and tribunals, although not immune from political interference and manipulation, present comparatively acceptable guarantees that the case will be investigated and prosecuted genuinely.

4. Capacity to address system criminality

In dealing with complex cases of system criminality over the last three decades, international criminal courts and tribunals have developed an institutional memory[19]

[15] Recall Chapter 4, Section B.2(c).

[16] This ground for refusal is listed in the UN Model Treaty on Extradition, Art 4(c).

[17] For an analysis of the contours of the principle *ne bis in idem* in different legal systems and in the international legal context, see Gerard Conway, '*Ne Bis in Idem* in International Law' (2003) 3 *International Criminal Law Review* 217. Within the EU, a European arrest warrant may not be executed 'if the executing judicial authority is informed that the requested person has been finally judged by a Member State in respect of the same acts': see Framework Decision on the European arrest warrant, Art 3(2). See also Art 9(2) of the European Convention on Extradition, as amended by Additional Protocol to the European Convention on Extradition, 15 October 1975, entered into force on 20 August 1979, ETS no 86. In France, foreign judicial decisions in criminal matters are considered *res judicata*, but only if concerning an offence committed in its entirety outside French territory: see Cass crim, 3 December 1998, App no 97-82.424, *Bull crim* (1998), no 331, p 962.

[18] Mark A Drumbl, *Atrocity, Punishment, and International Law* (Cambridge University Press, 2007), at 125.

[19] International criminal law as a discipline is said to have given birth to 'a professional class of legal entrepreneurs' and 'experts in horror' with 'a capacity simultaneously to respond and shape demand' for

which could usefully be harnessed to address state organized crime. The prosecution of senior officials involved in organized crime would require the know-how and expertise necessary to collect and analyse a massive volume of evidence from several states, to reconstruct intricate power structures involving informal networks, to define a prosecutorial strategy, and to conduct lengthy proceedings. Moreover, experience in substantive international criminal law as applied before international criminal courts and tribunals could be useful. Since the Nuremberg trials, international criminal courts and tribunals have developed a body of law specifically designed to address the complex mechanics of system criminality. Modes of liability such as joint criminal enterprise and superior responsibility are particularly well-suited to ascribe criminal responsibility in cases involving senior state officials, where the link between the offender and the physical perpetration of the crime is difficult to establish.[20] Furthermore, although the material and human resources of international criminal courts and tribunals are not always optimal, these institutions are comparatively better equipped to embark on long and complex proceedings than some of their domestic counterparts, especially in developing countries.

Yet expertise in financial crimes, which would be valuable in cases of state organized crime and which does exist at the domestic level in a number of states, remains underdeveloped and underexploited in international criminal courts and tribunals.

5. Expressive function

Normative considerations would also come into play when prosecuting state organized crime before an international criminal court or tribunal. International criminal courts and tribunals fulfil an expressive and symbolic function by signalling the common concern of a potentially large group of states for certain crimes and stressing the importance of the interests such courts and tribunals are designed to protect.[21] As such, they 'may be viewed as a rhetorical device'.[22] Their judgments fulfil a 'didactic function' aiming at 'strengthening a sense of accountability for international crime by exposure and stigmatization',[23] which in turn contributes to a 'norm-nurturing process' said to enhance the legitimacy of substantive international criminal law norms.[24] International criminal courts and tribunals have the potential

technical expertise. See Frédéric Mégret, 'Three Dangers of the International Criminal Court: A Critical Look at a Consensual Project' (2001) 12 *Finnish Yearbook of International Law* 193, at 242–43.

[20] See generally Héctor Olásolo, *The Criminal Responsibility of Senior Political and Military Leaders as Principals to International Crimes* (Hart Publishing, 2009).

[21] See Bassiouni and Blakesley (n 4), at 174.

[22] Leslie P Francis and John G Francis, 'International Criminal Court, the Rule of Law, and Prevention of Harm: Bringing Justice in Times of Injustice' in Larry May and Zachary Hoskins (eds), *International Criminal Law and Philosophy* (Cambridge University Press, 2010) 58, at 71. See also Mégret (n 12), at 743 ('the medium is the message').

[23] Mirjan Damaška, 'What Is the Point of International Criminal Justice?' (2008) 83 *Chicago-Kent Law Review* 329, at 345 ff.

[24] Diane-Marie Amman, 'Group Mentality, Expressivism, and Genocide' (2002) 2 *International Criminal Law Review* 93, at 95, 143. The expression is taken from Paul H Robinson, 'Why Does the Criminal Law Care What the Layperson Thinks Is Just? Coercive Versus Normative Crime Control' (2000) 86 *Virginia Law Review* 1839.

to induce behavioural change, not because of any deterrent effect they may have, but because of this expressive process. As Damaška points out,

> [b]y making criminal prohibitions operational, international criminal courts contribute to the emergence of a moral climate in which even big and powerful actors in the international arena find it increasingly difficult to ignore their verbal commitments. The evident discrepancy between word and deed may affect their reputation, or damage some of their perceived self-interests.[25]

This process operates slowly and may be unevenly and moderately effective. Yet the expressive impact of international criminal courts and tribunals should not be underestimated, and arguably stands at the core of the international criminal justice project. The expressive value of prosecuting offenders before an international criminal court or tribunal can outweigh the legal, practical, and political difficulties that come with the exercise of supranational criminal jurisdiction.[26]

Prosecuting senior state officials involved in organized crime before an international criminal court or tribunal would give teeth to a formal condemnation of state organized crime, signal offenders that using state resources to further a criminal agenda is considered of a particular gravity and entails consequences, and progressively shape a normative climate conducive to enhanced compliance with international norms.

B. Overview of Possible Mechanisms

International criminal justice mechanisms are based on different institutional models. The jurisdiction of international criminal courts and tribunals varies significantly in terms of its source (treaty-based or established by virtue of a Security Council decision), its scope (material, temporal, and territorial), and its relation vis-à-vis domestic jurisdictions (primacy or complementarity). These differences have a marked influence on how international criminal courts and tribunals operate and on their ability to exercise their jurisdiction in a particular case. The potential relevance of these factors for the prosecution of senior officials involved in state organized crime is examined, in turn, in the context of the ICC, of ad hoc tribunals, and of the ACJHR.

1. The International Criminal Court

The ICC is a treaty-based, permanent criminal court.[27] Whether the ICC may provide a suitable forum for the prosecution of senior public officials involved in state organized crime depends notably on the scope of its jurisdiction, on the conditions

[25] Damaška (n 23), at 364.

[26] Cf Boister (n 11), at 37 (discussing the symbolic value of using the ICC to prosecute treaty crimes such as drug trafficking).

[27] ICC Statute, Art 1.

under which the latter may be exercised, and on the Court's ability to secure the co-operation of states.

(a) *Jurisdiction* ratione materiae

The ICC has jurisdiction over the four 'core' international crimes, namely the crime of genocide, crimes against humanity, war crimes, and the crime of aggression.[28] During the drafting of the Rome Statute, several proposals were unsuccessfully submitted with a view to including drug trafficking within the jurisdiction of the ICC.[29] Being unable to reach an agreement, the Diplomatic Conference, upon adoption of the Rome Statute, 'recommend[ed] that a Review Conference [...] consider [...] drug crimes with a view to arriving at an acceptable definition and their inclusion in the list of crimes within the jurisdiction of the Court'.[30] At present, the Court does not have jurisdiction over drug offences or other organized crime offences most commonly encountered in cases of state organized crime, and in the current state of affairs it is unlikely that the Court will be granted jurisdiction over such crimes in the near future.

(b) *Conditions for the exercise of jurisdiction*

The ICC's jurisdiction is in principle limited to crimes committed in the territory or by nationals of a state party, or of any other state which accepts the exercise of the Court's jurisdiction with respect to particular crimes.[31] The Court may, however, exercise its jurisdiction over crimes committed in the territory of states not parties to the Rome Statute that have not consented to the exercise of the Court's jurisdiction, if the UN Security Council decides to refer a situation to the Court under Chapter VII of the Charter.[32]

Moreover, the ICC is complementary to national jurisdictions,[33] which means that it will exercise its jurisdiction only in the absence of a genuine investigation

[28] Ibid, Art 5.

[29] See Preparatory Committee on the Establishment of an International Criminal Court, *Proposal submitted by Costa Rica, Guyana, Jamaica and Trinidad and Tobago (Crimes involving the illicit traffic in narcotic drugs and psychotropic substances)*, 31 March 1998, UN Doc A/AC-249/1998/DP-10; United Nations Diplomatic Conference of Plenipotentiaries on the Establishment of an International Criminal Court, *Barbados, Dominica, Jamaica and Trinidad and Tobago: Proposal regarding article 5*, 3 July 1998, UN Doc A/CONF.183/C.1/L.48.

[30] *Final Act of the United Nations Diplomatic Conference of Plenipotentiaries on the Establishment of an International Criminal Court*, 17 July 1998, UN Doc A/CONF.183/10, Resolution E.

[31] ICC Statute, Art 12. [32] Ibid, Art 13(b).

[33] Ibid, preamble, 10th recital, and Art 1. On the principle of complementarity, see generally Carsten Stahn and Mohamed M El Zeidy (eds), *The International Criminal Court and Complementarity: From Theory to Practice* (Cambridge University Press, 2011); Jann K Kleffner, *Complementarity in the Rome Statute and National Criminal Jurisdictions* (Oxford University Press, 2008); Daniel Nsereko, 'The ICC and Complementarity in Practice' (2013) 26 *Leiden Journal of International Law* 427. See also Sarah M H Nouwen, *Complementarity in the Line of Fire: The Catalysing Effect of the International Criminal Court in Uganda and Sudan* (Cambridge University Press, 2013).

or prosecution by national authorities. While the Rome Statute acknowledges the primary right of states to investigate and prosecute,[34] a case under investigation or prosecution by domestic authorities will not necessarily be inadmissible before the ICC. Article 17 of the Statute, which governs the admissibility of cases before the Court,[35] reads, in relevant part, as follows:

1. Having regard to paragraph 10 of the Preamble and article 1, the Court shall determine that a case is inadmissible where:
   (a) The case is being investigated or prosecuted by a State which has jurisdiction over it, unless the State is unwilling or unable genuinely to carry out the investigation or prosecution;
   (b) The case has been investigated by a State which has jurisdiction over it and the State has decided not to prosecute the person concerned, unless the decision resulted from the unwillingness or inability of the State genuinely to prosecute;
   (c) The person concerned has already been tried for conduct which is the subject of the complaint, and a trial by the Court is not permitted under article 20, paragraph 3;

[...]

2. In order to determine unwillingness in a particular case, the Court shall consider, having regard to the principles of due process recognized by international law, whether one or more of the following exist, as applicable:
   (a) The proceedings were or are being undertaken or the national decision was made for the purpose of shielding the person concerned from criminal responsibility for crimes within the jurisdiction of the Court referred to in article 5;
   (b) There has been an unjustified delay in the proceedings which in the circumstances is inconsistent with an intent to bring the person concerned to justice;
   (c) The proceedings were not or are not being conducted independently or impartially, and they were or are being conducted in a manner which, in the circumstances, is inconsistent with an intent to bring the person concerned to justice.

In considering whether a case is admissible under Article 17 of the Statute, the Court first considers whether there are ongoing investigations or prosecutions or whether there have been investigations in a state concerning that case, before turning to the question of unwillingness and inability.[36] The Court has adopted a narrow understanding of the concept of 'case', ruling that domestic investigations 'must cover the same individual and substantially the same conduct as alleged in proceedings before

[34] Contrary to a common assumption (see e.g. Kleffner (n 33), at 235–308), the Rome Statute does not impose an obligation on states parties to investigate and prosecute crimes falling under the jurisdiction of the Court.

[35] For a discussion of the admissibility criteria as elaborated by the jurisprudence of the ICC, see Ben Batros, 'The Evolution of the ICC Jurisprudence on Admissibility' in Stahn and El Zeidy (n 33), vol I, 558; Nouwen (n 33), at 43–70.

[36] *Prosecutor v Germain Katanga and Mathieu Ngudjolo Chui*, Case no ICC-01/04-01/07, Judgment on the Appeal of Mr Germain Katanga against the Oral Decision of Trial Chamber II of 12 June 2009 on the Admissibility of the Case, 25 September 2009, para 78; *Prosecutor v Saif Al-Islam Gaddafi and Abdullah Al-Senussi*, Case no ICC-01/11-01/11, Judgment on the appeal of Libya against the decision of Pre-Trial Chamber I of 31 May 2013 entitled 'Decision on the admissibility of the case against Saif Al-Islam Gaddafi', 21 May 2014, para 213.

the Court'.[37] The concept of 'unwillingness' as defined by the jurisprudence of the Court 'concerns proceedings that are not genuine in that they are akin to sham or other proceedings that unjustly benefit the accused'[38] and 'would lead to a suspect evading justice'.[39]

The possibility of declaring admissible before the ICC a case already tried before a domestic court logically requires arrangements to the protection against double jeopardy. By derogation from the principle *ne bis in idem*, a person already tried before a domestic court for a crime under the jurisdiction of the ICC may be tried again before the latter if the domestic proceedings

(a) Were for the purpose of shielding the person concerned from criminal responsibility for crimes within the jurisdiction of the Court; or
(b) Otherwise were not conducted independently or impartially in accordance with the norms of due process recognized by international law and were conducted in a manner which, in the circumstances, was inconsistent with an intent to bring the person concerned to justice.[40]

As a matter of law, attempts on the part of a state to abuse its criminal justice system to shield an alleged offender from criminal responsibility before the ICC are therefore unlikely to succeed.

(c) Cooperation of states

States having accepted the ICC's jurisdiction are required to cooperate fully with the Court at all stages of the proceedings, and must comply with the Court's orders.[41] If a case is declared admissible, the ICC takes precedence over any concurrent request for surrender of the accused.[42] Yet states that are not parties to the Rome Statute are in principle under no obligation to cooperate with the Court.[43] In case of a referral of a situation to the Court by the UN Security Council, the Court may still request the Council's support to ensure a state's compliance with requests for cooperation.[44]

The cooperation of states parties is necessary notably for the freezing and confiscation of assets. The Court is empowered to request states parties to take 'protective measures' in view of the confiscation of assets at the pre-trial stage,[45] and may order the

[37] *Prosecutor v William Samoei Ruto and others*, Case no ICC-01/09-01/11, Judgment on the appeal of the Republic of Kenya against the decision of Pre-Trial Chamber II of 30 May 2011 entitled 'Decision on the Application by the Government of Kenya Challenging the Admissibility of the Case Pursuant to Article 19(2)(b) of the Statute', 30 August 2011, para 40. For an analysis of the ICC's case law on this point and an argument for departing from the 'same-conduct' test, see Nouwen (n 33), at 45–59.

[38] *Prosecutor v Saif Al-Islam Gaddafi and Abdullah Al-Senussi*, Case no ICC-01/11-01/11, Decision on the appeal of Mr Abdullah Al-Senussi against the decision of Pre-Trial Chamber I of 11 October 2013 entitled 'Decision on the admissibility of the case against Abdullah Al-Senussi', 24 July 2014, para 222.

[39] Ibid, para 218.

[40] ICC Statute, Art 20(3).

[41] Ibid, Arts 12 and 86 ff.

[42] Ibid, Art 90.

[43] Pursuant to Art 34 VCLT, '[a] treaty does not create either obligations or rights for a third State without its consent'. See generally Robert Cryer, 'The ICC and Its Relationship to Non-States Parties' in Carsten Stahn (ed), *The Law and Practice of the International Criminal Court* (Oxford University Press, 2015) 260.

[44] ICC Statute, Art 87(5)(b) and (7).

[45] Ibid, Art 57(3)(e).

forfeiture of proceeds of crime (but not instrumentalities) at sentencing.[46] States parties are accordingly required to comply with the Court's requests concerning '[t]he identification, tracing and freezing or seizure of proceeds, property and assets and instrumentalities of crimes for the purpose of eventual forfeiture'.[47] It is also incumbent on states parties to enforce the Court's orders for forfeiture in accordance with their domestic law.[48] The Court cannot order confiscation in value, but where their domestic law so permits, states 'unable to give effect to an order for forfeiture' may seize untainted property.[49] The tools available to the ICC for the confiscation of assets are considered to be limited and inadequate for tackling the financial dimension of international crimes.[50]

(d) Potential for prosecuting state organized crime

The main advantage of the ICC arguably resides in its formal legitimacy. The ICC is based on a widely ratified multilateral treaty, and its jurisdiction applies in principle only to states parties or states that have otherwise consented to the exercise of the Court's jurisdiction. Moreover, the ICC, being complementary to national criminal jurisdictions, will exercise its jurisdiction only in the absence of a genuine investigation or prosecution by national authorities. If states are ever to consent to the exercise of some form of supranational jurisdiction over cases of state organized crime, they would probably prefer a system with significant deference for state sovereignty resembling that of the ICC.

The ICC does not have jurisdiction over state organized crime or over the predicate offences most commonly encountered in cases of state organized crime, such as drug trafficking, corruption, or money laundering. The choice made by states to address such crimes through crime-suppression conventions relying on domestic law enforcement, and their decision not to include these crimes within the jurisdiction of the Court, show that states were not willing 'to commit themselves at the stage when the treaties were adopted to a more effective criminalization of conduct at the international level'.[51] Whether states may now be ready to make an even bolder move by granting the ICC jurisdiction over state organized crime is highly uncertain. The Court does, however, have jurisdiction over genocide, crimes against humanity, war crimes, and the crime of aggression—crimes which may amount to state organized crime where committed for profit purposes.[52] Situations involving state organized crime may therefore fall within the purview of the Court, and some such situations have recently become a matter of concern for the Office of the

[46] Ibid, Art 77(2)(b). [47] Ibid, Art 93(1)(k). [48] Ibid, Art 109(1).

[49] Ibid, Art 109(2).

[50] For an analysis of the legal framework concerning asset forfeiture at the ICC and its limits, see generally Manuel Galvis Martínez, 'Forfeiture of Assets at the International Criminal Court: The Short Arm of International Criminal Justice' (2014) 12 *Journal of International Criminal Justice* 193, at 204–16.

[51] Boister (n 11), at 34. See *Report of the International Law Commission* (47th sess), UN Doc A/50/10 in *Yearbook of the International Law Commission* (1995), vol II(2), at 29, para 113 (noting the view expressed by a number of states that 'the existing legal framework and international cooperation arrangements provided the necessary means and machinery for the suppression of illicit drug trafficking since most cases could be effectively prosecuted in the national courts', and that 'increased international cooperation in law enforcement would be a more effective way to deal with the problem').

[52] Recall Chapter 1, Section B.3.

Prosecutor of the ICC. When deciding whether to initiate an investigation or prosecution, the Office of the Prosecutor considers a range of factors, including the impact of the crimes.[53] In a 2016 policy paper on case selection, the Office of the Prosecutor laid out an innovative prosecutorial strategy:

> The impact of the crimes may be assessed in light of, *inter alia*, [...] the social, economic and environmental damage inflicted on the affected communities. In this context, the Office will give particular consideration to prosecuting Rome Statute crimes that are committed by means of, or that result in, *inter alia*, the destruction of the environment, the illegal exploitation of natural resources or the illegal dispossession of land.[54]

Placing emphasis on the relation between 'core' international crimes and the illegal exploitation of natural resources or the illegal dispossession of land represents a major step towards recognizing the existence of the economic and financial motives underlying crimes committed during armed conflict and other widespread human rights violations. Although perpetrators prosecuted pursuant to this case selection policy could only be charged for crimes falling within the Court's jurisdiction, the particular nature of the circumstances of such cases could induce an expansion of focus at trial, shedding light on the mechanics and impact of state organized crime. To that end, the prosecution could take advantage of certain crimes defined in the Court's Statute, whose constitutive elements reflect in part the elements of state organized crime. Such crimes include the war crimes of pillaging and unlawful appropriation or seizure of property,[55] which entail an element of personal enrichment,[56] and enslavement as a crime against humanity, which 'includes [conduct] in the course of trafficking in persons'.[57]

Be that as it may, several provisions of the Rome Statute would be likely to prove problematic in cases of state organized crime. First, even though jurisdictional immunities cannot be invoked before the Court by a defendant,[58] they still pose an obstacle to the arrest and surrender by a state party of a public official of another state. Article 98(1) of the Statute provides that 'the Court may not proceed with a request for surrender or assistance which would require the requested State to act inconsistently with its obligations under international law with respect to the State or diplomatic immunity of a person or property of a third State'. This provision was

[53] Regulations of the Office of the Prosecutor, 23 April 2009, Doc no ICC-BD/05-01-09, Regulation 29(2).

[54] *Policy Paper on Case Selection and Prioritisation*, 15 September 2016, para 41.

[55] For an argument that the illicit exploitation of natural resources may be prosecuted as a war crime under the Rome Statute, see Michael A Lundberg, 'The Plunder of Natural Resources during War: A War Crime?' (2008) 39 *Georgetown Journal of International Law* 495.

[56] Art 8(2)(b)(xvi) and (e)(v) of the Rome Statute prohibits 'pillaging a town or place', which notably requires appropriation of property by the perpetrator 'for private or personal use' (Elements of Crimes, in *Official Records of the Assembly of States Parties to the Rome Statute of the International Criminal Court*, 1st sess (New York, 3–10 September 2002), Doc no ICC-ASP/1/3, at 108 ff.). Art 8(2)(a)(iv), (b)(xiii), and (e)(xii) of the Statute further prohibits 'extensive [...] appropriation of property, not justified by military necessity and carried out unlawfully and wantonly' as well as 'seizing the enemy's property unless such [...] seizure be imperatively demanded by the necessities of the conflict'.

[57] ICC Statute, Art 7(1)(c) and (2)(c).

[58] Ibid, Art 27(2).

relied on by a number of African states to justify their decision not to arrest Sudanese President Omar Al-Bashir when he was present in their territory, in spite of the Court's questionable case-law on point holding jurisdictional immunities to be inapplicable in connection to proceedings before the Court, including in the relations of states parties *inter se* or in the relations between a state party and a state that is the object of a referral by the UN Security Council.[59] Moreover, pursuant to Article 72 any state can oppose the disclosure at any stage of the proceedings of information or documents if it reckons that such disclosure would 'prejudice its national security interests'—a provision that is likely to be relevant in matters involving a state's intelligence services. Lastly, pursuant to Article 16 the UN Security Council remains empowered to defer proceedings, which in effect allows a handful of powerful states to hinder investigations indefinitely if their interests appear to be compromised.[60]

Experience has shown that in cases involving serving senior state officials, the Court has faced tremendous difficulties in obtaining the cooperation of states, whether parties or not. It has been unable to secure the arrest and transfer of Sudanese President Omar al-Bashir, despite the Security Council's injunction requiring states to cooperate with the Court.[61] Charges against Kenyan Deputy President William Ruto were vacated after the Prosecution's case collapsed owing to witness interference and political intimidation.[62] Far from alleviating tensions, the ICC has been facing the frontal opposition of the AU, which denounced 'the politicization and misuse of indictments against African leaders by [the] ICC' and required AU member states not to cooperate with the Court.[63] Tensions culminated with the decision of several

[59] See *Prosecutor v Omar Hassan Ahmad Al Bashir*, Case no ICC-02/05-01/09, Decision pursuant to Article 87(7) of the Rome Statute on the Failure by the Republic of Malawi to Comply with the Cooperation Requests Issued by the Court with Respect to the Arrest and Surrender of Omar Hassan Ahmad Al Bashir, 12 December 2011; Decision Pursuant to Article 87(7) of the Rome Statute on the refusal of the Republic of Chad to comply with the cooperation requests issued by the Court with respect to the arrest and surrender of Omar Hassan Ahmad Al Bashir, 13 December 2011; Decision on the Cooperation of the Democratic Republic of the Congo Regarding Omar Al Bashir's Arrest and Surrender to the Court, 9 April 2014; and Decision under Article 87(7) of the Rome Statute on the non-compliance by South Africa with the request by the Court for the arrest and surrender of Omar Al-Bashir, 6 July 2017.

[60] The Security Council has made use of its powers under Chapter VII to prevent the ICC from investigating crimes committed by nationals of states not parties to the Rome Statute in the framework of peace-keeping operations. See e.g. Resolution 1970 (2011), para 6; Resolution 1487 (2003), 12 June 2003, UN Doc S/RES/1487 (2003); Resolution 1422 (2002), 12 July 2002, UN Doc S/RES/1422 (2002).

[61] See Resolution 1593 (2005), 31 March 2005, UN Doc S/RES/1593 (2005), para 2. It should be noted that no further measures were taken by the Council to sanction states that have failed to comply with their obligation to cooperate with the ICC.

[62] *Prosecutor v William Samoei Ruto and Joshua Arap Sang*, Case no ICC-01/09-01/11, Decision on Defence Applications for Judgments of Acquittal, 5 April 2016.

[63] See in particular Assembly Decision 1 (Oct. 2013), 'Decision on Africa's Relationship with the International Criminal Court', 12 October 2013 ('no charges shall be commenced or continued before any International Court or Tribunal against any serving AU Head of State or Government or anybody acting or entitled to act in such capacity during their term of office'); Decision 245 (XIII), 'Decision on the Report of the Commission on the Meeting of African States Parties to the Rome Statute of the International Criminal Court', 3 July 2009 ('AU Member States shall not cooperate pursuant to the provisions of Article 98 of the Rome Statute of the ICC relating to immunities, for the arrest and surrender of President Omar El Bashir').

African states to withdraw from the Rome Statute[64] and the adoption by the AU of a collective withdrawal strategy.[65]

Because the ICC is not vested with the authority and power to ensure the co-operation of states, it remains entirely reliant on goodwill. As Cryer put it, when the suspected offender is a sitting senior state official of the *locus delicti*, to be effective the ICC needs to 'persuade the perpetrators to help'.[66] To that extent, in cases of state organized crime the enforcement mechanisms of the Rome Statute would not necessarily be more adequate than the traditional extradition-based system of interstate cooperation in criminal matters.[67] Moreover, the expectation that the Court's legitimacy might compensate for its weak enforcement capability seems to have been frustrated by recent developments. In short, at present the ICC does not offer promising prospects for the prosecution of senior officials involved in state organized crime.

2. Ad hoc tribunals

Ad hoc tribunals are set up to investigate and prosecute particular crimes committed in a specific situation. International ad hoc tribunals were established by a resolution of the UN Security Council acting under Chapter VII of the Charter,[68] or by a treaty concluded between a state and the UN.[69] Their jurisdiction, both *ratione loci* and *ratione temporis*, is by definition circumscribed to a particular set of events.[70] The

[64] South Africa and Burundi deposited their instruments of withdrawal from the Rome Statute respectively on 19 and 27 October 2016, and Gambia notified its decision to withdraw on 8 November 2016. South Africa and Gambia eventually reversed their decision to withdraw.

[65] See Assembly Decision 622 (XXVIII), 'Decision on the International Criminal Court', 31 January 2017, para 8.

[66] Robert Cryer, 'Prosecuting the Leaders: Promises, Politics and Pragmatics' (2009) 1 *Göttingen Journal of International Law* 45, at 62–63.

[67] Cf Boister (n 11), at 34, 36 (discussing the advantages and problems of including treaty crimes such as drug trafficking within the ICC's jurisdiction, and arguing that '[e]xtradition to the ICC would face the same legal problems as extradition between states').

[68] See Resolution 808 (1993), 22 February 1993, UN Doc S/RES/808 (1993) and Resolution 827 (1993), 25 May 1993, UN Doc S/RES/827 (1993) (establishing the ICTY); Resolution 955 (1994) (establishing the ICTR); Resolution 1757 (2007), 30 May 2007, UN Doc S/RES/1757 (2007) (establishing the Special Tribunal for Lebanon (STL)). Although the STL was originally designed to be a hybrid tribunal established by an agreement with Lebanon, it was the Security Council that triggered the entry into force of the provisions of the agreement. The STL Trial Chamber accordingly found that 'the Tribunal exists solely as a result of the passing of Security Council Resolution 1757': see *Prosecutor v Salim Jamil Ayyash and others*, Case no STL-11-01, Decision on the Defence Challenges to the Jurisdiction and Legality of the Tribunal, 27 July 2012, paras 46–50.

[69] See Agreement between the United Nations and the Government of Sierra Leone on the establishment of the Special Court for Sierra Leone; Agreement between the United Nations and the Royal Government of Cambodia concerning the prosecution under Cambodian law of crimes committed during the period of Democratic Kampuchea, 6 June 2003, entered into force on 29 April 2005, 2329 UNTS 117. However, unlike the SCSL the ECCC is, in formal terms, a domestic tribunal.

[70] ICTY Statute, Art 8; ICTR Statute, Art 7; STL Statute, Art 1; SCSL Statute, Art 1(1). See also Law on the Establishment of the Extraordinary Chambers in the Courts of Cambodia for the Prosecution of Crimes Committed during the Period of Democratic Kampuchea, Art 2.

following analysis considers the potential value of establishing a tribunal with jurisdiction over a particular situation of state organized crime.

(a) *Jurisdiction* ratione materiae

To date, no international ad hoc tribunal has ever been granted jurisdiction over the offences typically encountered in cases of state organized crime. Lack of precedent on the international plane, however, does not in itself speak against establishing an ad hoc tribunal with jurisdiction over state organized crime. An international tribunal can be set up with subject-matter jurisdiction over any offence that states or the international organization responsible for its creation decide to include in its constituent instrument.[71] For instance, the Kosovo Specialist Chambers is vested with subject-matter jurisdiction over crimes identified in a 2011 Council of Europe report on inhuman treatment of people and illicit trafficking in human organs.[72] The Specialist Chambers may apply not only customary international criminal law, but also Kosovar domestic criminal law in force at the time of the conflict,[73] which criminalized, inter alia, participation in an organized criminal group.[74] While this latter example concerns a 'hybrid' ad hoc tribunal established within the domestic legal order of a state and not an international tribunal, it bears witness to the fact that no legal limitations exist as to the potential scope of an ad hoc tribunal's subject-matter jurisdiction and that ad hoc tribunals are considered suitable for the purpose of prosecuting crimes related to organized crime. It is therefore conceivable that an ad hoc tribunal, whether international or 'hybrid', could be established to exercise jurisdiction over a particular case of state organized crime.

(b) *Primacy over domestic courts*

Contrary to the ICC, the international ad hoc tribunals were granted full primacy over national criminal courts.[75] This means that domestic judicial authorities have the obligation to halt ongoing proceedings and immediately transfer the accused and forward all evidence materials, court records, and other relevant information to the international tribunal when requested to do so. In the case of tribunals established by the UN Security Council, a failure of domestic authorities to comply with a request for deferral may be sanctioned by the Security Council.[76] The ICTY

[71] See Roger O'Keefe, *International Criminal Law* (Oxford University Press, 2015), at 60.

[72] Law on Specialist Chambers and Specialist Prosecutor's Office, 3 August 2015, Law no 05/L-053, Arts 1(2) and 6(1). See Council of Europe, Committee on Legal Affairs and Human Rights, *Inhuman Treatment of People and Illicit Trafficking in Human Organs in Kosovo*, 7 January 2011.

[73] Law on Specialist Chambers and Specialist Prosecutor's Office, Arts 12 and 15.

[74] Decree on Proclamation of the Criminal Law of the Socialist Autonomous Province of Kosovo, 28 June 1977, PS no 011-25/77, Art 197 ('syndicated crime') and Art 200 ('participation in a group that commits a criminal act').

[75] ICTY Statute, Art 9(2); ICTR Statute, Art 8(2); STL Statute, Art 4(1). The SCSL had primary jurisdiction with respect to the domestic courts of Sierra Leone only: SCSL Statute, Art 8(2).

[76] ICTY Rules of Procedure and Evidence, as amended on 22 May 2013, Doc no IT/32/Rev. 49, Rule 11; ICTR Rules of Procedure and Evidence, as amended on 2 February 2009, Rule 11; STL Rules

had the authority to request deferral of a particular case or even retry a defendant if the facts under consideration had been characterized by domestic courts as ordinary crimes.[77] Deferral may also be requested or a retrial ordered if 'there is a lack of impartiality or independence, or the investigations or proceedings are designed to shield the accused from international criminal responsibility, or the case is not diligently prosecuted'.[78] Similarly, the SCSL could, with the authorization of the Security Council, exercise jurisdiction over crimes committed by members of peacekeeping forces present in Sierra Leone '[i]n the event the sending State is unwilling or unable genuinely to carry out an investigation or prosecution'.[79] Like the principle of complementarity, primacy is designed to prevent 'stratagems [that] might be used to defeat the very purpose of the creation of an international criminal jurisdiction'.[80] Last but not least, the principle of primacy enables international ad hoc tribunals to refer a case to domestic courts with jurisdiction over the crimes considered.[81] Primacy is sufficiently flexible to accommodate domestic jurisdictional claims if the circumstances in a particular case so dictate.

(c) Cooperation of states

The mode of creation of ad hoc tribunals has bearing on the legal regime governing the cooperation of states. In the case of a tribunal established by the UN Security Council, every state is obliged to cooperate at all stages of proceedings and to comply without delay with a request for assistance, for example concerning the surrender of wanted persons.[82] Because this obligation derives from an instrument annexed to a Security Council resolution adopted under Chapter VII of the UN Charter, it supersedes any other concurrent treaty obligation,[83] including obligations deriving from extradition treaties. Moreover, a state is not entitled to rely on national security concerns to withhold documentary evidence requested by ad hoc tribunals.[84]

of Procedure and Evidence, as amended on 9 April 2013, Doc no STL/BD/2009/01/Rev.6/Corr.1, Rule 20(C).

[77] ICTY Rules of Procedure and Evidence, Rule 9(i); ICTY Statute, Art 10(2)(a). The Tribunal warned against the 'perennial danger of international crimes being characterized as "ordinary crimes" ': see *Prosecutor v Duško Tadić*, Case no IT-94-1, Decision on the Defence Motion for Interlocutory Appeal on Jurisdiction, 2 October 1995, para 58.

[78] ICTY Rules of Procedure and Evidence, Rule 9(ii); ICTY Statute, Art 10(2)(b).

[79] SCSL Statute, Art 1(3).

[80] *Tadić* Decision on Jurisdiction (n 77), para 58.

[81] ICTY Rules of Procedure and Evidence, Rule 11*bis*; ICTR Rules of Procedure and Evidence, Rule 11*bis*; SCSL Rules of Procedure and Evidence, Rule 11*bis*.

[82] ICTY Statute, Art 29; ICTR Statute, Art 28. See also *Prosecutor v Tihomir Blaškić*, Case no IT-95-14, Judgment on the Request of the Republic of Croatia for Review of the Decision of Trial Chamber II of 18 July 1997, 29 October 1997 (ruling that the tribunal has the authority to issue compulsory subpoenas to a state).

[83] UN Charter, Arts 25 and 103.

[84] *Blaškić*, Judgment on the Request of the Republic of Croatia (n 82), paras 62–64.

(d) Potential for prosecuting state organized crime

The principal challenge to the establishment of an ad hoc tribunal with jurisdiction over state organized crime lies in the principle of non-retroactivity of the criminal law (*nullum crimen sine lege praevia*) enshrined in international human rights law.[85] When a tribunal is created to investigate and prosecute past events, its jurisdiction must be confined to crimes already established under the domestic law of the states concerned or under customary international law at the time of these events.[86] To conform with the principle of legality, the creation of an international criminal tribunal with jurisdiction over a particular situation of state organized crime would therefore require that the acts and omissions constitutive of state organized crime be already criminalized in the domestic law of the state of the *locus delicti* at the relevant period, for example further to the ratification by that state of the treaty proposed in Chapter 6.

Further difficulties may arise because of the geographical and temporal limitation of the jurisdiction of ad hoc tribunals. While limiting the tribunals' jurisdiction *ratione loci* and *ratione temporis* may seem adequate to address crimes such as genocide, crimes against humanity, and war crimes, which generally occur in a defined geographical and political context, it might prove unsuitable to address state organized crime, which often entails intricate transnational ramifications. Cases involving multiple actors situated in different jurisdictions and cross-border transactions would be likely to give rise to complex jurisdictional challenges which ad hoc tribunals may not be equipped to face. Even in the case of genocide, crimes against humanity, and war crimes, experience has shown that attempts to sever particular events from their broader geographical, temporal, and political context are prejudicial to the search for the truth. While the SCSL did prosecute former Liberian President Charles Taylor for his involvement in the conflict in Sierra Leone, other tribunals have been criticized for interpreting their jurisdiction too narrowly. Difficulties of this kind have arisen before the ICTR, where the defence unsuccessfully sought to introduce into evidence information concerning the involvement of foreign actors in crimes falling within the jurisdiction of the tribunals.[87] In view of the potential transnational ramifications of cases of state organized crime, states may

[85] ICCPR, Art 15(1); Convention for the Protection of Human Rights and Fundamental Freedoms, Art 7(1).

[86] See *Report of the Secretary-General pursuant to paragraph 2 of resolution 808 (1993)*, 3 May 1993, UN Doc S/25704 and Add.l, para 34 (stating that 'the application of the principle nullum crimen sine lege requires that the international tribunal should apply rules [...] which are beyond any doubt part of customary law so that the problem of adherence of some but not all States to specific conventions does not arise'); *Kaing Guek Eav alias Duch*, Case no 001/18-07-2007/ECCC, Appeal Judgment, 3 February 2012, para 91.

[87] See e.g. *Prosecutor v Casimir Bizimungu and others*, Case no ICTR-99-50, Requête de Casimir Bizimungu aux fins de communication par le Procureur du Rapport Bruguière (confidentielle), 24 February 2006 (seeking the disclosure of a report containing information relating, inter alia, to the involvement of Uganda in support of the Rwandan Patriotic Front), and Decision on Casimir Bizimungu's Requests for Disclosure of the Bruguière Report and the Cooperation of the Government of France, 25 September 2006 (rejecting the motion).

be unwilling to support the creation of, or to cooperate with, a tribunal vested with jurisdiction over such cases.[88]

Last but not least, although international tribunals established by the UN Security Council can always seek the assistance of the Council to obtain the cooperation of states, the ad hoc tribunals have faced difficulty in obtaining compliance with requests for assistance, especially concerning the arrest and transfer of high-profile suspects.[89] Nine years after its inauguration, the STL has still not been able to secure the arrest of a single accused, and has been reduced to initiating proceedings *in absentia*.[90]

In sum, the jurisdictional constraints that straitjacket ad hoc tribunals would present significant challenges in cases of state organized crime, especially in cases having far-reaching cross-border implications. Moreover, while ad hoc tribunals established pursuant to a Security Council resolution present the significant advantage of enjoying the support of the Council's power of coercion, this is not necessarily a recipe for success in politically sensitive cases.

3. The African Court of Justice and Human Rights

The Assembly of the AU has adopted a protocol amending the Statute of the ACJHR (known as the Malabo Protocol) to establish a criminal chamber with jurisdiction over a number of international crimes.[91] Several features of the Court's unique design are relevant to the prosecution of senior public officials involved in organized crime.

(a) *Jurisdiction* ratione materiae

The amendments to the ACJHR Statute grant the Court jurisdiction over traditional 'core' international crimes (genocide, crimes against humanity, and war crimes), as well as over other international crimes defined in crime-suppression conventions, such as corruption, money laundering, trafficking in persons, trafficking in drugs, trafficking in hazardous wastes, and illicit exploitation of natural resources.[92] The

[88] In the case of the STL, Syria's refusal to cooperate with the Tribunal can be explained in view of the suggestion by the UN International Independent Investigation Commission that the Syrian authorities may have been involved in the terrorist attack that killed former Lebanese President Rafik Hariri. See *Report of the International Independent Investigation Commission established pursuant to Security Council resolution 1595 (2005)*, annexed to UN Doc S/2005/662, 20 October 2005, para 216. See also Security Council Resolution 1636 (2005), preamble, 16th recital.

[89] See e.g. Security Council Resolution 1207 (1998), 17 November 1998, UN Doc S/RES/1207 (1998) (condemning Yugoslavia's failure to execute arrest warrants issued by the ICTY); Resolution 1503 (2003), 28 August 2003, UN Doc S/RES/1503 (2003) (noting the lack of cooperation of certain states with the ICTY and the ICTR).

[90] See *Prosecutor v Salim Jamil Ayyash and others*, Case no STL-11-01, Decision to Hold Trial *in Absentia*, 1 February 2012.

[91] Assembly Decision 529 (XXIII), 'Decision on the Draft Legal Instruments', 27 June 2014, para 2(e); Protocol on Amendments to the Protocol on the Statute of the African Court of Justice and Human Rights, 27 June 2014 (not yet in force).

[92] ACJHR Statute, Art 28A.

definition of crimes draws on the text of the relevant treaties. The definition of corruption (which includes trading in influence, abuse of functions, embezzlement of public funds, and illicit enrichment) as well as that of money laundering are almost identical to the provisions of the AU Convention on Corruption.[93] The definition of trafficking in persons is the same as that found in the UNCTOC Human Trafficking Protocol.[94] The definition of drug trafficking is also almost identical to that of the UN Drug Convention.[95] The crime of trafficking in hazardous wastes is defined by reference to the Bamako Convention.[96] A notable novelty is the definition of the crime of illicit exploitation of natural resources, formulated as follows:

For the purpose of this Statute, "Illicit exploitation of natural resources" means any of the following acts if they are of a serious nature affecting the stability of a state, region or the Union:

a. Concluding an agreement to exploit resources, in violation of the principle of peoples' sovereignty over their natural resources
b. Concluding with state authorities an agreement to exploit natural resources, in violation of the legal and regulatory procedures of the State concerned;
c. Concluding an agreement to exploit natural resources through corrupt practices;
d. Concluding an agreement to exploit natural resources that is clearly one-sided;
e. Exploiting natural resources without any agreement with the State concerned;
f. Exploiting natural resources without complying with norms relating to the protection of the environment and the security of the people and the staff; and
g. Violating the norms and standards established by the relevant natural resource certification mechanism.[97]

The ACHJR Statute, as amended by the Malabo Protocol, is the first international agreement to provide a definition for the crime of illicit exploitation of natural resources.

(b) *Individual criminal responsibility*

The modes of responsibility provided for in the amended ACJHR Statute differ markedly from those traditionally found in international criminal law. Article 28N reads as follows:

An offence is committed by any person who, in relation to any of the crimes or offences provided for in this Statute:

i. Incites, instigates, organizes, directs, facilitates, finances, counsels or participates as a principal, co-principal, agent or accomplice in any of the offences set forth in the present Statute;

[93] See and compare ACJHR Statute, Arts 28I and 28I*bis*, and AU Convention on Corruption, Arts 4 and 6.

[94] See and compare ACJHR Statute, Art 28J, and UNCTOC Human Trafficking Protocol, Art 3.

[95] See and compare ACJHR Statute, Art 28K, and UN Drug Convention, Art 3(1).

[96] See and compare ACJHR Statute, Art 28L, and Convention on the Ban of the Import into Africa and the Control of Transboundary Movement and Management of Hazardous Wastes within Africa, Art 2.

[97] ACJHR Statute, Art 28L*bis*.

ii. Aids or abets the commission of any of the offences set forth in the present Statute;
iii. Is an accessory before or after the fact or in any other manner participates in a collaboration or conspiracy to commit any of the offences set forth in the present Statute;
iv. Attempts to commit any of the offences set forth in the present Statute.

This provision causes a great deal of confusion by putting on the same level primary and ancillary modes of responsibility, and by including modes of responsibility previously unknown in international criminal law.[98] It also omits other modes of responsibility used by international criminal courts and tribunals, namely responsibility for planning, ordering, and participation in a joint criminal enterprise. Overall, the definition of the modes of responsibility is so broad that it could potentially cover any form of participation in the commission or preparation of a crime.

(c) *Conditions for the exercise of jurisdiction and jurisdictional immunities*

The international criminal law section of the ACJHR has jurisdiction when the crime was committed in the territory of a state party or by a national of a state party, when the victim is a national of a state party, and in the case of '[e]xtraterritorial acts by non-nationals which threaten a vital interest of [a state party]'.[99] Jurisdiction on the basis of passive personality and of the protective principle is a novelty for an international criminal court. The implications are far-reaching, as this allows the Court to exercise jurisdiction over acts committed by nationals of a state not party to its Statute in the territory of a state not party.

The ACJHR may exercise its jurisdiction over a specific 'situation' further to a referral by a state party, further to a referral by the Assembly of Heads of State and Government or by the Peace and Security Council of the AU, or in case of a *proprio motu* investigation by the Prosecutor.[100]

The exercise by the ACJHR of its criminal jurisdiction is subject to a number of significant limitations. First, the ACJHR Statute sets a jurisdictional requirement with respect to corruption offences and to the crime of illicit exploitation of natural resources: the acts in question must be 'of a serious nature affecting the stability of a state, region or the Union'.[101] While including a jurisdictional threshold for these offences is understandably necessary to maintain the Court's focus on the most serious cases, it is hard to understand why such a threshold is not required as a precondition to the exercise of the Court's jurisdiction over other economic crimes such

[98] See generally Chantal Melon, 'Modes of Responsibility (Art 28N), Individual Criminal Responsibility (Art 46B) and Corporate Criminal Liability (Art 46C)' in Werle and Vormbaum (n 9), at 144–48.

[99] ACJHR Statute, Art 46E*bis*.

[100] Ibid, Art 46F. In terms of the legitimacy of a referral by the AU Peace and Security Council, it is worth noting that the members of the Council are all elected and that decisions require a two-thirds quorum. See Protocol Relating to the Establishment of the Peace and Security Council of the African Union, 9 July 2002, entered into force on 26 December 2003, Art 5 and Art 8(8) and (13).

[101] ACJHR Statute, Arts 28I and 28L*bis*.

as drug trafficking or money laundering.[102] This clause could also potentially be abused to prevent the prosecution of politically sensitive cases of corruption or illicit exploitation of natural resources.

In addition, the functioning of the international criminal law section of the ACJHR is based on the principle of complementarity, leaving states parties the primary responsibility to investigate and prosecute cases falling within the Court's jurisdiction. The provisions spelling out the requirements for the admissibility of cases are almost the same as those of the Rome Statute, with one notable difference: the omission of the adverb 'genuinely' in the sentence referring to a state party's unwillingness or inability to investigate or prosecute.[103] As a result, it would seem that a case brought before the Court may be declared inadmissible if a state party has initiated an investigation, even if the investigation in question does not reflect a genuine effort on the part of the state to bring the suspects to justice.

Finally, and most controversially, the exercise of the Court's jurisdiction remains subject to very broad jurisdictional immunities. Article 46A*bis* provides:

> No charges shall be commenced or continued before the Court against any serving AU Head of State or Government, or anybody acting or entitled to act in such capacity, or other senior state officials based on their functions, during their tenure of office.

This provision recognizes immunity *ratione personae* as a valid bar to the exercise of the Court's jurisdiction. Whether the phrase 'based on their functions' was intended to refer to immunities *ratione materiae* remains ambiguous, which leaves open the question whether functional immunities may be applicable as a procedural bar before the ACJHR. Commentators have taken the view that the provision should be interpreted as referring only to immunities *ratione personae*.[104] Article 46A*bis* grants personal immunity to any 'senior state official', without offering a definition of this latter concept. This formulation goes way beyond the limited circle of officials entitled to immunity *ratione personae* from foreign criminal jurisdiction under customary international law.[105] Article 46A*bis* has attracted sharp criticism from human rights organizations arguing that 'the immunity clause will pose serious risks to [the] integrity, legitimacy and credibility [of the ACJHR]'.[106] Unfortunate as this provision may be, in the absence of a general rule of customary international law excluding jurisdictional immunities before international criminal courts and tribunals, states remain free to depart from the standards adopted in the constitutive instruments of other international tribunals.[107]

[102] Lovell D Fernandez, 'Corruption (Art 28I) and Money Laundering (Art 28I*bis*)' in Werle and Vormbaum (n 9), at 94–95.

[103] ACJHR Statute, Art 46H. On the admissibility of cases before the ICC, see Section B.1(b) of this chapter.

[104] See Tladi (n 9), at 206–207.

[105] Recall Chapter 4, Section B.4(a)(ii).

[106] See Amnesty International, *Malabo Protocol: Legal and Institutional Implications of the Merged and Expanded African Court* (London, 2016), at 26–27.

[107] Tladi (n 9), at 214–15. See also the authorities cited in n 10 in this chapter.

(d) Potential for prosecuting state organized crime

The amendments to the ACJHR Statute grant the Court exceptionally broad and far-reaching jurisdiction over conduct potentially constitutive of state organized crime. The Court has jurisdiction over a number of crimes commonly encountered in state organized crime, such as trafficking in drugs, human beings, and hazardous wastes, corruption, abuse of functions, embezzlement of public funds, money laundering, and illicit exploitation of natural resources. Perpetrators could be held responsible under a large variety of modes of responsibility, notably for organizing or participating in a conspiracy to commit crimes falling within the jurisdiction of the Court. Moreover, the Court could exercise its jurisdiction over crimes committed in part or even entirely outside the territory of a state party, such as in the case of a foreign covert operation designed to destabilize the government of a state party. However, in the case of crimes committed outside the territory of a state party and having a marked political dimension, the Court is likely to face almost insurmountable difficulties in securing the cooperation of the state concerned.[108]

Whether the Court would exercise its jurisdiction beyond the borders of the AU remains to be seen. It should be kept in mind that the project of granting jurisdiction over international crimes to the ACJHR is part of the broader efforts of the AU to oppose the use of the principle of universal jurisdiction against African leaders and the increasing involvement of the ICC in Africa.[109] Critics of the Court argue that the establishment of the international criminal law section of the ACJHR is merely intended to obstruct ICC proceedings and shield offenders from criminal responsibility.[110] That having been said, the idea of establishing a treaty-based regional court with international criminal jurisdiction is not without merit. If properly designed, it could have offered an innovative course of action against state organized crime. Unfortunately, the numerous preconditions to the exercise of the ACJHR's criminal jurisdiction and the rules on jurisdictional immunities would almost certainly bar the Court from exercising its jurisdiction over senior public officials involved in state organized crime. To date, the ACJHR is little more than ink on paper. Nine years after its adoption, only six states have ratified the Statute of the Court, out of the fifteen ratifications required for entry into force.[111] The Malabo Protocol itself has not been ratified by a single state.[112] Whether the international criminal law section of the ACJHR will one day be able to fulfil its mandate remains to be seen.

[108] Volker Nerlich, 'Preconditions to the Exercise of Jurisdiction (Art 46E*bis*), Exercise of Jurisdiction (Art 46F) and the Prosecutor (Art 46G)' in Werle and Vormbaum (n 9), at 169–70.

[109] See Decision 213 (XII), 'Decision on the Implementation of the Assembly Decision on the Abuse of the Principle of Universal Jurisdiction', 3 February 2009, para 9; Decision 245 (XIII), para 5; Decision 366 (XVII), 'Decision on the Implementation of the Assembly Decisions on the International Criminal Court', 1 July 2011, para 8.

[110] See e.g. Chacha Bhoke Murungu, 'Towards a Criminal Chamber in the African Court of Justice and Human Rights' (2011) 9 *Journal of International Criminal Justice* 1067, at 1086–87.

[111] See ratification status online at https://au.int/en/treaties/protocol-statute-african-court-justice-and-human-rights.

[112] See ratification status online at https://au.int/en/treaties/protocol-amendments-protocol-statute-african-court-justice-and-human-rights.

C. Conclusion

If vested with adequate subject-matter jurisdiction, an international criminal court or tribunal could play a role in prosecuting individuals suspected of being involved in state organized crime. Prosecution before an international criminal court or tribunal could overcome a number of obstacles undermining law enforcement at the domestic level. Recourse to an international criminal court or tribunal would present certain advantages, namely the potential unavailability of jurisdictional immunities as a procedural bar, the greater likelihood of a genuine investigation, the existence of formal rules to deal with concurrent claims of jurisdiction, the capacity to address complex cases of system criminality, and a distinct expressive potential. However, an examination of the respective features of the ICC, ad hoc tribunals, and the ACJHR suggests that while international criminal courts and tribunals may in some circumstances appear better equipped to deal with cases of state organized crime than their domestic counterparts, recourse to an international criminal court or tribunal would come with difficulties perhaps even greater than those associated with prosecuting offenders domestically. Nevertheless, such constraints are not unique to cases of state organized crime and should not discourage efforts to develop international legal responses to address this phenomenon.

9

Concluding Remarks

This volume has highlighted the distinctive criminological characteristics of state organized crime, a concept that emphasizes the commonality of wrongdoing involved in diverse forms of state criminality motivated by the pursuit of profit. Our examination of relevant rules and mechanisms of international law has suggested that, *de lege lata*, neither mechanisms of state responsibility nor existing crime-suppression conventions designed to prevent and punish the participation of individuals in organized crime and corruption are adequate for the purpose of suppressing state organized crime.

In the belief that new ways to conceive of criminal phenomena may require new normative approaches,[1] this book has made a case for establishing state organized crime as an international crime, and put forward proposals to develop international legal mechanisms designed to hold perpetrators responsible. It has suggested in particular that an international convention for the suppression of state organized crime, requiring states parties to criminalize the abuse of state authority by senior public officials using the resources of the state to participate in organized crime, would fulfil an important expressive function. It has also suggested that the UN Security Council, acting under Chapter VII of the UN Charter, could validly require member states to establish state organized crime as a criminal offence in their domestic law and to cooperate to bring offenders to justice, and to freeze the assets of state officials and entities suspected of being involved in state organized crime. Finally, it has discussed the potential role of international criminal courts and tribunals in holding perpetrators responsible, reaching the conclusion that while international criminal courts and tribunals may in some circumstances appear better equipped to deal with cases of state organized crime than their domestic counterparts, recourse to an international criminal court or tribunal would come with difficulties perhaps even greater than those associated with prosecuting offenders domestically.

An international legal framework for the suppression of state organized crime could also, subsidiarily, rest on mechanisms of state responsibility, but in order for such mechanisms to operate in any meaningful way, they would have to reflect the full extent of the wrong inherent in state organized crime. The proposed convention for the suppression of state organized crime addresses this issue by prohibiting the participation of states parties in a range of organized criminal activities. Another

[1] Recall Lemkin's study of genocide: Raphael Lemkin, *Axis Rule in Occupied Europe: Laws of Occupation, Analysis of Government, Proposals for Redress*, first published 1944 (The Lawbook Exchange, 2005).

possibility would be a formal recognition on the part of states of the existence of a primary norm of customary international law prohibiting states from participating in organized crime through their organs or agents. A development of the law in that direction is certainly desirable, as 'the state should not be permitted to hide its [responsibility] behind the punishment of individuals'.[2]

The choice to focus on state organized crime from the perspective of public international law was driven by the ambition to provide a normative justification for addressing this phenomenon at the international level, and by the belief that international law can be a force of change. I am very much mindful of the significant legal and political difficulties raised by this project. In view of these difficulties, it is uncertain whether international law may ever succeed in tackling state organized crime as such. Sceptics doubt international law's potential for addressing state criminality in general, arguing that 'the master's tools will never dismantle the master's house',[3] and that '[e]ffective resistance to and accountability for state crimes will not come from the current system of international law'.[4] It is certain that any endeavour to address state organized crime at the international level is bound to be confronted with international law's most enduring paradox: the ambivalence of states as both subjects and makers of international law.

It should be obvious that the suggestions put forward in this volume cannot be a panacea, and that the fight against state organized crime must encompass measures going well beyond the realm of international law.[5] While it is hard to downplay the significance of the obstacles standing in the way of the adoption of an international legal framework for the suppression of state organized crime, and of effective enforcement mechanisms to hold perpetrators responsible, I have argued that international law can and should play a role in addressing this phenomenon. It is hoped that this book will encourage reflection on possible avenues of action against state organized crime. It comes at a time of democratic crisis, when public distrust of government, fed by increasingly frequent reports of misconduct, is strong and deep-seated, and when established assumptions about the functioning and resilience of national and international institutions are being challenged.[6] This crisis, however,

[2] Nina H B Jørgensen, *The Responsibility of States for International Crimes* (Oxford University Press, 2000), at 155, 158.

[3] Raymond Michalowski, 'The Master's Tools: Can Supranational Law Confront Crimes of Powerful States?' in Elizabeth Stanley and Jude McCulloch (eds), *State Crime and Resistance* (Routledge, 2013) 210, at 210.

[4] Ronald C Kramer, 'State-Organized Crime, International Law and Structural Contradictions' (2016) 24 *Critical Criminology* 231, at 243; Michalowski (n 3), at 221.

[5] There is only so much international law can realistically be expected to achieve; as Drumbl put it, '[i]nternational law is to be studied, not venerated'. See Mark A Drumbl, *Atrocity, Punishment, and International Law* (Cambridge University Press, 2007), at 209. For a discussion of mechanisms of control of, and resistance to, state criminality in general, see Jeffrey Ian Ross (ed), *Controlling State Crime* (2nd edn, Transaction Publishers, 2000); Dawn L Rothe and Christopher W Mullins (eds), *State Crime: Current Perspectives* (Rutgers University Press, 2011), at 179–292; and Jeffrey Ian Ross, 'Controlling State Crime and Alternative Reactions' in Gregg Barak (ed), *The Routledge International Handbook of the Crimes of the Powerful* (Routledge, 2015) 492.

[6] In particular regarding present-day challenges to the international legal order, see James Crawford, 'The Current Political Discourse Concerning International Law' (2018) 81 *Modern Law Review* 1.

signals not so much a deterioration of the ethics of governance as the progressive entrenchment of certain legal and ethical norms at the international level. The time is ripe for debate. As governments ceremoniously proclaim their commitment to the rule of law and their concern over the persistence of armed conflicts and socio-economic inequalities, the misconduct and responsibility of our rulers ought to be addressed to their full extent.

APPENDIX

Proposed Provisions for a Convention for the Suppression of State Organized Crime

Criminalization

1. Each State Party shall adopt such legislative and other measures as may be necessary to establish as criminal offences the following, when committed by a public official in a position effectively to shape or influence the actions of a state, and acting in concert with a structured group for the purpose of obtaining, directly or indirectly, a financial or other material benefit:
   (a) using the material, financial, or human resources of that state to commit or facilitate the commission of any of the crimes listed in paragraph 2, knowing or having reason to know that such resources are used to commit or facilitate the commission of such crimes;
   (b) agreeing to use the material, financial, or human resources of that state to commit or facilitate the commission of any of the crimes listed in paragraph 2 and, where required by domestic law, involving an act undertaken by one of the participants in furtherance of the agreement.
2. For the purposes of paragraph 1, 'crimes' shall mean:
   (a) drug manufacturing and trafficking, as defined in Article 3, sub-paragraph 1(a), of the United Nations Convention against Illicit Traffic in Narcotic Drugs and Psychotropic Substances;
   (b) trafficking in human beings, as defined in Article 5, paragraph 1, and Article 3 of the Protocol to Prevent, Suppress and Punish Trafficking in Persons, Especially Women and Children, supplementing the United Nations Convention against Transnational Organized Crime;
   (c) sale of children and trafficking in child pornography, as defined in Article 3, paragraph 1, of the Optional Protocol to the Convention on the Rights of the Child on the Sale of Children, Child Prostitution and Child Pornography;
   (d) smuggling of migrants, as defined in Article 6, paragraph 1, and Article 3 of the Protocol against the Smuggling of Migrants by Land, Sea and Air, supplementing the United Nations Convention against Transnational Organized Crime;
   (e) trafficking in firearms, as defined in Article 5, paragraph 1, and Article 3 of the Protocol against the Illicit Manufacturing of and Trafficking in Firearms, Their Parts and Components and Ammunition, supplementing the United Nations Convention against Transnational Organized Crime;
   (f) illicit exploitation of natural resources, as defined in Article 28L*bis* of the Statute of the African Court of Justice and Human Rights, as amended by the Protocol on Amendments to the Protocol on the Statute of the African Court of Justice and Human Rights;

(g) trafficking in endangered species, as defined in Article VIII, sub-paragraph 1(a), of the Convention on International Trade in Endangered Species of Wild Fauna and Flora;
(h) illegal traffic in hazardous wastes, as defined in Article 9, paragraph 1, of the Convention on the Control of Transboundary Movements of Hazardous Wastes and their Disposal;
(i) illicit export and import of cultural property, as defined in Article 6, paragraph b, and Article 7, sub-paragraph b(i), of the Convention on the Means of Prohibiting and Preventing the Illicit Import, Export and Transfer of Ownership of Cultural Property;
(j) currency counterfeiting, as defined in Article 3 of the International Convention for the Suppression of Counterfeiting Currency;
(k) cybercrime, as defined in Articles 2 to 10 of the Council of Europe Convention on Cybercrime;
(l) corruption, as defined in Article 15 and Article 16 of the United Nations Convention against Corruption;
(m) trading in influence, as defined in Article 18 of the United Nations Convention against Corruption;
(n) embezzlement of public funds, as defined in Article 17 of the United Nations Convention against Corruption;
(o) laundering of the proceeds of crime, as defined in Article 6, paragraph 1, of the United Nations Convention against Transnational Organized Crime;
(p) genocide, as defined in Article II of the Convention on the Prevention and Punishment of the Crime of Genocide;
(q) crimes against humanity, as defined in Article 7 of the Rome Statute of the International Criminal Court;
(r) war crimes, as defined in Article 8 of the Rome Statute of the International Criminal Court;
(s) the crime of aggression, as defined in Article 8*bis* of the Rome Statute of the International Criminal Court.

3. The knowledge, purpose or agreement referred to in paragraph 1 may be inferred from objective factual circumstances.

Use of terms

For the purposes of this Convention,

(a) 'public official' shall mean (i) any person holding a legislative, executive, administrative or judicial office of a State Party, whether appointed or elected, whether permanent or temporary, whether paid or unpaid, irrespective of that person's seniority; (ii) any other person who performs a public function, including for a public agency or public enterprise, or provides a public service, as defined in the domestic law of the State Party and as applied in the pertinent area of law of that State Party; (iii) any other person defined as a 'public official' in the domestic law of a State Party;
(b) 'structured group' shall mean a group of three or more persons existing for a period of time that is not randomly formed for the immediate commission of an offence and that does not need to have formally defined roles for its members, continuity of its membership, or a developed structure;

(c) 'other material benefit' shall mean any material advantage, to the exclusion of the satisfaction of purely political motives;
(d) 'proceeds of crime' shall mean any property derived from or obtained, directly or indirectly, through the commission of any of the offences listed in sub-paragraphs 2(a) to (n) and (p) to (s) of [the provision defining state organized crime].

Jurisdiction

1. Each State Party shall adopt such measures as may be necessary to establish its jurisdiction over the offence established in accordance with this Convention when:
   (a) the offence is committed, in whole or in part, in its territory;
   (b) the offence is committed, in whole or in part, on board a vessel that is flying its flag or an aircraft that is registered under its laws at the time that the offence is committed; or
   (c) the offence is committed by one of its nationals.
2. For the purposes of sub-paragraph 1(a), the offence shall be regarded as having been committed in the territory of a State Party when one of the constitutive elements of the offence takes place in the territory of that State Party.
3. Subject to the fundamental principles of its domestic law, each State Party shall also adopt such measures as may be necessary to establish its jurisdiction over the offence established in accordance with this Convention when the offence is committed outside its territory,
   (a) with a view to the commission of one of the crimes listed in [the provisions defining the predicate offences of state organized crime] within its territory; or
   (b) when the offence affects its vital interests or otherwise has deleterious or harmful consequences or effects in its territory.
4. Each State Party shall also take such measures as may be necessary to establish its jurisdiction over the offence established in accordance with this Convention when the alleged offender is present in its territory and it does not extradite him or her.
5. If a State Party exercising its jurisdiction under this article has been notified, or has otherwise learned, that any other States Parties are conducting an investigation, prosecution or judicial proceeding in respect of the same conduct, the competent authorities of those States Parties shall, as appropriate, consult one another with a view to coordinating their actions.
6. This Convention shall not exclude the exercise of any criminal jurisdiction established by a State Party in accordance with its domestic law.

Extradition

1. A State Party in whose territory an alleged offender is found shall, if it does not extradite such person in respect of the offence defined in [the provision defining state organized crime], be obliged, without exception whatsoever, to submit the case without undue delay to its competent authorities for the purpose of prosecution.
2. The authorities referred to in paragraph 1 shall take their decision in the same manner as in the case of any other offence of a grave nature under the domestic law of that State

Party. The investigation shall be conducted independently and impartially and without unjustified delay, in a manner consistent with an intent to ascertain whether the person concerned should be prosecuted. [. . .]

Mutual legal assistance

States Parties may not decline to render assistance pursuant to this article by reference to an absence of double criminality. [. . .]

Participation of state organs or agents in organized crime

States Parties shall not knowingly participate in, support, or facilitate any of the activities listed in sub-paragraphs 2(a) to (o) of [the provision defining state organized crime], except to the extent permitted by the principles of their domestic law governing the use of controlled delivery and of other special investigative techniques for the purpose of collecting evidence regarding the commission of an offence.

Bibliography

'The Prospective Role of the United Nations in Dealing with the International Use of Force in the Post-Cold War Period: An Analysis in the Light of the Persian Gulf Crisis', Symposium (University of Georgia School of Law, 1–2 March 1991), (1992) 22 *Georgia Journal of International and Comparative Law* 9.

Adler, Matthew D, 'Expressive Theories of Law: A Skeptical Overview' (2000) 148 *University of Pennsylvania Law Review* 1363.

Akande, Dapo, 'The International Court of Justice and the Security Council: Is There Room for Judicial Control of Decisions of the Political Organs of the United Nations?' (1997) 46 *International and Comparative Law Quarterly* 309.

Akande, Dapo, 'International Law Immunities and the International Criminal Court' (2004) 98 *American Journal of International Law* 407.

Akande, Dapo and Shah, Sangeeta, 'Immunities of State Officials, International Crimes, and Foreign Domestic Courts' (2011) 21 *European Journal of International Law* 815.

Akhavan, Payam, *Reducing Genocide to Law: Definition, Meaning, and the Ultimate Crime* (Cambridge University Press, 2012).

Albini, Joseph L, *The American Mafia: Genesis of a Legend* (Appleton-Century-Crofts, 1971).

Alston, Philip (ed), *People's Rights (Collected Courses of the Academy of European Law)* (Oxford University Press, 2001).

Alvarez, José E, *International Organizations as Law-makers* (Oxford University Press, 2006).

Ambos, Kai, 'The Crime of Aggression after Kampala' (2010) 53 *German Yearbook of International Law* 463.

Ambos, Kai, *Treatise on International Criminal Law*, vol I: *Foundations and General Part* (Oxford University Press, 2013).

Amerasinghe, Chittharanjan F, *Principles of the Institutional Law of International Organizations* (2nd edn, Cambridge University Press, 2004).

Amman, Diane-Marie, 'Group Mentality, Expressivism, and Genocide' (2002) 2 *International Criminal Law Review* 93.

Anderson, Elizabeth S and Pildes, Richard H, 'Expressive Theories of Law: A General Restatement' (2000) 148 *University of Pennsylvania Law Review* 1503.

Anzilotti, Dionisio, *Cours de droit international*, vol I: *Introduction, Théories générales*, trans Gilbert Gidel (Libraire de Recueil Sirey, 1929).

Ascensio, Hervé, Decaux, Emmanuel, and Pellet, Alain (eds), *Droit international pénal* (2nd edn, Pedone, 2012).

Ashworth, Andrew, 'The Elasticity of *Mens Rea*' in Colin F H Tapper (ed), *Crime, Proof and Punishment: Essays in Memory of Sir Rupert Cross* (Butterworths, 1981) 45.

Aston, Jurij Daniel, 'Die Bekämpfung abstrakter Gefahren für den Weltfrieden durch legislative Maßnahmen des Sicherheitsrats – Resolution 1373 (2001) im Kontext' (2002) 62 *Zeitschrift für ausländisches öffentliches Recht und Völkerrecht* 257.

Augustine, Aurelius, *The City of God*, first published 426, trans Marcus Dods, vol 1 (T & T Clark, 1913).

Aust, Helmut Philip and Nolte, Georg, 'International Law and the Rule of Law at the National Level' in Michael Zürn, André Nollkaemper, and Randall Peerenboom (eds),

Rule of Law Dynamics in an Era of International and Transnational Governance (Cambridge University Press, 2012) 48.

Badié, Bertrand, *La fin des territoires : Essai sur le désordre international et sur l'utilité sociale du respect* (Fayard, 1995).

Ballot, Thomas, 'Réflexions sur les sanctions patrimoniales à la lumière du recouvrement des avoirs issus de la corruption transnationale' (2013) 77 *Revue de science criminelle et de droit pénal comparé* 321.

Barak, Gregg (ed), *Crimes by the Capitalist State: An Introduction to State Criminality* (State University of New York Press, 1991).

Barry, Mamadou Aliou, *Le commerce moderne des armes en Afrique : Données chiffrées, circuits et acteurs* (L'Harmattan, 2008).

Bartolus de Saxoferrato, *Tractatus represaliarum* (1354).

Bassiouni, M Cherif, 'The Penal Characteristics of Conventional International Criminal Law' (1983) 15 *Case Western Reserve Journal of International Law* 27.

Bassiouni, M Cherif, 'International Crimes: *Jus Cogens* and *Obligatio Erga Omnes*' (1996) 59 *Law and Contemporary Problems* 63.

Bassiouni, M Cherif, 'International Crimes: The *Ratione Materiae* of International Criminal Law' in M Cherif Bassiouni (ed), *International Criminal Law*, vol I: *Sources, Subject, and Contents* (3rd edn, Martinus Nijhoff, 2008) 120.

Bassiouni, M Cherif and Blakesley, Christopher L, 'The Need for an International Criminal Court in the New International World Order' (1992) 25 *Vanderbilt Journal of Transnational Law* 151.

Bassiouni, M Cherif and Wise, Edward M, *Aut Dedere Aut Judicare: The Duty to Extradite or Prosecute in International Law* (Martinus Nijhoff, 1995).

Batros, Ben, 'The Evolution of the ICC Jurisprudence on Admissibility' in Carsten Stahn and Mohamed M El Zeidy (eds), *The International Criminal Court and Complementarity: From Theory to Practice*, vol I (Cambridge University Press, 2011) 558.

Bayart, Jean-François, *L'État en Afrique : La politique du ventre* (rev edn, Fayard, 2006).

Bayart, Jean-François, trans Stephen Ellis, 'Africa in the World: A History of Extraversion' (2000) 99 *African Affairs* 217.

Bayart, Jean-François, Ellis, Stephen, and Hibou, Béatrice, *The Criminalization of the State in Africa* (Indiana University Press, 1999).

Bear, Margaret E (ed), *Critical Reflexions on Transnational Organized Crime, Money Laundering, and Corruption* (University of Toronto Press, 2003).

Behrens, Paul, 'Genocide and the Question of Motives' (2012) 10 *Journal of International Criminal Justice* 501.

Berdikeeva, Saltanat, 'Organized Crime in Central Asia: A Threat Assessment' (2009) 7 *China and Eurasia Forum Quarterly* 75.

Bernholz, Steven A, Bernholz, Martin J, and Herman, G Nicolas, 'International Extradition in Drug Cases' (1985) 10 *North Carolina Journal of International Law and Commercial Regulation* 353.

Birnbaum, Johann Michael Franz, 'Über das Erforderniß einer Rechtsverletzung zum Begriffe des Verbrechens, mit besonderer Rücksicht auf den Begriff der Ehrenkränkung' (1834) 15 *Archiv des Criminalrechts (Neue Folge)* 149.

Blackmore, Joshua D A, 'The Jurisdictional Problem of the Extraterritorial Conspiracy' (2006) 17 *Criminal Law Forum* 71.

Blundo, Giorgio, 'La corruption et l'État vus par les sciences sociales' in Giorgio Blundo and Jean-Pierre Olivier de Sardan (eds), *État et corruption en Afrique* (Karthala, 2007).

Boister, Neil, 'The Exclusion of Treaty Crimes from the Jurisdiction of the Proposed International Criminal Court: Law, Pragmatism, Politics' (1998) 3 *Journal of Conflict & Security Law* 27.

Boister, Neil, *Penal Aspects of the UN Drug Conventions* (Kluwer Law International, 2001).

Boister, Neil, ' 'Transnational Criminal Law'? ' (2003) 14 *European Journal of International Law* 953.

Boister, Neil, 'The Trend to Universal Extradition over Subsidiary Universal Jurisdiction in the Suppression of Transnational Crime' (2003) *Acta Juridica* 287.

Boister, Neil, *An Introduction to Transnational Criminal Law* (Oxford University Press, 2012).

Boyle, Alan, 'International Lawmaking? Towards a New Role for the Security Council' in Antonio Cassese (ed), *Realizing Utopia: The Future of International Law* (Oxford University Press, 2012) 172.

Briquet, Jean-Louis and Favarel-Garrigues, Gilles (eds), *Organized Crime and States: The Hidden Face of Politics* (Palgrave Macmillan, 2010).

Brzoska, Michael, 'From Dumb to Smart? Recent Reforms of UN Sanctions' (2003) 9 *Global Governance* 519.

Cahin, Gérard, 'La double incrimination dans le droit de l'extradition' (2013) 117 *Revue générale de droit international public* 579.

Caruso, Raul, 'The Impact of International Economic Sanctions on Trade: Empirical Evidence over the Period 1960–2000' (2005) 113 *Rivista internazionale di scienze sociali* 41.

Cassella, Stefan D, *Asset Forfeiture Law in the United States* (2nd edn, Juris, 2013).

Cassese, Antonio, 'On the Use of Criminal Law Notions in Determining State Responsibility for Genocide' (2007) 5 *Journal of International Criminal Justice* 875.

Cassese, Antonio, *International Criminal Law* (2nd edn, Oxford University Press, 2008).

Cassese, Antonio, Gaeta, Paola, and Jones, John R W D (eds), *The Rome Statute of the International Criminal Court: A Commentary*, vol I (Oxford University Press, 2002).

Ceccarelli, Alessandra, 'Clans, Politics and Organized Crime in Central Asia' (2007) 10 *Trends in Organized Crime* 19.

Cervell Hortal, María José, 'La explotación ilegal de los recursos naturales de un estado a la luz de la sentencia del Tribunal Internacional de Justicia sobre las actividades armadas en el territorio de Congo (2005)' (2006) 22 *Anuario Español de Derecho Internacional* 559.

Chabal, Patrick and Daloz, Jean-Pascal, *Africa Works: Disorder as Political Instrument* (Indiana University Press, 1999).

Chalmers, James and Leverick, Fiona, 'Fair Labelling in Criminal Law' (2008) 71 *Modern Law Review* 217.

Chambliss, William J, 'State-Organized Crime – The American Society of Criminology, 1988 Presidential Address' (1989) 27 *Criminology* 183.

Chambliss, William J, 'Commentary by William J. Chambliss' (1995) 26 *Society for the Study of Social Problems Newsletter* 9.

Chevallier, Jacques, 'État de droit et relations internationales' (2006) 7 *Annuaire français de droit international* 4.

Clagett, Brice M and Johnson, O Thomas, Jr, 'May Israel as a Belligerent Occupant Lawfully Exploit Previously Unexploited Oil Resources of the Gulf of Suez?' (1978) 72 *American Journal of International Law* 558.

Clinard, Marshall B and Quinney, Richard, *Criminal Behavior Systems: A Typology* (Holt, Rinehart and Winston, 1967).

Cogan, Jacob Katz, 'Stabilization and the Expanding Scope of the Security Council's Work' (2015) 109 *American Journal of International Law* 324.

Cohen, Stanley, 'Human Rights and Crimes of the State: The Culture of Denial' (1993) 26 *Australian & New Zealand Journal of Criminology* 97.

Conway, Gerard, '*Ne Bis in Idem* in International Law' (2003) 3 *International Criminal Law Review* 217.

Coolidge, Jacqueline and Rose-Ackerman, Susan, 'High-Level Rent Seeking and Corruption in African Regimes: Theory and Cases', World Bank Working Paper (1999).

Cooper, John, *Raphael Lemkin and the Struggle for the Genocide Convention* (Palgrave Macmillan, 2008).

Cooter, Robert, 'Expressive Law and Economics' (1998) 27 *Journal of Legal Studies* 585.

Corten, Olivier, 'L'arrêt rendu par la CIJ dans l'affaire du *Crime de génocide (Bosnie-Herzégovine c. Serbie)* : vers un assouplissement des conditions permettant d'engager la responsabilité d'un État pour génocide ?' (2007) 53 *Annuaire français de droit international* 249.

Corten, Olivier, 'L'État de droit en droit international : quelle valeur juridique ajoutée ?' in Société française de droit international, *L'État de droit en droit international – Colloque de Bruxelles* (Pedone, 2009) 11.

Corten, Olivier and Klein, Pierre (eds), *The Vienna Conventions on the Law of Treaties: A Commentary* (Oxford University Press, 2011).

Cortright, David and Lopez, George A, *The Sanction Decade: Assessing UN Strategies in the 1990s* (Lynne Rienner, 2000).

Cortright, David and Lopez, George A, *Sanctions and the Search for Security: Challenges to UN Action* (Lynne Rienner, 2002).

Cortright, David and Lopez, George A (eds), *Smart Sanctions: Targeting Economic Statecraft* (Rowman & Littlefield, 2002).

Cot, Jean-Pierre, Pellet, Alain, and Forteau, Mathias (eds), *La Charte des Nations Unies : Commentaire article par article* (3rd edn, Economica, 2005).

Craig, Paul, 'Formal and Substantive Conceptions of the Rule of Law: An Analytical Framework' (1997) *Public Law* 467.

Craven, Matthew, 'Humanitarianism and the Quest for Smarter Sanctions' (2002) 13 *European Journal of International Law* 43.

Crawford, James (ed), *The Rights of Peoples* (Clarendon Press, 1988).

Crawford, James (ed), *State Responsibility: The General Part* (Cambridge University Press, 2013).

Crawford, James, 'The Current Political Discourse Concerning International Law' (2018) 81 *Modern Law Review* 1.

Crawford, James, Pellet, Alain, and Olleson, Simon (eds), *The Law of International Responsibility* (Oxford University Press, 2010).

Cryer, Robert, *Prosecuting International Crimes: Selectivity and the International Criminal Law Regime* (Cambridge University Press, 2005).

Cryer, Robert, 'The Doctrinal Foundations of International Criminalization' in M Cherif Bassiouni (ed), *International Criminal Law*, vol I: *Sources, Subject, and Contents* (3rd edn, Martinus Nijhoff, 2008) 107.

Cryer, Robert, 'Prosecuting the Leaders: Promises, Politics and Pragmatics' (2009) 1 *Göttingen Journal of International Law* 45.

Cryer, Robert, 'The ICC and Its Relationship to Non-States Parties' in Carsten Stahn (ed), *The Law and Practice of the International Criminal Court* (Oxford University Press, 2015) 260.

Cryer, Robert, Friman, Håkan, Robinson, Darryl, and Wilmshurst, Elizabeth (eds), *An Introduction to International Criminal Law and Procedure* (3rd edn, Cambridge University Press, 2014).

Damaška, Mirjan, 'What Is the Point of International Criminal Justice?' (2008) 83 *Chicago-Kent Law Review* 329.

d'Aspremont, Jean, *Formalism and the Sources of International Law: A Theory of the Ascertainment of Legal Rules* (Oxford University Press, 2011).

David, Éric, 'Portée et limites du principe de non-intervention' (1990) 23 *Revue belge de droit international* 350.

David, Éric, 'Les valeurs, politiques et objectifs du droit pénal international à l'heure de la mondialisation' in Association internationale de droit pénal, *International Criminal Law: Quo Vadis?*—Proceedings of the International Conference held in Siracusa, Italy, 28 November – 3 December 2002, Nouvelles études pénales no 19 (Érès, 2004) 157.

de la Cuesta, José Luis (ed), *Resolutions of the Congresses of the International Association of Penal Law (1926–2004)* (Érès, 2009).

Delbez, Louis, 'La responsabilité internationale pour crimes commis sur le territoire d'un État et dirigés contre la sûreté d'un État étranger' (1930) 4 *Revue générale de droit international public* 461.

Delmas-Marty, Mireille (ed), *Corpus Juris: Introducing Penal Provisions for the Purpose of the Financial Interests of the European Union* (Economica, 1997).

Denis, Catherine, *Le pouvoir normatif du Conseil de sécurité des Nations Unies : portée et limites* (Bruylant, 2004).

de Wet, Erika, *The Chapter VII Powers of the United Nations Security Council* (Hart Publishing, 2004).

Dinstein, Yoram, 'International Criminal Law' (1985) 20 *Israel Law Review* 206.

Dominicé, Christian, 'Quelques observations sur l'immunité de juridiction pénale de l'ancien chef d'État' (1999) 103 *Revue générale de droit international public* 297.

Donnedieu de Vabres, Henri, *Les principes modernes du droit pénal international*, first published 1928 (reprinted edn, Panthéon-Assas, 2004).

Dormoy, Daniel (ed), *La corruption et le droit international* (Bruylant, 2010).

Driver, Julia, 'Normative Ethics' in Frank Jackson and Michael Smith (eds), *The Oxford Handbook of Contemporary Philosophy* (Oxford University Press, 2007) 31.

Drumbl, Mark A, *Atrocity, Punishment, and International Law* (Cambridge University Press, 2007).

Dubber, Markus D (ed), *Foundational Texts in Modern Criminal Law* (Oxford University Press, 2014).

Duff, Robin Antony, *Trials and Punishments* (Cambridge University Press, 1986).

Dupuy, Pierre-Marie, 'Some Reflections on Contemporary International Law and the Appeal to Universal Values: A Response to Martti Koskenniemi' (2005) 16 *European Journal of International Law* 131.

Dupuy, Pierre-Marie, 'A Crime without Punishment' (2016) 14 *Journal of International Criminal Justice* 879.

Dupuy, Pierre-Marie and Hoss, Cristina, '*Trail Smelter* and Terrorism: International Mechanisms to Combat Transboundary Harm' in Rebecca M Bratspies and Russell A Miller (eds), *Transboundary Harm in International Law: Lessons from the Trail Smelter Arbitration* (Cambridge University Press, 2006) 225.

Dupuy, René-Jean (ed), *The Future of International Law in a Multicultural World* (Martinus Nijhoff, 1984).

Earl Childress, Donald, III (ed), *The Role of Ethics in International Law* (Cambridge University Press, 2012).

Elberling, Björn, 'The *Ultra Vires* Character of Legislative Action by the Security Council' (2005) 2 *International Organizations Law Review* 337.

Eriksson, Michael, *Targeting Peace: Understanding UN and EU Targeted Sanctions* (Ashgate, 2011).

Farrall, Jeremy Matam, *United Nations Sanctions and the Rule of Law* (Cambridge University Press, 2007).

Feinberg, Joel, *Doing and Deserving: Essays in the Theory of Responsibility* (Princeton University Press, 1970).

Feinberg, Joel, *The Moral Limits of the Criminal Law*, vol 1: *Harm to Others* (Oxford University Press, 1987).

Feldman, Daniel L, 'Conflict Diamonds, International Trade Regulation, and the Nature of Law' (2003) 24 *University of Pennsylvania Journal of International Economic Law* 835.

Ferrari Bravo, Luigi, 'Méthodes de recherche de la coutume internationale dans la pratique des États' (1985) 192 *Recueil des cours de l'Académie de droit international* 233.

Fischer, Georges, 'La souveraineté sur les ressources naturelles' (1962) 8 *Annuaire français de droit international* 516.

Foakes, Joanne, *The Position of Heads of State and Senior Officials in International Law* (Oxford University Press, 2014).

Fox, Hazel and Webb, Philippa, *The Law of State Immunity* (3rd edn, Oxford University Press, 2013).

Francis, Leslie P and Francis, John G, 'International Criminal Court, the Rule of Law, and Prevention of Harm: Bringing Justice in Times of Injustice' in Larry May and Zachary Hoskins (eds), *International Criminal Law and Philosophy* (Cambridge University Press, 2010).

Friedrichs, David O (ed), *State Crime*, vol I: *Defining, Delineating and Explaining State Crime* (Ashgate, 1998).

Gaeta, Paola, 'On What Conditions Can a State Be Held Responsible for Genocide?' (2007) 18 *European Journal of International Law* 631.

Gaeta, Paola, 'When Is the Involvement of State Officials a Requirement for the Crime of Torture?' (2008) 6 *Journal of International Criminal Justice* 183.

Gaeta, Paola, 'International Criminalization of Prohibited Conduct' in Antonio Cassese (ed), *The Oxford Companion to International Criminal Justice* (Oxford University Press, 2009) 63.

Gaeta, Paola (ed), *The UN Genocide Convention: A Commentary* (Oxford University Press, 2009).

Gaeta, Paola, 'Immunity of States and State Officials: A Major Stumbling-Block to Judicial Scrutiny?' in Antonio Cassese (ed), *Realizing Utopia: The Future of International Law* (Oxford University Press, 2012) 227.

Gallant, Kenneth S, *The Principle of Legality in International and Comparative Criminal Law* (Cambridge University Press, 2009).

Galvis Martínez, Manuel, 'Forfeiture of Assets at the International Criminal Court: The Short Arm of International Criminal Justice' (2014) 12 *Journal of International Criminal Justice* 193.

Gambetta, Diego, *The Sicilian Mafia: The Business of Private Protection* (Harvard University Press, 1996).

Gardiner, Richard, *Treaty Interpretation* (Oxford University Press, 2008).

Geisinger, Alex and Stein, Michael Ashley, 'A Theory of Expressive International Law' (2007) 60 *Vanderbilt Law Review* 75.

Gianaris, William N, 'The New World Order and the Need for an International Criminal Court' (1992) 16 *Fordham International Law Journal* 88.

Gill, Terry D, 'Legal and Some Political Limitations on the Power of the UN Security Council to Exercise Its Enforcement Powers under Chapter VII of the Charter' (1995) 26 *Netherlands Yearbook of International Law* 33.

Gilmore, William C, *Dirty Money: The Evolution of International Measures to Counter Money Laundering and the Financing of Terrorism* (4th edn, Council of Europe, 2011).

Gilmore, William C and McClean, David, *Commentary on the United Nations Convention against Illicit Traffic in Narcotic Drugs and Psychotropic Substances, 1988* (United Nations, 1998).

Godson, Roy (ed), *Menace to Society: Political-Criminal Collaboration around the World* (Transaction Publishers, 2003).

Godson, Roy, *Dirty Tricks or Trump Cards: U.S. Covert Action and Counterintelligence* (3rd edn, Transaction Publishers, 2004).

Golash, Deidre, 'The Justification of Punishment in the International Context' in Larry May and Zachary Hoskins (eds), *International Criminal Law and Philosophy* (Cambridge University Press, 2010) 201.

Goldsmith, Jack L and Posner, Eric A, 'Moral and Legal Rhetoric in International Relations: A Rational Choice Perspective' (2002) 31 *Journal of Legal Studies* 115.

González, Emilio T, 'The Cuban Connection: Drug Trafficking and the Castro Regime' (1997) 2 *Cuban Studies Association Occasional Paper Series*, paper no 7.

Goodrich, Leland, Hambro, Edvard, and Simons, Anne, *Charter of the United Nations: Commentary and Documents* (3rd edn, Columbia University Press, 1969).

Gowlland-Debbas, Vera, 'Security Council Enforcement Action and Issues of State Responsibility' (1994) 43 *International and Comparative Law Quarterly* 55.

Gowlland-Debbas, Vera, 'The Functions of the United Nations Security Council in the International Legal System' in Michael Byers (ed), *The Role of Law in International Politics: Essays in International Relations and International Law* (Oxford University Press, 2000) 277.

Green, Penny and Ward, Tony, *State Crime: Governments, Violence and Corruption* (Pluto Press, 2004).

Greenberg, Michael, *British Trade and the Opening of China 1800–42* (reprinted edn, Cambridge University Press, 1969).

Gregorie, Richard D, 'Extraterritorial Jurisdiction: Its Use, Its Roots and Its Viability' (1991) 15 *Nova Law Review* 625.

Guggenheim, Paul, 'Les principes de droit international public' (1952) 80 *Recueil des cours de l'Académie de droit international* 1.

Guzman, Andrew T, 'Saving Customary International Law' (2005) 27 *Michigan Journal of International Law* 115.

Hafen, Jonathan O, 'International Extradition: Issues Arising under the Dual Criminality Requirement' (1992) *Brigham Young University Law Review* 191.

Happold, Matthew, 'Security Council Resolution 1373 and the Constitution of the United Nations' (2003) 16 *Leiden Journal of International Law* 593.

Harper, Keith, 'Does the United Nations Security Council Have the Competence to Act as Court and Legislature?' (1994) 27 *New York University Journal of International Law and Politics* 103.

Hart, Herbert L A, *The Concept of Law* (2nd edn, Clarendon Press, 1994).

Hauck, Pierre and Peterke, Sven, 'Organized Crime and Gang Violence in National and International Law' (2010) 92 *International Review of the Red Cross* 407.

Hauck, Pierre and Peterke, Sven (eds), *International Law and Transnational Organized Crime* (Oxford University Press, 2016).

Hefendehl, Roland, *Kollektive Rechtsgüter im Strafrecht* (Heymanns, 2002).

Hefendehl, Roland, 'Die Materialisierung von Rechtsgut und Deliktsstruktur' (2002) 149 *Goltdammer's Archiv für Strafrecht* 21.

Hefendehl, Roland, von Hirsch, Andreas, and Wohlers, Wolfgang (eds), *Die Rechtsgutstheorie: Legitimationsbasis des Strafrechts oder dogmatisches Glasperlenspiel?* (Nomos, 2003).

Heller, Kevin Jon, 'Retreat from Nuremberg: The Leadership Requirement in the Crime of Aggression' (2007) 18 *European Journal of International Law* 477.

Heller, Kevin Jon, 'What Is an International Crime? (A Revisionist History)' (2017) 58 *Harvard International Law Journal* 353.

Henckaerts, Jean-Marie and Debuf, Els, 'The ICRC and the Clarification of Customary International Humanitarian Law' in Brian D Lepard (ed), *Reexamining Customary International Law* (Cambridge University Press, 2017) 161.

Henckaerts, Jean-Marie and Doswald-Beck, Louise, International Committee of the Red Cross, *Customary International Humanitarian Law*, vol I: *Rules* (3rd rev edn, Cambridge University Press, 2009).

Hibou, Béatrice (ed), *Privatising the State* (C Hurst & Co, 2004).

Hmoud, Mahmoud, 'Negotiating the Draft Comprehensive Convention on International Terrorism: Major Bones of Contention' (2006) 4 *Journal of International Criminal Justice* 1031.

Hobbes, Thomas, *Leviathan, or The Matter, Forme and Power of a Common-whealth Ecclesiasticall and Civill* (London, 1651).

Hobe, Stephan, 'Evolution of the Principle on Permanent Sovereignty over Natural Resources: From Soft Law to a Customary Law Principle?' in Marc Bungenberg and Stephan Hobe (eds), *Permanent Sovereignty over Natural Resources* (Springer, 2015) 1.

Husak, Douglas N, *Philosophy of Criminal Law* (Rowman & Littlefield, 1987).

Hutchinson, D N, 'Solidarity and Breaches of Multilateral Treaties' (1988) 59 *British Yearbook of International Law* 151.

Jakobs, Günther, 'Kriminalisierung im Vorfeld einer Rechtsgutsverletzung' (1985) 97 *Zeitschrift für die gesamte Strafrechtswissenschaft* 751.

Jennings, John M, *The Opium Empire: Japanese Imperialism and Drug Trafficking in Asia, 1895–1945* (Praeger, 1997).

Jescheck, Hans-Heinrich and Weigend, Thomas, *Lehrbuch des Strafrechts: Allgemeiner Teil* (5th edn, Duncker & Humblot, 1996).

Johnstone, Ian, 'Legislation and Adjudication in the UN Security Council: Bringing Down the Deliberative Deficit' (2008) 102 *American Journal of International Law* 275.

Jones, Peter, 'Human Rights, Group Rights and Peoples' Rights' (1999) 21 *Human Rights Quarterly* 80.

Jørgensen, Nina H B, *The Responsibility of States for International Crimes* (Oxford University Press, 2000).

Kadelbach, Stefan, '*Jus Cogens*, Obligations *Erga Omnes* and Other Rules – The Identification of Fundamental Norms' in Christian Tomuschat and Jean-Marc Thouvenin (eds), *The Fundamental Rules of the International Legal Order: Jus Cogens and Obligations Erga Omnes* (Martinus Nijhoff, 2006) 21.

Kahan, Dan M, 'What Do Alternative Sanctions Mean?' (1996) 63 *University of Chicago Law Review* 591.

Kahan, Dan M, 'The Secret Ambition of Deterrence' (1999) 113 *Harvard Law Review* 413.

Kan, Paul Rexton, Bechtol, Bruce E, Jr, and Collins, Robert M, *Criminal Sovereignty: Understanding North Korea's Illicit International Activities* (Strategic Studies Institute, US Army War College, March 2010).

Kaplan, David E and Dubro, Alec, *Yakuza: Japan's Criminal Underworld* (University of California Press, 2003).

Katsouris, Christina and Sayne, Aaron, *Nigeria's Criminal Crude, International Options to Combat the Export of Stolen Oil* (Chatham House, The Royal Institute of International Affairs, September 2013).

Keitner, Chimène I, 'Categorizing Acts by State Officials: Attribution and Responsibility in the Law of Foreign Official Immunity' (2016) *Duke Journal of Comparative & International Law* 451.

Kelman, Herbert C, 'The Policy Context of International Crimes' in André Nollkaemper and Harmen van der Wilt (eds), *System Criminality in International Law* (Cambridge University Press, 2009) 26.

Kelsen, Hans, 'The Principle of Sovereign Equality of States as a Basis for International Organization' (1944) 53 *Yale Law Journal* 207.

Kelsen, Hans, *The Law of the United Nations: A Critical Analysis of Its Fundamental Problems* (Stevens & Sons, 1951).

Kemp, Gerhard, 'The United Nations Convention against Transnational Organized Crime: A Milestone in International Criminal Law' (2001) 14 *African Journal of Criminal Justice* 152.

Kirgis, Frederic L, 'Custom on a Sliding Scale' (1987) 81 *American Journal of International Law* 146, at 149.

Kleffner, Jann K, *Complementarity in the Rome Statute and National Criminal Jurisdictions* (Oxford University Press, 2008).

Kofele-Kale, Ndiva, 'Patrimonicide: The International Economic Crime of Indigenous Spoliation' (1995) 28 *Vanderbilt Journal of Transnational Law* 45.

Kofele-Kale, Ndiva, *Combating Economic Crimes: Balancing Competing Rights and Interests in Prosecuting the Crime of Illicit Enrichment* (Routledge, 2012).

Kofele-Kale, Ndiva, *The International Law of Responsibility for Economic Crimes: Holding State Officials Individually Liable for Acts of Fraudulent Enrichment* (2nd edn, Routledge, 2016).

Koh, Jean Kyongun, 'Reservations to Multilateral Treaties: How International Legal Doctrine Reflects World Vision' (1982) 23 *Harvard International Law Journal* 71.

Kolb, Robert, 'La bonne foi en droit international public' (1998) 31 *Revue belge de droit international* 661.

Kondoch, Boris, 'The Limits of Economic Sanctions under International Law: The Case of Iraq' (2001) 7 *International Peacekeeping* 267.

Koskenniemi, Martti, '"The Lady Doth Protest Too Much": Kosovo, and the Turn to Ethics in International Law' (2002) 65 *Modern Law Review* 159.

Koskenniemi, Martti, 'International Law and Hegemony: A Reconfiguration' (2004) 17 *Cambridge Review of International Affairs* 197.

Koskenniemi, Martti, *From Apology to Utopia: The Structure of International Legal Argument* (2nd edn, Cambridge University Press, 2005).

Kramer, Ronald C, 'State-Organized Crime, International Law and Structural Contradictions' (2016) 24 *Critical Criminology* 231.

Kramer, Ronald C, Michalowski, Raymond J, and Kauzlarich, David, 'The Origins and Development of the Concept and Theory of State-Corporate Crime' (2002) 48 *Crime & Delinquency* 263.

Kubiciel, Michael, 'Core Criminal Law Provisions in the United Nations Convention against Corruption' (2009) 9 *International Criminal Law Review* 139.

Kulesza, Joanna, *Due Diligence in International Law* (Brill Nijhoff, 2016).

Kupatadze, Alexander, *Organized Crime, Political Transitions and State Formation in Post-Soviet Eurasia* (Palgrave Macmillan, 2012).

Labrousse, Alain and Koutouzis, Michel, *Géopolitique et géostratégies des drogues* (Economica, 1996).

Lacher, Wolfram, *Organized Crime and Conflict in the Sahel-Sahara Region* (Carnegie Endowment for International Peace, 2012).

Lapidoth, Ruth, 'Some Reflections on the Law and Practice Concerning the Imposition of Sanctions by the Security Council' (1992) 30 *Archiv des Völkerrechts* 114.

Lauterwein, Carl Constantin, *The Limits of Criminal Law: A Comparative Analysis of Approaches to Legal Theorizing* (Ashgate, 2010).

Lemkin, Raphael, *Axis Rule in Occupied Europe: Laws of Occupation, Analysis of Government, Proposals for Redress*, first published 1944 (The Lawbook Exchange, 2005).

Leong, Angela Veng Mei, *The Disruption of International Organized Crime: An Analysis of Legal and Non-Legal Solutions* (Ashgate, 2007).

Le Page, Jean-Marc, *Les services secrets en Indochine* (Nouveau Monde, 2012).

Lewis, Peter and Stein, Howard, 'Shifting Fortunes: The Political Economy of Financial Liberalization in Nigeria' (1997) 25 *World Development* 5.

Licht, Sonja, 'The Threat of Organized Crime to State and Human Security' in *State and Human Security in the "Age of Terrorism": The Role of Security Sector Reform*—Compilation of presentations made at the second joint seminar of the United Nations Office at Geneva (UNOG) and the Geneva Centre for the Democratic Control of Armed Forces (DCAF) held on 26 January 2004 (United Nations Office at Geneva, 2004).

Lledó Vásquez, Rodrigo, 'Comentarios sobre la Sentencia de Extradición de Alberto Fujimori Fujimori' (2008) 4 *Anuario de Derechos Humanos* 107.

Luban, David, 'A Theory of Crimes against Humanity' (2004) 29 *Yale Journal of International Law* 85.

Lundberg, Michael A, 'The Plunder of Natural Resources during War: A War Crime?' (2008) 39 *Georgetown Journal of International Law* 495.

Lunsford, Virginia W, *Piracy and Privateering in the Golden Age Netherlands* (Palgrave MacMillan, 2005).

Lupsha, Peter A, 'Transnational Organized Crime versus the Nation-State' (1996) 2 *Transnational Organized Crime* 21.

McClean, David, *Transnational Organized Crime: A Commentary on the UN Convention and Its Protocols* (Oxford University Press, 2007).

McConville, Molly, 'A Global War on Drugs: Why the United States Should Support the Prosecution of Drug Traffickers in the International Criminal Court' (2000) 37 *American Criminal Law Review* 75.

McCoy, Alfred W, *The Politics of Heroin: CIA Complicity in the Global Drug Trade* (rev edn, Lawrence Hill Books, 2003).

McDougall, Carrie, *The Crime of Aggression under the Rome Statute of the International Criminal Court* (Cambridge University Press, 2013).

MacGaffey, Janet, *The Real Economy of Zaire: The Contribution of Smuggling and Other Unofficial Activities to National Wealth* (University of Pennsylvania Press, 1991).

Mack, Andrew and Khan, Asif, 'UN Sanctions: A Glass Half-Full?' in Richard M Price and Mark W Zacher (eds), *The United Nations and Global Security* (Palgrave Macmillan, 2004) 156.

MacPherson, Bryan F, 'Building an International Criminal Court for the 21st Century' (1998) 13 *Connecticut Journal of International Law* 1.

Makarenko, Tamara, 'The Crime-Terror Continuum: Tracing the Interplay Between Transnational Organized Crime and Terrorism' (2004) 6 *Global Crime* 129.

Maljević, Almir, *'Participation in a Criminal Organization' and 'Conspiracy': Different Legal Models against Criminal Collectives* (Duncker & Humblot, 2011).

Manes, Vittorio, *Il principio di offensività nel diritto penale. Canone di politica criminale, criterio ermeneutico, parametro di ragionevolezza* (Giappichelli, 2005).

Mann, Frederick Alexander, 'The Doctrine of Jurisdiction in International Law' (1964) 111 *Recueil des cours de l'Académie de droit international* 1.

Marat, Erica, 'The State-Crime Nexus in Central Asia: State Weakness, Organized Crime, and Corruption in Kyrgyzstan and Tajikistan', Silk Road Paper (Central Asia-Caucasus Institute and Silk Road Studies Program, 2006).

Marcel, Valérie, 'ISIS and the Dangers of Black Market Oil' (2014) 57 *Middle East Economic Survey* 19.

Maruko, Eiko, 'Mediated Democracy: *Yakuza* and Japanese Political Leadership' in Felia Allum and Renate Siebert (eds), *Organized Crime and the Challenge to Democracy* (Routledge, 2003) 202.

May, Larry, *Crimes against Humanity: A Normative Account* (Cambridge University Press, 2005).

Mbembe, Achille, 'At the Edge of the World: Boundaries, Territoriality, and Sovereignty in Africa' (2000) 12 *Public Culture* 259.

Mbembe, Achille, *On Private Indirect Government* (Council for the Development of Social Research in Africa, 2000).

Mbembe, Achille, *On the Postcolony* (University of California Press, 2001).

Mégret, Frédéric, 'Three Dangers of the International Criminal Court: A Critical Look at a Consensual Project' (2001) 12 *Finnish Yearbook of International Law* 193.

Mégret, Frédéric, 'In Defense of Hybridity: Towards a Representational Theory of International Criminal Justice' (2005) 38 *Cornell International Law Journal* 725.

Merrien, Jean, *Histoire des corsaires* (L'Ancre de Marine, 1992).

Merton, Robert K, 'Social Structure and Anomie' (1938) 3 *American Sociological Review* 672.

Meyer, Frank, *Strafrechtsgenese in Internationalen Organizationen: Eine Untersuchung der Strukturen und Legitimationsvoraussetzungen strafrechtlicher Normbildungsprozesse in Mehrebenensystemen* (Nomos, 2012).

Michalowski, Raymond, 'The Master's Tools: Can Supranational Law Confront Crimes of Powerful States?' in Elizabeth Stanley and Jude McCulloch (eds), *State Crime and Resistance* (Routledge, 2013) 210.

Mill, John Stuart, *On Liberty* (London, 1859).

Moore, Michael S, *Placing Blame: A Theory of the Criminal Law* (Oxford University Press, 2010).

Morice, Alain, 'Guinée 1985 : État, corruption et trafics', *Les Temps Modernes*, no 487 (February 1987) 108.

Morin, Jacques-Yvan, 'L'État de droit : émergence d'un principe du droit international' (1995) 254 *Recueil des cours de l'Académie de droit international* 9.

Murungu, Chacha Bhoke, 'Towards a Criminal Chamber in the African Court of Justice and Human Rights' (2011) 9 *Journal of International Criminal Justice* 1067.

Nadelmann, Ethan A, 'Global Prohibition Regimes: The Evolution of Norms in International Society' (1990) 44 *International Organization* 479.

Naylor, Robin Thomas, 'Follow-the-Money Methods in Crime Control Policy' in Margaret E Beare (ed), *Critical Reflections on Transnational Organized Crime, Money Laundering, and Corruption* (University of Toronto Press, 2003) 256.

Naylor, Robin Thomas, 'Towards a General Theory of Profit-Driven Crimes' (2003) 43 *British Journal of Criminology* 81.

Nelken, David and Levi, Michael, 'The Corruption of Politics and the Politics of Corruption: An Overview' (1996) 23 *Journal of Law and Society* 1.

Ninčić, Djura, *The Problem of Sovereignty in the Charter and in the Practice of the United Nations* (Martinus Nijhoff, 1970).

Nollkaemper, André and van der Wilt, Harmen (eds), *System Criminality in International Law* (Cambridge University Press, 2009).

Nouwen, Sarah M H, *Complementarity in the Line of Fire: The Catalysing Effect of the International Criminal Court in Uganda and Sudan* (Cambridge University Press, 2013).

Noyer, M Lawrence, 'High Seas Narcotics Smuggling and Section 955a of Title 21: Overextension of the Protective Principle of International Jurisdiction' (1982) 50 *Fordham Law Review* 688.

Nsereko, Daniel, 'The ICC and Complementarity in Practice' (2013) 26 *Leiden Journal of International Law* 427.

Obokata, Tom, *Transnational Organized Crime in International Law* (Hart Publishing, 2010).

O'Keefe, Roger, 'Universal Jurisdiction: Clarifying the Basic Concept' (2004) 2 *Journal of International Criminal Justice* 735.

O'Keefe, Roger, 'An "International Crime" Exception to Immunity of State Officials from Foreign Criminal Jurisdiction: Not Currently, Not Likely' (2015) 109 *AJIL Unbound* 167.

O'Keefe, Roger, *International Criminal Law* (Oxford University Press, 2015).

O'Keefe, Roger and Tams, Christian J (eds), *The United Nations Convention on Jurisdictional Immunities of States and Their Property: A Commentary* (Oxford University Press, 2013).

Olásolo, Héctor, *The Criminal Responsibility of Senior Political and Military Leaders as Principals to International Crimes* (Hart Publishing, 2009).

Olukoshi, Adebayo O, 'The Elusive Prince of Denmark: Structural Adjustment and the Crisis of Governance in Africa' in Thandika Mkandawire and Charles C Soludo (eds), *African Voices on Structural Adjustment: A Companion to Our Continent, Our Future* (Council for the Development of Social Research in Africa, 2003) 229.

Orakhelashvili, Alexander, 'The Power of the UN Security Council to Determine the Existence of a 'Threat to the Peace'' (2006) 1 *Irish Yearbook of International Law* 61.

Orakhelashvili, Alexander, *Collective Security* (Oxford University Press, 2011).

Owen, David Edward, *British Opium Policy in China and India* (Yale University Press, 1934).

Paoli, Letizia and vander Beken, Tom, 'Organized Crime: A Contested Concept' in Letizia Paoli (ed), *The Oxford Handbook of Organized Crime* (Oxford University Press, 2014) 13.

Pape, Robert A, 'Why Economic Sanctions Do Not Work' (1997) 22 *International Security* 90.

Pella, Vespasien V, 'La répression de la piraterie' (1926) 15 *Recueil des cours de l'Académie de droit international* 145.

Petersen, Niels, 'Customary Law without Custom: Rules, Principles, and the Role of State Practice in International Norm Creation' (2008) 23 *American University International Law Review* 275.

Pickard, Daniel, 'When Does Crime Become a Threat to International Peace and Security?' (1998) 12 *Florida Journal of International Law* 1.

Pieth, Mark, Low, Lucinda A, and Cullen, Peter J (eds), *The OECD Convention on Bribery: A Commentary* (Cambridge University Press, 2007).

Popovski, Vesselin and Fraser, Trudy (eds), *The Security Council as Global Legislator* (Routledge, 2014).
Przetacznik, Franciszek, *Protection of Officials of Foreign States According to International Law* (Martinus Nijhoff, 1983).
Puente Egido, José, 'L'extradition en droit international : problèmes choisis' (1991) 231 *Recueil des cours de l'Académie de droit international* 9.
Radi, Yannick, 'Du « dilemme du prisonnier » au « jeu d'intégration » : l'internationalisation de l'incrimination pénale de la corruption active transnationale' in Daniel Dormoy (ed), *La corruption et le droit international* (Bruylant, 2010) 169.
Reinisch, August, 'European Court Practice Concerning State Immunity from Enforcement Measures' (2006) 14 *European Journal of International Law* 803.
Reisman, W Michael, 'Editorial Comments: Harnessing International Law to Restrain and Recapture Indigenous Spoliations' (1989) 83 *American Journal of International Law* 56.
Reno, William, *Corruption and State Politics in Sierra Leone* (Cambridge University Press, 1995).
Reno, William, *Warlord Politics and African States* (Lynne Rienner, 1999).
Robinson, Paul H, 'Why Does the Criminal Law Care What the Layperson Thinks Is Just? Coercive Versus Normative Crime Control' (2000) 86 *Virginia Law Review* 1839.
Roht-Arriaza, Naomi, 'Prosecutions of Heads of State in Latin America' in Ellen L Lutz and Caitlin Reiger (eds), *Prosecuting Heads of State* (Cambridge University Press, 2009) 46.
Ross, Jeffrey Ian (ed), *Controlling State Crime* (2nd edn, Transaction Publishers, 2000).
Ross, Jeffrey Ian, 'Controlling State Crime and Alternative Reactions' in Gregg Barak (ed), *The Routledge International Handbook of the Crimes of the Powerful* (Routledge, 2015) 492.
Rothe, Dawn L, *State Criminality: The Crime of All Crimes* (Lexington Books, 2009).
Rothe, Dawn L and Friedrichs, David O, 'The State of the Criminology of Crimes of the State' (2006) 33 *Social Justice* 147.
Rothe, Dawn L and Mullins, Christopher W (eds), *State Crime: Current Perspectives* (Rutgers University Press, 2011).
Roujou de Boubée, Gabriel, 'Compétence française pour des détournements de fonds publics commis au préjudice d'États africains', *Recueil Dalloz* (2009) no 22, p 1520.
Roxin, Claus, *Strafrecht: allgemeiner Teil*, vol I: *Grundlagen. Der Aufbau der Verbrechenslehre* (4th edn, C.H. Beck, 2006).
Sachariew, Kamen, 'State Responsibility for Multilateral Treaty Violations: Identifying the 'Injured State' and Its Legal Status' (1988) 35 *Netherlands International Law Review* 273.
Sandiford, Roberto, 'Évolution du droit de la guerre maritime et aérienne' (1939) 68 *Recueil des cours de l'Académie de droit international* 555.
Scharf, Michael P, 'Seizing the "Grotian Moment": Accelerated Formation of Customary International Law in Times of Fundamental Change' (2010) 43 *Cornell International Law Journal* 439.
Schatzberg, Michael G, *The Dialectics of Oppression in Zaïre* (Indiana University Press, 1988).
Schrager, Laura Shill and Short, James F, 'Toward a Sociology of Organizational Crime' (1977) 25 *Social Problems* 407.
Schreuer, Christoph, 'State Sovereignty and the Duty of States to Cooperate – Two Incompatible Notions?' in Jost Delbrück (ed), *International Law of Cooperation and State Sovereignty*—Proceedings of the International Symposium of the Kiel Walther-Schücking-Institute of International Law, May 23–26, 2001 (Duncker & Humblot, 2002) 163.
Schrijver, Nico, *Sovereignty over Natural Resources: Balancing Rights and Duties* (Cambridge University Press, 1997).

Schrijver, Nico, 'Reforming the UN Security Council in Pursuance of Collective Security' (2007) 12 *Journal of Conflict & Security Law* 127.

Schulze, Götz (ed), *Kulturelle Relativität des internationalen Rechts* (Nomos, 2014).

Scott, Peter Dale and Marshall, Jonathan, *Cocaine Politics: Drugs, Armies, and the CIA in Central America* (updated edn, University of California Press, 1998).

Simester, Andrew and von Hirsch, Andreas, *Crimes, Harms, and Wrongs: On the Principles of Criminalization* (Hart Publishing, 2011).

Simma, Bruno, 'From Bilateralism to Community Interest in International Law' (1994) 250 *Recueil des cours de l'Académie de droit international* 217.

Simma, Bruno, Khan, Daniel-Erasmus, Nolte, Georg, and Paulus, Andreas (eds), *The Charter of the United Nations: A Commentary* (3rd edn, Oxford University Press, 2012).

Singer, Michael, 'The Act of State Doctrine of the United Kingdom: An Analysis, with Comparisons to United States Practice' (1981) 75 *American Journal of International Law* 283.

Spencer, John R, 'The *Corpus Juris* Project and the Fight against Budgetary Fraud' (1998) 1 *Cambridge Yearbook of European Legal Studies* 77.

Sproule, D W and St-Denis, Paul, 'The UN Drug Trafficking Convention: An Ambitious Step' (1989) 27 *Canadian Yearbook of International Law* 263.

Stahn, Carsten and El Zeidy, Mohamed M (eds), *The International Criminal Court and Complementarity: From Theory to Practice* (Cambridge University Press, 2011).

Stein, Torsten, *Die Auslieferungsausnahme bei politischen Delikten: Normative Grenzen, Anwendung in der Praxis und Versuch einer Neuformulierung* (Springer, 1983).

Stern, Brigitte, 'Immunities for Heads of State: Where Do We Stand?' in Mark Lattimer and Philippe Sands (eds), *Justice for Crimes against Humanity* (Hart Publishing, 2003) 73.

Stessens, Guy, *Money Laundering: A New International Law Enforcement Model* (Cambridge University Press, 2000).

Stewart, David P, 'Internationalizing the War on Drugs: The UN Convention against Illicit Traffic in Narcotic Drugs and Psychotropic Substances' (1990) 18 *Denver Journal of International Law & Policy* 387.

Stewart, Gwyneth G, 'Enforcement Problems in the Endangered Species Convention: Reservations Regarding the Reservation Clauses' (1981) 14 *Cornell International Law Journal* 429.

Strange, Susan, *The Retreat of the State: The Diffusion of Power in the World Economy* (Cambridge University Press, 1996).

Strudler, Alan, 'The Power of Expressive Theories of Law' (2001) 60 *Maryland Law Review* 492.

Sundack, Tracie A, '*Republic of the Philippines v Marcos*: The Ninth Circuit Allows a Former Ruler to Invoke the Act of State Doctrine against a Resisting Sovereign' (1988) 38 *American University Law Review* 225.

Sunstein, Cass R, 'Incommensurability and Valuation in Law' (1994) 92 *Michigan Law Review* 779.

Sunstein, Cass R, 'On the Expressive Function of Law' (1996) 144 *University of Pennsylvania Law Review* 2021.

Szasz, Paul C, 'The Security Council Starts Legislating' (2002) 96 *American Journal of International Law* 901.

Tallgren, Immi, 'The Sensibility and Sense of International Criminal Law' (2002) 13 *European Journal of International Law* 561.

Talmon, Stefan, 'The Security Council as World Legislature' (2005) 99 *American Journal of International Law* 175.

Talmon, Stefan, 'Security Council Treaty Action' (2009) 62 *Revue héllénique de droit international* 65.

Thouvenin, Jean-Marc, 'Le principe de non extradition des nationaux' in SFDI, *Droit international et nationalité – Colloque de Poitiers* (Pedone, 2012) 127.

Tilly, Charles, 'War Making and State Making as Organized Crime' in Peter B. Evans, Dietrich Rueschemeyer, and Theda Skocpol (eds), *Bringing the State Back In* (Cambridge University Press, 1985) 169.

Tomuschat, Christian, 'Obligations Arising for States without or against Their Will' (1993) 241 *Recueil des cours de l'Académie de droit international* 195.

Trapp, Kimberley N, *State Responsibility for International Terrorism* (Oxford University Press, 2011).

Triffterer, Otto, *Dogmatische Untersuchungen zur Entwicklung des materiellen Völkerstrafrechts seit Nürnberg* (E. Albert, 1966).

Tsoutsos, Athos G, 'Facteurs déterminant la notion du crime international' (1954) 7 *Revue hellénique de droit international* 164.

van Alebeek, Rosanne, *The Immunity of States and Their Officials in International Criminal Law and International Human Rights Law* (Oxford University Press, 2008).

van Brabant, Koenraad, *Can Sanctions Be Smarter? The Current Debate*—Report of a conference held in London, 16–17 December 1998 (Overseas Development Institute, May 1999).

van den Wijngaert, Christine, *The Political Offence Exception to Extradition: The Delicate Problem of Balancing the Rights of the Individual and the International Public Order* (Kluwer, 1980).

van Sliedregt, Elies and Keijzer, Nico (eds), *The European Arrest Warrant in Practice* (TMC Asser, 2010).

Vetter, Greg R, 'Command Responsibility of Non-Military Superiors in the International Criminal Court (ICC)' (2000) 25 *Yale Journal of International Law* 89.

Villiers, Patrick, *Les corsaires : des origines au traité de Paris du 16 avril 1856* (Jean-Paul Gisserot, 2007).

Villiger, Mark E, *Commentary on the 1969 Vienna Convention on the Law of Treaties* (Martinus Nijhoff, 2009).

Watts, Arthur, 'The International Rule of Law' (1993) 36 *German Yearbook of International Law* 15.

Watts, Arthur, 'The Legal Position in International Law of Heads of States, Heads of Governments and Foreign Ministers' (1994) 247 *Recueil des cours de l'Académie de droit international* 9.

Weckel, Philippe, 'Le Conseil de sécurité et la coopération judiciaire internationale' (2013) 117 *Revue générale de droit international public* 623.

Wedel, Janine R, 'Corruption and Organized Crime in Post-Communist States: New Ways of Manifesting Old Patterns' (2001) 7 *Trends in Organized Crime* 3.

Weigend, Thomas, '*Societas delinquere non potest*? A German Perspective' (2008) 6 *Journal of International Criminal Justice* 927.

Werle, Gerhard, *Principles of International Criminal Law* (2nd edn, TMC Asser, 2009).

Werle, Gerhard and Vormbaum, Moritz (eds), *The African Criminal Court: A Commentary on the Malabo Protocol* (TMC Asser, 2016).

Williams, Glanville, 'Convictions and Fair Labelling' (1983) 42 *Cambridge Law Journal* 85.

Williams, Phil, 'Transnational Organized Crime and the State' in Rodney Bruce Hall and Thomas J Biersteker (eds), *The Emergence of Private Authority in Global Governance* (Cambridge University Press, 2002) 161.

Wilsher, Dan, 'Inexplicable Wealth and Illicit Enrichment of Public Officials: A Model Draft That Respects Human Rights in Corruption Cases' (2006) 45 *Crime, Law & Social Change* 27.

Wise, Judith and Jensen, Eric L, 'International Drug Pollution? Reflections on *Trail Smelter* and Latin American Drug Trafficking' in Rebecca M Bratspies and Russell A Miller (eds), *Transboundary Harm in International Law: Lessons from the Trail Smelter Arbitration* (Cambridge University Press, 2006) 281.

Wollbrink, Stephan, *A Violation of International Law as a Necessary Element of a 'Threat to the Peace' under the UN Charter* (Nomos, 2014).

Wood, Michael C, 'The Interpretation of Security Council Resolutions' (1998) 2 *Max Planck Yearbook of United Nations Law* 73.

Xiaodong Yang, *State Immunity in International Law* (Cambridge University Press, 2012).

Yarnold, Barbara M, 'Doctrinal Basis for the International Criminalization Process' (1994) 8 *Temple International and Comparative Law Journal* 85.

Zürn, Michael, Nollkaemper, André, and Peerenboom, Randall (eds), *Rule of Law Dynamics in an Era of International and Transnational Governance* (Cambridge University Press, 2012).

Index